BERTOLT BRECHT

COLLECTED PLAYS

Volume 7

BERTOLT

Bertolt Brecht: Plays, Poetry, & Prose

Edited by

Ralph Manheim and John Willett

Wolfgang Sauerlander, Associate Editor

BRECHT

COLLECTED PLAYS

VOLUME 7

The Visions of Simone Machard

Schweyk in the Second World War

The Caucasian Chalk Circle

The Duchess of Malfi

Vintage Books, *A Division of Random House, New York*

VINTAGE BOOKS EDITION, JANUARY 1975

Library of Congress Cataloging in Publication Data

Brecht, Bertolt, 1898–1956.   Collected plays.

(His Plays, poetry, & prose)
CONTENTS: v. 1. Baal. Drums in the night. In the jungle of cities. The life of Edward II of England. The wedding. The beggar, or the dead dog. He drives out a devil. Lux in tenebris. The catch.—
v. 5. Life of Galileo. The trial of Lucullus. Mother Courage and her children.—
v. 7. The visions of Simone Machard. Schweyk in the Second World War. The Caucasian chalk circle. The Duchess of Malfi.
v. 9. Adaptations: The tutor. Coriolanus. The trial of Joan of Arc at Rouen, 1431. Don Juan. Trumpets and drums.

I. Willett, John, ed. II. Manheim, Ralph, ed.
PT2603.R397A29 1971   832'.9'12   71-113718
ISBN 0-394-71670-1 (v. 1)
     0-394-71216-1 (v. 7)

Manufactured in the United States of America

Contents

Introduction

The American plays 1942–46

1

The plays in this volume are the ones which Brecht wrote during his six-year stay in the United States. He arrived on July 21, 1941, by ship from Vladivostok, after having set out from Helsinki two months earlier via Moscow and the Trans-Siberian railway. He left again by air on October 31, 1947, to return to Europe and in due course Berlin. Most of the time in between he spent living in the Los Angeles area where he had landed, though he also made prolonged visits to New York.

As in Munich nearly a quarter of a century earlier, his mentor in this new world was the now internationally successful novelist Lion Feuchtwanger, who persuaded him to remain on the West Coast where he would be close to Hollywood and its large German film colony, several of whom (like Fritz Lang and William Dieterle) were subscribing to the fund on which he and his family initially lived. Besides the three original plays which we print, therefore, and the *Duchess of Malfi* adaptation given in the appendix, his output in this period also embraced a number of rejected film outlines and synopses, including the story "Caesar and his Legionary," which was later taken into *Tales from the Calendar*, as well as an undetermined portion of the material for the film *Hangmen Also Die*, which Fritz Lang actually made. To this must be added the American version of *Galileo*, whose evolution is covered in volume 5, and a trickle of very fine but mostly rather short poems. His theoretical writing seems to have dried up almost entirely; major prose projects like the Caesar and "Tui" novels went into cold storage; and he gave up writing short stories. So it is mainly on the contents of the present volume that his American experience must be judged.

To start with, its impact on his work was disastrous. This was due above all to something that had happened on the journey: the death of his aide Margarete Steffin in Moscow from tuberculosis. Both the group of poems which he wrote "After the death of my collaborator M.S." (included in the selected *Poems*) and his own private notes and journal entries suggest that this was among the severest blows he ever suffered; a month later he could write commenting on it.

> for nearly a year i have been feeling deeply depressed as a result of the death of my comrade and collaborator steffin. up to now i have avoided thinking at all deeply about it. i'm not frightened so much of feeling pain as of being ashamed of the fact. but above all i have too few thoughts about it. i know that no pain can offset this loss, that all i can do is close my eyes to it. now and again i have even drunk a tot of whisky when her image rose before me. since i seldom do this even one tot affects me strongly. in my view such methods are just as acceptable as others that are better thought of. they are only external, but this is a problem which i don't see how to resolve internally. death is no good; all is not necessarily for the best. there is no inscrutable wisdom to be seen in this kind of thing. nothing can make up for it.

Very soon after arriving, too, he learned of the fate of another close friend, Walter Benjamin, who had killed himself on the French frontier in 1940 rather than risk being handed over to the Gestapo. At the same time, however, the atmosphere of southern California was hardly such as to relieve his depression. This was partly a matter of its utter remoteness from the war—"Tahiti in urban form" he called it soon after arriving—though Pearl Harbor that autumn brought reality closer; partly a deep-seated resentment of its artificiality and underlying commercial ethos. Thus a journal entry of March 1942 (one of many to the same effect):

> extraordinary in these parts how a universally demoralizing

cheap prettiness stops one from leading anything like a cultivated, i.e., dignified life.

On top of this came the often degrading experience of working for the films, which bore particularly painfully on him as he became drawn into the making of Fritz Lang's Czech resistance movie during the summer of 1942. Taking stock towards the end of April, he listed all the factors hampering him, from his loss of Steffin to his lack of money, and concluded that "for the first time in ten years I am not doing any proper work."

Yet even while he was battling over that film (for adequate representation of the Czech people, for his theme song, for a part for Helene Weigel and a scriptwriter's credit for himself: on all of which points he failed), his prospects in other ways were beginning to improve. Materially, he and his family no longer had to live on $120 a month, but were able to move into a bigger and very much pleasanter house in Santa Monica (1063 26th Street; it is still there, though the area has been much built up) on the strength of the $10,000 which Lang got for him. Once again he was working with the composer Hanns Eisler, who had arrived there in April and for whom he now wrote his "Hollywood Elegies," condensing much of what he felt about the civilization around him. He was also in touch with a young lecturer at UCLA called Eric Bentley, who differed from the rest of his friends in being neither central European nor involved in show business, and who seems immediately to have helped him to widen his English reading. From Feuchtwanger he heard that the Zurich Schauspielhaus wished to stage *The Good Person of Szechwan*, while Thornton Wilder had seen and been impressed by their production of *Mother Courage*. Still more changed for him when El Alamein was followed by Stalingrad (for it should never be forgotten how closely and continuously Brecht followed the war news). And during that October he and Feuchtwanger began collaborating on the war play, a modern Saint Joan story, which was to become *The Visions of Simone Machard*.

Like the other two original plays in this book, *Simone Machard* derived from a scheme which Brecht had brought in

his head with him from Europe. Already perhaps inspired by
the basic idea of Anna Seghers' radio play (which he was later
to adapt for the Berliner Ensemble, as described in volume 9),
he had conceived it in outline two years earlier, soon after the
collapse of France:

> a young frenchwoman in orléans, working at a filling sta-
> tion while her brother is away, dreams and daydreams of
> being joan of arc and undergoing her fate. for the germans
> are advancing on orléans. the voices joan hears are voices
> of the people—the things the blacksmith and the peasant
> are saying. she obeys these voices and saves france from
> the enemy outside, but is conquered by the enemy within.
> the court that sentences her is packed with pro-english
> clerics: victory of the fifth column.

Returning to it just before Christmas 1941, he sketched out a
play in nine scenes under the title *The Voices*, whose social
points should be (a) that vox dei is really vox populi, and (b)
that "owners and criminals stand shoulder to shoulder against
anyone who rejects the idea of property." Exactly at what
stage he first discussed this with Feuchtwanger is not clear,
but he now laid the plan aside in order to read *The Devil in
France*, the book in which the novelist described his own experiences in 1940, when he had been interned outside Aix-en-
Provence, then managed to escape across the Pyrenees at the
point where Benjamin was turned back. Other readings about
the French débâcle followed, though Feuchtwanger, who had
spent all the early part of his exile in that country, remained
in essential ways better informed about it than Brecht. Their
systematic collaboration began at the end of October, just before the shooting of *Hangmen Also Die*, which Brecht occasionally went to watch in the afternoons. They worked mostly
in Feuchtwanger's house, a quiet Spanish-style mansion on the
mountains overlooking Santa Monica and the sea, which has
now been made over to the University of Southern California.
The curfew imposed after Pearl Harbor, together with their
status as enemy aliens, prevented their meeting at night.

In one way the work went easily. The two men got on well
together, and despite their disagreement as to Simone's age
(for which see the Notes, pp. 246 and 271) the division of responsibility seems to have given no trouble. Brecht set up the

play's structure, which was then filled out in discussion between them—Feuchtwanger evidently doing his best to see
that the events were probable and the details authentic—after
which the actual writing of the scenes would be done by
Brecht and checked over at the next meeting. "He has a good
sense of structure," wrote Brecht approvingly,

> appreciates linguistic refinements, is also capable of making
> poetic and dramaturgical suggestions, knows a lot about
> literature, pays attention to arguments and is pleasant to
> deal with, a good friend.

At the same time, however,

> he wants to have nothing to do with the technical or social
> aspects (epic portrayal, A-effect, characters made up of so-
> cial rather than biological ingredients, class conflicts built
> into the story and so on), and tolerates all that merely as
> my personal style . . .

Perhaps because of the effect of the previous fifteen months of
largely pointless work ("that kind of thing can indeed be bad
for one's handwriting," noted Brecht of the role allotted by
Hollywood to its authors) he was less able than usual to resist
the pressure of convention, for aside from the dream element
(itself not particularly daring by local standards) the play is
quite Aristotelian in its observance of the unities. Moreover
the collaborators almost certainly had Hollywood's demands
in mind, both in the play and in the somewhat pot-boiling
novel which Feuchtwanger subsequently wrote on the same
theme (it appeared in 1944 and is briefly summarized on pp.
271–73). Before Brecht left for New York in February 1943,
leaving the ending of the play still not finally settled, an
agreement was drawn up between himself, Ruth Berlau (who
is neither named as a collaborator nor known to have had any
direct role in the work), and the Feuchtwangers, dividing the
stage and screen rights equally and giving Feuchtwanger all
rights to the proposed novel. Thereafter William Dieterle
took an interest, and arranged for a rough translation into English, which had been completed by April. On the strength of
this (so Feuchtwanger then wrote to Brecht) the agents
Curtis Brown were hoping to persuade either Ashley Dukes
or the Muirs to make a good English version. At Columbia

Pictures the story editor was favorably impressed. Not so Hanns Eisler, who had watched the development of the play throughout and made occasional suggestions, and was now embarking on the music. He told Brecht in May that he disliked Simone's instinctive patriotism and saw her as the poor victim of a patriotic upbringing. Brecht had failed to show that she was being exploited.

2

His visit to New York, which lasted from February to late May 1943, launched Brecht on the writing of *Schweyk in the Second World War* as well as on the first stage of *The Duchess of Malfi* adaptation. There is a long history to Brecht's fascination with Jaroslav Hašek's Good Soldier Švejk or Schweyk, arguably the outstanding fictional figure of our century; and his involvement in Erwin Piscator's dramatization of 1928 is discussed in our notes on the play. From then on he was repeatedly returning to the theme, first hoping that Piscator would film it in the USSR in the early 1930's, then expecting to be involved in the same director's scheme to film it elsewhere in 1937; "you really mustn't do it without me," he told Piscator that spring. Though these projects came to nothing, Piscator never abandoned his interest in this theme, and by 1943 was engaged in discussions with the Theater Guild in New York with a view to a new stage production. Brecht may well not have been informed about this, but the fact that *Hangmen Also Die* was a story of the Czech resistance (for Brecht and Lang were presumably unaware that Heydrich's— the hangman in question—assassins were for better or worse agents from Britain) almost certainly helped to turn his mind back to Hašek's anti-militarist epic, since it was during his work with Lang that he noted in his journal that

> once again i would like to do *Schweyk*, interspersed with scenes from [Karl Kraus's] *The Last Days of Mankind* so people can see the ruling forces up top with the private soldier down below surviving all their vast plans.

The man who actually got him to work on this project was
Ernst-Josef Aufricht, the former Berlin impresario who had
first staged *The Threepenny Opera* in 1928 and was now in
New York after escaping from Unoccupied France. Partly
involved in the Office of War Information German broad-
casts, he was also on the lookout for a libretto to interest Kurt
Weill, who had become well established on Broadway with
Lady in the Dark. He helped to put on a mixed program at
Hunter College (in New York) on April 3 in which Weill
and Lotte Lenya performed some of the Brecht songs, including "Und was bekam des Soldaten Weib?" which Weill had
recently set; this finished with a turn by the Czech clowns
George Voskovec and Jan Werich entitled "Schweyk's spirit
lives on." At some point he reintroduced the two former collaborators, and proposed that they should make a Schweyk
musical, quickly raising the necessary $85,000 from émigrés
who remembered their previous success.

According to Brecht's journal he then spent a week staying
with the Weills at New City, where he outlined a version of
The Good Person of Szechwan which the composer thought
of producing; the Zurich première having taken place on February 4, just before Brecht came to New York. For a $500
advance (Hanns Eisler later recalled) he agreed to provide the
Schweyk libretto, of which he wrote Weill an outline in May
(it is printed on pp. 275–85). Having reread Hašek's novel
in the train back to Los Angeles, he quickly settled down to
work on the play and had finished the first three scenes by
June 9 and the whole thing by the end of the month. Though
it is quite untrue to say as Aufricht does (in his memoirs) that
"Brecht had copied whole pages of dialogue from the Schweyk
book" the work clearly flowed very much more easily than
Simone Machard, without the awkward changes and compromises that mar that work. Brecht himself thought well enough
of it to term it (again, in his journal),

> a counterpart to *Mother Courage*. compared with the
> schweik which i wrote for piscator around 27 (a pure
> montage based on the novel) the present second world war
> version is a lot sharper, and corresponds to the shift from

the hapsburgs' well-ensconced tyranny to the nazis' invasion.

He and Weill met again in Hollywood to discuss it. Then at the beginning of July he sent Weill the finished script, assuring him that it was not especially important that Schweyk himself should talk as he does in the German version of the novel, where he speaks a now-defunct kind of Prague German. Paul Selver's translation, he found, managed to be comic without this, and without attempting to find Anglo-Saxon equivalents for the social and political setting. He recommended getting the American poet Alfred Kreymborg to do a version of the play, saying that he was known to Ruth Berlau and "has the right sort of opinions (liberal)." It is not clear whether Weill agreed, though apparently he was already nervous that the script would prove too un-American for Broadway. Brecht, however, went ahead and commissioned Kreymborg, paying him out of a loan from his friend the actor Peter Lorre, who he hoped might play the name part. The translation was finished by September 4, all except for the "Moldau Song," which Brecht himself was still struggling to get right. The unavoidable effect was to infuriate Piscator, who not only regarded *Schweyk* almost as his own property—and indeed had spent much time in negotiations with the Hašek lawyer, who now gave the rights to Aufricht—but was expecting Kreymborg to translate the 1928 version for the Theater Guild.

However, the finished play never appealed to Weill, despite assurances that the publican's part had been written for Lotte Lenya and that he was welcome to get in an American lyric writer for the songs; there is no sign that he composed a note of music for it. Nor did he pursue the *Good Person of Szechwan* project, about which Brecht still hoped they might come to a formal agreement. By August it seems that Aufricht had lost interest, but Brecht none the less went carefully over Kreymborg's translation when it arrived and sent it back to New York for him and Ruth Berlau to revise. This had been done by the time of Brecht's return to New York in mid-November. Shortly afterwards Weill, now in California, wrote to Brecht to summarize his objections. He could only collaborate, he said, on three conditions:

1. if the play is written by a top-class American author in the Ben Hecht category and put on by a top-class American producer.
2. if Lenya plays the publican.
3. if the play is written as a "musical play," with more openings for music than the present version, as I do not under any circumstances wish to write incidental music.

As it stood, he thought that it

has no prospect of succeeding on the American stage without major alterations, unless there is some prominent American author (in the Ben Hecht category) who can find a way of rendering the humor of your script in American terms. Nor do I think the rights position clear enough to ensure the backing for a first-class Broadway production. But these are entirely private opinions, and I'm only telling you them because I don't want you to waste time and energy on a project which in my view hasn't much chance.

Similarly with *The Good Person of Szechwan*, where any agreement must be conditional on getting hold of an American writer. Their "collaboration on the present version of Szechwan" was now at an end.

3

Around October, when *Schweyk* was still uppermost in his mind, Brecht went to visit Luise Rainer, who was living in Westwood not far from his 26th Street house, and without any personal acquaintance with him had signed the affidavit allowing him to come to the United States. She was then at the height of her fame after her performance in the film of *The Good Earth*, and as they were walking on the beach Brecht asked her what, of all plays, she would most like to appear in. When she named the *Chalk Circle* he instantly responded, for once again this was a theme which (as the editorial note will show) he had been taking up intermittently for several years previously; indeed, he told her that he had suggested it in the first place to Klabund, whose adaptation had so successfully been performed by Elisabeth Bergner in Berlin in 1925. Miss Rainer in turn got in touch with a New York backer called Jules Leventhal, who was anxious to bring her to Broadway in a suitable work, and advised him that it would be worth commissioning Brecht and paying him a monthly salary till he had finished the play. This was formally arranged during Brecht's second New York visit, which lasted from mid-November to the middle of March. But he does not seem to have given Leventhal much information about his plans for the play, so that when the actress returned from performing to the troops in the Mediterranean she saw Brecht in New York to find out what was happening. According to her, he reacted so disagreeably as to make her call off her participation. None the less Brecht got down to the writing very soon after his return to Santa Monica, finishing the play in something close to its final version by June 5, when he sent it off to her (so he noted in his journal). She was then ill with the after-effects of jaundice and malaria from her Mediterranean tour, and can no longer even recollect its arrival. She was, however, aware that the play had developed an extra act since Brecht started on it, and that this was connected with his wish to give his friend Oscar Homolka a good part as Azdak, something that had not originally been bargained for.

In the meantime Brecht's financial circumstances, which nine months before had been very precarious, had changed as a result of the sale of the film rights of *Simone Machard* to MGM in February. This seems to have been due entirely to Feuchtwanger, who when Sam Goldwyn failed to understand the play got him to read the much more conventional *Simone* novel, buy the rights, and then buy those of the play as well. Brecht and Feuchtwanger had $50,000 to divide, in return for which there could be no stage production without Goldwyn's permission for the next three and a half years. Perhaps this is one reason why Brecht seemed so little discouraged by the collapse of the original *Chalk Circle* plan (which was not yet Caucasian when his journal first mentions it in March) as to carry his preoccupation with it right through the summer of

1944. Thus he reworked the character of Grusha, whose goodness, like Simone's patriotism, had seemed too arbitrary, and tried to make her tougher; he rewrote the prologue; and he asked neighbor Christopher Isherwood (who refused) to make a translation. Then at some point James and Tanya Stern, who had first translated the play for Leventhal and Broadway, made a new version with W. H. Auden, who was sharing a house with them on Fire Island. (Part of this new version appeared in spring, 1946, in *The Kenyon Review.*) By September 1944, Brecht seems to have more or less finished the fully revised script, which was to remain virtually unchanged for the next ten years. That month his child by Ruth Berlau, called Michel like the child in the play, was born and died in Los Angeles. Coincidentally or not, he laid the play aside and by the end of the year was deeply involved instead in the *Galileo* project with Charles Laughton, who had recently become very taken with Brecht's work.

4

Galileo apart—and it must be remembered that for all the effort Brecht put into it over the next two and a half years this was just a revision of a previous play—the only one of his "American" works to reach the professional stage was *The Duchess of Malfi*, a play whose text has never formed part of the German collected works; it is printed for the first time as an appendix to the present volume. This interesting but largely frustrated adaptation was the result of Brecht's keenness to write something for the most famous of all the exiled German actresses, Elisabeth Bergner, whom he had first met in his Munich days. Soon after his arrival in the United States he had shown her the script of *The Good Person of Szechwan*, which she found boring; the trouble (so he later noted in his journal) being that she could not conceive of the theater audience as a group of people who would change the world—

so that the basic climate of this kind of theater is alien to her: the beginner's enthusiasm for a new millennium, the spirit of inquiry, the urge to unshackle *everybody's* productivity. in her eyes it is all a new "style," a matter of fashion, something arbitrary.

None the less she and her producer-husband, Paul Czinner, shared the Brechts' first family Christmas in Santa Monica, entertained them in turn on New Year's Eve, and set Brecht to work on a film story, now lost, which according to him was successfully plagiarized by some other (unidentified) writer.

One of his projects for her was an adaptation of Heywood's *A Woman Killed with Kindness*, with which he apparently thought of asking Feuchtwanger to help him. Instead, however, they tackled *Simone Machard*, and by the time that was finished and Brecht had set off for New York, either he or Miss Bergner had decided that another Elizabethan work would suit her better, Webster's *The Duchess of Malfi*. Once in New York, Brecht got in touch with the poet H. R. Hays, a friend of Hanns Eisler's who had already translated *Mother Courage* and *Lucullus* (first two of his major plays to be published in the U.S.) and also provided immigration affidavits. It was arranged with the Czinners that Hays and Brecht should adapt the play together, Hays doing the actual writing while Brecht concentrated on story and structure. The work began in April 1943, and by June 26, when Brecht was back in Santa Monica finishing *Schweyk*, a first script had been completed and copyrighted in both collaborators' names. Though Brecht then showed it to Eisler and asked him to write the music nothing more seems to have been done till he returned to New York that winter, when he went back (in the words of his journal) to

> work with hays and bergner on the *Duchess of Malfi*. not completely finished, since bergner is short of time.

Meanwhile he asked W. H. Auden to collaborate, seemingly without mentioning or consulting Hays. "I have been treating Webster's text with great care," he wrote on December 5,

> but I had to add a few new scenes and verses. These are now available in English, but it seems advisable to improve

> them and I have told Miss Bergner that no one could do it
> as well as you.

When Czinner told Hays of this proposal he walked out, leaving Auden to carry on as and when he could. The whole project now seems to have simmered for some eighteen months till in mid-summer of 1945 Brecht, who had come to New York a third time to help stage *The Private Life of the Master Race*, went to the Czinners' summer place near Woodstock, Vermont, to finish it off "in the rough." There is no more mention of it in his journal after that point, but a final Brecht-Auden script was copyrighted in April 1946, and it was at last decided to go ahead with its production. Spurred by the production of the original play at the Haymarket Theater in London a year earlier, with Peggy Ashcroft as the Duchess and John Gielgud as Ferdinand, the Czinners engaged as director George Rylands, a friend of Auden's and an eminent Cambridge Elizabethan scholar, but almost ludicrously out of tune with Brecht's personality and ideas. The Duchess was of course Miss Bergner; Bosola, the black actor Canada Lee playing with a whitened face; John Carradine and Robert Speaight were also in the cast; the music was by Benjamin Britten, "arranged" by Ignatz Strasfogel; Harry Bennett did the sets. Brecht's reactions can be gauged from the ultimatum which he sent Czinner after seeing the Boston production that September (see pp. 423-24). His criticisms were disregarded and at the Broadway opening at the Ethel Barrymore Theater on October 15 his contribution—which no critic could have detected once Rylands had chosen mainly to return to Webster —was no longer mentioned, credit being given to Auden alone. It is not known whether he even attended, despite his strong condemnatory note. The play got a bad press and ran only a few days.

Such was the one tangible result of Brecht's four attempts to write for Broadway. As for the others, the *Simone Machard* film was never made, first because Teresa Wright, whom MGM had cast for the part of the adolescent girl, was inappositely expecting a baby, and then because the liberation of France in 1944 made the theme so much less topical. It re-

mained MGM's property, so Feuchtwanger told Brecht as late
as 1956, when the latter wanted to propose it to Cavalcanti,
director of the previous year's second-rate *Puntila* film.
Around the same time there were various inquiries about the
play—from Akimov in Leningrad, from Norman Lloyd in
New York, and from Jean-Marie Serreau and Benno Besson
for a mixed German-French tour—and these led Brecht to
stress that

> the most important thing for any production of Simone is
> that the title part must on no account be played by a young
> actress—not even one that looks like a child. It must be an
> eleven-year-old, and one that looks like a child.

This principle was followed in the eventual première of the
play at Frankfurt in March 1957, which Brecht of course
never saw. For there Simone was played by a child who had
been trained specially for the part by Ruth Berlau in Berlin.
Eisler, who had started writing the music in 1943, now finished
it off and the whole production was a great success. None the
less Eisler himself once again did not like it. "The play's too
heroic for me," he told Hans Bunge later. It was "a tribute
to heroism. And that's not right. I don't need to tell you how
utterly contrary to Brecht's whole way of looking at things
that is." Nor did the Berliner Ensemble ever stage it, though
there was an East German television version that included a
number of the Ensemble actors.

Schweyk remained a play, which Brecht never amended so
as to provide the greater musical opportunities which Weill
had asked for. None the less in the autumn of 1947, when
Wolfgang Langhoff at the Deutsches Theater in (East) Berlin
was planning to present it, it was to Weill that Brecht turned
for the incidental music. Once again Weill put him off, and
there is no further record of this plan. Eighteen months later,
however, when Brecht was setting up his Ensemble, he hoped
to get Peter Lorre to come to Berlin to create the part. Again,
it was not possible to organize a production before Brecht's
death in 1956, though in 1955 (if we are to believe Hanns
Eisler's slightly erratic recollections) he had asked Eisler to
start writing the music and to give it priority over that for

Simone Machard. "Interesting that you can be so amusing," he told Eisler when he brought him the result a few weeks before he died.

> He made me play it, and I still see him smiling at my weaknesses and his advantages.

In the event the play was first staged not in Germany at all but at the Polish army theater in Warsaw, where Ludwik René directed it in January 1957. This was nearly fourteen years after it had been written. The *Duchess of Malfi* adaptation has never been performed again.

The Caucasian Chalk Circle was put on in America by students at Northfield, Minnesota, under the direction of Henry Goodman (now of UCLA Drama Department) who had been bitten with Brecht on seeing the *Galileo* production of July 1947. This took place in May 1948 after Brecht had left the country, and used Eric and Maja Bentley's translation, which had apparently superseded that by the Sterns and Auden. Two and a half years later, when Brecht was back in Berlin, he saw the Austrian composer Gottfried von Einem in Munich and tentatively arranged for a German-language première at the Salzburg festival, to be directed by Berthold Viertel with Homolka as Azdak and Käthe Gold as Grusha. Though their plan never materialized, he managed to interest Carl Orff in the idea of writing the music: something that Hanns Eisler found uncongenial. This was partly because there was no real certainty of a production, but above all because in his view "Brecht was pursuing a chimera":

> Brecht said he wanted a kind of music to which lengthy epics can be narrated. After all, Homer was sung. He used to say, "Isn't it possible to write a setting or note down a cadence that would permit the delivery of a two-hour epic?"

By his own account Eisler made one or two sketches before deciding that this was beyond him. In 1953 therefore when Brecht determined to stage the play himself with the Ensemble he went instead to Paul Dessau, who had already in America been interested enough in "The Augsburg Chalk Circle" version of the story to draft out the framework of an oratorio. Following very much the requirements posed by Brecht in the note on pp. 297–98, Dessau provided him with the kind of orientally-derived music which he wanted for his recycling of a popular narrative tradition still observable in North Africa and the Far East. The production itself took about eight months to rehearse before its première in June 1954. Though it fell foul of the party critics in East Germany it made a great impression at the Paris International Theater Festival the following year; since then the play has been among the best-known of Brecht's works. After 1964 it was even one of those most performed in the USSR, though according to the critic Kats (reported by Henry Glade), the prologue (or first scene) is simply not playable before a Soviet audience, presumably because it gives too unreal a picture of conditions there.

5

Particularly among those who disapprove of his decision to settle finally in East Germany, it has become common to contrast Brecht's six years in America with his seven years in East Berlin. And certainly the latter were not productive so far as his actual writing went. But his American record is not all that impressive either, at least by the standards which he had set himself in Scandinavia and before that in pre-Nazi Berlin. Of course his initial difficulties did not last forever, and some of the poems which he wrote from 1942 on show new qualities of concentrated observation which were a genuine gain; nor were they any the less deeply political for being independent of day-to-day party tactics. Though he always remained in some measure dependent on the goodwill of his fellow exiles—it is difficult, for instance, to think of his involvement in *The Duchess of Malfi* as due to anything less than a wish to help on the Czinners' part—he did gradually make his mark among the non-Germans with whom he came in contact, and here his addiction to English literature, whether classical or criminal, must surely have helped. He worked hard and systematically, witness the "plan for the day" which he drew up on concluding *The Caucasian Chalk Circle* in Santa Monica in 1944:

> get up 7 A.M. newspaper, radio. make coffee in the little copper pot. morning: work. light lunch at twelve. rest with crime story. afternoon: work or pay visits. evening meal at 7 P.M. then visitors. night: half a page of shakespeare or waley's collection of chinese poems. radio. crime story.

But three of our four plays are to a greater or lesser extent flawed, and there was only one which he chose to stage himself when he had the chance. Thus *Simone Machard* not only reflects Brecht's uncertainties while writing it (as our editorial note attempts to show), but is in essential ways inconsistent with his own attitude, just as Eisler—a judge whom he always respected—pointed out. (Of course some audiences like it all the better for that.) *Schweyk*, despite its success in capturing Hašek's tone of voice, has none of the panoramic sweep of the novel, or even of the Piscator adaptation, while there is something deeply inappropriate about pitting the amiable Good Soldier—so perfect an instrument for undermining the whiskered Emperor Franz Josef—against political psychopaths and mass murderers. Both plays, moreover, take a romanticized view of the resistance movements, whose topical appeal they were in some measure surely designed to exploit. Since *The Duchess of Malfi* was so mangled that there is difficulty in reconstructing Brecht's conception of it—something that he never seems to have wished to do himself, to judge from the absence of any German version—the only one of the American plays to succeed in Brecht's own terms is *The Caucasian Chalk Circle*. Despite its awkward combination of two largely unrelated stories (though these had long been married up in the author's mind) and the uncharacteristic sweetness of the heroine, it is a truly epic work, embodying many of Brecht's special ideas, tastes, and talents. In many opinions it is a masterpiece.

It is significant that although this play was originally commissioned for a Broadway production Brecht himself could attribute its structure to "a revulsion against the commercialized dramaturgy of Broadway." For everything else that Brecht wrote in America, apart from his poems, was written for more or less commercial ends; and if he kicked against the commercial spirit it was surely because he knew that he was being conditioned by it. Most obviously this was so of his film stories, which were without exception what he termed "daily bread and butter work" even though he could hardly help imbuing them with some of his own qualities (whence, no doubt, their ill success). But *Simone Machard* too was written with one eye at least to the film industry; *Schweyk* was to be a Broadway musical, while not only the other two plays but also the adaptation of *Galileo* were written with Broadway productions in view. For the first time in the fourteen years since the success of *The Threepenny Opera*, Brecht was writing exclusively for the commercial stage in its most nakedly competitive form; nor was anything that he is known to have written in America (apart possibly from a short unpublished ballet libretto for Lotte Goslar) performed by the students, musicians, or left-wing amateurs who had helped to shape some of his most original works. He was never particularly good at working for the box office or respecting other people's conventions, while his natural cussedness made him spoil any chance he might have had of succeeding: witness his wanton (was it unconsciously deliberate?) antagonizing of Leventhal and Luise Rainer. One might almost say that it was his very failures that justify this group of plays.

Why then did he never make contact with any other form of theater (or cinema) in the United States during those years? Perhaps it was the result of his experiences over the New York production of *Mother* in 1935 that alienated him so from the American left-wing stage; certainly he seems to have had little use for the ideas of Odets or John Howard Lawson, while even so good a friend as Gorelik was largely in disagreement with him. Nor was university theater then anything like so active as it has since become. Perhaps too the identification of Hollywood and Broadway with the war effort was itself misleading, for Brecht was always primarily concerned to see the Nazis beaten. *Hangmen, Simone,* and *Schweyk* all deal with the same theme of European resistance to Hitler, while the revised prologue to *The Caucasian Chalk Circle* sets it too within the framework of the war, despite the remoteness of the legend. Oddly enough he never again took up those American themes which had fascinated him earlier, from *In the Jungle of Cities* to *Arturo Ui*, in other words from Munich days right up to his departure from Europe. As Professor James Lyon has pointed out, he did come to take a good deal of interest in the affairs of his half-adopted country and at one point considered basing a script on Edgar Lee Masters's *Spoon River Anthology;* but the only direct reflection of his surroundings is in his poems. Much must have been due to his lack of money and dependence on the German colony's esteem for him; much too to the lack of his two most-valued women collaborators, Margarete Steffin and Elisabeth Hauptmann (though the latter was then living elsewhere in the U.S.). One can only speculate what might have happened if he had come into contact with the student movement as it later developed, or chosen to associate himself with the blacks. As it was he did not.

He already seems to have decided to return to Germany well before his summons to appear before the House Un-American Activities Committee in 1947. 1946 is a mysteriously blank year in his life, when he wrote virtually no poems, worked on no plays other than *Galileo*, and made no entries in his journal (unless the relevant pages have somehow been lost). But by that winter he was already planning his return, to judge from his correspondence with Piscator and Caspar Neher, to whom he reported receiving offers "to be able to use the Theater am Schiffbauerdamm for certain purposes." His hearing by J. Parnell Thomas's committee the following autumn was in some measure a by-product of their investigation of the motion-picture industry, though his only real link with the so-called Hollywood Ten was his friendship with Donald Ogden Stewart and his wife. What clearly was of more interest to the investigators was his association with Hanns Eisler and through him with his brother Gerhart, the one genuinely important international Communist functionary whom they were able to unearth. This was in some measure due to the Eislers' sister Ruth Fischer, who had been one of the leaders of the German Communist Party in her youth, knew Brecht, and now coined the pleasant phrase for him "minstrel of the GPU." Hanns was effectively deported in February 1948; Gerhart (whose prosecution was called for by Richard Nixon in his maiden speech as a Representative) left the U.S. on a Polish liner and was lucky to escape arrest. Brecht stood up well under examination, made the committee laugh, and left for Europe under his own steam a day later. He never came back.

THE EDITORS

The Visions of
Simone Machard

Play

This play was written in collaboration with Lion Feuchtwanger

Translator: Ralph Manheim

CHARACTERS

PHILIPPE CHAVEZ, mayor of
   Saint-Martin (King
   Charles VII in the dreams)
HENRI SOUPEAU, owner of the
   hostelry (the constable)
MARIE SOUPEAU, his mother
   (Isabeau, the queen
   mother)
CAPTAIN HONORÉ FÉTAIN, a
   wealthy vineyard owner
   (the duke of Burgundy)
THE COLONEL (bishop of
   Beauvais)
A GERMAN CAPTAIN (an
   English general)

SIMONE MACHARD (the Maid
   of Orleans in the dreams)
MAURICE and ROBERT, truck
   drivers
GEORGES, PÈRE GUSTAVE,
   employees of the hostelry
MADAME MACHARD, MONSIEUR
   MACHARD, Simone's parents
A SERGEANT
REFUGEES
SUPPORTING CHARACTERS
   (soldiers and people in
   the dreams)
THE ANGEL

*The scene represents the yard of the "Au Relais" hostelry.
The background consists of the garage, a low building. To the
right of the audience is the hostelry with its back door. To the
left the storehouse, with rooms for the truck drivers. Between
the storehouse and the garage a rather large gate, opening out
on the street. The garage is conceived as a large one, since the
hostelry also operates a trucking business.*

   *The action takes place in June 1940, in Saint-Martin, a small
town on one of the main roads from Paris to the south of
France.*

1

The Book

Georges, a soldier, is sitting smoking. His right arm is bandaged. Beside him old Père Gustave is mending a tire. The brothers Maurice and Robert, truck drivers employed by the hostelry, are looking intently at the sky. Airplanes are heard. It is the evening of June 14.

ROBERT They must be ours.

MAURICE They're not ours.

ROBERT (*calling over to Georges*) Georges, are they ours or are they Boches?

GEORGES (*gingerly moving his bandaged arm*) Now it's gone numb above the elbow.

PÈRE GUSTAVE Don't move it; that's no good.

(*Simone Machard comes in. She is a young teenager; her skirt is too long and her shoes are too big. She is carrying a heavy basket full of washing*)

ROBERT Heavy?

(*Simone nods and carries the basket as far as the gas pump. Smoking, the men watch her*)

GEORGES (*to Père Gustave*) Think it could be the bandage? It's got stiffer since yesterday.

PÈRE GUSTAVE Simone, go get Monsieur Georges some cider out of the storehouse.

SIMONE (*puting down her basket*) What if Monsieur Soupeau catches me again?

PÈRE GUSTAVE Do as you're told.

(*Simone goes out*)

ROBERT (*to Georges*)   Can't you answer a question? The guy wears a uniform and he doesn't even look up when he hears a plane! With soldiers like you they'll lose the war.

GEORGES   What do *you* think, Robert? Now it's numb above the elbow too. Père Gustave thinks it's only the bandage.

ROBERT   I asked you about those planes.

GEORGES (*without looking up*)   Germans. Ours don't get off the ground.

(*Simone has come back with a bottle of cider, from which she pours a glass for Georges*)

SIMONE   Do you think we're going to lose the war, Monsieur Georges?

GEORGES   Win or lose, I'm going to need two arms.

(*Monsieur Henri Soupeau, the owner of the hostelry, comes in from the street. Simone quickly hides the cider. Monsieur Soupeau stops in the gateway, looks to see who is in the yard, and motions to someone in the street. A gentleman in a long dust coat appears. Monsieur Soupeau escorts him across the yard, carefully shielding him from the others, and disappears with him into the hostelry*)

PÈRE GUSTAVE   Did you see that dust coat? That's an officer. A colonel. One more who's beat it from the front. They don't want to be seen. But they eat like a horse.

(*Simone has gone over to her basket and sat down on the support of the gas pump; she starts reading a book that was on top of her basket*)

GEORGES (*over his cider*)   Robert gives me a pain. He says they'll lose the war with soldiers like me. But thanks to me, they've won something else, you can't deny it. A gentleman in Tours has made good money on my shoes and a gentleman in Bordeaux on my helmet. My jacket brought in a castle on the Riviera, and my leggings seven race horses. France was making a good thing out of me before the war even started.

PÈRE GUSTAVE   And now it's being lost. By the dust coats.

GEORGES   Exactly. There are 200 hangars with 1000 fighter planes, paid for, tested and manned, but in the hour of France's peril they never get off the ground. The Maginot Line cost 10 billion; steel and concrete, 700 miles long, seven stories deep, in open country. And when the battle started, our colonel hopped into his car and drove to the rear, followed by two cars full of food and wine. Two million men waiting for orders, ready to die, but the war minister's mistress was on the outs with the prime minister's mistress, so no orders came. Our forts are dug in, they don't move; their forts are on wheels, they roll over us. Nothing is going to stop their tanks as long as they have gas, and they get gas from our gas stations. Tomorrow they'll be here at your station, Simone, drinking up your gas. Thanks for the cider.

ROBERT   Don't talk about tanks (*with a motion of his head in Simone's direction*) when she's around. Her brother's at the front.

GEORGES   She's busy with her book.

PÈRE GUSTAVE (*to Robert*)   How about a game of belote?

ROBERT   I've got a headache. All day we've been driving the captain's wine barrels through crowds of refugees. A regular migration.

PÈRE GUSTAVE   The captain's wine is the most important refugee of all. Can't you get that through your head?

GEORGES   Everybody knows the man's a fascist. His pals on the general staff must have told him that something's gone wrong again up front.

ROBERT   Maurice is fit to be tied. He says he's good and sick of driving those damn wine barrels through women and children. I'm hitting the hay. (*He goes out*)

PÈRE GUSTAVE   Those crowds of refugees are ruinous for warfare. Tanks can get through any swamp, but in a human swamp they bog down. The civilian population has turned out to be a terrible nuisance in wartime. When a war breaks out they ought to be moved to another planet, they're only in the way. One or the other has got to be abolished: the people or the war; you can't have both.

GEORGES (*has sat down beside Simone; reaching into the basket*)   You've taken the washing down dripping wet.

SIMONE (*still reading*)   The refugees keep stealing the tablecloths.

GEORGES   Probably for diapers or to wrap their feet in.

SIMONE (*still reading*)   Madame counts them just the same.

GEORGES (*pointing at the book*)   Is it still the Maid of Orleans? (*Simone nods*) Who gave you this book?

SIMONE   Monsieur Soupeau. But I never get a chance to read. I'm only up to page 72, where the Maid defeats the English and crowns the king in Rheims. (*Goes on reading*)

GEORGES   Why do you read that old-fashioned stuff?

SIMONE   I want to know what happens next.—Monsieur Georges, is it true that France is the fairest land on earth?

GEORGES   Is that what it says in the book? (*Simone nods*) I've never seen the rest of the world. But they say the fairest land is the one you live in.

SIMONE   What's the Gironde like, for instance?

GEORGES   I think they grow wine there too. They say France is the biggest wine drinker in the world.

SIMONE   Are there a lot of barges on the Seine?

GEORGES   About a thousand.

SIMONE   And Saint-Denis, where you were working. What's it like?

GEORGES   Nothing to write home about.

SIMONE   But all in all it's the fairest land.

GEORGES   It's good for bread, wine, and fish. I wouldn't say anything against the cafés with their orange awnings. Or the food markets with all the meat and fruit, especially in the early morning. Never mind the bistros with their pernod. The country fairs and the brass bands at ship launchings are all right. And who could object to the poplars we play boules under? Have you got to take food parcels to the schoolhouse again today?

SIMONE   If only the engineers get here before I have to go.

GEORGES   What engineers?

SIMONE   They're expecting engineer troops in the kitchen. Their field kitchen got lost in the crowd of refugees. They're from the 132nd.

GEORGES   Isn't that your brother's regiment?

SIMONE   Yes. They're moving up to the front.—It says in the book that the angel commanded the Maid to slay all the enemies of France, God wills it.

GEORGES   You'll be getting your nightmares again if you go on reading that bloodthirsty stuff. Why do you think I took the newspapers away from you?

SIMONE Do their tanks really plow through crowds of people, Monsieur Georges?

GEORGES Yes. And now you've done enough reading.

(*He tries to take the book away from her. Monsieur Soupeau steps into the door from the hostelry*)

MONSIEUR SOUPEAU Georges, you're not to let anyone into the breakfast room. (*To Simone*) You're reading at your work again, Simone. That's not what I gave you the book for.

SIMONE (*has begun to count the tablecloths eagerly*) I was only taking a quick look while I was counting the washing. I'm sorry, Monsieur Henri.

PÈRE GUSTAVE I wouldn't have given her that book if I were you, Monsieur Henri; it's getting her all upset.

MONSIEUR SOUPEAU Nonsense. In times like these it won't hurt her to learn something about the history of France. These youngsters don't even know what France is. (*Speaking over his shoulder back into the house*) Jean, take the hors d'oeuvres to the breakfast room. (*Again to those in the yard*) It wouldn't hurt you to read about the spirit they had in those days. God knows we could use a Maid of Orleans.

PÈRE GUSTAVE (*affecting interest*) Where would she come from?

MONSIEUR SOUPEAU Where would she come from! From anywhere. It could be anybody. You! Or Georges! (*Indicating Simone*) She could be the one. Any child could tell them what needs to be done, it's simple. Even she could tell the country.

PÈRE GUSTAVE (*looking Simone over*) Maybe kind of small for a Maid of Orleans.

MONSIEUR SOUPEAU Kind of small, kind of young, kind of big, kind of old: where the spirit is lacking there's always an alibi. (*Over his shoulder into the house*) Jean, did you serve the Portuguese sardines?

PÈRE GUSTAVE (*to Simone*) How about it? Would you like to change your job? I'm only afraid no angels would come along these days.

MONSIEUR SOUPEAU That will do, Père Gustave. I wish you'd keep your cynicism to yourself in front of the child. Let her read her book; she can do without your nasty remarks.

(*On his way into the hostelry*) But it doesn't have to be during work hours, Simone. (*Goes out*)

PÈRE GUSTAVE (*grinning*)   Hey, Georges, can you beat that? Now he wants his kitchen maid to learn how to be the Maid of Orleans, on her own time of course. They cram kids full of patriotism. And they disguise themselves in dust coats. Or hide their hoarded gasoline in certain brickyards instead of handing it over to the army.

SIMONE   Monsieur Soupeau isn't doing anything wrong.

PÈRE GUSTAVE   No, he's a public benefactor. He gives you twenty francs a week, so your people "won't be left entirely high and dry."

SIMONE   He keeps me on so my brother's job will be waiting for him.

PÈRE GUSTAVE   And gets a gas station attendant, a waitress, and a dishwasher out of it.

SIMONE   That's because there's a war on.

PÈRE GUSTAVE   Which doesn't hurt him any, does it?

MONSIEUR SOUPEAU (*appears in the doorway of the hostelry*) Père Gustave, a half bottle of the '23 Chablis for the gentleman with the trout. (*Back into the hostelry*)

PÈRE GUSTAVE   The gentleman in the dust coat, alias the colonel, desires a bottle of Chablis before the fall of France. (*Out into the storehouse. During the following, he takes the bottle of Chablis across the yard into the hostelry*)

A WOMAN'S VOICE (*from the second floor of the hostelry*) Simone, where are those tablecloths?
(*Simone picks up the basket and starts toward the hostelry. At this moment a sergeant and two soldiers come in from the street with a large stew pot*)

SERGEANT   We've come to pick up rations. The people at the town hall said they'd phoned.

SIMONE (*beaming, eagerly*)   It must be ready by now. Go right into the kitchen. (*To the sergeant, while the two soldiers go in*) Monsieur, my brother André Machard is with the 132nd. Do you know why we haven't heard from him?

SERGEANT   Everything's in a muddle up front. We lost contact with the front line the day before yesterday.

SIMONE   Is the war lost, monsieur?

SERGEANT   Of course not, mademoiselle. A few enemy tanks have broken through, that's all. The monsters are bound to run out of gas pretty soon. Then they'll be stuck.

SIMONE   They say they'll never get as far as the Loire.

SERGEANT   No, nothing to worry about. It's a long way from the Seine to the Loire. The only trouble is the crowds of refugees. We can hardly move. And we've got to repair the bombed bridges, or the reserves won't get through. (*The two soldiers come back with the pot; the sergeant looks inside it*)

SERGEANT   Is that all? It's a disgrace. Take a look, mademoiselle. It's not even half full. This is the third restaurant we've been sent to. The first two gave us nothing at all. Here we get this.

SIMONE (*looks into the pot with consternation*)   There must be some mistake. We've got plenty, lots of lentils and smoked pork. I'll speak to Monsieur Soupeau myself. Your pot will be full. Just a minute. (*She rushes inside*)

GEORGES (*offering cigarettes*)   Her brother's only seventeen. He was the only one in Saint-Martin to volunteer. She's very fond of him.

SERGEANT   Damn this war. What kind of a war is it anyway? The army's treated like an enemy in its own country. And the premier says on the radio: "The army is the people."

PÈRE GUSTAVE (*who has come out of the house*)   "The army is the people." And the people are the enemy.

SERGEANT (*hostile*)   What do you mean by that?

GEORGES (*looks into the half-empty pot*)   Why do you stand for it? Go get the mayor.

SERGEANT   We know mayors; they don't do a thing.

SIMONE (*comes out slowly; without looking at the sergeant*)   Monsieur Soupeau says he can't give you any more on account of all the refugees.

PÈRE GUSTAVE   And we can't give them anything because the troops get it all.

SIMONE (*in despair*)   Monsieur Soupeau is angry because the mayor is always making demands.

SERGEANT (*wearily*)   It's the same all over.

MONSIEUR SOUPEAU (*comes into the doorway and gives Simone a folded check*) Here's the check for the gentleman with the trout. Tell him we're giving him the strawberries at cost price, say your parents sold them to the hostelry. (*He shoves her into the house*) What's the matter? You're not satisfied? Would you kindly stop to think of the civilian population? We've been bled white, and every day they ask more of us. God knows that nobody feels for France more than I do, but . . . (*With a sweeping gesture of help-lessness*) I have to make big sacrifices to keep this business going. Look at the help I've got. (*With a gesture in the direction of Père Gustave and Georges*) An old man and a cripple. And a child. I employ them because they'd starve if I didn't. I can't feed the French army into the bargain.

SERGEANT And I can't send my men out in the night on an empty stomach to work under fire for your benefit. Repair your own bridges. I'll wait for my field kitchen. If it takes seven years. (*Goes out with his men*)

MONSIEUR SOUPEAU What can I do? You can't please every-body. (*Making up to the help*) Friends, thank your stars that you don't own a restaurant. You see how it is? Like fighting off wolves. After all the trouble we've had getting two stars in the guidebook. (*Since Père Gustave and Georges show little sympathy for his troubles, angrily*) Don't stand there like bumps on a log. (*Calls back into the house*) Monsieur, there's no one in the yard now.

COLONEL (*the gentleman in the dust coat—comes out of the hostelry. To Monsieur Soupeau who is escorting him across the yard to the road*) Your prices are outrageous, mon-sieur. One hundred and sixty francs for a meal.

GEORGES (*goes in the meantime into the hostelry and drags out Simone, who is burying her face in her hands*) They left long ago. You don't have to hide in the hallway any more. It's not *your* fault, Simone.

SIMONE (*drying her tears*) It's only because they're from the 132nd, Monsieur Georges. The boys at the front are waiting for help, and the engineers have to repair the bridges first.

MONSIEUR SOUPEAU (*returns from the street*) Foie gras,

trout, roast lamb, asparagus, Chablis, coffee, brandy, Martell '84. In times like these. And when the check comes, they make a face a mile long. But the service has to be double quick, because they can't wait to get out of the war zone. An officer! A colonel! Poor France! (*Sees Simone; with a guilty conscience*) And you, don't butt in. What goes on in the kitchen is none of your business! (*Out into the hostelry*)

GEORGES (*to Père Gustave, pointing at Simone*)   She's ashamed on account of the engineers.

SIMONE   What will they think of our hostelry, Monsieur Georges?

GEORGES (*to Simone*)   You have no reason to be ashamed. The hostelry will cheat people as sure as God made little red apples, and the boss will charge scandalous prices as sure as a dog farts. You're not the hostelry. When a guest praises the wine, you've got nothing to be pleased about; when the roof caves in, you've got nothing to cry about. It wasn't you that chose the bed linen. It wasn't you that refused them food. See?

SIMONE (*not convinced*)   Yes, Monsieur Georges.

GEORGES   André knows you took the job on his account. That's enough. And now go on over to the schoolhouse to see little François. But don't let his mother scare you with her talk about the stukas, or you'll dream half the night that you're on the battlefield. (*He pushes her gently into the hostelry; to Père Gustave*) Too much imagination.

PÈRE GUSTAVE (*mending his tire*)   She doesn't like going to the schoolhouse. They insult her because the food parcels are too expensive.

GEORGES (*with a sigh*)   As I know her, she probably sticks up for the boss. She's a loyal one.

MONSIEUR SOUPEAU (*comes out of the hostelry and calls out in the direction of the storehouse, clapping his hands*)   Maurice, Robert!

ROBERT'S VOICE (*from the storehouse, sleepily*)   Yes?

MONSIEUR SOUPEAU   Captain Fétain just called up. He wants you to take the rest of the wine barrels to Bordeaux right away.

ROBERT'S VOICE   Tonight? That's impossible, Monsieur Henri.
We've been on the road for two days.

MONSIEUR SOUPEAU   I know. I know. But what can I do? The
captain thinks we're being too slow about his shipments.
Of course it's because of the clogged roads. I really hate to
deprive you of your night's sleep, but . . . (*A gesture of
helplessness*)

ROBERT'S VOICE   The roads are clogged at night too, and we
have to drive with blackout lights.

MONSIEUR SOUPEAU   C'est la guerre. We can't antagonize our
best customers. Mother insists. So get started. (*To Père
Gustave*) Aren't you through with that tire yet? (*Monsieur Chavez, the mayor, has come in from the street, with
a briefcase under his arm. He is very much excited*)

PÈRE GUSTAVE   (*calling Monsieur Soupeau's attention to him*)
Monsieur le maire.

MAYOR   Henri, it's about your trucks again. I'm sorry. You've
got to let me have them for the refugees.

MONSIEUR SOUPEAU   But I've told you that I'm under contract
to haul Captain Fétain's wine. I can't refuse him. He and
mother are childhood friends.

MAYOR   "The captain's wine!" Henri, you know I don't like
to interfere with anyone's business activities, but at a time
like this I can't worry my head over your relations with
that fascist Fétain.

(*Simone has come out of the hostelry. A tray full of large
parcels is slung round her neck, and she is carrying two
baskets full of parcels*)

MONSIEUR SOUPEAU   (*menacingly*)   Philippe, watch your step
about calling the captain a fascist.

MAYOR   (*angrily*)   "Watch your step!" That's all you and
your captain can think of, with the Germans on the Loire.
France is going to the dogs!

MONSIEUR SOUPEAU   What! Where are the Germans?

MAYOR   (*emphatically*)   On the Loire. And the Ninth Army
can't get through to relieve our boys because Route 20 is
clogged with refugees. Your trucks are confiscated along
with every other truck in Saint-Martin; I want them ready

tomorrow morning to evacuate the refugees in the school-house. That's official. (*He takes a small red poster out of his briefcase and starts fastening it to the garage door*)

SIMONE (*horrified, in a low voice to Georges*) The tanks are coming, Monsieur Georges.

GEORGES (*puts his arm over her shoulder*) Yes, Simone.

SIMONE They're on the Loire. They'll be coming to Tours.

GEORGES Yes, Simone.

SIMONE They'll come here too, won't they?

MONSIEUR SOUPEAU Now I see why the captain was in such a hurry. (*Shaken*) The Germans on the Loire, that's terrible. (*Goes over to the mayor who is still posting his notice*) Philippe, never mind about that. Come inside with me. I want to talk to you in private.

MAYOR (*angrily*) No, Henri, I'm through talking with you in private. I want your employees to know that your trucks are confiscated and your gas too. I've looked the other way long enough.

MONSIEUR SOUPEAU Are you out of your mind? Confiscating my trucks in this situation! Anyway, I haven't got any gas. Except for the few gallons I've got here.

MAYOR What about the black-market stuff you haven't declared?

MONSIEUR SOUPEAU What's that? Are you accusing me of illegally hoarding gas? (*Furious*) Père Gustave, have we any illegal gas?

(*Père Gustave pretends not to hear and starts rolling his tire into the garage*)

MONSIEUR SOUPEAU (*shouting*) Maurice! Robert! Come down here this minute! Père Gustave! (*Père Gustave stops*) Speak up! Have we any illegal gas around here?

PÈRE GUSTAVE I don't know anything about it. (*To Simone, who is staring at him*) Attend to your work and stop listening to other people's business.

MONSIEUR SOUPEAU Maurice! Robert! Where are you!

MAYOR If you have no extra gas, what do you truck the captain's wine with?

MONSIEUR SOUPEAU You can't catch me with that one, monsieur le maire. I truck the captain's wine with the captain's gas. Georges, did you ever hear of my having any illegal gas?

GEORGES (*with a look at his arm*) I've only been back from the front for four days.

MONSIEUR SOUPEAU That's right, you wouldn't know. But there's Maurice and Robert. (*Maurice and Robert have entered*) Maurice and Robert! Monsieur Chavez has been accusing us of hiding gasoline. I ask you in the presence of Monsieur Chavez: is that true?

(*The brothers hesitate*)

MAYOR Maurice and Robert. You know me. I'm not a policeman, I don't like to meddle in other people's business. But France needs gasoline. I'm asking you to testify that there is gasoline here. You're decent young fellows.

MONSIEUR SOUPEAU Well?

MAURICE (*sullenly*) We never heard of any gas.

MAYOR So that's your answer. (*To Simone*) Your brother's at the front, isn't he? But I presume you won't tell me either that there's gas hidden here?

(*Simone stands motionless, then starts to cry*)

MONSIEUR SOUPEAU Oh, now you're asking children to give evidence against me? Monsieur le maire, you have no right to undermine this child's respect for her employer. (*To Simone*) Run along, Simone.

MAYOR (*wearily*) Sending some of your fraudulent food parcels to the schoolhouse? Robbing the refugees again? You only filled the soldiers' pot half full. How can the refugees get anywhere if they're robbed of their last sou all along the line?

MONSIEUR SOUPEAU This is a restaurant, not a charitable institution.

MAYOR I see. Only a miracle can save France. It's rotten to the core. (*He goes out. Silence*)

MONSIEUR SOUPEAU All right, Simone. Get going!

(*Simone goes out slowly and hesitantly toward the gate, repeatedly looking back. The book which she has hidden in the tray falls to the ground. She picks it up on the sly and goes out through the gate with her tray and baskets*)

Simone Machard's First Dream

The night of June 14.

Music. The angel emerges from the darkness. He stands on the garage roof. His face is golden and expressionless. In his hand he holds a small drum. Three times he cries out in a loud voice: "Joan!" Then the stage lights up. Simone is standing in the deserted yard with her wash basket on her arm, looking up at the angel.

THE ANGEL
Daughter of France, Joan: something must be done
Or our great France will perish before two weeks have run.
The Lord our God has looked around for aid
And now His eyes have fallen on His little Maid.
Here is a drum. God sends it. Beat it mightily
To shake the people from their lethargy.
But to be heard, you must set this drum upon the ground
As though to make the soil of France itself resound.
Now drum, and wake this people from its trance
Till rich and poor take pity on their mother France.
For shipping call on the bargemen of the Seine
On the peasants of Gironde to feed our fighting men.
For tanks you will go to the metal workers of Saint-Denis
And to pull the bridges down before the enemy
Round up the carpenters of Lyons. Tell them all
That France, the mother they have scoffed at, sends this call
That France the great toiler and wine drinker is in need
And peril. Go now and seek them out. Godspeed!

SIMONE (*looks around to see if anyone else is there*)   Do I have to, monsieur? Aren't I too little to be a Saint Joan?
THE ANGEL   No.
SIMONE   Then I'll do it.
THE ANGEL   It will be hard. Leftit cribble clump.
SIMONE (*timidly*)   Are you my brother André?
(*The angel is silent*)
SIMONE   How are you getting along?

(*The angel disappears. But Georges comes sauntering out of the garage, bringing Simone his helmet and bayonet*)

GEORGES Helmet and sword. You'll need them. It's not the job for you, but the boss hasn't got anybody but a cripple and a kid. Forget about your work; listen, the tanks are breaking through like meat choppers: no wonder your brother's already an angel.

SIMONE (*takes the helmet and bayonet*) Should I clean them for you, Monsieur Georges?

GEORGES No, you'll be needing them now that you're the Maid of Orleans.

SIMONE (*puts on the helmet*) You're right. I've got to go to the king in Orleans right away. It's twenty miles, the tanks do fifty an hour, and my shoes are full of holes, I won't get new ones until Easter. (*Turns to go*) Would you wave to me as I go down the road, Monsieur Georges? I'll be afraid if you don't, war is old-fashioned, bloodthirsty stuff.

(*Georges tries to wave with his bandaged arm, and disappears. Simone starts on her way to Orleans, marching in a small circle*)

SIMONE (*sings loudly*)
On my way to Saint-Nazaire
I had lost my breeches.
All the people shouted loud:
"Where'd you put your breeches?"
I said: hard by Saint-Nazaire
Look, the sky is azure
And the oats are much too high
And the sky too azure.

(*Suddenly the truck drivers Maurice and Robert start trotting behind her, in overalls but with medieval weapons*)

SIMONE What are you doing here? Why are you following me?

ROBERT We're following you because we're your bodyguard. But kindly stop singing that song, it's indecent. We're betrothed to you, Joan, so be dignified.

SIMONE Am I betrothed to Maurice too?

MAURICE Yes, secretly.

(*Père Gustave comes toward them in primitive medieval armor. He looks away and begins to pass them by*)

SIMONE   Père Gustave!

PÈRE GUSTAVE   You leave me out of this. Expecting me to man guns at my age. Ridiculous! Live on tips and die for France!

SIMONE (*softly*)   But France, your mother, is in *danger*.

PÈRE GUSTAVE   My mother was Madame Poirot, the washerwoman. She was coming down with pneumonia. But what could I do? I had no money for all the medicines.

SIMONE (*shouting*)   Then I command you, in the name of God and the angel, to come back and take charge of the guns. (*In a kindlier tone*) I'll clean them for you.

PÈRE GUSTAVE   All right. That's something else again. Here, carry my pike. (*He gives her his pike and trots along with the others*)

MAURICE   How much farther is it, Simone? It's all for the capitalists anyway. Workers gobbie girl, belie! (*Simone also answers in a dream language unintelligible to the audience. She speaks with great force of conviction*)

MAURICE (*who has understood her*)   That's God's truth. All right, we'll keep going.

ROBERT   You're limping, Simone. That hardware is too heavy for you.

SIMONE (*suddenly exhausted*)   I'm sorry. It's only because I didn't get much breakfast. (*Stops and dries her sweat*) I'll be all right in a minute. Robert, do you remember what I'm supposed to say to the king?

ROBERT (*says something unintelligible in the dream language; then*)   That's all.

SIMONE   Of course. Thanks. Look, there are the towers of Orleans.

(*The colonel enters in armor with the dust coat over it. He sneaks across the yard*)

PÈRE GUSTAVE   A fine beginning. The marshals are leaving town, they're clearing out.

SIMONE   Why are the streets so empty, Père Gustave?

PÈRE GUSTAVE   I suppose they're all having supper.

SIMONE   And Père Gustave, why aren't they ringing the bells if the enemy's coming?

PÈRE GUSTAVE   I suppose Captain Fétain has sent the bells to
   Bordeaux.
   (*Monsieur Soupeau is standing in the entrance to the hostelry. He is wearing a helmet with a red plume and around
   his chest something of glittering steel*)

MONSIEUR SOUPEAU   Joan, you're to take the fraudulent parcels
   to the schoolhouse this minute.

SIMONE   But Monsieur Henri, France, our mother, is in danger. The Germans are on the Loire and I must speak to the
   king.

MONSIEUR SOUPEAU   This is an outrage. I'm doing all I can.
   Don't forget the respect you owe to your employer. (*A
   man in a purple garment appears in the garage*)

SIMONE   (*proudly*)   Look, Monsieur Henri, there's King
   Charles VII. (*The man in purple proves to be the mayor,
   who is wearing the royal cloak over his suit*)

MAYOR   Good morning, Joan.

SIMONE   (*astonished*)   Are you the king?

MAYOR   Yes. I'm here on official business. I hereby confiscate
   the trucks. We wish to speak to you in private, Joan. (*The
   drivers, Père Gustave, and Monsieur Soupeau disappear in
   the darkness. Simone and the mayor sit down on the stone
   support of the gasoline pump*)

MAYOR   Joan, it's all over. The marshal has gone off without
   leaving his address. I've written to the constable for guns,
   but my letter with the royal seal has been returned un-
   opened. The master of the horse says he's been wounded in
   the arm, though no one has ever seen the wound. They're
   all rotten to the core. (*He weeps*) I know, you've come
   here to scold me, to tell me I'm a weakling. And so I am.
   But what about you, Joan? First of all I want you to tell me
   where that illegal gas is.

SIMONE   In the brickyard, of course.

MAYOR   I know I've been looking the other way. But you're
   robbing the refugees of their last sou with your fraudulent
   parcels.

SIMONE   I do it because I have to keep a job for an angel,
   King Charles.

MAYOR   And is it to keep their jobs that the drivers have been trucking Captain Fétain's wine instead of refugees?

SIMONE Yes. And because the boss has registered them as indispensable to keep them out of the army.

MAYOR Ah yes, my bosses and nobles. They're the ones that have given me my gray hairs. The nobility is against the king. It says so in your book. But you've got the people behind you, especially Maurice. Couldn't we make a pact, Joan, you and I?

SIMONE Why not, King Charles? (*Hesitantly*) Only you've got to interfere with people's business activity and make sure the stew pots are always full.

MAYOR I'll see what I can do. I've got to watch my step, though, or they'll cut off my royal salary. You see, I'm the man who looks the other way, so naturally when I say something nobody listens. I'm expected to do all the dirty work. Take those engineers. Instead of taking their rations from the hostelry by force, they come to me: "Repair your own bridges. We'll wait for our field kitchen." Is it any wonder that the duke of Burgundy deserts me and goes over to the English?

MONSIEUR SOUPEAU (*stands in the doorway*) King Charles, I hear you're dissatisfied? Would you kindly stop to think of your civilian population? We've been bled white. Nobody feels for France more than I do, but . . . (*Gesture of helplessness; goes out*)

MAYOR (*with resignation*) Then how do you expect us to defeat the English?

SIMONE I'll just have to beat my drum. (*She sits down on the ground and beats her invisible drum. Every stroke resounds as though it came out of the earth*) Come on, you bargemen of the Seine! Come on, you metal workers of Saint-Denis. You carpenters of Lyons, come on. The enemy is coming.

MAYOR What do you see, Joan?

SIMONE They're coming. Stand fast, men. First comes the drummer with the voice of a wolf, *his* drum is made out of a Jew's skin; he's got a vulture on his shoulder, with the face of Fauche, the Lyons banker. Right behind him comes Field Marshal Firebug. He's on foot, a fat clown in seven uniforms, and he doesn't look human in any of them. It's easy to recognize the two devils, because there's a canopy of newspapers over them. Behind them ride the executioners and marshals. A swastika is branded on their low foreheads, and behind them as far as the eye can see come tanks and guns and railroad trains, and cars with altars on them and torture chambers, all very fast, on wheels. The battle wagons in the lead and behind them the loot wagons. The people get mowed down, but the grain gets gathered. Wherever they go, cities collapse, and every place they leave is a naked desert. But now they're done for, because here stand King Charles and the Maid of God, that's me.

(*All the Frenchmen who have appeared or will appear in the play have arrived, all with medieval weapons and odd pieces of armor*)

SIMONE (*radiant*)   See, King Charles, they've all come.

MAYOR   Not all, Joan. I don't see my mother Isabeau, for instance. And the constable has gone away in anger.

SIMONE   Don't be afraid. Now I must crown you king, then the whole French people will be united. I've brought you a crown. See?

(*She takes a crown out of the basket*)

MAYOR   But who am I going to play rummy with if the constable doesn't come back?

SIMONE   Ockal grisht burlap. (*Simone sets the crown on the king's head. In the background the engineers appear, pounding their stew pot with ladles and making a loud noise*)

MAYOR   What's that sound?

SIMONE   It's the bells of Rheims cathedral.

MAYOR   Isn't it the engineer troops that I sent to the hostelry for food?

SIMONE   They didn't get any. That's why their pots are empty. The empty pots are your coronation bells, King Charles.

MAYOR   Clidder dunk frim. Klemp!

ALL   Long live the king and Joan, the Maid, who has crowned him.

MAYOR   Many thanks, Simone. You have saved France.

(*The stage darkens. The voice of a radio announcer mingles with the confused music*)

2

The Handshake

It is early morning. Maurice and Robert, Père Gustave, and Georges are eating breakfast. The radio is heard from the hostelry.

RADIO We repeat the war ministry bulletin issued at three-thirty this morning. Due to an unexpected crossing of the Loire by German tank formations the strategically important highways of central France have been swamped by new waves of refugees. The civilian population is requested to stay put, so the roads can be open for reinforcements.

MAURICE It's time to get out of here.

GEORGES The waiter and the rest of them cleared out at five; they'd worked all night packing the china. The boss threatened to call the police. It didn't do him any good.

ROBERT (*to Georges*) Why didn't you wake us up?
(*Georges is silent*)

MAURICE The boss told you not to, eh? (*Laughs*)

ROBERT Aren't you clearing out, Georges?

GEORGES No. I'll take off my uniform and stay. They feed me here. I've given up hope of my arm getting better.
(*Monsieur Soupeau comes bustling out of the hostelry. He is carefully dressed. Simone comes trotting behind him, carrying his suitcases*)

MONSIEUR SOUPEAU (*clapping his hands*) Maurice, Robert, Gustave, get moving. The china has to be loaded. Everything in the storehouse goes into the trucks. Pack the hams in salt. But load the vintage wines first. You can have your coffee later, there's a war on. We're going to Bordeaux.
(*The help go on with their breakfast. Maurice laughs*)

MONSIEUR SOUPEAU What's the matter? Didn't you hear me? The trucks have got to be loaded.

MAURICE (*negligently*) The trucks have been requisitioned.

MONSIEUR SOUPEAU   Requisitioned? Nonsense. (*With a grand gesture*) That was yesterday. The German tanks are heading for Saint-Martin. That changes everything. Yesterday's arrangements don't apply any more.

PÈRE GUSTAVE (*in an undertone*)   Right.

MONSIEUR SOUPEAU   Stop drinking when I'm talking to you. (*Simone has put the suitcase down and crept back into the hostelry*)

MAURICE   Let's have another coffee, Robert.

ROBERT   Right, how do we know when we'll eat again?

MONSIEUR SOUPEAU (*repressing his anger*)   Be reasonable. Help your boss pack his belongings. There's a tip in it for you. (*When no one looks up*) Père Gustave, come on now. Get started on the china. Well?

PÈRE GUSTAVE (*stands up hesitantly*)   I haven't finished my breakfast yet. Don't look at me like that. It won't do you any good now. (*Angrily*) You can stick your china up your ass for all I care. (*He sits down again*)

MONSIEUR SOUPEAU   Are you crazy, too? At *your* age? (*He looks from one to the other, then at the motorcycle; angrily*) So that's it? You're waiting for the Germans? Your boss is through? Is that the affection and respect you owe your employer? (*To the drivers*) Three times I've signed statements that you were indispensable to my trucking business; if I hadn't, you'd be at the front, and this is how you thank me. This is my reward for treating my help as if we were all one happy family. (*Over his shoulder*) Simone, get me some brandy! I feel weak. (*When there is no answer*) Simone, where are you?—Now she's gone too. (*Simone comes out of the hostelry, wearing a jacket, dressed to go out; she tries to sneak past Monsieur Soupeau*)

MONSIEUR SOUPEAU   Simone! (*Simone keeps going*)

MONSIEUR SOUPEAU   What, you won't answer me? Are you crazy? (*Simone starts to run and goes out. Monsieur Soupeau shrugs his shoulders and points at his forehead*)

GEORGES   What's got into Simone?

MONSIEUR SOUPEAU (*turns back to the truck drivers*)   So you refuse to obey orders?

MAURICE   Not at all. As soon as we've finished our breakfast, off we go.

MONSIEUR SOUPEAU   And the china?

MAURICE   We'll take it. If you'll load it.

MONSIEUR SOUPEAU   Me?

MAURICE   Yes, you. It's yours, isn't it?

ROBERT   Of course we can't guarantee that we'll get to Bordeaux, can we, Maurice?

MAURICE   Who can guarantee anything these days?

MONSIEUR SOUPEAU   This is an outrage. Do you know what will happen to you if you disobey orders in the face of the enemy? I'll have you shot right here, up against this wall! (*Simone's parents come in from the street*)

MONSIEUR SOUPEAU   What do *you* want?

MADAME MACHARD   Monsieur Soupeau, we've come on account of our Simone. We hear the Germans will be here soon and that you're leaving. Simone is a little girl, and Monsieur Machard is worried about the twenty francs.

MONSIEUR SOUPEAU   She's run away, God knows where.

GEORGES   Didn't she go home, Madame Machard?

MADAME MACHARD   No, Monsieur Georges.

GEORGES   That's funny.

(*The mayor comes in with two policemen. Simone is hiding behind them*)

MONSIEUR SOUPEAU   You've come at the right time, Philippe. (*With a grand gesture*) Philippe, I'm faced with rebellion. Do something.

MAYOR   Henri, Mademoiselle Machard has informed me that you're planning to abscond with your trucks. That is illegal. I shall use every means at my disposal to prevent it. Including the police. (*Points at the policemen*)

MONSIEUR SOUPEAU   Simone, you had the gall . . . ? Gentlemen, I employed this creature out of kindness for her family!

MADAME MACHARD   (*shakes Simone*)   Now look what you've done! (*Simone is silent*)

MAURICE   I sent her.

MONSIEUR SOUPEAU   I see. And you took orders from Maurice?

MADAME MACHARD   Simone, how could you!

SIMONE I wanted to help monsieur le maire, mother. They need our trucks.

MONSIEUR SOUPEAU *Our* trucks!

SIMONE (*growing confused*) André's roads are clogged. (*Unable to continue*) Please, monsieur le maire, you explain.

MAYOR Henri, try to keep your selfishness within bounds. The child was right in calling me. At a time like this everything we own belongs to France. My sons are at the front and so is her brother. In other words, even our own sons don't belong to us.

MONSIEUR SOUPEAU (*beside himself*) So order has ceased to exist. Property doesn't exist any more. Why don't you give my hostelry to the Machards? Maybe my truck drivers here would like to help themselves to the contents of my safe? This is anarchy! Permit me to remind you, Monsieur Chavez, that my mother went to school with the prefect's wife. And there's still such a thing as a telephone.

MAYOR (*weakening*) Henri, I'm only doing my duty.

MONSIEUR SOUPEAU Philippe, be reasonable. You talk about the property of France. What about my supplies, my precious china, my silverware? Aren't they the property of France? Do you want them to fall into the hands of the Germans? Not one coffee cup must fall into enemy hands, not one ham, not one can of sardines. Wherever they go they must find a desert. Have you forgotten that? You're the mayor. You should have come to me and said: Henri, it's your duty to safeguard your possessions from the Germans. And my answer would have been: Philippe, in that case I need my trucks.

(*The sound of a crowd is heard from the street. A bell rings in the hostelry, and there is pounding on one of the doors*)

MONSIEUR SOUPEAU What's going on? Georges, go see what's going on. (*Georges goes into the hostelry*) And to my staff, who have forgotten their duty so far as to leave my possessions in the lurch, you must say (*to the drivers*): Gentlemen, I appeal to you as Frenchmen. Go pack the china.

GEORGES (*coming back*) It's a crowd of people from the schoolhouse, Monsieur Henri. They heard the trucks were being sent away. They're all excited, they want to speak to the mayor.

MONSIEUR SOUPEAU (*turning pale*) There you have it, Philippe. It's all Simone's fault. Quick, Georges, shut the gate. (*Georges goes to close the gate*) Quick, quick! Run!—This is the result of the agitation about my food parcels. The mob. (*To the policemen*) Do something! This minute! Philippe, you've got to phone for reinforcements, you owe me that. They'll kill me, Philippe. Help me! Please, Philippe.

MAYOR (*to the policemen*) Guard the gate. (*To Monsieur Soupeau*) Nonsense, they won't hurt you. You heard him, they only want to talk to me. (*Since there is pounding on the gate*) Admit a delegation, not more than three.

(*The policemen open the gate a crack and talk with the crowd. Then they admit three people, two men and a woman with a babe in arms*)

MAYOR What is it?

ONE OF THE REFUGEES (*excitedly*) Monsieur le maire, we demand the trucks!

MONSIEUR SOUPEAU Haven't you heard that the roads have to be kept clear?

THE WOMAN For you? What do you want us to do? Wait here for the German bombers?

MAYOR (*to the refugees*) Madame, messieurs, don't panic. It's all settled about the trucks. Monsieur Soupeau merely wants to save a few valuable possessions from the threat of enemy action.

THE WOMAN (*indignantly*) You see? There you have it! They want to evacuate crates instead of people.

(*The sound of planes is heard*)

VOICES (*from outside*) Stukas!

MONSIEUR SOUPEAU They're diving.

(*The noise grows deafening. The planes have dived. All throw themselves on the ground*)

MONSIEUR SOUPEAU (*when the planes have gone*) That's dangerous. I've got to get out of here.

VOICES (*from outside*) Give us the trucks!—Do they want us all to be killed?

MONSIEUR SOUPEAU They're not loaded yet! Philippe!

SIMONE (*angrily*) This is no time to think of your supplies!

MONSIEUR SOUPEAU (*flabbergasted*) How dare you, Simone!

SIMONE Why not give the food to the people?

THE REFUGEE Oh, it's food? It's food they want to load in the trucks?

MAURICE That's right.

THE WOMAN And we couldn't even get soup this morning.

MAURICE It's not the Germans he wants to save his supplies from. It's the French.

THE WOMAN (*runs back to the gate*) Open up! (*When the policemen hold her back, she shouts over the wall*) It's the hotel's food supplies that's going in the trucks!

MONSIEUR SOUPEAU Philippe! Don't let her broadcast that.

VOICES (*from outside*) They're evacuating the food supplies! —Break down the gate!—Aren't there any men here?— They're taking away the food and they're leaving us for the German tanks!

(*The refugees break through the gate. The mayor goes toward them*)

MAYOR Messieurs, mesdames, no violence! Everything will be straightened out.

(*While the mayor argues by the gate, a violent dispute arises in the yard. Two main groups form. On the one side Monsieur Soupeau, one of the male refugees, the woman refugee, and Simone's parents. On the other side, Simone, the two truck drivers, the second refugee, and Père Gustave. Georges does not take part, but goes on with his breakfast*)

(*Unnoticed, old Madame Soupeau has come out of the hostelry. She is very old, dressed all in black*)

THE WOMAN There's still at least eighty people without transportation.

MONSIEUR SOUPEAU You're taking your bundles, madame. Why should I leave everything behind? They're my trucks, aren't they?

MAYOR How much space

SIMONE You know the roads. You can go around the back way so's to leave Route 20 clear for the troops.

ROBERT What makes you think we're going to drive his supplies through the flood for him?

do you need, Monsieur Soupeau?

MONSIEUR SOUPEAU Enough for at least sixty crates. There'll be room for about thirty refugees in the other truck.

THE WOMAN So you want to leave fifty of us behind. Is that it?

MAYOR Let's say you'll manage with half a truck. Then at least there'll be room for the children and sick people.

THE WOMAN Do you want to break up families? You wicked man!

MONSIEUR SOUPEAU Eight or ten of them can sit on the crates. (*To Madame Machard*) Your daughter's to blame for all this.

THE WOMAN The child has more heart than the whole lot of you put together.

MADAME MACHARD You must forgive our Simone, Monsieur Henri. She got these ideas from her brother. It's dreadful.

SIMONE But you'll take the children and sick people?

ROBERT Refugees—that's something else again.

PÈRE GUSTAVE You keep out of this, Simone. That's my advice to you.

SIMONE But our fair France is in danger, Père Gustave.

PÈRE GUSTAVE She got that out of that damn book! "Is our fair France not in danger?"

ROBERT Here comes Madame Soupeau. She wants you.
(*Simone goes over to Madame Soupeau*)

THE WOMAN (*to the crowd in the doorway*) Why don't we take the trucks and the food too?

MADAME SOUPEAU Here's the key, Simone. Let the people take all the food they want. Père Gustave, Georges, give them a hand.

MAYOR (*in a loud voice*) Bravo, Madame Soupeau!

MONSIEUR SOUPEAU Mother, how can you? What are you doing down here anyway? You'll catch your death in this draft. There are vintage wines and 70,000 francs worth of supplies in the cellars.

MADAME SOUPEAU (*to the mayor*) The township is free to use them as it sees fit. (*To Monsieur Soupeau, coldly*) Would you rather have looting?

SIMONE (*to the woman with the baby*) There's going to be food for you.

MADAME SOUPEAU Simone! At your suggestion, my son has just made all the hostelry's food supplies available to the township. That leaves only the china and silverware, which won't take up much room. Will somebody load them for us?

THE WOMAN What about room for us in the trucks?

MADAME SOUPEAU Madame, we'll take as many of you as possible, and as for those who are left behind, the hostelry will be honored to feed them.

A REFUGEE (*calling out toward the gate*) Gaston! Would the old Creveux couple and the Meuniers stay behind if they're fed?

SHOUT FROM OUTSIDE Maybe they would, Jean!

THE WOMAN Hey, if they'll feed us, I'd like to stay myself.

MADAME SOUPEAU You'll be welcome.

MAYOR (*in the gateway*) Messieurs, mesdames, help yourselves. The hostelry's supplies are yours.

(*A few of the refugees go hesitantly into the storehouse*)

MADAME SOUPEAU And bring us a few bottles of brandy, Simone, the 1884 Martell.

SIMONE Yes, madame. (*She motions to the refugees and goes with them, Père Gustave, and Georges into the storehouse*)

MONSIEUR SOUPEAU Mother, this is going to be the death of me.

ONE OF THE REFUGEES (*drags out a crate with Georges; in high spirits parodies a market crier*) Fruit, ham, chocolate! Provisions for your trip! Absolutely free of charge!

MONSIEUR SOUPEAU (*looking indignantly at the cans that the refugees and Georges are carrying across the yard to the gate*) But those are delicacies! That's foie gras!

MADAME SOUPEAU (*under her breath*) Shut up! (*To the refugee, politely*) I hope you enjoy it, monsieur. (*With Père*

Gustave's help the other refugee hauls baskets of food across the yard)

MONSIEUR SOUPEAU (*lamenting*) My Pommard 1915. And that's caviar. And this is . . .

MAYOR This is a time for making sacrifices, Henri. (*In a choked voice*) We must let our hearts speak.

MAURICE (*imitating Monsieur Soupeau's outcry*) "My Pommard!" (*Laughing uproariously, slaps Simone on the back*) Just for that I'll load your china for you, Simone.

MONSIEUR SOUPEAU (*offended*) I fail to see what's so funny. (*Pointing at the vanishing baskets*) This is looting.

ROBERT (*good-naturedly with a basket*) Don't let it get you down, Monsieur Henri. We'll load your china to make up for it.

MADAME SOUPEAU It's a deal. (*She picks up some cans and bottles of wine and takes them to Simone's parents*) Here. You have some too. And get glasses for your parents, Simone. (*Simone does so; then she gets a stool, puts it down by the wall and hands provisions from a basket to the refugees on the other side of the wall*)

MADAME SOUPEAU Maurice, Robert, Père Gustave, go get yourselves glasses. (*Pointing to the policemen*) I see that the law is already served. (*To the woman with the baby*) Won't you join us in a drink, madame? (*To all*) Mesdames, messieurs, I propose a toast to our fair France.

MONSIEUR SOUPEAU (*standing alone and excluded*) What about me? Are you going to drink a toast to France without me?

(*He pours himself a glass and joins the group*)

MAYOR (*to Madame Soupeau*) In the name of the township of Saint-Martin, I wish to thank the hostelry for its generosity. (*He raises his glass*) To France and to the future.

GEORGES But where's Simone?

(*Simone is still busy handing provisions over the wall to the refugees*)

MAYOR Simone!

(*Simone is flushed. She approaches hesitantly*)

MADAME SOUPEAU Go get a glass, Simone. All of use here owe you a debt of gratitude.

(*All drink*)

MONSIEUR SOUPEAU (*to the drivers*)   Are we friends again?
Did you think I objected to transporting refugees in my
trucks? Maurice and Robert, I like to get my own way, but
I respect noble motives when I see them. I'm willing to admit a mistake. You do the same. Let's forget our little personal differences and stand together, shoulder to shoulder,
against the common enemy. Shake on it.

(*He begins with Robert, who gives him his hand with a
sheepish grin; next Georges gives him his left hand. Then
Monsieur Soupeau embraces the woman with the baby.
Grumbling, still angry, Père Gustave gives him his hand.
Finally, Monsieur Soupeau turns to Maurice, who, however,
makes no move to give him his hand*)

MONSIEUR SOUPEAU   Oh la la. Are we Frenchmen, or aren't
we?

SIMONE (*reproachfully*)   Maurice!

MAURICE (*hesitantly giving Monsieur Soupeau his hand; ironically*)   Long live our new St. Joan, come to unite the
French people.

(*Monsieur Machard gives Simone a slap in the face*)

MADAME MACHARD (*explains*)   That's for your obstinacy, for
disobeying your employer.

MONSIEUR SOUPEAU (*to Machard*)   Don't, monsieur. (*He puts
his arms around Simone consolingly*) Simone is my pet, madame. I've got a weakness for her. (*To the drivers*) But
come on, boys, let's start loading. I'm sure Monsieur Machard will help us.

MAYOR (*to his policemen*)   How about you fellows giving
monsieur a hand?

MONSIEUR SOUPEAU (*bows to the woman with the baby*)
Madame!

(*The group breaks up, the crowd outside also drifts away.
Only Monsieur Soupeau, the mayor, Madame Soupeau,
Simone, the two truck drivers, and Georges remain on the
stage*)

MONSIEUR SOUPEAU   Friends, I wouldn't have missed that for
anything. Damn the caviar and the Pommard. I'm for unity.

MAURICE   What about the brickyard?

MAYOR (*cautiously*)   That's right, Henri. Something's got to be done about the brickyard.

MONSIEUR SOUPEAU (*distressed*)   What? What more do you want? All right, send any trucks that are out of gas to the brickyard. They can fill up. Now are you satisfied?

ROBERT   In Abbeville the German tanks got their gas from the filling stations. That's why they get ahead so fast.

GEORGES   Our 132nd had tanks on its tail before they had time to look around. They made mincemeat out of two regiments.

SIMONE (*frightened*)   But not the Seventh?

GEORGES   No, not the Seventh.

MAYOR   Gasoline stocks have to be destroyed, Henri.

MONSIEUR SOUPEAU   Aren't you in a bit too much of a hurry? We can't destroy everything just like that. Maybe we'll throw the enemy back. What do you say, Simone? Tell Monsieur Chavez that France isn't lost yet, not by a long shot. (*To Madame Soupeau*) And now good-bye, mother. I hate to leave you here. (*Kisses her*) But Simone will be a great help to you. Good-bye, Simone. I'm not ashamed to thank you. You're a real Frenchwoman. (*Kisses her*) As long as you're here, nothing will fall into the hands of the Germans, I can be sure of that. I want the whole place stripped bare, understand? I know you'll carry out my wishes. Good-bye, Philippe, old man. (*Embraces him, picks up his bags. Simone wants to help him, he waves her away*) Never mind. Have a talk with mother, decide what to do about our supplies.

(*Goes out in the direction of the street*)

SIMONE (*runs after the two truck drivers*)   Maurice, Robert. (*She kisses them both on their cheeks. Then finally Maurice and Robert go out too*)

VOICE OF THE RADIO ANNOUNCER   Attention! Attention! German tank formations have reached Tours. (*The announcement is repeated several times until the end of the scene*)

MAYOR (*pale, beside himself*)   Then we can expect them here by tonight.

MADAME SOUPEAU   Don't be such an old woman, Philippe.

SIMONE   Madame, I'll run over to the brickyard with Père Gustave and Georges. We'll destroy the gasoline.

MADAME SOUPEAU   You've heard your employer's orders. He told us not to be in too much of a hurry. You must leave certain decisions to us, my dear.

SIMONE   But madame, Maurice says the Germans go so fast.

MADAME SOUPEAU   That will do, Simone. (*Turns to go*) There's a nasty draft here. (*To the mayor*) Thank you, Philippe, for all you've done for the hostelry today. (*In the doorway*) Besides, Simone, now that they're all gone, I'll probably close the hostelry. Give me the key to the store-house. (*Simone, stunned, gives her the key*) I think you'd better go home to your parents. I've been satisfied with you.

SIMONE   (*does not understand*)   But can't I help when the people from the town hall come to get supplies?

(*Without a word Madame Soupeau goes into the hostelry*)

SIMONE   (*after a silence, haltingly*)   Have I been fired, monsieur le maire?

MAYOR   (*comfortingly*)   I'm afraid so. But you mustn't feel badly. You heard her say she was satisfied with you. Coming from her, that means a good deal, Simone.

SIMONE   (*tonelessly*)   Yes, monsieur le maire.

(*The mayor goes out dejectedly*)

(*Simone looks after him*)

Simone Machard's Second Dream

The night of June 15.

Confused, festive music. A waiting group emerges from the darkness: the mayor in his royal cloak, Monsieur Soupeau and the colonel, both in armor and with marshal's batons; the colonel is wearing his dust coat over his armor.

COLONEL   Our Joan has now taken Orleans and Rheims after clearing Route 20 for our advancing troops. She must be suitably honored, that much is plain.

MAYOR I, the king, will see to that, monsieur. The dignitaries and great families of France, who are to assemble here today, will bow down to the ground before her.

(*From now until the end of the scene the titles and names of France's dignitaries and leading families are called out backstage, as though they were assembling*)

MAYOR By the way, I hear she's been fired? (*Discreetly*) At the behest of the queen mother, the proud Queen Isabeau, so I hear.

MONSIEUR SOUPEAU I don't know anything about that, I wasn't there. If you ask me, it's not right. She's my pet. I say she stays.

(*The mayor says something unintelligible, apparently evasive, in the dream language*)

COLONEL Here she comes.

(*Simone strides in with sword and helmet, preceded by her bodyguard, consisting of Maurice, Robert, and Georges. The three are in armor. From the darkness have emerged Simone's parents and the staff of the hostelry: "the people." The bodyguard pushes the people back with long pikes*)

ROBERT Make way for the Maid.

MADAME MACHARD (*craning her neck*) It's her. That helmet looks pretty good on her.

MAYOR (*steps forward*) Dear Joan, what can we do for you? Tell me your wishes.

SIMONE (*with a bow*) My first request, King Charles, is to go on feeding my beloved native town with the hostelry's supplies. You know I've been sent to help the poor and needy. Their taxes must be remitted.

MAYOR That goes without saying. What else?

SIMONE In the second place, Paris must be taken. The second campaign must begin at once, King Charles.

MONSIEUR SOUPEAU (*astonished*) A second campaign?

COLONEL What will old Madame Soupeau, the proud Queen Isabeau, say to that?

SIMONE You must give me an army, King Charles, with which to defeat the enemy completely before the year is out.

MAYOR (*smiling*) Dear Joan, we are very well satisfied with

you. Coming from us, that means a good deal. That will do.
You must leave certain decisions to us. I shall now close the
hostelry, and you will go home. But first of course you will
be ennobled. Give me your sword, I've mislaid mine, and I
shall dub you a lady of France.

SIMONE (*gives him the sword and kneels*) Here's the key.
(*Confused music, organ and chorus, indicates festive church
rites in the distance*)
(*The mayor solemnly touches Simone's shoulder with the
sword*)

BODYGUARD AND PEOPLE Long live the Maid! Long live the
great lady of France!

SIMONE (*when the mayor starts to leave*) Just a minute, King
Charles. Don't forget to give me back my sword. (*Urgently*) The English haven't been defeated yet, the Burgundians are raising a new army, more formidable than the first.
The hardest is yet to come.

MAYOR Many thanks for the offer. And many thanks for
everything else, Joan. (*Gives Simone's sword to Monsieur
Soupeau*) Take it to Bordeaux, Henri, there it will be safe.
We for our part must now have a confidential talk with
Madame Soupeau, the proud Queen Isabeau. Farewell, Joan,
it has been a pleasure! (*Goes out with Monsieur Soupeau
and the colonel*)

SIMONE (*in terror*) But the enemy's coming, don't you see!
(*The music sinks to a murmur, the light grows dim, the
people vanish in the darkness*)

SIMONE (*stands motionless. Then*) André! Help! Archangel,
come down! Speak to me! The English are raising an army,
the Burgundians have turned traitor, and our men are running away.

THE ANGEL (*appears on the garage roof; reproachfully*)
Where is your sword, Joan?

SIMONE (*confused, apologetically*) They dubbed me a noble
lady with it and they never gave it back. (*Softly, ashamed*)
I've been fired.

THE ANGEL I see. (*After a silence*) Maid of France, don't let them send you away. Hold out. France wishes it. Don't go back to your parents yet, they'd eat their hearts out about your being fired. Besides, you promised to keep your brother's job in the garage for him; because one day he'll be coming back. Stay, Joan. How can you leave your post when the enemy may burst in from one minute to the next?

SIMONE   Should we go on fighting if the enemy has already won?

THE ANGEL   Is the night wind blowing?

SIMONE   Yes.

THE ANGEL   Isn't there a tree in the yard?

SIMONE   Yes, the poplar.

THE ANGEL   Do its leaves rustle when the wind blows?

SIMONE   Oh yes.

THE ANGEL   Then you should fight, even if the enemy has won.

SIMONE   But how can I fight when I have no sword?

THE ANGEL

Hark:

When the conqueror comes to your town or village
Let there be nothing left for him to pillage.
Let no one give him a key
He's vermin, not company.
Let there be nothing for him to feed on
No chair to sit on and no bed to sleep on.
Hide what you cannot burn. Bury the bread and meat
Pour out the milk, let the dearth be complete.
Let him curse his fate, for Monster is his name
Let him eat earth and dwell in flame.
Let there be no court where he can plead
For mercy; let your city be gone, demolished, dead.
Let him find emptiness at every step. Let it be
As though there had never been a hostelry.
Go forth and destroy.

(*The stage grows dark. Confused music. Intermittently one hears the angel's soft but insistent "Go forth and destroy" and, very distinctly, the rumble of heavy tanks*)

3

The Fire

(a)

Old Madame Soupeau all in black, and behind her Thérèse the chambermaid and Père Gustave wearing his Sunday suit, are waiting in the gateway for the German captain. Georges, now in civilian clothes, is leaning against the garage wall. Simone is inside the garage hiding from Madame Soupeau and listening to him. The clanking of passing tanks is heard from outside.

SIMONE   She's as white as a sheet. She's scared.

GEORGES   She thinks they'll arrest her as a hostage and shoot her. She's been having fits all night. Thérèse heard her screaming: "The butchers will kill us all." But that didn't keep her from staying here, it's her greed, and now she's waiting for the German captain—I really don't understand why you don't want her to see you. Is anything wrong?

SIMONE   *(lying)*   No, no. Except she'd send me away if she saw me. For fear the Germans might hurt me.

GEORGES   *(suspiciously)*   Is that the only reason you don't want her to see you?

SIMONE   *(changing the subject)*   Do you think the Germans have caught up with Maurice and Robert?

GEORGES   Maybe.—Say, why have you moved out of your room upstairs?

SIMONE   *(lying)*   There's room for me in the storehouse now that the drivers have gone away.—Do you think André will be coming back soon?

GEORGES   Probably.—She hasn't fired you, Simone?

SIMONE   *(lying)*   No.

GEORGES   Here come the Germans.

   (The German captain comes in from the street, accompanied

by Captain Fétain. In the gateway Madame Soupeau exchanges polite greetings with the two officers. Their conversation cannot be heard)

GEORGES The captain and secret fascist has the honor of introducing the enemy to madame. All too polite for words. They're sniffing, they don't seem to dislike each other's smell. The enemy is a gentleman. Madame seems enormously relieved. (*Whispers*) They're coming.

(Simone steps back. Madame Soupeau leads the two officers across the yard to the hostelry; Thérèse the chambermaid follows)

PÈRE GUSTAVE (*to whom Madame Soupeau has whispered something, goes over to Georges and Simone*) Madame doesn't want the mob from the schoolhouse in the hostelry any more. The German officers might not like it. But it looks as if the boss could just as well have stayed.

GEORGES The first thing they announced over the radio was: "No one who observes law and order has anything to fear."

PÈRE GUSTAVE The one in there says "please" when he wants something. "Please show my orderly my rooms."

SIMONE He's the enemy all the same.

(Père Gustave goes out into the storehouse)

GEORGES Has your cousin had another dream?

SIMONE Yes, last night.

GEORGES About the Maid again?

SIMONE (*nods*) They dubbed her a lady.

GEORGES That must have been a big thing for her.

SIMONE Her native place has had its taxes remitted, the same as in the book.

GEORGES (*rather harshly*) But actually the hostelry's supplies are not being distributed to the people, as promised.

SIMONE (*flustered*) My cousin didn't say anything about that.

GEORGES Oh.

SIMONE Monsieur Georges. If in a dream like my cousin has now and then a certain person appears as an angel—does it mean the person must be dead?

GEORGES I don't think so. It probably just means that the dreamer is afraid this person might be dead.—Tell me, what more is your cousin expected to do?

SIMONE   Lots of things.

GEORGES   Did something bad happen in the dream?

SIMONE   Why?

GEORGES   Because you're telling me so little.

SIMONE *(slowly)*   No, nothing bad.

GEORGES   I'm asking, Simone, because it seems to me now and then that another person might take these dreams seriously and forget that we're living in broad daylight and not in a dream.

SIMONE *(violently)*   Then I won't talk about my cousin's dreams with you any more, Monsieur Georges.

(The woman with the baby and another refugee from the schoolhouse come into the yard)

SIMONE   They're coming for food. Tell them nicely, Monsieur Georges. *(She hides and looks on)*

GEORGES *(steps forward)*   Madame.

THE WOMAN   The tanks are here.

THE MAN   There are three of them outside the town hall.

THE WOMAN   Big ones. Twenty feet long.

THE MAN *(indicating the German sentry)*   Watch out!

MADAME SOUPEAU *(steps into the doorway of the hostelry)*   Georges! Père Gustave. Take the hors d'oeuvres to the breakfast room for the Herr Hauptmann.—What have you come for?

THE WOMAN   We've come to see about the food, madame. There are twenty-one people left in the schoolhouse.

MADAME SOUPEAU   Georges, didn't I tell you to keep beggars out of the hostelry?

THE MAN   What do you mean, beggars?

MADAME SOUPEAU   Why haven't you told these people that from now on they'll be dealing with the German commandant and not with us? Those happy days are over.

THE WOMAN   You want us to tell that to the people in the schoolhouse after we advised them all to stay here so you could send your china away?

MADAME SOUPEAU   Madame, I wouldn't start denouncing people if I were you.

THE WOMAN   Madame, don't hide behind the Germans.

MADAME SOUPEAU *(calls over her shoulder)*   Honoré!

THE WOMAN   Me and my baby could have been in Bordeaux with my sister by now. You promised to feed us, madame.

MADAME SOUPEAU   I was blackmailed into it, madame.

CAPTAIN FÉTAIN (*coming up behind her*)   The place was being looted, neither more nor less! But now, my friends, there's going to be order and discipline around here. (*Motioning toward the German sentries*) Do you want me to have you driven out of here with bayonets? Don't get worked up, Marie; remember your heart.

THE WOMAN   You bastards!

THE MAN (*holds her back and leads her away*)   Madame, this won't last forever.

MADAME SOUPEAU   It's beginning to stink of sewage around here. The gutters of the northern cities are pouring their rats into our peaceful villages. We're getting the riffraff from their cheap wine rooms. They'll have to pay for this, in blood. Père Gustave, breakfast for four.

CAPTAIN FÉTAIN (*to Georges*)   Hey you! The mayor will be coming here. Tell him I want to speak to him before he sees the Herr Hauptmann. (*He leads Madame Soupeau back into the hostelry*)

(*When the two are gone, Simone runs after the refugees*)

GEORGES   Père Gustave! The hors d'oeuvres for the Herr Hauptmann.

PÈRE GUSTAVE'S VOICE (*from the storehouse*)   I heard you. Nothing's too good for the Herr Hauptmann.

(*Simone comes back out of breath*)

GEORGES   What did you say to them?

SIMONE   To tell the people in the schoolhouse that they'll get their food. I'll take it to them tonight.

GEORGES   Yes, you've still got the key.

SIMONE   It was promised to them.

GEORGES   Just be very careful. That's theft.

SIMONE   Didn't the boss say: "As long as you're here, Simone, nothing will fall into the hands of the Germans, I can be sure of that"?

GEORGES   But now his mother's singing a different tune.

SIMONE   Maybe they're forcing her.

(*The mayor appears in the gateway*)

SIMONE (*rushes up to him; in a whisper*)   Monsieur le maire, what's going to happen now?

MAYOR   What do you think, Simone? I have good news for you: at my suggestion your father's being taken on as bailiff. You've deserved it, Simone. Now it won't matter that you lost your job.

SIMONE (*in a whisper*)   Monsieur le maire, is it true that there are three tanks outside the town hall? (*Still more softly*) The gas is still there.

MAYOR (*absently*)   Yes, that's bad. (*Suddenly*) But Simone, why are you still here?

SIMONE   Something has to be done about the gas, monsieur le maire. Can't you do something? They're sure to ask Madame Soupeau for it.

MAYOR   I don't think we have to worry about Madame Soupeau, Simone.

SIMONE   I could do something. I know my way around the brickyard.

MAYOR (*vaguely*)   I hope you're not thinking of doing anything foolish, Simone. I've got a great responsibility for the town of Saint-Martin. Do you understand?

SIMONE   Yes, monsieur le maire.

MAYOR   I don't know why I'm talking to you like this. You're still a child, Simone. But I think each one of us has to do his best. Don't you?

SIMONE   Oh yes, monsieur le maire. If the brickyard were to burn down . . .

MAYOR   Good God! You mustn't even think of such things. But now I have to go in. This is the hardest thing I've done in all my life. (*He starts to go in*)
(*Captain Fétain comes out*)

CAPTAIN FÉTAIN   Monsieur Chavez. You're just in time for breakfast.

MAYOR   I've had my breakfast.

CAPTAIN FÉTAIN   That's unfortunate. You don't quite seem to understand. A good many unpleasant things happened here yesterday, with the connivance of the authorities. It is regrettable that no immediate measures were taken to stop the shameless attempts of certain elements to exploit the downfall of France for their own advantage. The least our German guests can expect is a polite gesture from us. The German commandant, for instance, has already been informed about certain supplies that are stored in a brickyard. Maybe you ought to take that into account, Chavez. Maybe that will improve your appetite? After you, monsieur le maire.

MAYOR (*very unsure of himself*)   After you, mon capitaine. (*The two go into the hostelry. Père Gustave comes out of the storehouse and follows them*)

PÈRE GUSTAVE (*going in with the hors d'oeuvres*)   Fair weather and happy journey! Rich birds flock together, eh, Georges? They're selling France the same as they sell their wine and hors d'oeuvres! (*Goes out*)
(*Simone has followed the last exchange. She has sat down*)

GEORGES   Simone! What's the matter with you? Simone!
(*Simone does not answer. Georges stands rigidly, preserving the gesture with which he has tried to shake her into consciousness. During Simone's daydream, Père Gustave's "Rich birds flock together" is repeated mechanically and more faintly*)

Simone Machard's Daydream

On June 20.

Confused martial music. The back wall of the hostelry becomes transparent. Before an enormous tapestry the mayor as King Charles, Captain Fétain as the duke of Burgundy, the German captain with his sword across his knees as the English general, and Madame Soupeau as Queen Isabeau are seated playing belote on a marble table.

MADAME SOUPEAU   I wish to see the mob no more, my lord.

GERMAN CAPTAIN   Hide behind us, Queen Isabeau. I'll have them all cleared out of the yard. Then we'll have order. My trick.

MAYOR   Hark! Do I hear the sound of drums?
(*Joan's drum is heard in the distance*)

CAPTAIN FÉTAIN   I hear nothing. Play your ace of clubs. (*The drumming stops*)

MAYOR (*doubtfully*)   No? Duke of Burgundy, I'm afraid my Joan is in trouble and needs help.

CAPTAIN FÉTAIN   Ten of hearts. I need peace, so I can sell my wines.

GERMAN CAPTAIN   What is the price of your hors d'oeuvres, madame?

MADAME SOUPEAU   Whose deal? Ten thousand pieces of silver, my lord.

MAYOR   This time I'm sure. She must be in danger, mortal danger. I must hasten to her help and destroy everything. (*He stands up with his cards in hand*)

CAPTAIN FÉTAIN   I should be careful if I were you. If you go now, it's the last time. You don't understand. How can we play if we're disturbed all the time? Jack of clubs.

MAYOR (*sits down again*)   Very well.

MADAME SOUPEAU (*slaps him in the face*)   That's for being so independent.

GERMAN CAPTAIN   By your leave, Queen Isabeau. (*He lays coins down on the table*) One, two, three . . .

(*Georges shakes Simone out of her daydream, while the German captain goes on counting*)

GEORGES   Simone! Now you're dreaming with your eyes open.

SIMONE   Will you come, Monsieur Georges?

GEORGES (*stares at his bandaged arm; joyfully*)   Simone, I can move it again.

SIMONE   That's good. But we have to go to the brickyard, Monsieur Georges. We haven't got much time. Père Gustave, you come too. Quick.

PÈRE GUSTAVE (*coming back out of the hostelry*)   Me? They've put up a notice: Anyone destroying essential war material will be shot. They mean business.

SIMONE   The mayor wants us to.

PÈRE GUSTAVE   The mayor's an asshole.

SIMONE   But you'll come, Monsieur Georges? It's for André.

I wouldn't know how to destroy all that gas. Will we have to set fire to the whole brickyard?

GEORGES Don't you understand? I can move it again.

SIMONE (*looks at him*) So you won't come?

PÈRE GUSTAVE Here comes another one.

(*A German soldier comes into the yard, hauling baggage. As soon as she sees him, Simone runs away in a fright*)

THE GERMAN SOLDIER (*throws down the baggage; he is in a sweat. He lifts his steel helmet and, taking a friendly attitude, tries to communicate with gestures*) Hauptmann? Inside?

GEORGES (*with gestures*) In there. In the hostelry. Cigarette?

THE GERMAN SOLDIER (*takes the cigarette and grins*) War— merde. (*Gesture of shooting, disparaging wave of the hand*)

GEORGES (*laughing*) Boom boom. (*Farts with his lips, both laugh*)

THE GERMAN SOLDIER Hauptmann—asshole.

GEORGES What's that?

THE GERMAN SOLDIER (*mimes the German captain with the monocle*) Merde.

GEORGES (*understands. Happily mimes Captain Fétain and Madame Soupeau*) All merde.

(*They laugh again, then the German soldier takes the baggage and goes in*)

GEORGES (*to Père Gustave*) Oh la la, wouldn't it be easy for us to understand each other?

PÈRE GUSTAVE Better watch your step.

GEORGES Don't worry. Now that my arm is mending.

(*The German captain, Captain Fétain, the mayor, and Madame Soupeau come out of the hostelry*)

CAPTAIN FÉTAIN Herr Hauptmann, I am glad to see that we understand each other so well.

GERMAN CAPTAIN Madame, I wish to thank you for voluntarily offering us your gasoline. Not that the Wehrmacht needs it. But we accept your offer, because it demonstrates your good will and desire to cooperate.

MADAME SOUPEAU It's not far to the brickyard.

GERMAN CAPTAIN I'll send the tanks.

(*The sky has turned red. The group freezes into immobility.*

Explosions in the distance)
GERMAN CAPTAIN   What's that?
CAPTAIN FÉTAIN (*in a hoarse voice*)   The brickyard.

(b)

It is night. Pounding on the gate. Georges comes out of his room and opens for Monsieur Soupeau and the two drivers.

MONSIEUR SOUPEAU   How's it going, Georges? Is mother all right? Looks like the place is still standing. I feel like after the Flood. Hello, Simone.
(*Simone enters scantily dressed from the drivers' room. Robert hugs her. Père Gustave has also appeared*)
ROBERT   Have you been making yourself at home in our room? (*He dances around with her, singing in an undertone*)
Jo the strangler came back home
Rosa was still there
Mama had a green chartreuse
And Papa had a beer.
MONSIEUR SOUPEAU   What's been going on?
GEORGES   We've got a German captain here. Madame Soupeau's kind of tired from the investigation about the brickyard. The German captain . . .
MONSIEUR SOUPEAU   What investigation?
SIMONE   Monsieur Henri, everything has been done the way you wanted it. And last night I managed to take some food to the schoolhouse.
MONSIEUR SOUPEAU   I asked about the brickyard.
GEORGES (*hesitantly*)   It's burned down, Monsieur Henri.
MONSIEUR SOUPEAU   Burned down?—The Germans? (*Georges shakes his head*) An accident? (*He looks from one to the other. No answer*) Orders from town hall?
GEORGES   No.
MONSIEUR SOUPEAU   The scum from the schoolhouse?
GEORGES   No, Monsieur Henri.

MONSIEUR SOUPEAU Then it was arson. (*Bellowing as if his foot had been cut off*) Who did it? (*No one answers*) Aha, you're all in it together. (*In cold rage*) So now you've started committing crimes? Isn't that nice? I might have expected it after the proofs of gratitude you gave me on my last day here. "You can stick your china up your ass" —remember, Père Gustave? All right, I'll take up the challenge. We'll see.

GEORGES It was on account of the Germans, Monsieur Henri.

MONSIEUR SOUPEAU (*sarcastically*) I see. It so happens it was my brickyard, but you set it on fire to spite the Germans. In other words, you were so blinded by hate, so intent on destruction, that you slaughtered the cow that gave you milk. (*abruptly*) Simone!

SIMONE Yes, monsieur.

MONSIEUR SOUPEAU Tell me this instant who did it.

SIMONE Me, monsieur.

MONSIEUR SOUPEAU What? You dared . . . ? (*Clutches her arm*) Who told you? Who was behind it?

SIMONE Nobody, monsieur.

MONSIEUR SOUPEAU Don't lie! I won't stand for . . .

GEORGES Please, Monsieur Henri, leave her alone. She's not lying.

MONSIEUR SOUPEAU Who told you to do it?

SIMONE I did it for my brother, monsieur.

MONSIEUR SOUPEAU Ah, André! So he incited you against your employer? "We underdogs," is that it? I always knew he was a Red. Who helped you?

SIMONE Nobody, monsieur.

MONSIEUR SOUPEAU But why did you do it?

SIMONE On account of the gasoline, sir.

MONSIEUR SOUPEAU And for that you had to set fire to the whole brickyard? Why didn't you just open the taps?

SIMONE I didn't know, Monsieur Henri.

GEORGES She's a child, Monsieur Henri.

MONSIEUR SOUPEAU Firebugs? The whole lot of you! Criminals! Get off my place, Père Gustave! Georges, you're fired! You're worse than Germans.

GEORGES Very well, Monsieur Henri. (*He goes to stand beside Simone*)

MONSIEUR SOUPEAU Weren't you saying something about an investigation? What kind of investigation?

GEORGES The Germans are investigating.

MONSIEUR SOUPEAU You mean it happened after the Germans got here?

GEORGES Yes.

MONSIEUR SOUPEAU (*has to sit down; in despair*) That's all I needed. The hostelry will be ruined! (*Props his head in his hands*)

PÈRE GUSTAVE Monsieur Henri, yesterday afternoon all Saint-Martin was saying nice things about the hostelry. "Right under the Germans' noses!" they were saying.

MONSIEUR SOUPEAU I'll be court-martialed. That's what you've done to me. (*in despair*) I'll be shot.

SIMONE (*steps forward*) You won't be shot, monsieur, because I did it. Come to the German captain with me, and I'll take it all on myself.

MAURICE That's out of the question.

MONSIEUR SOUPEAU Why is it out of the question? She's a child. They won't touch her.

MAURICE You can tell the Germans she did it, but we're going to take her away. Get dressed, Simone.

MONSIEUR SOUPEAU That would make us accomplices.

SIMONE Maurice, I've got to stay. I'm sure André wants me to.

MONSIEUR SOUPEAU It all depends on whether she did it after the Germans got here or before. Before they came, we were at war, then they can't do anything to her.

PÈRE GUSTAVE (*fawningly*) They put up a notice right away, Monsieur Henri, saying that anyone committing a hostile act would be shot.

MONSIEUR SOUPEAU Did you see that notice, Simone?

SIMONE Yes, Monsieur Henri.

MONSIEUR SOUPEAU What did it look like?

SIMONE It was on red paper.

MONSIEUR SOUPEAU Is that right? (*Père Gustave nods*) Now comes the question the Germans will ask you, Simone. Did you read it after you set the fire? In that case it wasn't sabotage, Simone, and they can't do anything to you.

SIMONE   I saw it first, monsieur.

MONSIEUR SOUPEAU   You don't understand. If you didn't see it until afterwards, the Germans will probably just hand you over to the mayor, because then it's a matter that concerns only the French. And then you'll be all right, Simone. Do you understand?

SIMONE   Yes, monsieur. But I saw it before.

MONSIEUR SOUPEAU   She's confused. Père Gustave, you were in the yard at the time. When did Simone leave?

PÈRE GUSTAVE   Before, Monsieur Henri. Of course. Before the notice was put up.

MONSIEUR SOUPEAU   See?

SIMONE   You're wrong, Père Gustave. You told me yourself before I went that the notice said it was forbidden.

PÈRE GUSTAVE   I told you nothing of the kind.

MONSIEUR SOUPEAU   Of course not.

MAURICE   Monsieur Henri, can't you see that the child wants no part in your tricks? She's not ashamed of what she did.

SIMONE   Monsieur Soupeau is only trying to help me, Maurice.

MONSIEUR SOUPEAU   That's right. Then you trust me, Simone? Now listen carefully. It's the enemy we'll be speaking to now, Simone. That makes a big difference, you can see that. They'll ask a lot of questions, but you'll only say what's good for Saint-Martin and France. Isn't that simple enough?

SIMONE   Yes, monsieur. But I don't want to say anything that's not right.

MONSIEUR SOUPEAU   I understand. You don't want to tell an untruth. Not even to the enemy. Very well. I give in. I'll only ask one thing of you: don't say anything, leave it to us. Leave it to me. (*Almost in tears*) I'll stand behind you to the last, you know that. We're all behind you. We're Frenchmen.

SIMONE   Yes, monsieur.

(*Monsieur Soupeau takes Simone by the hand and goes into the hostelry with her*)

MAURICE   She didn't read her book right.

4

The Trial

(a)

Simone Machard's Fourth Dream

The night of June 21.

Confused music. In the yard stand the German captain in armor and Simone as the Maid of Orleans, surrounded by soldiers in black mail with red swastikas; one, recognizable as the German captain's orderly, is holding a swastika banner.

GERMAN CAPTAIN   We've got you now, Joan of Orleans. You will be handed over to a high court which will decide why you will be condemned to death at the stake.
   (*All go out with the exception of Simone and the standard bearer*)
SIMONE   What kind of court is it?
THE STANDARD BEARER   Not an ordinary one. An ecclesiastical court.
SIMONE   I'll confess nothing.
THE STANDARD BEARER   That's all very well, but the trial seems to be over already.
SIMONE   You mean I've been sentenced before they've even tried me?
THE STANDARD BEARER   Yes. Of course.
   (*A number of people who have apparently attended the trial come out of the hostelry and cross the yard to the street*)
PÈRE GUSTAVE (*while crossing the yard, to Thérèse*)   To death! At her age!

THÉRÈSE My, who'd have expected such a thing only two days ago!

SIMONE (*plucks at her sleeve*) Is Hitler himself here?

(*Thérèse does not seem to notice her; she goes out with Père Gustave*)

(*Simone's parents cross the yard, the father in uniform, the mother in black*)

MADAME MACHARD (*sobbing*) Even as a little girl she was so obstinate. Just like her brother. It's a terrible blow to Monsieur Machard. And in his position as bailiff! The disgrace! (*Both go out*)

(*The brothers Maurice and Robert cross the yard*)

ROBERT She looked pretty good.

MAURICE Especially in the blue one with the ruffles.

SIMONE (*plucks Robert's sleeve*) Did you see the trial?

ROBERT (*nonchalantly*) Yes, of course.

SIMONE Will I see it too?

ROBERT Certainly. The judges will be coming out to break the staff over you. (*Both go out*)

A LOUD VOICE Quiet! Make way! The Maid will now be sentenced. By the ecclesiastical court of the high bishops and cardinals of Rouen. First the staff will be broken over the Maid.

(*A judge in resplendent cardinal's robes steps out of the hostelry. He holds a breviary in front of his face, so that he is not recognizable. He crosses the yard, stops behind a bronze tripod with a kettle on it, turns his back, claps the breviary shut, takes a small staff out of his sleeve, solemnly breaks it, and throws the pieces into the kettle*)

THE LOUD VOICE His Eminence, the bishop of Beauvais. For liberating the city of Orleans: death.

(*Before going further, he looks back indifferently over his shoulder. It is the colonel*)

SIMONE Monsieur le colonel!

(*A second judge steps out of the hostelry and repeats the ceremony*)

THE LOUD VOICE For liberating the city of Orleans and feeding the rats of the city of Orleans—with stolen goods: death.

(*The second judge likewise shows his face. It is Captain Fétain*)

SIMONE   Monsieur le capitaine!
  (*A third judge steps out of the hostelry and repeats the
  ceremony*)
THE LOUD VOICE   For attacking the city of Paris and the black-
  market gasoline: death.
  (*The third judge is Monsieur Soupeau*)
SIMONE   But Monsieur Henri, it's me you're condemning!
  (*Monsieur Soupeau makes his gesture of helplessness; a
  fourth judge steps out of the hostelry and repeats the cere-
  mony*)
THE LOUD VOICE   For uniting the whole French people: death.
  (*The fourth judge is holding his breviary so convulsively
  that he drops it. He hurriedly bends down to pick it up and
  is recognized; it is the mayor*)
SIMONE   Heavens, the mayor. Oh, Monsieur Chavez!
THE LOUD VOICE   Your high judges have spoken, Joan.
SIMONE   But they're all Frenchmen. (*To the standard bearer*)
  It's a mistake!
THE STANDARD BEARER   No, mademoiselle, the high court is
  French. (*The four judges have stopped in the gateway*)
MAYOR   You must know that from your book. Naturally, the
  Maid is condemned by French judges, that's as it should be,
  because she's French.
SIMONE (*confused*)   That's true. I know from the book that
  I'm condemned to death. But I'd like to know why. I've
  never really understood that part of it.
MAYOR (*to the judges*)   She demands a trial.
CAPTAIN FÉTAIN   What's the point of a trial when the sentence
  has already been read?
MAYOR   Well, then at least the defendant will have been
  examined, questioned, and weighed in the balance.
COLONEL   And found wanting. (*Shrugging his shoulders*) But
  very well, if you insist.
MONSIEUR SOUPEAU   But we're not prepared.
  (*They put their heads together and deliberate in whispers.
  Père Gustave brings out a table and puts dishes and candles
  on it. The judges sit down at the table*)
PÈRE GUSTAVE   The refugees from the schoolhouse are outside.
  They wish to be admitted to the trial.
MONSIEUR SOUPEAU   Impossible. I'm expecting mother. She

says they stink.

CAPTAIN FÉTAIN (*in the direction of the gate*) The trial will take place behind closed doors. In the interests of the state.

MONSIEUR SOUPEAU Where are the records? Probably gone down the drain, like everything else in this country.

MAYOR Where is the complainant?

(*The judges look at each other*)

MAYOR It can't be official without a complainant.

MONSIEUR SOUPEAU Père Gustave, get a complainant out of the storehouse.

PÈRE GUSTAVE (*stands in the gateway and calls out toward the street*) The high court of Rouen calls on each one of you to put forward his complaint against the Maid.—Nobody? (*He repeats the summons; then to the judges*) The complainant: Isabeau, the queen mother, partisan of the renegade duke of Burgundy and of the mortal enemy.

MADAME SOUPEAU (*in armor, comes out of the hostelry and greets the judges, who bow low. With the practiced affability of a high-class hotelkeeper*) Good evening, Herr Hauptmann. No, don't get up. (*Over her shoulder toward the hostelry*) One Alsace-Lorraine for the Herr Hauptmann, well done. How would you like your peasants, constable? Are you satisfied with the service, colonel? (*Pointing to Simone*) Everything would have been saved if this Maid of Orleans hadn't upset the negotiations. Everything: France and the brickyard as well. You're too weak, gentlemen. Who makes the decisions around here, the church or one of the hostelry's kitchen maids? (*Begins to scream furiously*) I demand that this person be executed at once for heresy, disobedience, and obstinacy. Heads must roll. Blood must flow. She must be bloodily exterminated. A bloody example must be set. (*Exhausted*) My drops.

CAPTAIN FÉTAIN A chair for the queen mother.

(*Père Gustave brings a chair*)

MONSIEUR SOUPEAU Isn't that armor too tight for you, mother? Why are you in armor anyway?

MADAME SOUPEAU I'm making war too.

MONSIEUR SOUPEAU What kind of a war is that?

MADAME SOUPEAU My war. Against the seditious Maid, who incited those people in the schoolhouse.

CAPTAIN FÉTAIN (*sharply*)   Shh! (*To Simone*) Maid, by what
right did you incite the French people to make war?

SIMONE   An angel told me to, venerable bishop of Beauvais.
(*The judges exchange looks*)

MONSIEUR SOUPEAU   Oh. An angel? What kind of an angel?

SIMONE   The one in the church. On the left side of the altar.

CAPTAIN FÉTAIN   Never seen him.

MAYOR (*friendly*)   What did this angel look like, Simone?
Describe him.

SIMONE   He was very young and he had a lovely voice, your
worships. He said I should . . .

COLONEL (*interrupting*)   What he said is of no interest. What
sort of dialect did he speak? Like an educated person? Or
some other way?

SIMONE   I don't know. The way people speak.

CAPTAIN FÉTAIN   Aha.

MONSIEUR SOUPEAU   How was this angel dressed?

SIMONE   He was beautifully dressed. He was dressed in a kind
of material you'd pay twenty or thirty francs a yard for in
Tours.

CAPTAIN FÉTAIN   Have I understood you correctly, Simone, I
mean Joan? This angel was not one of the magnificent
angels whose clothes cost maybe two or three hundred
francs a yard?

SIMONE   I don't know.

COLONEL   In what condition was the robe? Rather worn?

SIMONE   The angel was just a little crumbled away, in the
sleeve.

COLONEL   Aha. Crumbled away in the sleeve. As if he'd had
to wear his robe at work, eh? Would you say torn?

SIMONE   No, not torn.

CAPTAIN FÉTAIN   But crumbled. Couldn't the sleeve in the
crumbled part have been torn, from work? Maybe you
couldn't see it, because the paint had crumbled away. But
wouldn't you say that was possible?
(*Simone is silent*)

COLONEL   Did the angel say anything that a person of rank
could have said? Think before you answer.

SIMONE   Plain, simple things.

MAYOR Did the angel look like anybody you know?

SIMONE (*softly*) My brother André.

COLONEL Private André Machard! Gentlemen, now we know. A very peculiar angel, to say the least.

MADAME SOUPEAU A barroom angel, a gutter Gabriel! Now at least we know what to think of those "voices." They come from the cheap wine rooms and manure pits.

SIMONE You oughtn't to say bad things about the angel, venerable bishops and cardinals.

MONSIEUR SOUPEAU On page 124 of your book you will find that we are the ecclesiastical court, the highest authority on earth, so to speak.

COLONEL Don't you think that we, the high cardinals of France, know better what God wants than some low-class angel?

CAPTAIN FÉTAIN Where is God, Joan? Down below or up above? And where did *your* so-called angel come from? From down below. So who sent him? God? Or could it have been the evil one?

MADAME SOUPEAU The devil! Joan of Orleans, the voices you heard came from the devil!

SIMONE (*in a loud voice*) No! No! Not from the devil!

CAPTAIN FÉTAIN Why don't you call your angel? Maybe he will defend the great Maid of Orleans. Usher, do your duty.

PÈRE GUSTAVE (*cries out*) The high ecclesiastical court of Rouen hereby summons the angel, name unknown, who allegedly appeared to the Maid on various nights, to testify in her behalf.

(*Simone looks up toward the roof of the garage. It remains empty. Père Gustave repeats his summons. In great distress Simone looks at the smiling judges. Then she crouches down and in her confusion begins to beat the ground. But no sound is heard and the garage roof remains empty*)

SIMONE It doesn't sound here. What has happened? It doesn't sound. The French earth doesn't sound any more! It doesn't sound here!

MADAME SOUPEAU (*steps up to her*) Have you any idea who France is?

(b)

The morning of June 22. Over the gate a French flag at half-mast, hung with crape. Georges, Robert, and Père Gustave are listening to Maurice, who is reading from a newspaper edged with black.

MAURICE   The marshal says the armistice conditions leave the honor of France intact.

PÈRE GUSTAVE   That makes me feel better.

MAURICE   It would. The marshal goes on to say that the French people must rally round him as round a father. A new order and discipline are needed.

PÈRE GUSTAVE   That's right. André has stopped fighting, they have laid down his arms. What he needs now is strict discipline.

GEORGES   It's good Simone has got away.

(The German captain, without his hat and sword-belt, comes out of the hostelry, smoking his after-breakfast cigar. He casts an indifferent glance at those present and saunters toward the gate. He looks out for a moment, turns around, and now walking more quickly, goes back into the hostelry)

PÈRE GUSTAVE   It always bothered him that she's only a child.

GEORGES   I can't get over her running away. She always said she'd stay no matter what. Something must have scared her. She just crawled through the window of the laundry room.

(Monsieur Soupeau comes out of the hostelry, rubbing his hands)

MONSIEUR SOUPEAU   Maurice, Robert. Unload the china and silverware! (*In an undertone, after looking around him*) I'm not going to ask you whether any of my staff helped a certain person to escape last night. What's done is done. I'll even go so far as to say that maybe it wasn't such a bad solution. Not that there was any real danger. The Germans aren't cannibals, and your boss knows how to handle them. Only this morning at breakfast I was saying to the German captain: "A farce! Before the notice, after the notice, what's the sense in all that? A child! What do they expect? Maybe a little soft in the head, psychopathic! Tanks! Stop them! Destroy everything! And naturally the fascination of matches. A political act? Nonsense! Pure childishness!"

GEORGES *(looking at the others)* Childishness, Monsieur Henri? Childishness?

MONSIEUR SOUPEAU I told mother the same thing: a child!

GEORGES That child was the only one of us here at the hostelry to do her duty; nobody else lifted a finger. And the people of Saint-Martin won't forget it, Monsieur Henri.

MONSIEUR SOUPEAU *(disgruntled)* You just do *your* duty. Unload those crates. I'm only glad the matter is settled. I'm sure the captain won't waste much time looking for Simone. And now to work! That's what our poor France needs now! *(Goes out)*

GEORGES Relief all along the line: she's gone!

MAURICE And it had nothing to do with patriotism or anything like that. That would have been unpleasant. "The Germans aren't cannibals." We were just getting ready to make a noble gesture, to give the Germans the gasoline we'd been withholding from our own army, when the rabble steps in and gets patriotic.

(The mayor comes in through the gate. He is pale and does not answer their greetings. Goes toward the hostelry)

MAYOR *(turning around)* Are there sentries in the corridor outside Madame Soupeau's room?

PÈRE GUSTAVE No, Monsieur Chavez.

(The mayor goes out)

PÈRE GUSTAVE He's probably come because the Germans want the schoolhouse evacuated. Unless it's Madame Soupeau that wants it.

ROBERT The new order and discipline!

PÈRE GUSTAVE About Simone, Maurice: it had to be common arson, because in that case the insurance company has to pay up. They don't overlook things like that. *(Simone comes in through the gate between two German soldiers with fixed bayonets)*

GEORGES Simone! What's happened?

SIMONE *(stops, very pale)* I was in the schoolhouse.

ROBERT   Don't be afraid. The Germans won't hurt you.

SIMONE   When they questioned me last night they said I'd be handed over to the French authorities.

GEORGES   Then why did you run away?

(*Simone does not answer. The soldiers push her into the hostelry*)

MAURICE   So the Germans haven't washed their hands of it. Monsieur Henri was mistaken.

(*Monsieur and Madame Machard come in through the gate, the former in his bailiff's uniform*)

MADAME MACHARD   Have they already brought her here? That's terrible. Monsieur Machard is beside himself. It's not just because the rent is due; it's the disgrace that's killing him. I always knew it would end like this; it's reading all those books that drove her mad. At seven o'clock this morning there's a knocking at the door and the Germans are outside. "Messieurs," I say, "if our daughter can't be found, she's done something to herself. Fire or not, she'd never have left the hostelry otherwise. If only for her brother's sake she'd have stayed."

(*Monsieur Soupeau comes out of the hostelry*)

MONSIEUR SOUPEAU   It's too much, Madame Machard! She's cost me 100,000 francs. Not to mention the wear and tear on my nerves.

(*Madame Soupeau comes out of the hostelry. She has a powerful hold on Simone's arm and drags her, despite her resistance, to the storehouse. Behind them the mayor and Captain Fétain. All go into the storehouse. Those present in the yard look on in amazement*)

MAYOR   (*at the storehouse door*)   Machard, run over to the schoolhouse and get them to evacuate quietly. Tell them the Germans need the premises. (*Out into the storehouse*)

MADAME MACHARD   Yes, monsieur le maire.

(*The two Machards go out with dignity*)

ROBERT   What do they want of her in the storehouse? What are they doing to her, Monsieur Henri?

MONSIEUR SOUPEAU   Don't ask questions. We have an enormous responsibility. One false step and the hostelry is ruined.

MADAME SOUPEAU (*comes out of the storehouse with Simone, followed by the mayor and Captain Fétain*) Monsieur le maire, I believe I have convinced you, you've seen it with your own eyes, that she left the cellars, with supplies including vintage wines valued at 50,000 francs, unlocked. How many cases of other goods have been lost I can only surmise. To deceive me, she handed me the key in your presence. (*Turns to Simone*) Simone, I hear that you yourself took whole baskets full of food to the schoolhouse. What did they pay you for it? Where is the money?

SIMONE I didn't take money, madame.

MADAME SOUPEAU Don't lie. And that's not all. The morning Monsieur Henri left, the mob threatened him because someone had spread a rumor that we were about to move our trucks. Did you spread that rumor?

SIMONE I told monsieur le maire, madame.

MADAME SOUPEAU Who was in the mayor's office at the time? Refugees?

SIMONE Yes, I think so.

MADAME SOUPEAU Oh, you think so. Then when the mob came here, what did you advise them to do about the supplies belonging to the hostelry where you were employed? (*Simone does not understand*) Did you or did you not advise them to take what they wanted?

SIMONE I don't remember, madame.

MADAME SOUPEAU So . . .

MAYOR What are you driving at, madame?

MADAME SOUPEAU Simone, who were the first to help themselves? Exactly, your parents. They took plenty.

ROBERT This is too much. (*To Madame Soupeau*) You yourself forced the stuff on the Machards.

GEORGES (*at the same time*) You told monsieur le maire to dispose of your supplies as he saw fit.

MAYOR That's right, madame.

MADAME SOUPEAU (*ignoring the last remarks, to Simone*) You were insolent, disloyal, and obstinate. For that reason I discharged you. Did you leave the hostelry when I ordered you to?

SIMONE No, madame.

MADAME SOUPEAU No, you just hung around, and then to get even with me for discharging you, you set fire to the brick-yard. Out of pure vindictiveness. Is that right?

SIMONE (*excitedly*) I did it because of the Germans.

ROBERT Everybody in Saint-Martin knows that.

MADAME SOUPEAU Oh, because of the Germans? Who told you the Germans would ever find out about the gasoline?

SIMONE I heard monsieur le capitaine telling monsieur le maire.

MADAME SOUPEAU Ah, you heard that we were going to declare the gasoline?

SIMONE Monsieur le capitaine wanted you to.

MADAME SOUPEAU So you burned the gasoline to keep us from handing it over. That's exactly what I wanted to know.

SIMONE (*in despair*) I did it because of the enemy! There were three tanks on the square outside the town hall.

MADAME SOUPEAU And they were the enemy? Or could it have been someone else?

(*Two nuns appear in the gate, accompanied by a police-man*)

MAYOR What brings you here, Jules?

THE POLICEMAN The ladies are from the Sisters of St. Ursula.

CAPTAIN FÉTAIN I phoned St. Ursula's in your name, Chavez. (*To the nuns*) Mes soeurs, this is the Machard girl.

MAYOR How dare you . . . ?

CAPTAIN FÉTAIN Monsieur Chavez, you can't be thinking of letting this girl run around loose? (*Sharply*) The least our guests can expect is that we clean up the dangerous elements in Saint-Martin. You don't seem to have studied the marshal's address. France is facing a period fraught with peril. Insubordination is contagious, and it is our duty to nip it in the bud. One such fire in Saint-Martin is enough, Chavez.

MAURICE Oh, now we're expected to do the Germans' dirty work for them. And it looks like we're only too glad to.

MADAME SOUPEAU (*coldly*) Obviously the girl must be formally committed. I shall apply to the public prosecutor in Tours. For sordid personal motives she set fire to *our* brick-yard.

GEORGES   How could Simone have personal motives?

MAYOR (*shaken*)   Do you want to destroy the child?

ROBERT (*menacingly*)   Who's being vindictive now?

MONSIEUR SOUPEAU   Don't start in again, Robert. She's a minor. She's being entrusted to the sisters' care. That's all there is to it.

MAURICE (*horrified*)   But they beat the inmates.

SIMONE (*screaming*)   No!

MAYOR   You can't send Simone to a home for the feeble-minded. It's a house of mental torture! A hell! Do you realize you're condemning her to madness?

MAURICE (*pointing at the brutish nuns*)   Just look at those ladies.

(*The nuns' faces remain masklike and unmoved*)

GEORGES   You'd have done better to let the Germans execute her.

SIMONE (*imploring help*)   That's where people's heads swell up and the spit runs out of their mouths, monsieur le maire. They tie you up!

MAYOR (*energetically*)   Madame Soupeau, I will testify before the board in Tours and tell them what the child's actual motives were. Don't worry, Simone, everyone knows your motives were patriotic.

MADAME SOUPEAU (*in an outburst*)   You want to make a national saint out of this little pétroleuse. Is that it? France is saved by fire. On one side the German tanks, on the other Simone Machard, the daughter of a common laborer.

CAPTAIN FÉTAIN   In view of your past, Monsieur Chavez, the judges of the new France are not likely to attach much importance to your testimony. Besides, the road to Tours has become rather unsafe for people of your stamp.

MAURICE (*angrily*)   Now I get it: you're clearing Saint-Martin of any suspicion that it has Frenchmen in it.

MADAME SOUPEAU   Frenchmen? (*Seizes Simone and shakes her*)   Do you think you can teach us what patriotism is? The Soupeaus have owned the hostelry for two hundred years. (*To all*)   Do you want to see a patriot? (*Pointing to Captain Fétain*)   Here he is. We're quite capable of telling you when war is necessary, and we can also tell you when peace is better. You want to do something for France? Fine. *We* are France. Understand?

CAPTAIN FÉTAIN   You're working yourself up, Marie.—Monsieur le maire, will you or will you not let them take the girl away?

MAYOR   Me? *You* seem to have taken over the power here. (*Turns to go*)

SIMONE (*frightened*)   Don't go away, monsieur le maire!

MAYOR (*helplessly*)   Chin up, Simone! (*Broken, he staggers off*)

MADAME SOUPEAU (*breaking the silence, to Captain Fétain*)   Honoré, get this scandalous business over with!

CAPTAIN FÉTAIN (*to the policeman*)   On my responsibility. (*The policeman seizes Simone*)

SIMONE (*terrified, softly*)   Not to St. Ursula's!

ROBERT   Swine! (*Wants to strike the policeman*)

MAURICE (*holds him back*)   Don't be a fool, Robert. There's nothing we can do to help her. They've got their police, and they've got the Germans. Poor Simone, too many enemies.

MADAME SOUPEAU   Simone, get your things.

(*Simone looks around. Her friends stand silent, with downcast eyes. Bewildered, she goes into the storehouse*)

MADAME SOUPEAU (*half to the personnel, calmly, explaining*)   The child is insubordinate, incapable of accepting authority. It is our painful duty to teach her order and discipline.

(*Simone comes back carrying a tiny suitcase, with her apron over her arm. She hands the apron to Madame Soupeau*)

MADAME SOUPEAU   And now open your suitcase. We want to see what you're taking with you.

MONSIEUR SOUPEAU   Is that necessary, mother?

(*One of the nuns has already opened the suitcase. She takes out Simone's book*)

SIMONE   Not the book!

(*The nun hands Madame Soupeau the book*)

MADAME SOUPEAU   This is the property of the hostelry.

MONSIEUR SOUPEAU   I gave it to her.

MADAME SOUPEAU   It wasn't much good to her. (*To Simone*) Say good-bye to the staff.

SIMONE   Good-bye, Monsieur Georges.

GEORGES   Will you be brave, Simone?

SIMONE   Oh yes, Monsieur Georges.

MAURICE   Stay well.

SIMONE   Yes, Maurice.

GEORGES   I won't forget your cousin.

(*Simone smiles at him. She looks up at the garage roof. The light dims. Music announces the apparition of the angel. Simone looks up at the garage roof and sees the angel*)

THE ANGEL

Daughter of France, don't be afraid
None will endure who fight the Maid.
The Lord will blast the arm
That does you harm.
Where they take you it matters not
France is wherever you set foot.
The day will soon be coming when
Glorious France will rise again.

(*The angel vanishes. Full light. The nuns take Simone by the arms. Simone kisses Maurice and Robert and is led off. All look on in silence*)

SIMONE (*in the gateway, struggling desperately*)   No, no! I won't go! Help me! Not to St. Ursula's! André! André! (*She is dragged away*)

MADAME SOUPEAU   Henri, my drops!

MONSIEUR SOUPEAU (*frowning*)   Maurice, Robert, Georges, Père Gustave! Back to work! Don't forget, we're at peace now!

(*Monsieur Soupeau and Captain Fétain lead Madame Soupeau into the hostelry. Maurice and Robert go out through the gate. Père Gustave rolls a tire out into the yard to mend it. Georges examines his bad arm. The sky begins to turn red. Père Gustave points this out to Georges. Monsieur Soupeau comes rushing out of the hostelry*)

MONSIEUR SOUPEAU   Maurice, Robert! Find out what's burning. (*Goes out*)

PÈRE GUSTAVE   It must be the schoolhouse. The refugees! It looks like they've learned something.

GEORGES   The car can't have reached St. Ursula's yet. Simone must be able to see the fire from the car.

Schweyk in the Second World War

Play

Translators: Max Knight and Joseph Fabry

CHARACTERS

SCHWEYK, dog hustler in
   Prague
BALOUN, photographer, his
   friend
ANNA KOPECKA, owner of
   the "Flagon"
YOUNG PROCHAZKA, a butcher's
   son, her admirer
ANNA, a maidservant
KATI, her girl friend

BRETTSCHNEIDER, Gestapo
   agent

BULLINGER, SS platoon leader
SS MAN MÜLLER 2
THE ARMY CHAPLAIN

HITLER
HIMMLER
GÖRING
GOEBBELS
VON BOCK

SUPPORTING CHARACTERS

Prelude in the Higher Regions

Martial music. Hitler, Göring, Goebbels, and Himmler around a globe. All are larger than life-size except Goebbels who is smaller than life-size.

HITLER

Gentlemen, dear party members. Now that with iron hand
I have subjugated our own German land
I am fixing to conquer the whole world plus population
In my opinion, a mere problem of tanks, stukas, and con-
centration.
But now, before I forget in my great eagerness
Tell me, dear chief of police and SS
The Little Man—what does he think of me
Not only in Germany
Also in Czechovakia or whatever name
Those little countries used to be called (they're all the
same)?
Is he for me? Or does he—love me?
Will he stand by me? Or will he—come to my help in an
emergency?
Does he revere me, grand master of all art, strategist most
noted?
In short, what is his attitude?

HIMMLER

Devoted.

HITLER

Will he make sacrifices? Will he make concessions
I mean, of his possessions

Which I need to make my war, for though a shining ge-
    nius, I
Still am only a man.

HIMMLER

That I deny.

HITLER

Thanks. I should hope so. But as I've said
When this damn insomnia agitates my head
Then I wonder: Where does the humble Little Man in
    Europe stand?

HIMMLER

My Führer, he worships you on one hand
As he would worship God. Meanwhile
On the other, he loves you just as dearly as the Germans
    do.

GÖRING, GOEBBELS, HIMMLER

Heil!

1

*Schweyk and Baloun are drinking their morning beer at the
"Flagon." Mrs. Anna Kopecka, the owner, is serving a drunken
SS man. At the bar sits young Prochazka.*

MRS. KOPECKA   You've had five Pilsners, and I'd rather not
    give you a sixth because you're not used to it.
SS MAN   Give me one more. That's an order. You know what
    that means. If you're sensible and carry it out, I'll let you
    in on a secret. You won't regret it.
MRS. KOPECKA   I don't want to hear it. That's why I'm not
    giving you any more beer. If you start blabbing your
    secrets, I'll be in trouble.
SS MAN   That's very smart of you, take it from me. Anybody
    who knows this secret will be shot. They tried to kill

Adolf in Munich. A hair's breadth and he'd have been a goner.

MRS. KOPECKA You just keep quiet. You're drunk.

SCHWEYK (*amiably from the next table*) Which Adolf was that? I know two Adolfs. One was a salesman in Prusha's drugstore, he's in a concentration camp because he wouldn't sell concentrated hydrochloric acid to anybody but Czechs, the other is Adolf Kokoschka, that collects dog shit and he's in a concentration camp too for saying—so I'm told—that the shit of the English bulldog is best. No great loss, either of them.

SS MAN (*rises and salutes*) Heil Hitler!

SCHWEYK (*also rises and salutes*) Heil Hitler!

SS MAN (*threateningly*) You don't like it?

SCHWEYK Beg to report, sir, I like it fine.

MRS. KOPECKA (*arrives with beer*) Here's your Pilsner, it makes no difference now. But sit down and don't spill your Führer's secrets that nobody wants to know. No politics around here. (*She points to a sign saying: "Drink your slivovitz, drink your beer/but don't talk politics in here"*) I'm a businesswoman. If somebody orders a beer, I draw it for him, but that's all.

YOUNG PROCHAZKA (*when she returns to the bar*) Mrs. Anna, why can't you let your customers have a little fun?

MRS. KOPECKA Because the Nazis will shut the place down on me, Mr. Prochazka.

SCHWEYK (*who is again seated*) If it was Hitler they tried to kill, that would be a good one.

MRS. KOPECKA You keep still, too, Mr. Schweyk. It's none of your business.

SCHWEYK If it happened, maybe it's because we're running short of potatoes. People don't go for that. The trouble is we've got so much order, everything has its place, every bunch of soup greens is a coupon in the ration book, that's order. I'm told that Hitler brought us more order than anybody ever thought possible. When there's plenty, there's no order. For instance, when I've sold a dachshund, my money is all mixed up in my pocket, bills and five and ten heller pieces, but when I'm broke all I've got is one little bill and one five-heller piece: how can you have disorder in that? In Italy when Mussolini came along the trains started running on schedule. They've tried to bump him off seven or eight times.

MRS. KOPECKA   Stop shooting your mouth off and drink your beer. If something's happened, we'll all catch it.

SCHWEYK   What I don't understand, Baloun, is why you're so down at the mouth about the news. I'll bet there aren't many like you in Prague.

BALOUN   It's all very well to say that food is short in wartime. But with all these ration books and half a pound of meat a week, I haven't had a square meal since Corpus Christi last year. (*Pointing to the SS man*) It's all right for those fellows, look how well fed they are. Got to ask him a few questions. (*He walks over to the SS man*) What did you have for lunch, neighbor, that made you so thirsty, if I may ask? I bet it was something good and spicy—goulash maybe?

SS MAN   That's none of your business, it's a military secret. Meat loaf.

BALOUN   With gravy. And fresh vegetables? I don't want you to give away a secret, but if it was cabbage, was it well chopped? That makes all the difference. Dear me, one time in Przlov, before Hitler—begging your pardon—I had a meat loaf at the "Swan," I tell you, it was better than at "Plattner's."

MRS. KOPECKA   (*to Schweyk*) Can't you get Baloun away from that SS man? Yesterday he kept asking Herr Brettschneider of the Gestapo—funny he hasn't shown up yet—about the helpings in the German army; they almost arrested him as a spy.

SCHWEYK   You can't stop him. Food is his vice.

BALOUN   (*to the SS man*) Do you happen to know if the Germans in Prague are taking on volunteers for the Russian campaign, and if the helpings are as big as in the German army, or is it a false rumor?

MRS. KOPECKA   Mr. Baloun, don't bother the gentleman, he's here as a private citizen and you as a Czech ought to be ashamed of yourself asking such questions.

BALOUN   (*guiltily*) I don't mean any harm, or I wouldn't be asking questions so innocently; I know your opinions, Mrs. Kopecka.

MRS. KOPECKA   I haven't any opinions, I have a tavern. All I ask of my customers is common decency. And I have a terrible time with you, Mr. Baloun.

SS MAN   You want to volunteer?

BALOUN   I'm only asking.

SS MAN   If you're interested, I'll take you to the recruiting office. The food is excellent, if you want to know. The Ukraine is going to be the granary of the Third Reich. When we were in Holland, I sent so many packages home there was even enough for my aunt that I can't stand. (*Rises*) Heitler.

BALOUN (*also rises*) Heil Hitler.

SCHWEYK (*joining them*)   Don't say "Heil Hitler," say "Heitler" like this gentleman, who must know: that shows you're used to it and even say it at home in your sleep.

MRS. KOPECKA (*puts a schnapps down in front of the SS man*) Here, one for the road.

SS MAN (*embracing Baloun*)   So you want to volunteer against the Bolsheviks, that is good to hear; you're a lousy Czech but a smart one. I'll take you to the recruiting office.

MRS. KOPECKA (*pushes him back into his chair*)   Drink your slivovitz, that will calm you down. (*To Baloun*) I have a good mind to throw you out on your ear. You have no dignity, that comes from your unnatural passion for food. You know the song they're singing? I'll sing it for you, you've only had two beers, you must have some sense left in you. (*She sings* "The Song of the Nazi Soldier's Wife")

And what did the mail bring the soldier's wife
From the ancient city of Prague?
From Prague it brought her some high-heeled shoes
A letter with news and high-heeled shoes—
That's what she got from the town of Prague.

And what did the mail bring the soldier's wife
From Warsaw, the town on the plains
From Warsaw it brought her a nice linen blouse

It was all on the house, that nice Polish blouse
That's what she got from the Polish plains.

And what did the mail bring the soldier's wife
From Oslo, across the sound?
From Oslo it brought her an elegant fur
Just the thing for her, that elegant fur
That's what she got from over the sound.

And what did the mail bring the soldier's wife
From opulent Rotterdam?
From Rotterdam it brought her a hat
How nice to look at, that little Dutch hat
That's what she got from Rotterdam.

And what did the mail bring the soldier's wife
From Brussels, the city of sprouts?
From Brussels it brought her some delicate lace.
Oh, it flattered her face, that delicate lace
That's what she got from the city of sprouts.

And what did the mail bring the soldier's wife
From Paris, city of light?
From Paris it brought her a silken dress
She loved to impress with that silken dress—
Sent from Paris, the city of light.

And what did the mail bring the soldier's wife
From Libyan Tripoli?
From Tripoli it brought her a charm
To shield her from harm, a copper-chained charm—
That's what she got from Tripoli.

And what did the mail bring the soldier's wife
From the land of Russia?
From Russia it brought her a widow's weeds
That's all she needs, a widow's weeds
That's what she got from Russia.

(*The SS man triumphantly nods at the end of each stanza,*

but before the last one his head drops onto the table because he is now completely drunk)

SCHWEYK   A very nice song. (*To Baloun*) It shows that you'd better think twice before doing anything rash. Don't take it into your head to march to Russia with Hitler on account of the big helpings, you'll only freeze to death, you damn fool.

BALOUN (*shaken by the song, puts his head on his elbow and starts crying*)   Holy Jesus and Mary, what's going to become of me and my appetite? You've got to do something for me or I'll crack up. How can I be a good Czech on an empty stomach?

SCHWEYK   If you'd swear by the Virgin Mary that you'll never volunteer, you'd keep your oath. (*To Mrs. Kopecka*) He's religious. But would you swear? No.

BALOUN   I can't swear just like that, it's no joke.

MRS. KOPECKA   Terrible. You're a grown-up man.

BALOUN   But a weak one.

SCHWEYK   If somebody put a dish of roast pork in front of your nose and said: "There, eat, you hopeless degenerate, but swear you'll always be a good Czech," you'd swear, as I know you. You'd swear if they kept a good hold on the dish and snatched it away if you didn't swear. With you that would work.

BALOUN   I guess it would, but they'd have to hold on tight.

SCHWEYK   And you'd only keep your oath if you'd gone down on your knees and sworn on the Bible in front of a lot of people? Am I right?

(*Baloun nods*)

MRS. KOPECKA   I'm almost tempted to try it. (*She goes back to young Prochazka*)

YOUNG PROCHAZKA   Just hearing you sing, I can hardly breathe.

MRS. KOPECKA (*absently*)   Why?

YOUNG PROCHAZKA   Love.

MRS. KOPECKA   How can you tell it's love and not just a passing fancy?

YOUNG PROCHAZKA   I can tell, Mrs. Anna. Yesterday I wrapped up a customer's purse instead of a schnitzel because I was thinking of you, and my father didn't like that at all. And every morning I have a headache. It's love.

MRS. KOPECKA   The question is: how much love?

YOUNG PROCHAZKA   What do you mean by that, Mrs. Anna?

MRS. KOPECKA   I mean, how far would your love go? Maybe only as far as blowing your nose; that's been known to happen.

YOUNG PROCHAZKA   Mrs. Anna, don't crush my heart with cold suspicions. My love would go to the ends of the earth if it were only requited. But it isn't.

MRS. KOPECKA   I wonder, for instance, if it would go as far as two pounds of smoked butt.

YOUNG PROCHAZKA   Mrs. Anna! How can you be so materialistic at a time like this?

MRS. KOPECKA (*turning away to count bottles*)   See? Any favor is too much.

YOUNG PROCHAZKA (*shaking his head*)   I don't understand you, Mrs. Anna. Ships that pass in the night.

BALOUN (*hopelessly*)   It didn't start with this war, it's an old weakness, this craving for food. To cure it, my sister and her kids, where I was living then, went to the Klokota church fair. But even Klokota was no good. My sister and the kids come home from the fair and right away she counts the chickens. One or two were missing. But I just can't help myself. I knew she needed them for eggs, but I go outside and it's like I'm in love. Suddenly, so help me, I feel a bottomless pit in my stomach and an hour later I'm all right again and the chicken is gone. I'm probably hopeless.

YOUNG PROCHAZKA   Were you serious?

MRS. KOPECKA   Very serious.

YOUNG PROCHAZKA   Mrs. Anna, when do you want the smoked butt? Tomorrow?

MRS. KOPECKA   Aren't you being a little rash? You'll have to take it from your father's shop, without permission and without meat coupons. That's called black-marketing nowadays. You'll get shot if they find out.

YOUNG PROCHAZKA   Do you really think I'd mind being shot if I knew you'd love me for it?

(*Schweyk and Baloun have followed the conversation*)

SCHWEYK (*appreciatively*) That's the way a man in love should behave. In Pilsen a young man hanged himself from a rafter for a widow who wasn't even so young any more, because she remarked one day that he'd never done anything for her. And at the "Bear" a man slashed his wrist in the toilet because the waitress poured more beer in another customer's glass—a family man at that. A few days later two men jumped into the Moldau off Charles Bridge because of a woman, but that was on account of her money. Seems she was rich.

MRS. KOPECKA I must admit, Mr. Prochazka, that a woman doesn't get to hear such things very often.

YOUNG PROCHAZKA That's God's truth. I'll bring it tomorrow noon. Will that be soon enough?

MRS. KOPECKA I don't like you to take the risk but it's for a good cause, it's not for me. You heard what Mr. Baloun said: he needs a square meal with meat in it, or he gets terrible ideas.

YOUNG PROCHAZKA So you don't like me to take risks? That slipped out of you, didn't it? You do care if I get shot. You've made me happy, so don't take it back, Mrs. Anna. It's all settled—you can count on the smoked butt even if they blow my brains out for it.

MRS. KOPECKA Be here for lunch tomorrow, Mr. Baloun. I won't promise, but it looks like you'll get a meal.

BALOUN If I get just one more meal, I'll forget all my terrible ideas. But I won't start drooling before I see it. I've suffered too much.

SCHWEYK (*referring to the SS man*) I don't think he'll remember a thing when he wakes up; he's drunk. (*He shouts into the SS man's ear*) Hurrah for Beneš! (*When the man does not move*) That's the most reliable sign that he's out cold, or he'd make hash out of me because that's what they're scared of.

(*The Gestapo agent Brettschneider has entered*)

BRETTSCHNEIDER Who's scared?

SCHWEYK (*firmly*) The SS men. Sit down with us, Herr Brettschneider. A Pilsner for the gentleman, Mrs. Kopecka. It's hot today.

BRETTSCHNEIDER   And what are they scared of, in your opinion?

SCHWEYK   Of not being careful enough and letting a seditious remark slip by or some such thing. But maybe you want to read your newspaper in peace and I'm bothering you?

BRETTSCHNEIDER (*sits down with the paper*)   Nobody bothers me if he's got something interesting to say. Mrs. Kopecka, you're looking like a spring blossom again today.

MRS. KOPECKA (*putting a mug of beer down in front of him*) Better say a summer bloom.

YOUNG PROCHAZKA (*when she returns to the bar*)   If I were you, I wouldn't let him get so fresh.

BRETTSCHNEIDER (*opening his paper*)   This is a special edition. There's been an attempt to assassinate the Führer, with a bomb, in a Munich beerhall. What do you think of that?

SCHWEYK   Did he suffer long?

BRETTSCHNEIDER   He wasn't hurt, the bomb exploded too late.

SCHWEYK   Probably a cheap bomb. Nowadays they do everything with mass production methods, and then people are surprised that the workmanship is no good. Those things just aren't made with the same loving care as in the old days when they made them by hand, am I right? But imagine not picking a better bomb for a job like that? I call that negligence. I remember one time in Česky Krumlov, a butcher . . .

BRETTSCHNEIDER (*interrupting*)   You call it negligence when the Führer almost loses his life?

SCHWEYK   A word like "almost" can be tricky, Herr Brettschneider. In '38 when they sold us out at Munich, we almost went to war, but then we almost lost everything because we didn't. In the First World War, Austria almost conquered Serbia, and Germany almost conquered France. You can't rely on "almost."

BRETTSCHNEIDER   Keep on talking, it's interesting. You have interesting customers, Mrs. Kopecka. So well informed about politics.

MRS. KOPECKA   One customer is like another. For a businesswoman like me there's no such thing as politics. And see here, Herr Brettschneider, I'll thank you not to needle my customers into making political statements so you can arrest them afterwards. And you, Mr. Schweyk, as long as you pay for your beer, you're free to sit down and shoot off your mouth as much as you like. But right now, Mr. Schweyk, you've shot it off enough for two glasses of beer.

BRETTSCHNEIDER I have the impression that you wouldn't consider it a great loss for the Protectorate if the Führer were dead.

SCHWEYK It would be a loss all right, you can't deny it. A terrible loss. You couldn't replace Hitler with any old idiot. A lot of people gripe about Hitler. It doesn't surprise me.

BRETTSCHNEIDER (*hopefully*) What do you mean by that?

SCHWEYK (*with animation*) As the editor of *Field and Garden* once wrote, great men are always unpopular with the common people. The masses don't understand them, they think all those things are unnecessary, even heroism. The little man doesn't give a shit about a great era. All he wants is to drop into the bar now and then and eat goulash for supper. Naturally a statesman gets riled at bums like that, when it's his job to get his people into the schoolbooks, the poor bastard. To a great man the common people are a ball and chain. It's like offering Baloun here, with his appetite, a small Hungarian sausage for supper, what good is that? I wouldn't want to listen in when the big shots get together and start griping about us.

BRETTSCHNEIDER Are you, by any chance, of the opinion that the German people grumble, that they're not behind the Führer?

MRS. KOPECKA Please, gentlemen, talk about something else. There's no point in it, the times are too serious.

SCHWEYK (*takes a big swig of beer*) The German people are behind the Führer, Herr Brettschneider, nobody can deny it. As Reich Marshal Göring said one time: "People don't always understand the Führer at first, he's too great." Göring must know. (*Confidentially*) It's amazing, the way even the big shots cross Hitler up every time he gets one of his ideas. Last fall, I'm told, he wanted to put up a building that would reach all the way from Leipzig to Dresden—a memorial temple to Germany after it collapsed according to his great plan that he'd worked out in every detail, but they shook their heads at the ministry. They said it was "too great," because they've got no appreciation for the incomprehensible things that a genius thinks up when he's got nothing else to do. He managed to get them into this war, but only by telling them that all he wanted was the city of Danzig, not an inch more. And, mind you, that's the higher-ups and the educated people, the generals and the directors of I. G. Farben who shouldn't give a damn, because, hell, do *they* pay for it? The common man is a lot worse. If they ask him to die for a great cause, he says it louses up his plans, he gripes and bellyaches, and pokes his spoon around in his tripe as if he didn't like the taste of it, and no wonder the Führer gets fed up, when he's gone out of his way to think up something really new for them, conquering the world for instance. What more is there to conquer? The world is limited like everything else. It's just as well.

BRETTSCHNEIDER   Then you maintain that the Führer wants to conquer the world? That his aim is not just to defend Germany against its Jewish enemies and the plutocrats?

SCHWEYK   Don't take it that way; he doesn't mean any harm. Conquering the world is nothing special for him, it's like drinking beer for you, he gets a kick out of it, so he thinks he'll give it a try. Woe to perfidious Albion, I won't say a word more.

BRETTSCHNEIDER (*rises*)   You don't need to say any more. Just come with me to Gestapo headquarters at the Petschek Bank, we'll have something to say to you.

MRS. KOPECKA   But Herr Brettschneider, Mr. Schweyk only made a few innocent remarks. Don't get him in trouble.

SCHWEYK   I'm so innocent that I get arrested. I had two beers and a slivovitz. (*He pays, then says to Brettschneider amiably*) I beg your pardon for going out ahead of you, it's to help you keep an eye on me and guard me.

(*Brettschneider and Schweyk leave*)

BALOUN   Maybe they'll shoot him.

MRS. KOPECKA   Better have a slivovitz, Mr. Prochazka. It's given you a bad shock, too, hasn't it?

YOUNG PROCHAZKA   They're very quick about arresting people.

2

Gestapo headquarters at the Petschek Bank. Schweyk and Gestapo agent Brettschneider are facing Platoon Leader Ludwig Bullinger. In the background an SS man.

BULLINGER   This "Flagon" seems to be a regular hotbed of subversive characters.

BRETTSCHNEIDER (*quickly*)   Not at all, Herr Platoon Leader. Frau Kopecka, who owns the place, is a very respectable woman who keeps her nose out of politics; Schweyk is a dangerous exception among her customers. I've had my eye on him for quite some time.

(*The telephone on Bullinger's desk rings. He lifts the receiver. The caller's voice can be heard*)

TELEPHONE VOICE   Motorized squad. Banker Krusha denies making any remarks about the attempted assassination. Says he couldn't have read the news because he was arrested before it happened.

BULLINGER   Is he the Commercial Bank? In that case, give him ten on the ass. (*To Schweyk*) So you're one of those bastards, are you? First, let me ask you a question. If you don't know the answer, you swine, Müller 2 (*pointing at the SS man*) will take you down to the cellar and educate you, understand? The question is: Do you shit thin or do you shit thick?

SCHWEYK   Beg to report, Herr Platoon Leader, I shit the way you want me to.

BULLINGER   Answer correct. But you made remarks endangering the security of the German Reich, referred to the Führer's defensive war as a war of conquest, criticized the rationing system, and so on and so on. What have you to say for yourself?

SCHWEYK   That's a good deal. You can have too much of a good thing.

BULLINGER (*with heavy irony*)   I'm glad you're aware of that.

SCHWEYK I'm aware of a lot of things. There's got to be discipline. Without discipline nobody would get nowhere, like our sergeant told us in the 91st: "If somebody doesn't chew you out, you'll throw your pants away and start climbing trees." That's what I said to myself last night when they were manhandling me.

BULLINGER So you were manhandled—you don't say.

SCHWEYK In the cell. A gentleman from the SS came in and hit me over the head with a leather strap, and when I groaned he shined his flashlight in my face and said, "It's a mistake, it's not him." And he was so mad about making a mistake that he hit me again in the back. That's human nature: a man makes mistakes till his dying day.

BULLINGER I see. And you confess that you made the remarks recorded here? (*Pointing at Brettschneider's report*)

SCHWEYK If you want me to confess, Your Excellency, I'll confess, it can't hurt me. But if you say, "Schweyk, don't confess," I'll talk myself out of it till they tear me to pieces.

BULLINGER (*shouting*) Shut up! Take him away!

SCHWEYK (*when Brettschneider has taken him to the door, raising his right hand, loudly*) Hurrah for our Führer Adolf Hitler. We're going to win this war!

BULLINGER (*startled*) Are you feebleminded?

SCHWEYK Beg to report, Herr Platoon Leader, I can't help it, I was discharged from the army for idiocy. A military commission officially declared me an idiot.

BULLINGER Brettschneider! Didn't you notice that this man is an idiot?

BRETTSCHNEIDER (*hurt*) Herr Platoon Leader, the way Schweyk talked at the "Flagon" he sounded like an idiot who puts his seditious remarks in such a way that you can't prove anything.

BULLINGER And it's your opinion that we've been listening to the remarks of a man who knows what he's talking about?

BRETTSCHNEIDER Herr Bullinger, that is still my opinion. But if for any reason you don't want him, I'll take him back. It's just that at Investigation we haven't got much time to waste either, you know.

BULLINGER And my opinion, Brettschneider, is that you're a shitass.

BRETTSCHNEIDER   Herr Platoon Leader, I don't have to take that from you.

BULLINGER   And I want you to confess it. It's not much, and it would make you feel better. Admit that you're a shitass.

BRETTSCHNEIDER   I don't know what makes you feel that way about me, Herr Bullinger. I do my duty down to the slightest detail, I . . .

TELEPHONE VOICE   Motorized squad. Krusha is willing to take in your brother as a partner in the Commercial Bank but definitely denies that he made those remarks.

BULLINGER   Ten more on the ass, I need the remarks. (*To Brettschneider, almost pleading*) Look, don't you see how little I'm asking of you? If you admit it, it won't hurt your reputation, it's just between you and me. You are a shitass, why not admit it? If I practically get down on my knees? (*To Schweyk*) You persuade him.

SCHWEYK   Beg to report, sir, I wouldn't want to come between you gentlemen, but I know what you mean, Herr Platoon Leader. On the other hand it's hard on Herr Brettschneider because he's such a good bloodhound, and he doesn't really deserve it.

BULLINGER   (*sadly*)   So you're betraying me, too, you swine. "And the cock crew a third time," as it says in the Jew Bible. I'll squeeze it out of you yet, Brettschneider, but right now I haven't any time for private affairs, I've got ninety-seven more cases to take care of. Throw out this idiot and try to bring me something better next time.

SCHWEYK   (*steps up to him and kisses his hand*)   A thousand thanks, the Lord bless you. If you ever need a nice little pooch, let me know. Dogs are my business.

BULLINGER   Concentration camp. (*Brettschneider is about to take Schweyk away*) Stop! Leave me alone with this man. (*Brettschneider leaves angrily. The SS man leaves too*)

TELEPHONE VOICE   Motorized squad. Krusha has confessed to the remarks, but only that the attempted assassination was all one to him. Not that he was happy about it, or that the Führer's a clown, but only that he's human like everybody else.

BULLINGER   Five more until he's happy and the Führer's a stinking clown. (*To Schweyk, who smiles at him amiably*)

You realize, I hope, that in the concentration camp we tear you limb from limb if you try playing any jokes on us, you bastard!

SCHWEYK   I know all about that. They shoot you before you can count to four.

BULLINGER   So you're a dog hustler. In the park the other day I saw a purebred spitz that appealed to me, with a white spot on one ear.

SCHWEYK (*interrupts*)   Beg to report, sir, I am professionally acquainted with the animal. A lot of people have asked for him. He's got a whitish spot on his left ear, right? He belongs to Undersecretary Voyta. That dog is the apple of his eye, he won't eat unless you beg him on bended knee, and it has to be breast of veal. That proves he's a purebred. Mongrels are smarter, but purebreds are racially superior and favored by dog thieves. Usually they're so dumb they need two or three maids to tell them it's time to shit or open their mouths to eat. High-class people are the same way.

BULLINGER   That's enough about racial superiority, you bastard. I want the spitz, and that's that.

SCHWEYK   You can't have him; Voyta won't sell. How about a police dog? The kind that sniffs out everything you want to know and leads you straight to the scene of the crime. A butcher in Vrshovitz has one, and it pulls his cart for him. That dog missed his calling, so to speak.

BULLINGER   I told you I wanted the spitz.

SCHWEYK   If Undersecretary Voyta were only Jewish, you could simply take the dog, and no questions asked. But he's an Aryan, with a blond beard, kind of moth-eaten.

BULLINGER (*interested*)   Is he a genuine Czech?

SCHWEYK   It's not the way you think, he doesn't commit sabotage and curse Hitler, that would be simple. Off to the concentration camp, just like with me when I was misunderstood. But he's a collaborationist, they even call him a Quisling, which is a headache as far as the spitz is concerned.

BULLINGER (*takes a gun from his drawer and cleans it ostentatiously*)   I see, you don't want to get me the spitz, you saboteur.

SCHWEYK   Beg to report, sir, I do want to get you the dog.

(*Lecturing*) There are several systems, Herr Platoon Leader. The way to steal a lap dog or a toy terrier is to cut its leash in a crowd. You can get a mean German spotted mastiff by using a bitch in heat for bait. A fried horse-meat sausage is almost as good. But some dogs are as spoiled and pampered as an archbishop. I remember a salt-and-pepper pinscher I needed for the dog kennel up over the Klamovka —he wouldn't take any sausage. Three days I tried, until I couldn't stand it any more and I went up to the woman who walked the dog and asked her what in the world he ate that made him so pretty. The woman was flattered and said he liked chops best. So I bought a schnitzel, that was even better, I thought. But do you know, that damn dog didn't even give it a second look because it was veal. He was used to pork. So I had to buy a pork chop. I let the dog sniff at it, then I ran, and the dog ran after me. And the woman shouted, "Puntik! Puntik!" But hell, her dear Puntik ran around the corner after the chop, I snapped a chain around his neck, and the next day he was in the Klamovka kennel. —But suppose people start asking you where you got your dog when they see the spot on his ear?

BULLINGER   I don't believe anybody will ask me where I got my dog. (*He rings the bell*)

SCHWEYK   Maybe not. It wouldn't get them very far.

BULLINGER   In my opinion you were spoofing when you claimed to be a certified idiot; but I'll give you a break, in the first place because Brettschneider is a shitass, and in the second place if you'll get me the dog for my wife, you criminal.

SCHWEYK   Herr Platoon Leader, if you'll allow me, it's true about my certificate, but I was spoofing a little too. As the innkeeper said in Budweis, "I'm an epileptic but I've also got cancer," which was only his way of not letting on that he was bankrupt. Or, as the saying goes, "An athlete's foot seldom comes singly."

TELEPHONE VOICE   Motorized squad 4. Mrs. Moudra, the grocer, denies overstepping the ordinance that shops must not be opened before nine A.M. She claims she opened at ten.

BULLINGER   Lock her up for a couple of months, the lazy

bitch, for *under*-stepping the ordinance. (*To the SS man who has entered, pointing at Schweyk*) Released until further notice!

SCHWEYK   Before I leave for good, I'd like to put in a word for a gentleman who is waiting outside. He was brought in with the rest of us, but he'd rather not sit on the same bench because he's afraid of being mistaken for a political offender. He's only here for attempting to rob and murder a peasant in Holitz.

BULLINGER (*shouting*)   Get out!

SCHWEYK (*at attention*)   Yes, sir. I'll bring the spitz as soon as I get him. Good morning, everybody.

(*Leaves with the SS man*)

Interlude in the Nether Regions

Schweyk and SS man Müller 2 talking on their way from the Petschek Bank to the "Flagon."

SCHWEYK   If I ask Mrs. Kopecka, she'll do it for you. I'm glad to hear you say the Führer doesn't chase skirts but saves his strength for important matters of state, and never touches liquor. What he's done, he's done with a cool head, which is more than a lot of people I know could say. And not eating anything but a little vegetables and cake is a good idea too, there isn't too much to go around what with the war and all, that makes one less mouth to feed. I knew a peasant in Moravia, he had a kink in the gut which spoiled his appetite, his hired hands were all as thin as a rail. The people in the village started gossiping, but the peasant went around saying, "At my place the hired hands eat the same as I do." Drinking is a vice, I'll admit that, Budova the leather dealer wanted to cheat his brother, and then when he was full of booze he signed over the inheritance to him, instead of the other way round. There are two sides to everything, and as far as I'm concerned, Hitler doesn't have to go without women. I wouldn't ask that of anybody.

3

At the "Flagon" Baloun is waiting for his meal. Two other guests are playing checkers, a fat lady shopkeeper is drinking a small slivovitz, and Mrs. Kopecka is embroidering.

BALOUN It's ten after twelve, and no Prochazka. I knew it.

MRS. KOPECKA Give him time. Haste makes waste, you've got to have the right mixture of hurrying and taking it easy. You know "The Song of the Gentle Breeze"?
(*She sings*)

Haste to me, love, my dearest guest
No one dearer do I know.
But when within your arms I rest
Then rather take it slow.
   Learn from the plums in autumn
   Ripe to be plucked with ease.
   They fear the mighty tempest
   They love the gentle breeze.
   Ah, you hardly feel the little breeze
   It gently rocks you round.
   The plums want anyway to fall
   And lie upon the ground.

O reaper stop, you've done enough.
Let one stalk stand, just one!
Don't drink your wine in one swift draft
Don't kiss me on the run.
   Learn from the plums in autumn
   Ripe to be plucked with ease.
   They fear the mighty tempest
   They love the gentle breeze.
   Ah, you hardly feel the breeze
   It gently rocks you round.

The plums want anyway to fall
And lie upon the ground.

BALOUN (*walks nervously over to the checker players*) You're
doing fine. Would you gentlemen be interested in postcards? I work for a photographer. We've got a hot series.
"German cities," we call it.

FIRST CUSTOMER I'm not interested in German cities.

BALOUN Then you'll like this series. (*He shows the postcards
furtively as if they were pornographic*) This is Cologne.

FIRST CUSTOMER It looks terrible. I'll take them. Nothing but
bomb craters.

BALOUN Fifty hellers. But be careful about showing them
around. People have been stopped by the police patrol for
showing them to each other, they think they're dirty pictures, the kind they like to confiscate.

FIRST CUSTOMER Here's a funny caption. "Hitler is one of the
greatest architects of all time." And it shows a heap of
wreckage that used to be Bremen.

BALOUN I sold two dozen to a German sergeant. He smiled
when he looked at them; I liked that. I told him to meet me
in the park in front of Havliček. I kept my knife open in
my pocket, in case he was a stool pigeon. But he was on the
level.

THE FAT WOMAN Them that live by the sword, die by the
sword.

MRS. KOPECKA Careful!

(*Schweyk enters with the huge SS man Müller 2 who has
escorted him from Bullinger's office*)

SCHWEYK Hello, everybody. This gentleman is off duty. Give
us a glass of beer.

BALOUN I didn't expect you back for a couple of years, but
a man can make mistakes. Herr Brettschneider is usually so
efficient. Last week when you weren't here, he left with the
upholsterer from around the corner, and *he* never came
back.

SCHWEYK Probably a sap that didn't knuckle under. Herr
Brettschneider will think twice before he misunderstands
me again. I've got influence.

THE FAT WOMAN Are you the man they took away yesterday?

SCHWEYK (*proudly*) The same. In times like these you have
to knuckle under. It's a matter of practice. I licked his hand.
In the old days, they sprinkled salt on the prisoners' faces.
They were tied, and then big German shepherds were sicked
on them, and the dogs licked their whole faces off. Nowadays people aren't so cruel any more except when they get
mad. But I forgot: this gentleman (*referring to the SS man*)
would like to know what joys the future holds in store for
him, Mrs. Kopecka. And two beers. I told him you were a
fortune-teller and it gave me the creeps. I advised him
against it.

MRS. KOPECKA You know I don't like to do it, Mr. Schweyk.

SS MAN Why don't you like to do it, young woman?

MRS. KOPECKA A gift like that is a responsibility. How do I
know how a customer is going to take it, and will he always
have the strength to bear it? Because sometimes a look at
the future gives people the holy horrors, and they blame me.
Like Czaka the brewer when I had to tell him his wife was
going to be unfaithful, and right away he smashes my valuable wall mirror.

SCHWEYK She made a fool of him all right. We predicted the
same thing to Blaukopf the schoolteacher, and it happened
again. When she predicts things like that they always happen. It's uncanny if you ask me. The time you told Council-
man Czerlek that his wife . . . remember, Mrs. Kopecka?
It came true.

SS MAN Then you have a rare gift, it shouldn't go to waste.

SCHWEYK I told her to tell the whole city council the same
thing. I wouldn't be surprised if it came true.

MRS. KOPECKA Mr. Schweyk, don't joke about things we
know nothing about except that they happen. They're
supernatural.

SCHWEYK The time you told engineer Bulova right to his
face that he'd be torn to pieces in a train wreck? His wife
is already remarried. Women stand up better to predictions.
They have more strength of character, I'm told. Mrs. Las-
laczek on Hus Street had so much strength of character

that her husband declared right out in public, "Anything is better than living with her," and went to work in Germany. But the SS can also stand a good deal, I'm told, they have to, what with concentration camps and interrogations where they need nerves of steel. Am I right? (*The SS man nods*) That's why you needn't have any qualms about foretelling this gentleman's future, Mrs. Kopecka.

MRS. KOPECKA   If he promises to take it as a harmless bit of fun, and not to worry about it, I might take a look at his palm.

SS MAN (*suddenly hesitating*)   I don't want to force you. You say you don't like to.

MRS. KOPECKA (*brings him his beer*)   That's a fact. Forget it and drink your beer.

THE FAT WOMAN (*in a low voice to the checker players*)   If you suffer from cold feet, try cotton.

SCHWEYK (*sitting down with Baloun*)   I've got a little ness to discuss with you. I'm doing some work wit Germans in connection with a dog, and I need you.

BALOUN   I'm not in the mood for anything.

SCHWEYK   There'll be something in it for you. Wh get the dough, you can take your appetite to th market and get something in no time.

BALOUN   Young Prochazka isn't coming. Nothing but soggy potatoes again. Another disappointment like this will be the end of me.

SCHWEYK   It seems to me we could set up a little club, six or eight men. All of them would agree to pool their eighth of a pound of meat, and you'd have a meal.

BALOUN   But how would we find them?

SCHWEYK   You're right, it won't work. They'll say, for a stinker like you, a Czech without any willpower, they wouldn't think of giving up a meal.

BALOUN   That's true, they wouldn't give a shit about me.

SCHWEYK   Can't you pull yourself together and think of the honor of your country when temptation raises its head and all you can see in the world is a leg of veal or a roasted tenderloin with a little red cabbage, or maybe a few pickles? (*Baloun groans*) Think what a disgrace it would be if you weakened!

BALOUN Can't help it. (*Silence*) Anyway I'd rather have cabbage than pickles.

(*Young Prochazka enters with a briefcase*)

SCHWEYK Here he is. You've been too pessimistic, Baloun. Good afternoon, Mr. Prochazka, how's business?

MRS. KOPECKA (*with a glance at the SS man*) Sit down with the gentlemen, I've got something to attend to. (*To the SS man*) You know, I think your palm might interest me, may I take a look? (*Takes his hand*) I thought so: your palm is very very interesting. I mean, it's the kind of palm that's almost irresistible for us astrologists and chiropracticians, really interesting. How many other men are there in your squad?

SS MAN (*painfully, as if having a tooth pulled*) In the storm squad? Twenty. Why?

MRS. KOPECKA I thought so. It's written in your palm. You're tied up for life and death with twenty men.

SS MAN Can you really see that in my palm?

SCHWEYK (*has joined them, cheerfully*) You'll be surprised at all the things she can see. But she's cautious, she only says things that are absolutely sure.

MRS. KOPECKA There's something electrifying about your palm, you're lucky with women, the well-developed mount of Venus shows that. They throw themselves at you, kind of, but then they get a pleasant surprise and they wouldn't have missed it for the world. You're a serious man, you've got a way of talking that's almost severe. Your success line is tremendous.

SS MAN What does that mean?

MRS. KOPECKA Nothing to do with money, much more than that. You see this H, these three lines here? That's an act of heroism, something you're going to do very soon.

SS MAN Where? Can you see where?

MRS. KOPECKA Not around here. Or in your own country either. Far away. Here's a strange thing that I don't quite understand. There's something mysterious about this act of heroism, as if only you and the men with you would know about it. Nobody else, not even afterwards, never.

SS MAN How can that be?

MRS. KOPECKA (*sighs*) I don't know, maybe it'll be on the

battlefield, in an advanced position or something. (*As if in confusion*) But that's enough now, isn't it? I've got to get back to my work, it's only in fun anyway, you promised not to take it seriously.

SS MAN But you can't stop now. I want to know more about the secret, Mrs. Kopecka.

SCHWEYK He's right, Mrs. Kopecka. You oughtn't to leave him up in the air like that. (*Mrs. Kopecka winks at him in such a way that the SS man can see it*) But, then, maybe you've told him enough at that. It's better not to know about some things. Varczek the schoolteacher once looked in the dictionary to find out what schizziphonia was, and after a while they had to put him in the insane asylum in Ilmenau.

SS MAN You saw more in my palm.

MRS. KOPECKA No, no, that's all. Leave me be.

SS MAN You won't tell me what you saw. And you winked at this gentleman here, I saw you, to make him stop pushing you, because you didn't want to say any more. But you won't get away with it.

SCHWEYK That's a fact, Mrs. Kopecka, the SS won't let you get away with it. When I was at the Gestapo, I had to speak up, like it or not. Right away I confessed that I wished the Führer a long life.

MRS. KOPECKA Nobody can force me to tell a customer disagreeable things, so he'll never come back.

SS MAN You see, you know something and won't tell me, you've given yourself away.

MRS. KOPECKA But the second H is very faint, ninety-nine people out of a hundred wouldn't even have noticed it.

SS MAN What's this about a second H?

SCHWEYK Another beer, Mrs. Kopecka. This is so exciting, it makes me thirsty.

MRS. KOPECKA It's always the same, it only gets you in trouble to give in and examine a palm to the best of your knowledge and ability. (*Brings Schweyk a beer*) I didn't expect the second H, but if it's there what can I do? If I tell you, it'll make you miserable, you can't do anything about it anyway.

SS MAN About what?

SCHWEYK (*amiably*) It must be something terrible. As long as I've known Mrs. Kopecka, I've never seen her like this— and she's read a lot of things in palms. Are you sure you can take it, do you feel strong?

SS MAN (*hoarsely*) What is it?

MRS. KOPECKA Suppose I have to tell you that the second H means a hero's death, that's what it usually means, and suppose it upsets you? You see, now you feel miserable. I knew it. Three beers—that will be two crowns.

SS MAN (*pays, crushed*) Palm reading is all a lot of nonsense. There's nothing in it.

SCHWEYK You're perfectly right. Don't give it a second thought.

SS MAN (*leaving*) Heil Hitler!

MRS. KOPECKA (*calling after him*) Promise me at least that you won't tell the other gentlemen.

SS MAN (*stops*) What other gentlemen?

SCHWEYK The ones on your squad! You know, the twenty.

SS MAN What business is it of theirs?

MRS. KOPECKA Oh, only because they're tied up with you for life and death. No use getting them all worried over nothing!

(*SS man leaves, cursing*)

MRS. KOPECKA Come again!

THE FAT WOMAN (*laughing*) You're all right, Mrs. Kopecka. Keep it up.

SCHWEYK We knocked out the whole platoon. Open your briefcase, Mr. Prochazka, Baloun can't stand it another minute.

MRS. KOPECKA Yes, Rudolf, hand it over, nice of you to bring it.

YOUNG PROCHAZKA (*weakly*) I haven't got it. When I saw them taking Schweyk away, it shook me up. I saw the scene all night. Good afternoon, Mr. Schweyk, I see you're back. I didn't have the nerve, I admit it. I feel terrible on account of you, Mrs. Kopecka, giving you a black eye in front of all these people, but I couldn't help it. (*Desperate*) Please, say something, anything is better than saying nothing.

BALOUN   Nothing.

MRS. KOPECKA   Well, so you haven't got it. But when you came in and I motioned that I had to get rid of the SS man first, you nodded as if you had it.

YOUNG PROCHAZKA   I didn't have the nerve . . .

MRS. KOPECKA   That's enough. I know your kind. You flunked your test as a man and a Czech. Get out, you coward, and never set foot here again.

YOUNG PROCHAZKA   I don't deserve to be treated any better. (*Slinks away*)

SCHWEYK (*after a moment's silence*) Talking about palm reading: Krish, the barber from Mnishek—you know Mnishek?—did a little palm reading at the parish fair and got drunk on the money he made, and a young peasant took him home with him, so he could tell him his future when he came to. Before falling asleep, Krish asked the peasant: "What's your name? Take my notebook out of my pocket. So your name is Kunert. Come back in fifteen minutes and you'll find the name of your future wife on a slip of paper." Then he started snoring, but woke up again and scribbled something in his notebook. He tore out the page, threw it on the floor, and put his finger on his lips and said, "Not yet, in another fifteen minutes. It's best if you look for the slip of paper blindfolded!" And do you know what he'd written on the slip of paper? "Your future wife's name will be Mrs. Kunert."

BALOUN   That Prochazka is a criminal.

MRS. KOPECKA (*angrily*) Don't be a fool. The criminals are the Nazis who threaten and torture people until they go against their better nature. (*Looking out the window*) That fellow coming now is a criminal, Rudolf Prochazka is only a weakling.

THE FAT WOMAN   We're guilty too, I tell you. Seems to me we could do more than drink slivovitz and crack jokes.

SCHWEYK   Don't ask too much of yourself. It's quite a job just to be around nowadays. Keeps you so busy just staying alive, you haven't much time for anything else.

(*Brettschneider enters with yesterday's SS man*)

SCHWEYK (*cheerfully*) I wish you a good afternoon, Herr

Brettschneider. Will you have a beer? I'm working with the SS now, it can't hurt me.

BALOUN (*spitefully*)   Out!

BRETTSCHNEIDER   What do you mean by that?

SCHWEYK   We were talking about food, and Mr. Baloun thought of the chorus from a popular song we were trying to remember. They mostly sing this song at church fairs, it's about the way they fix radish around Mnishek. They grow those big black ones, you must have heard about them, they're famous. Why don't you sing the song for Herr Brettschneider, Baloun? It'll cheer you up. He's got a good voice, he even sings in the church choir.

BALOUN (*sullenly*)   I'll sing it. It's about radishes.

(*Baloun sings* "The Song of How to Fix a Black Radish." *During the entire song Brettschneider, at whom everyone is looking, is trying to make up his mind whether to take action. Several times he gets up and sits down again*)

BALOUN (*sings*)

You'd better take a black one, a big full one
And tell him gaily: "Brother, get on out!"
Don't leave your hands bare when you pull one
By the snout.
  Better put gloves on, this black radish lives in rot.
  Not a doubt! Must be got
  Out!

And you can also buy one (at low prices)
And don't forget, first wash his dirty skin.
When you have cut him up in little slices
Put salt in.
  And rub it in the wound, no matter how he frets.
  Salt him down till he sweats.
  Put salt in.

Interlude in the Higher Regions

Hitler and Reich Marshal Göring in front of a tank model. Both are larger than life-size. Martial music.

HITLER

My dearest Göring, we're now in the fourth year
And victory is ours, at least pretty near.
But my war keeps spreading to more and more vast new
    regions.
I therefore now need more tanks, bombers, and new legions.
Which means the people have just got to stop lying around
    and snoring
They've got to labor for my war until sweat and blood are
    pouring.
So tell me now if you can:
How do things stand in Europe with the Little Man?
Will he work hard and long when no one's paying?

GÖRING

My Führer, that in times like these goes without saying.
The Little Man in Europe will work for your great war as
    cheerfully
As the Little Man does in Germany.
Labor Service will see to that.

HITLER

Good. To such an organization I gladly take off my hat.

4

On a bench in a park along the Moldau. Evening. Two lovers enter, stop for a moment, stand closely embraced, gaze at the Moldau in the background, and go on. Schweyk and his friend Baloun come in. They look back.

SCHWEYK That Voyta is mean to his servants. This is his
third maid since Candlemas, and I hear she wants to quit,
the neighbors are mean to her because she works for a
quisling. It'll be all the same to her if she comes home without the dog as long as it's not her fault. You'd better sit

down before she gets here, she doesn't like to sit down on a bench with nobody on it.

BALOUN   Don't you want me to hold the sausage?

SCHWEYK   And have you gobble it up on me? Go on, sit down.

(*Baloun sits down on the bench. Two maidservants enter, Anna and Kati, the first with a spitz on the leash*)

SCHWEYK   Excuse me, miss, how do I get to Palacky Street from here?

KATI (*suspiciously*)   You cross Havliček Square. Come on, Anna.

SCHWEYK   Pardon me if I ask where the square is. I'm a stranger here.

ANNA   I'm a stranger here myself. Go on, Kati, tell him.

SCHWEYK   So you're a stranger, too, miss? That's a good one. I'd never have known you weren't from the city, and such a nice little dog. Where are you from?

ANNA   I'm from Protivin.

SCHWEYK   Then we're practically neighbors. I'm from Budweis.

KATI (*tries to pull her away*)   Come along, Anna.

ANNA   Just a second. Then you must know Pejchara the butcher, on the main street, in Budweis?

SCHWEYK   Of course I know him! He's my brother. Everybody likes him, he's honest and helpful, he has fresh meat, and he throws in an extra bone for soup.

ANNA   Yes.

(*Silence, Kati waits mockingly*)

SCHWEYK   What a coincidence running into each other like this, so far from home! Have you got a moment? We've got to talk about Budweis, here's a bench with a nice view. That's the Moldau.

KATI   Really? (*Ironically*) That's news to me.

ANNA   Somebody's sitting there.

SCHWEYK   A gentleman enjoying the view. You better keep a close watch on your dog.

ANNA   Why?

SCHWEYK   Don't quote me, but the Germans are crazy about dogs, it's amazing, especially the SS. A dog like that is gone

before you can look twice, they send them home. I was
talking to a platoon leader myself the other day, name of
Bullinger, he wanted a spitz for his missus in Cologne.

KATI So you run around with platoon leaders and people like
that? Come along, Anna, that's enough now.

SCHWEYK I talked to him when I was under arrest for remarks endangering the security of the Third Reich.

KATI Really? Then I take it back. We still have a little time,
Anna.

(*She walks ahead to the bench. All three sit down next to
Baloun*)

KATI What kind of remarks did you make?

SCHWEYK (*indicates that he cannot talk about it in the presence of the stranger, and speaks with pointed innocence*)
Do you like it in Prague?

ANNA Oh yes. But you can't trust the men around here.

SCHWEYK That's only too true. I'm glad you realize that.
People in the country are more honest, am I right? (*To
Baloun*) A fine view, isn't it, neighbor?

BALOUN Not bad.

SCHWEYK Something for a photographer.

BALOUN As a background.

SCHWEYK A photographer could do something with it.

BALOUN I am a photographer. In the studio where I work we
painted the Moldau on a screen, but a little more pictur-
esque. We use it for the Germans, mostly the SS men who
pose in front of it for a souvenir when they have to leave
and can't come here any more. Only it's not the Moldau,
it's just some lousy river.

(*The girls laugh approvingly*)

SCHWEYK That's very interesting. Couldn't you snap a picture of the ladies, in bust, excuse me, that's what they call it.

BALOUN I could.

ANNA That would be nice. But not in front of your Moldau,
eh?

(*They laugh abundantly at the joke, then silence*)

SCHWEYK You know this one? A Czech on the Charles Bridge
hears somebody shouting for help in German from the
Moldau. He leans over the rail and calls down: "Shut up,

you should have learned swimming instead of German!"
(*The girls laugh*)

SCHWEYK Yes, that's the Moldau. A lot of immorality goes
on along its banks in wartime.

KATI In peacetime too.

BALOUN And at spring fairs.

SCHWEYK Out in the open until after All Saints' Day.

KATI And I suppose nothing happens indoors?

BALOUN Oh yes, plenty.

ANNA And at the movies.

(*Again they all laugh*)

SCHWEYK Ah yes, the Moldau. Do you know the song,
"Henry Slept beside his Newly-wedded"? They sing it a lot
in Moravia.

ANNA You mean the one that goes on "Heiress to a castle on
the Rhine?"

SCHWEYK That's it. (*To Baloun*) Got something in your eye?
Don't rub. Could you take care of the gentleman, miss?
Use the corner of your handkerchief, that's the best way.

ANNA (*to Schweyk*) Would you mind holding the dog?
You've got to be careful in Prague. The air is full of soot.

SCHWEYK (*ties the dog loosely to the lamppost beside the
bench*) Excuse me, I've got to be going now, to Palacky
Street, on business. I'd like to hear you sing, but I can't.
Good afternoon. (*Leaves*)

KATI (*while Anna tries to fish something out of Baloun's eye
with a handkerchief*) He's really in a hurry.

ANNA I can't find anything.

BALOUN I feel better already. What's that song about?

ANNA Would you like us to sing it for you? Before we go?
Oh, keep quiet, Lux. I'll sure be glad to see the last of you
and your master. (*To Baloun*) He's too fond of the Germans. I'll start. (*The two girls sing the ballad "Henry Slept
beside his Newly-wedded"* with much feeling. Meanwhile
Schweyk, behind a bush, uses a tiny sausage to lure the dog
to him, and leaves with the animal*)

BALOUN (*after the song*) You sang that beautifully.

KATI We have to go now. Jesus, where's the dog?

---

* [The text of this ballad is given at the end of the play.]

ANNA Holy Virgin, he's gone. He never runs away. What will Mr. Voyta say?

BALOUN He'll call up his German friends, that's all. Don't worry, it's not your fault. I guess that gentleman didn't tie him very well, it seems to me I saw a shadow while you were singing.

KATI Quick, we'll go to the lost-and-found.

BALOUN Drop in some Saturday night at the "Flagon," 7 Hus Street. (*They nod to Baloun and leave quickly. Baloun looks at the view again. The lovers come back, but no longer holding each other tight. Then Schweyk enters with the spitz on the leash*)

SCHWEYK He's a typical quisling's dog—bites the second you look away. Been giving me a terrible time on the way. When I was crossing the railroad tracks, he lay down and wouldn't budge. Maybe he wanted to be run over, the scoundrel. Come along, now.

BALOUN Did he go for the horse sausage? I thought you only ate veal?

SCHWEYK War is no bed of roses. Not even for purebred dogs. I won't give him to Bullinger unless he puts the cash on the line, or he'll swindle me. They can't have collaboration for nothing.

(*A tall, sinister-looking man has appeared in the background and has been watching the two. Now he approaches them*)

THE INDIVIDUAL Taking a walk, gentlemen?

SCHWEYK That's right. What business is it of yours?

THE INDIVIDUAL Would you please identify yourselves? (*He shows them an official badge*)

SCHWEYK I've got nothing on me. Have you?

BALOUN (*shakes his head*) We haven't done anything.

THE INDIVIDUAL I haven't stopped you for doing anything but because it seems to me that you're not doing anything. I'm from the Voluntary Labor Service.

SCHWEYK Are you one of those gentlemen who stroll around in beer gardens and outside movie houses, picking up people to work in the factories?

THE INDIVIDUAL What is your occupation?

SCHWEYK I'm in the dog business.

THE INDIVIDUAL Have you a certificate that your enterprise is essential for the war effort?

SCHWEYK No, Your Excellency. But it is essential for the war effort. Same in war as in peace, a dog is a friend in need, what do you say, spitz? People are much calmer during an air raid if a dog looks at them as if to say, "Is this really necessary?" And this gentleman is a photographer, maybe that's even more essential for the war effort. He photographs soldiers, so the folks at home at least have pictures of their loved ones, which is better than nothing, you've got to admit.

THE INDIVIDUAL I think I'd better take you to headquarters. I wouldn't advise you to give them any of your applesauce.

BALOUN But we caught the dog on orders from higher up. Tell him.

SCHWEYK It's no use. The gentleman has orders from higher up too.

(*They go with him*)

SCHWEYK So your job is catching people?

5

Noon break at the freight station in Prague. On the rails sit Schweyk and Baloun, now railroad workers in Hitler's service, guarded by a German soldier armed to the teeth.

BALOUN I wonder where Mrs. Kopecka is with the grub. I hope nothing's happened to her.

A TRANSPORTATION CORPS LIEUTENANT (*passing by, to the soldier*) Guard! If anybody asks you which of these freight cars goes to Lower Bavaria, remember it's this one, number 4268.

SOLDIER (*at attention*) Yes, sir.

SCHWEYK With the Germans, organization is everything.

The world has never seen anything like the organization they have now. If Hitler pushes a button, it's the end of China, for instance. They've got the pope in Rome in their files, with everything he ever said about them, he's a dead duck. Even an underling, an SS leader for instance, has his buttons to push, and the next thing you know your ashes are delivered to your widow. It's lucky for us that we're here with a heavily armed guard watching us to keep us from committing sabotage and getting shot.

(*Mrs. Kopecka hurriedly enters with enamel dishes. The soldier absentmindedly studies her pass*)

BALOUN   What is it?

MRS. KOPECKA   Carrot cutlet and potato sausage. (*While the two men eat, dishes on knees, softly*) The dog has got to go. He's getting political. Don't stuff yourself like that, Mr. Baloun, you'll get ulcers.

BALOUN   Not from potatoes. Maybe from a capon.

MRS. KOPECKA   The morning paper had a story that the disappearance of Undersecretary Voyta's dog was an act of vengeance by the population against a civil servant friendly to the Germans. They're looking for him, they want to smoke out the nest of subversive elements. He can't stay at the "Flagon" another day.

SCHWEYK (*eating*)   It's a little inconvenient now. Yesterday I wrote a special-delivery letter to Platoon Leader Bullinger telling him that my price is two hundred crowns, and I won't deliver till I get them.

MRS. KOPECKA   Mr. Schweyk, you're taking your life in your hands writing a letter like that.

SCHWEYK   I don't think so, Mrs. Kopecka. Herr Bullinger is a fat pig but he'll say it's perfectly natural, business is business, or where would we be; the story is that he needs the spitz for his missus in Cologne. Collaborationists don't work for nothing. The fact is they're making more than ever, because their countrymen despise them. I've got to be paid for this thing or there's no point in it.

MRS. KOPECKA   But you can't do business while you're locked up.

SCHWEYK (*amiably*)   I won't grow moss around here. I've

already cost them a carload of soap. It's easy. One time in Austria, when they made a law against strikes, the railroad workers tied everything up for eight hours just by observing all the safety regulations.

MRS. KOPECKA (*firmly*) That dog can't stay at the "Flagon," Mr. Schweyk, and that's that. I can count on a certain amount of protection from Herr Brettschneider, he's still hoping to get somewhere with me, but it doesn't amount to much.

(*Schweyk listens to her only with half an ear because two German soldiers have passed by carrying a large, steaming cauldron and have ladled out some goulash soup into the soldier's mess tin. Baloun, who has finished his meal long since, stands up and takes a few steps as in trance, sniffing the soup*)

SCHWEYK I'll pick him up. Say, take a look at that!

GERMAN SOLDIER (*calling sharply after Baloun*) Halt!

MRS. KOPECKA (*to Baloun who returns disgruntled and agitated*) Pull yourself together, Mr. Baloun.

SCHWEYK There was a doctor in Budweis with such a bad case of diabetes that all they let him eat was a sip of rice soup—and he was built like an ox. He couldn't stand it, he kept sneaking into the pantry to stuff himself on leftovers, and he knew what he was doing. Then he got good and sick of it all and he told his housekeeper to bring him a seven-course meal, with pastry and all, she was blubbering so bad she could hardly serve him, and he made her play a funeral march on the gramophone, and it really did him in. It'll be the same with you, Baloun. You'll end up under a Russian tank.

BALOUN (*still trembling all over*) They're dishing out goulash.

MRS. KOPECKA I've got to go. (*She takes the dishes and leaves*)

BALOUN I just want to take a look. (*To the eating soldier*) Are the helpings always that big in the army, Herr Soldier? That's a pretty big one you've got. But maybe only for guards to keep you awake, or maybe we'd run away, wouldn't we? Couldn't I take just one sniff?

(*The soldier sits there eating, but moves his lips between bites*)

SCHWEYK   Don't ask him questions. Can't you see he's got to learn the number by heart, or the wrong freight car will go to Lower Bavaria on him, you dope. (*To the soldier*) You're right to keep thinking about it, all sorts of things can happen. They've stopped painting the destination on freight cars because the saboteurs wipe it off and put wrong addresses on instead. What number is it? 4268, isn't it? Well, you don't have to sit here for half an hour counting with your lips. I'll tell you how to do it, I got it from a clerk in the license bureau: this is the way he explained it to a peddler who couldn't keep his number in his head. I'll show you with your own number and you'll see how easy it is. 4268. The first number is a four, the second a two. So remember 42, that's two times 2, I mean from front to back 4, divided by 2, and that gives you 4 and 2 next to each other again. Don't panic! How much is two times 4? 8, isn't it? So keep well in mind that the 8 in number 4268 is the last in the row, all you've got to remember is that the first number is a 4, the second a 2, and the fourth an 8. Now you've only got to find a good way to remember the 6 that comes before the 8. It's easy. The first number is a 4, the second a 2, 4 plus 2 is 6. So now you're sure as shooting that the second from the end is a 6. As the gentleman from the license bureau would have said, the order of those numbers will never fade from your memory. There's an even simpler way of getting the same result. He explained that one to the peddler, too. I'll show you with your own number.

(*The soldier has listened with wide-open eyes. His lips have stopped moving*)

SCHWEYK   8 take away 2 is 6. That gives him the 6 already. Six take away 2 is 4, so he knows the 4 too. 8 and the 2 in between makes it 4-2-6-8. There's still another easy way, with multiplication and division. This is how it works: just remember, I'm quoting the clerk again, that two times 42 is 84. The year has 12 months. So you take away 12 from 84, and you get 72, and another 12 months, that's 60. That definitely gives us 6, we cross out the zero. So we know 42-6-84. When we cross out the zero, we also cross out the 4 in back. And again our number is complete. It works with division too, and I'll show you the way it goes. Now, what was our number?

VOICE (*from behind*) Guard, what's the number of that freight car that's supposed to go to Lower Bavaria?

SOLDIER What is it?

SCHWEYK Just a second, I'll try the method with the months. There are 12 of them, aren't there? We agree on that.

SOLDIER (*desperately*) Tell me the number.

VOICE Guard! Are you asleep?

SOLDIER (*calling*) Forgot. I for-got! (*To Schweyk*) Damn your hide!

VOICE (*gruffly*) That car's got to leave for Passau with the 12:50.

SECOND, MORE DISTANT VOICE Take this one. This is the one, I think.

BALOUN (*satisfied, referring to the soldier who looks back in a fright*) He wouldn't even let me sniff at his goulash.

SCHWEYK Maybe now they'll be sending a carload of machine guns to Bavaria. (*Philosophically*) But maybe by that time they'll need harvesting machines in Stalingrad and machine guns in Bavaria. Why not?

6

Saturday night at the "Flagon." Among the customers are Baloun, Anna, Kati, young Prochazka and off to one side, two SS men. Dancing to the music of the electric piano.

KATI (*to Baloun*) When Herr Brettschneider questioned me, I told him I'd heard the SS was after the spitz. I didn't mention you, only your friend, Mr. Schweyk. And I didn't say anything about Mr. Schweyk pretending not to know you so he could start up a conversation with us. Was that all right?

BALOUN   Anything is all right with me. You won't see me very long around here. Man, won't they be surprised to see me!

ANNA   You mustn't talk so glum, Mr. Baloun, it doesn't help. And that SS man over there will ask me to dance if I'm just sitting here. You'd better ask me.

(*Baloun is about to get up when Mrs. Kopecka steps forward and claps her hands*)

MRS. KOPECKA   Ladies and gentlemen, it's almost half past eight, which is time for the beseda (*half to the SS men*), the folk dance we dance among ourselves. Some people don't like it, but we do. The music is on the house.

(*Mrs. Kopecka puts a coin into the piano and those present dance the beseda, stamping very loudly. Baloun and Anna dance, too. The purpose of the dance is to drive the SS men away, bumping into their table, etc.*)

BALOUN (*sings*)
Strikes the midnight hour, smack
Jumps the barley from the sack.
Yuppidiyah, yuppidoh.
Every girl lets go.

THE OTHERS (*joining in*)
Lets the fellows tweak her cheeks,
Almost all have got four cheeks.
Yuppidiyah, yuppidoh.
Every girl lets go.

(*The SS men get up, cursing, and make their way to the door. After the dance Mrs. Kopecka comes back from the adjoining room and continues washing her glasses. Kati brings the First Customer from scene 3 with her to the table*)

THE FIRST CUSTOMER   Folk dancing is something new at the "Flagon" and very popular because the regular customers know that while it's going on Mrs. Kopecka tunes in on Radio Moscow.

BALOUN   There won't be any more dancing for me. Where I'm going they don't dance the beseda.

ANNA They tell me we should have thought twice before going to the park. It's dangerous on account of the German deserters that attack you.

THE FIRST CUSTOMER They only attack men. Deserters need civilian clothes. Every morning these days you can find German uniforms in Stromovka Park.

KATI If you lose a suit it's not easy to get another. They say the clothing control office made a rule against paper suits and hats. On account of the paper shortage.

THE FIRST CUSTOMER The Germans are crazy about those kind of offices. They pop up like mushrooms. They make jobs for themselves to keep them out of the war. They'd rather pester the Czechs with milk control, food control, paper control, and so on. Keeps them out of the draft.

BALOUN They'll be too much for me. I can see my future. It's inevitable.

ANNA I don't know what you're talking about.

BALOUN You'll know soon enough, Miss Anna. I'm sure you know the song, "Countless Gates and Hallways," about the painter who died young. Sing it for me, will you. I'm just in the mood for it.

ANNA (*sings*)

Countless gates and hallways he was painting always
Meanwhile giving kisses to the little misses.
Now his painting's over, he is pushing clover.

Is that it?

BALOUN That's it.

ANNA Goodness, you're not going to do something to yourself?

BALOUN What I'm going to do to myself will give you the cold shivers, miss. I won't lay a hand on myself, I'm going to do something worse.

(*Schweyk enters with a package under his arm*)

SCHWEYK (*to Baloun*) Here I am with the goulash meat. Don't thank me, I'm swapping it for the cot you've put up in the kitchen.

BALOUN Let's see, is it beef?

SCHWEYK (*firmly*) Hands off. We're not going to unpack

it here. Good evening, ladies, you here too?

ANNA   Good evening, we know the whole story.

SCHWEYK (*draws Baloun into a corner*)   What did you blab to them this time?

BALOUN   Only that we knew each other and pretending not to was a trick. I didn't know what to tell them. My cot is yours. You're saving a friend from the abyss, just let me sniff at it, through the paper. Mrs. Mahler across the street offered me twenty crowns for it, I wouldn't even consider it. How did you get it?

SCHWEYK   It's from the black-market, from a midwife that got it from the country. Around 1930 she delivered a baby at a peasant's house. The baby had a little bone in his mouth, she started crying and said, "It means we'll all be starving." She said that before the Germans came; and every year the peasant woman has been sending her a little package to keep her from starving, but this year the midwife needed the money for taxes.

BALOUN   If only Mrs. Kopecka has some real paprika!

MRS. KOPECKA (*joining them*)   Go back to your table, in half an hour I'll call you into the kitchen. Meanwhile act as if nothing had happened. (*To Schweyk, after Baloun has returned to his table*) What kind of meat is it?

SCHWEYK (*reproachfully*)   Mrs. Kopecka, I'm surprised at you.

(*Mrs. Kopecka takes the package from him and cautiously peeks in*)

SCHWEYK (*seeing that Baloun is talking to the girls with big, excited gestures*)   Baloun is getting too excited to suit me. Put in a lot of paprika to make it taste like beef. It's horsemeat. (*She looks at him sharply*) All right, it's Mr. Voyta's spitz. I had to do it, because the "Flagon" would be disgraced if starvation made one of your steady customers join the Germans.

A CUSTOMER AT THE BAR   Service!

(*Mrs. Kopecka hands Schweyk the package to hold so that she can quickly serve her customer. At that moment the sound of a large car is heard. SS men enter, led by Platoon Leader Bullinger*)

BULLINGER (*to Schweyk*) Your housekeeper was right that you'd be at the tavern. (*To the SS men*) Clear the floor! (*To Schweyk while the SS men push the other guests back*) What have you done with the dog, you stinker?

SCHWEYK Beg to report, Herr Platoon Leader, the papers said he was stolen. Haven't you read about it?

BULLINGER Is this more of your impudence?

SCHWEYK Beg to report, Herr Platoon Leader, I only wish to say that if you don't keep up with the daily papers, you might miss something and then you won't be able to take vigorous action.

BULLINGER I don't know why I bother with you, there must be something wrong with me. I probably want to see how far a character like you can go before he dies.

SCHWEYK Yes, sir, Herr Platoon Leader, and because you want the dog.

BULLINGER You admit you wrote me a letter asking me to pay two hundred crowns for that dog?

SCHWEYK Herr Platoon Leader, I admit that I wanted the two hundred crowns because I'd have had expenses if the dog hadn't been stolen.

BULLINGER We'll talk about that at the Petschek Bank. (*To the SS men*) Search tavern for spitz! (*One SS man leaves*) (*The sound of furniture being overturned, objects smashed, and so on, comes from the adjoining room. Schweyk waits in stoic calm, his package under his arm*)

SCHWEYK (*suddenly*) We've also got good slivovitz here.

(*An SS man jostles a little man in passing. While drawing back, the latter steps on a woman's foot and says, "Pardon me," whereupon the SS man turns, knocks him down with a club, and, at a nod from Bullinger, carries him out with the help of another SS man. An SS man comes in with Mrs. Kopecka*)

SS MAN Tavern searched, dog not present.

BULLINGER (*to Mrs. Kopecka*) This innocent tavern of yours is a hornet's nest of subversive activity. But I'll smoke you out.

SCHWEYK Yes, sir, Herr Platoon Leader, Heil Hitler. If you don't, we might get fresh and snap our fingers at the regulations. Mrs. Kopecka, you've got to run your tavern so everything's as clear as fresh spring water, like Chaplain Vyvoda said when he . . .

BULLINGER   Shut up, you bastard. I have a good mind to pull you in and shut your place down, Mrs. Kosheppa.

BRETTSCHNEIDER (*who has appeared at the door*)   Herr Platoon Leader Bullinger, may I have a word with you in private?

BULLINGER   I can't see anything to talk to you about. You know what I think of you.

BRETTSCHNEIDER   The Gestapo has received new information concerning the whereabouts of Voyta's missing dog. I thought it might be of interest to you, Herr Platoon Leader Bullinger.

(*The two men go to a corner and begin to gesticulate wildly. Brettschneider seems to be intimating that Bullinger has the dog, Bullinger seems to be saying "Me?" and to grow angry, etc.*)

(*Mrs. Kopecka has calmly resumed washing glasses. Schweyk stands there unconcerned and amiable. Unfortunately Baloun now embarks on a maneuver to get hold of his package and succeeds. At a sign from him a customer takes it from Schweyk and passes it on. It reaches Baloun and he fingers it, having lost all self-control.*)

(*An SS man has watched the wandering package with interest*)

SS MAN   Hey, what's going on here? (*With a few steps he is at Baloun's side, and takes away the package*)

SS MAN (*handing the package to Bullinger*)   Herr Platoon Leader, this package has been smuggled to one of the customers, that man over there.

BULLINGER (*opens the package*)   Meat! Owner, step forward!

SS MAN (*to Baloun*)   You there, you opened the package.

BALOUN (*bewildered*)   It was handed to me. It doesn't belong to me.

BULLINGER   Oh, it doesn't belong to you? Ownerless meat, huh? (*Suddenly shouting*) Why did you open it then?

SCHWEYK (*when Baloun doesn't know how to answer*)   Beg

to report, Herr Platoon Leader, this dumbbell must be innocent because he wouldn't have peeked if it was his; he'd have known what was in it.

BULLINGER (*to Baloun*)   Who did you get it from?

SS MAN (*when Baloun again fails to answer*)   The first thing I noticed was this man (*pointing at the customer who took the package from Schweyk*) passing the package.

BULLINGER   Where did you get it from?

THE CUSTOMER (*unhappily*)   It was handed to me, I don't know by whom.

BULLINGER   This tavern seems to be a branch of the black-market. (*To Brettschneider*) And if I'm not mistaken, Herr Brettschneider, you vouched just a minute ago for the woman who owns it?

MRS. KOPECKA (*stepping forward*)   Gentlemen, the "Flagon" is not a black-market.

BULLINGER   No? (*Slaps her face*) I'll show you, you Czech swine!

BRETTSCHNEIDER (*excitedly*)   Mrs. Kopecka is known to me as an unpolitical person. I'll have to ask you not to pass judgment on her without a hearing.

MRS. KOPECKA (*very pale*)   Don't you dare strike me!

BULLINGER   What's this? Backtalk? (*Slaps her again*) Take her away!

(*As Mrs. Kopecka prepares to haul off at Bullinger, the SS man hits her on the head. She falls*)

BRETTSCHNEIDER (*bending over her*)   You'll have to answer for this, Bullinger. You're only trying to distract attention from Voyta's dog, but you won't get away with it.

SCHWEYK (*steps forward*)   Beg to report, sir, I can explain everything. The package doesn't belong to anybody here. I know because I laid it down myself.

BULLINGER   So it's you.

SCHWEYK   A gentleman gave it to me to hold, then he said he was going to the toilet. Man of medium height with a blond beard.

BULLINGER (*amazed at the explanation*)   Say, are you feeble-minded?

SCHWEYK (*looking him earnestly in the eye*)   Yes, sir, as I've already told you. I was officially certified an idiot by a commission. I was fired from the Voluntary Labor Service for the same reason.

BULLINGER But you're intelligent enough for the black-market, huh? Maybe when we get you to Gestapo headquarters you'll begin to realize that it won't do you a damn bit of good, even if you can show a hundred certificates.

SCHWEYK (*softly*) Beg to report, Herr Platoon Leader, I realize it won't do me a damn bit of good, because ever since I was a kid I've always gotten into a mess when I had the best of intentions and only wanted to help people. Like in Lubova one time, when I tried to help this school caretaker's wife to hang out her washing. If you'll step out in the hall with me, I'll tell you what happened. I got into this black-market business same as Pontius Pilate got into the Creed.

BULLINGER (*staring at him*) I don't know why I listen to you, and this isn't the first time. You've probably got me hypnotized, because I never saw such a villain before.

SCHWEYK It must be like you suddenly saw a lion on Karlova Street where it's unusual, or like in Chotebor when a postman caught his wife with the janitor and stabbed her one two three. He went straight to the police station to give himself up, and when they asked him what he did after the crime, he said that the minute he stepped out of the house he'd seen a naked man turning the corner, so they decided he was mentally deranged and let him go. But two months later they found out that a lunatic really had escaped from the asylum stark naked. The postman had told the truth, but they hadn't believed him.

BULLINGER (*amazed*) I'm still listening. I can't tear myself away. I know what you're thinking. You think the Third Reich is good for a year, or maybe ten years, but I'm here to tell you that ten thousand years is probably more like it. Makes your eyes pop out, doesn't it?

SCHWEYK That's a long time, like the sexton said when the lady that runs the "Swan" married him and dropped her teeth into the water glass for the night.

BULLINGER Do you piss yellow or do you piss green?

SCHWEYK (*amiably*) Beg to report, Herr Platoon Leader, I piss yellowish-green.

BULLINGER But now you're coming with me even if certain people (*referring to Brettschneider*) vouch for you till they're blue in the face.

SCHWEYK Yes, sir, Herr Platoon Leader. There's got to be order. Black-marketing is an evil and it won't stop until there's nothing left. Then we'll have order right away, am I right?

BULLINGER And we'll find the dog too.

(*He leaves with the package under his arm. The SS men seize Schweyk and take him along*)

SCHWEYK (*while leaving, good-naturedly*) I only hope you won't be disappointed. Some customers are so keen on a dog they move heaven and earth to get him, and once they have him, they don't like him any more.

BRETTSCHNEIDER (*to Mrs. Kopecka who has recovered consciousness*) Mrs. Kopecka, you have been the victim of certain conflicts between certain sections of the Gestapo and the SS. I say no more. However, you are under my protection, I'll be back to talk this over with you in private. (*Leaves*)

MRS. KOPECKA (*staggering back to the bar where she ties a dish towel around her bleeding forehead*) Does anybody want some beer?

KATI (*looking at Schweyk's hat still hanging over the table*) They didn't even let him take his hat.

THE CUSTOMER He'll never come off alive.

(*Young Prochazka enters shyly. He is horrified at the sight of Mrs. Kopecka's blood-soaked bandage*)

YOUNG PROCHAZKA What's happened to you, Mrs. Kopecka? I saw the SS driving away—did the SS do it?

CUSTOMERS They clubbed her on the head because they said the "Flagon" was a black-market.—Even Herr Brettschneider of the Gestapo stood up for her, or they'd have pulled her in.—They took one man away.

MRS. KOPECKA Mr. Prochazka, you have no business here at the "Flagon." This is a place for real Czechs.

YOUNG PROCHAZKA Believe me, Mrs. Anna, I've been miser-

able and I've learned my lesson. Can't I hope to make it up
to you?

(*Mrs. Kopecka's icy look makes him shudder and he sneaks
guiltily away*)

KATI They're nervous at the SS, too, because yesterday they
fished another SS man out of the Moldau, with a hole in his
left side.

ANNA They throw in plenty of Czechs.

CUSTOMER That's only because things are going badly for
them in the East.

THE FIRST CUSTOMER (*to Baloun*) Wasn't it your friend they
took away?

BALOUN (*bursts into tears*) It's all my fault. That's what I
get for my gluttony. I've prayed and prayed to the Virgin
Mary to give me strength and somehow shrink my stomach,
but it's no use. I dragged my best friend into this and maybe
they'll shoot him tonight, or if he's lucky tomorrow morning.

MRS. KOPECKA (*puts down a slivovitz in front of him*) Drink
that. Bawling won't help.

BALOUN God bless you. You broke with your admirer on account of me, you won't find a better one, he's only weak,
same as me. If I'd taken that oath you asked me to, things
wouldn't look so desperate. If I could take it now—but can
I? On an empty stomach? Good God, what's going to happen now?

MRS. KOPECKA (*goes back to the bar and starts washing
glasses*) Somebody put a nickel into the piano. I'll tell you
what's going to happen.

(*A customer puts a coin into the electric piano. A light
goes on inside, a transparency shows the moon over the
majestically flowing Moldau. Washing her glasses, Mrs.
Kopecka sings "The Song of the Moldau"*)

The stones on the Moldau's bottom go shifting
In Prague three emperors molder away.
The top won't stay top, for the bottom is lifting
The night has twelve hours and is followed by day.

The times will be changing. The intricate plotting
Of people in power must finally fail.
Like bloodthirsty cocks though today they are strutting
The times will be changing, force cannot prevail.

The stones on the Moldau's bottom go shifting
In Prague three emperors molder away.
The top won't stay top, for the bottom is lifting
The night has twelve hours and is followed by day.

Interlude in the Higher Regions

*Hitler and General von Bock, known as "The Killer," facing
a map of the Soviet Union. Both men are larger than life-size.
Military music.*

VON BOCK
Respected Herr Hitler, your expedition
In Russia's costing a lot of bombers, guns, tanks, and ammunition
To say nothing of men. "The Killer" is what they now call me.
To be thought a spoil-sport would appall me
But if you think you will get to Stalingrad, you're very much mistaken.

HITLER
Herr General von Bock, Stalingrad will be taken
I've given the German people my promise.

VON BOCK
Herr Hitler, the winter is nearly on us
And when it starts to snow out here in the east you know it's snowing.
If we're stuck when the north winds start blowing . . .

HITLER
Herr von Bock, I will throw the peoples of Europe into the disaster
And the Little Man will extricate his master.
Herr von Bock, don't let me down, you would not dare.

VON BOCK
As for replacements . . .

HITLER
That's my care.

7

Cell in a military prison with Czech prisoners waiting to be drafted into military service, among them Schweyk. They are waiting, stripped to the waist, and are simulating the most pitiful ailments. One of them, for instance, is lying on the floor as if he were dying.

A STOOPED MAN   I talked to my lawyer, he was very encouraging. They can't put us in the army if we're not willing. It's illegal.

A MAN WITH CRUTCHES   Then why do you double up like that, if you don't expect to be taken?

THE STOOPED MAN   Just in case.

(*The man with crutches laughs scornfully*)

THE DYING MAN (*on the floor*)   They wouldn't dare, we're all invalids. They're unpopular enough already.

A NEARSIGHTED MAN (*triumphantly*)   One night in Amsterdam a German officer was crossing what they call the Gracht, it was almost eleven and he was beginning to feel nervous. He asked a Dutchman for the time. The Dutchman gives him a solemn look and all he says is: "My watch has stopped." The officer walks on, feeling pretty glum, and stops a second man. Before he can even ask the question, the man says he left his watch home. They say the officer shot himself.

THE DYING MAN   He couldn't take it. All that contempt.

SCHWEYK   They're more likely to shoot other people than themselves. In Vralava a tavern keeper's wife was carrying on with his brother. He punished them with contempt. He found a pair of her panties in his brother's wagon and put them on the bedside table, he thought that would make her feel ashamed. They went to the district court and had him declared legally incompetent, then they sold the tavern out from under him and went away together. But in a way he was right, because his wife admitted to her girl friend that she was almost ashamed to take his lined winter coat.

THE STOOPED MAN   What are you here for?

SCHWEYK   Black-marketing. They could have shot me but the Gestapo needed me as a witness against the SS. The big shots are at loggerheads and I benefited. They told me I was lucky about my name, because it's Schweyk with a "y". If I wrote it with a plain "i", I'd be of German descent and then I could be drafted.

THE MAN WITH CRUTCHES   They're even drafting them out of jail these days.

THE STOOPED MAN   Only if they're of German descent.

THE MAN WITH CRUTCHES   Or if they volunteer to be of German descent like him over there.

THE STOOPED MAN   The only hope is to be a cripple.

THE NEARSIGHTED MAN   I'm nearsighted, I could never recognize an officer and salute.

SCHWEYK   They can put you at a listening post reporting enemy planes. In that line of work blindness is an advantage, the blind develop extra-special hearing. A peasant in Socz, for instance, cut out his dog's eyes to improve his hearing. In other words you're fit for service.

THE NEARSIGHTED MAN (*in despair*)   I know a chimney sweep in Brevnov who can give you such a fever for ten crowns that you'll jump out of the window.

THE STOOPED MAN   That's nothing. There's a midwife in Vrshovitz who can dislocate your leg so good for twenty crowns that you'll be a cripple the rest of your life.

THE MAN WITH CRUTCHES   I got my leg dislocated for five crowns.

THE DYING MAN   I didn't have to pay anything. I've got a genuine strangulated hernia.

THE MAN WITH CRUTCHES   Then they'll operate on you in Pankratz hospital, and then what will you do?

SCHWEYK (*cheerfully*) Listening to you people, somebody
could get the idea that you're trying to keep out of this war
that's got to be fought to defend civilization against Bolshevism.

(*A soldier enters and busies himself with the pail*)

SOLDIER You got crap all over the bucket again, you pigs.
You haven't even learned how to shit.

SCHWEYK We're discussing Bolshevism. Do you fellows know
what Bolshevism is? It's the sworn ally of Wall Street which
has planned our destruction under the leadership of the Jew
Rosenfeld in the White House. (*The soldier keeps busy
with the pail in order to listen, and Schweyk continues pa-
tiently*) But they don't know us. Do you know the song
about the cannoneer from Przemysl in the First World War,
which was fought against the tsar? (*He sings*)

Standing behind the gun
He loads from sun to sun.
Standing behind the gun
He loads from sun to sun.
Then a bullet comes on swiftly
Carries both his hands off deftly.
But he stands by his gun
Loading from sun to sun.
Stands steady at his gun
Loading from sun to sun.

The Russians fight because they have to. They got no
agriculture, because they wiped out the big land-owners,
and their industry is ruined because they want everybody to
be equal and that's depressing and because the thoughtful
workers are bitter about the big salaries of the bureaucrats.
You see, there's nothing there, and once we get there, the
Americans will be too late. Am I right?

SOLDIER Shut up. Conversation is prohibited.

(*He leaves angrily with the pail*)

THE DYING MAN Seems to me you're a stoolpigeon.

SCHWEYK (*cheerfully*) I'm not a stoolpigeon. I only listen
regularly to the German radio. You ought to listen, once in
a while. It's a scream.

THE DYING MAN   It is not. It's a disgrace.

SCHWEYK (*firmly*)   It's a scream.

THE NEARSIGHTED MAN   There's no reason to crawl up their asses.

SCHWEYK (*lecturing*)   Don't say that. It's an art. A lot of small animals would be glad if they could squeeze into a tiger. That way he couldn't get at them and they'd feel relatively safe; only it's hard to get in.

THE STOOPED MAN   Don't be vulgar. It's not pretty to see the Czechs putting up with everything.

SCHWEYK   Like this Jaroslav Vaniek said to the consumptive peddler. The owner of the "Swan" in Budweis, a big tall fellow, filled the peddler's glass only half full, and when the little runt didn't say anything, Vaniek gave him hell: "How can you take it lying down?—that makes you a partner in the offense." The peddler socked Vaniek, and that was the end of it. And now I'm going to ring the bell and make them hurry up with their war, I've got no time to waste. (*He stands up*)

A SHORT, FAT MAN (*who has been sitting apart from the others*) You will not ring the bell.

SCHWEYK   Why not?

THE FAT MAN (*with authority*)   Because things are going fast enough to suit us.

THE DYING MAN   That's right. What did they pick you up for?

THE FAT MAN   Because somebody stole my dog.

SCHWEYK (*interested*)   Was it a spitz?

THE FAT MAN   What do you know about it?

SCHWEYK   I bet your name is Voyta. I'm glad to meet you. (*He proffers his hand which the fat man overlooks*) My name is Schweyk. Maybe that doesn't mean anything to you, but you can shake hands with me. I bet you're not a German-lover any more since they brought you here.

THE FAT MAN   On the strength of what my maid told me, I accused the SS of kidnaping my dog. Is that enough for you?

SCHWEYK   Plenty. At home in Budweis we had this teacher who was accused by a student he'd been picking on of having the newspaper on his music rack while he was playing the organ in church. The teacher was a religious man, and he made his wife miserable by not letting her wear short skirts. But by the time they were through pestering him with questions, he said he didn't even believe in the Marriage at Cannae anymore. So you'll march to the Caucasus and shit on Hitler—only, like the owner of the "Swan" said, it all depends where you shit on what.

THE FAT MAN If your name is Schweyk, when they were leading me through the gate, a young fellow sidled up to me. He only had a chance to whisper, "Ask for Mr. Schweyk," then they opened the gate. He must still be down there.

SCHWEYK I'll have a look right away. I always thought there'd be a crowd down there in the morning, the owner of the "Flagon," who wouldn't want to miss the chance, and maybe a big fat fellow, waiting for Schweyk, but in vain. Give me a hand, one of you gentlemen!

(*He goes to the little cell window and climbs onto the back of the man with the crutches, to look out*)

SCHWEYK It's young Prochazka. I doubt if he can see me. Give me your crutches.

(*He gets them and waves them. Young Prochazka seems to have noticed him, and Schweyk communicates with him with sweeping gestures. He indicates a tall man with a beard—Baloun—and makes the gestures of stuffing food into his mouth and of carrying something under his arm. Then he climbs down off the back of the man with crutches*)

SCHWEYK You're probably wondering what I was doing up there. We made a gentleman's agreement, that's why he came here. I always knew he was a decent sort. I was only repeating his gestures, so he'd know I caught on. He probably didn't want me marching off to Russia with a weight on my mind.

(*Orders are heard from outside, and marching steps; a band begins to play the* "Horst Wessel" *march*)

THE DYING MAN What's going on? Did you see anything?

SCHWEYK A lot of people at the gate. Probably a battalion, marching off.

THE STOOPED MAN That music is terrible.

SCHWEYK   I think it's pretty because it's sad and rousing.

THE MAN WITH CRUTCHES   We'll soon be hearing it more often. They play the "Horst Wessel" march every time they get a chance. It was written by a pimp. I wish I knew what the words mean.

THE FAT MAN   I can oblige you with a translation. The flag raised high/ and tightly closed the columns/ Storm troops march on with firm and steady tread./ The comrades who have shed their heroes' blood before us/ March on with us in spirit straight ahead.

SCHWEYK   I know another version we used to sing at the "Flagon."

(*He sings accompanied by the military band. He sings the chorus to the tune, the preceding stanzas to the drums*)

After the drummer come
Sheep in great masses.
The skin for the drumhead
Comes from their asses.
 The butcher calls. With eyelids tightly shuttered
 The sheep march on with firm and steady tread.
 And those who at the yard have shed their blood before
  them
 March on with them in spirit straight ahead.

They lift up their hands to show
What rough work they do
Already stained with blood
And empty too.
 The butcher calls. With eyelids tightly shuttered
 The sheep march on with firm and steady tread.
 And those who at the yard have shed their blood before
  them
 March on with them in spirit straight ahead.

They carry a blood-red flag
Which has a cross on it.
A cross with a hook to hang
Poor people upon it.
 The butcher calls. With eyelids tightly shuttered

The sheep march on with firm and steady tread.
And those who at the yard have shed their blood before
them
March on with them in spirit straight ahead.

(*The other prisoners have joined in the chorus from the
second stanza on. At the end the door opens and a German
army doctor appears*)

THE ARMY DOCTOR It's nice to hear you all singing so happily.
You'll be glad to know that I consider you well enough
to join the army. You're accepted. Everybody up. Put your
shirts on. Be ready to march in ten minutes. (*He leaves*)
(*The prisoners, crushed, put on their shirts*)

THE STOOPED MAN Without a medical examination, that's absolutely illegal.

THE DYING MAN I have a stomach ulcer, I can prove it.

SCHWEYK (*to the fat man*) I hear they'll put us in different
outfits to keep us from being together and making trouble.
Good-bye, Mr. Voyta, I was glad to meet you, I'll see you
at the "Flagon" at six o'clock, after the war.
(*Overcome with emotion, he shakes hands all around as the
cell door opens. Schweyk marches out first with military
bearing*)

SCHWEYK Heitler! On to Moscow!

8

*Weeks later. Deep inside the wintry steppes of Russia the good
Hitler soldier Schweyk is marching to join his company near
Stalingrad. Because of the cold he is wrapped in many layers
of miscellaneous garments.*

SCHWEYK (*sings*)
Onward to Jaromersh hoofing
Probably you think I'm spoofing

We arrived there just about
Almost dinner time.

(*A German patrol stops him*)

FIRST SOLDIER   Halt. Password!

SCHWEYK   Victory! Can you tell me the way to Stalingrad? Something went wrong, I got separated from my company, and I've been hiking all day.

(*The first soldier examines his papers*)

SECOND SOLDIER (*hands him his canteen*) Where are you from?

SCHWEYK   Budweis.

SECOND SOLDIER   Then you're a Czech.

SCHWEYK (*nods*) I hear things aren't going so well up front.

(*The two soldiers who have been exchanging looks give an ugly laugh*)

FIRST SOLDIER   What's a Czech like you looking for at the front?

SCHWEYK   I'm not looking for anything. I only want to help defend civilization against Bolshevism, same as you, if we don't, it's a bullet in the chest, am I right?

FIRST SOLDIER   You could be a deserter.

SCHWEYK   Oh no, you'd shoot me right away for breaking my soldier's oath and not dying for the Führer, Heil Hitler.

SECOND SOLDIER   What? You still believe that stuff? (*Takes back his canteen*)

SCHWEYK   I believe as much as Tonda Novotny in Vysočan who went to the parish house to apply for a job as a sexton. He didn't know if the church was Protestant or Catholic, but the minister was in suspenders and there was a woman in the room, so he said he was Protestant, and guess what: he was wrong.

FIRST SOLDIER   Why does it have to be Stalingrad, you fishy ally?

SCHWEYK   Because that's where my regimental headquarters is, comrades, and I need a stamp to show that I reported for duty, or my papers won't be any good and I won't be able to show my face in Prague. Heil Hitler!

FIRST SOLDIER   And suppose we said "Shit on Hitler," we're deserting to the Russians and want to take you with us because you understand Russian because it's supposed to be like Czech.

SCHWEYK   Czech is very similar. But I advise you against it. I don't know my way around here, gentlemen, I'd rather you told me how to get to Stalingrad.

FIRST SOLDIER   Maybe you don't trust us. Is that it?

SCHWEYK (*amiably*)   In my opinion you're good soldiers because, if you were deserters, you'd have something for the Russians, a machine gun or maybe a good field glass, something they could use, and you'd hold it up in the air so they wouldn't start shooting right away. That's the way it's done, I'm told.

FIRST SOLDIER (*laughs*)   You mean they'd catch on, even if it wasn't Russian? I see, you're the cautious kind. So you think it's better to ask the way to your grave in Stalingrad. Go in that direction. (*He shows him*)

SECOND SOLDIER   And if anybody asks you: we're an army patrol and we gave you a good grilling. Just in case.

FIRST SOLDIER (*leaving*)   And your advice isn't bad, brother.

SCHWEYK (*waves after them*)   Glad to help, and good-bye!

(*The soldiers leave quickly. Schweyk starts in the direction indicated but is seen to deviate from it. He disappears into the twilight. When he emerges on the other side, he stops for a moment in front of a signpost and reads, "Stalingrad —30 miles." He shakes his head and marches on. The drifting clouds in the sky are now reddish from a distant conflagration. He watches them with interest while marching*)

SCHWEYK (*sings*)

Thought that in the service
We would have a ball
Thought the war would last a week or two or three weeks
But that would be all.

(*Smoking his pipe, he keeps on marching. The clouds pale, and Schweyk's table at the "Flagon" emerges in a pink light.*

His friend Baloun is kneeling on the floor. Beside him stands Mrs. Kopecka with her embroidery. At a table, behind a glass of beer, sits Anna, the maidservant)

BALOUN *(in the tone of a litany)*   I swear without hesitation and on an empty stomach, because all efforts by various people to get me some meat have failed; without a square meal under my belt, I swear to the Virgin Mary and all the saints that I'll never volunteer for the Nazi army, so help me God Almighty. I swear in memory of my friend Schweyk who is now marching over the icy steppes of Russia in faithful fulfillment of his duty, because there's no help for it. He was a good man.

MRS. KOPECKA   All right, you can get up now.

ANNA *(takes a sip from the glass of beer, stands up, and hugs him)*   And the wedding can take place as soon as the papers from Protivin get here. *(After kissing him, to Mrs. Kopecka)* Too bad there's no happy ending for you.

(Young Prochazka stands in the door, a package under his arm)

MRS. KOPECKA   Mr. Prochazka, I forbade you ever to darken my door again. It's all over between us. Now that I know your grand passion isn't even good for two pounds of smoked butt.

YOUNG PROCHAZKA   But suppose I've brought it? *(Shows it)* Two pounds of smoked butt.

MRS. KOPECKA   What, you've got it? In spite of the heavy penalties?

ANNA   But we don't really need it any more. Mr. Baloun took the oath without.

MRS. KOPECKA   But you've to admit that it shows true love. Rudolf!

(She embraces him passionately)

ANNA   That would make Mr. Schweyk happy, if he only knew, the good soul! *(She looks tenderly at Schweyk's bowler hanging over his table)* Take good care of that hat, Mrs. Kopecka, I'm sure Mr. Schweyk will come and get it after the war.

BALOUN *(sniffing at the package)*   It would be good with lentils.

(The "Flagon" disappears. A drunken man, wearing two heavy sheepskins and a steel helmet, staggers from the background. Schweyk meets him)

THE DRUNK   Halt! Who are you? I see you're one of ours and not a gorilla, thank God. I'm Chaplain Ignaz Bullinger from Metz. Would you happen to have some kirsch?

SCHWEYK   Beg to report, sir, I haven't.

CHAPLAIN   That's hard to believe. I don't need it to drink, as you may have thought, you stinker. Admit it, that's what you think of your priest. I need it for my car back there, the portable altar's in it; I've run out of gas. In Rostov they're trying to save gas on God, that'll cost them plenty when they step up to God's throne and he asks them in a thundering voice: "You motorized my altar, but where was the gas?"

SCHWEYK   I don't know, Your Reverence. Can you tell me the way to Stalingrad?

CHAPLAIN   God only knows. Do you know the one about the bishop who asks the captain during a storm, "Will we get through?" And the captain answers, "We're in the hands of God, bishop." And the bishop only says, "Is it as bad as all that?" and bursts into tears! *(He sits down in the snow)*

SCHWEYK   Is Platoon Leader Bullinger your brother?

CHAPLAIN   Yes, God help us, then you know him? You haven't any kirsch or vodka?

SCHWEYK   No, and you'll catch cold if you sit in the snow.

CHAPLAIN   It doesn't matter what happens to me. They want to save on gas, do they, let them see how long they can fight a war without God and God's word. On land, in the air, and on the sea, etcetera. I joined their stupid Nazi League for German Christians, but with a very troubled conscience. To suit them, I stopped saying that our Lord Jesus was a Jew, in my sermons I make him a thumping one hundred percent Christian, with blue eyes. I throw in Wotan for good measure, and I tell them the world has got to be German, even if the price is an ocean of blood, because I'm a renegade swine who's betrayed his faith for wages, and they don't give me enough gas, and now see where it's got me.

SCHWEYK To the Russian steppes, Your Reverence. You'd better go back to Stalingrad with me and sleep it off. (*He pulls him up and drags him along a few feet*) But you'll have to use your own legs too, or I'll drop you right here. I've got to get back to my company. Hitler needs me.

CHAPLAIN I can't leave my altar here, it'll be captured by the Bolsheviks, and then what? They're heathen. I passed a hut back there, there was smoke coming out of the chimney, I wonder if they've got any vodka. Just hit them over the head with your rifle butt, that'll do it. Are you a German Christian?

SCHWEYK No, the plain kind. Don't puke all over yourself, it freezes on you.

CHAPLAIN Yes, I'm frozen stiff. I'll make it hot for them at Stalingrad.

SCHWEYK First you've got to get there.

CHAPLAIN I'm not very optimistic. (*Calmly, almost soberly*) Do you realize—what's your name anyway?—that they laugh in my face, me a priest of God, when I threaten them with hell? The only way I can explain it is that they think they're there already. Religion is going to the dogs, it's all Hitler's fault, don't tell anybody I said so.

SCHWEYK Hitler's a fart, I can tell you because you're drunk. And who's to blame for Hitler? The people who handed him Czechoslovakia in Munich, in the name of "peace in our lifetime," which turned out to be a blitz peace. But the war turned out to be a long one, and for quite a lot of people a lifetime. That's the kind of mistakes people make.

CHAPLAIN Then you're against this war that it's our duty to fight against the godless Bolsheviks, you stinker. Do you know that I'm going to have you shot when we get to Stalingrad?

SCHWEYK If you don't pull yourself together and walk like a human being, you'll never make it to Stalingrad. And I'm not against the war, I'm not marching to Stalingrad for the fun of it, but because, "Where the bullets fly, the grub stands by," as Naczek the cook said in the First World War.

CHAPLAIN Don't tell me fairy tales. Deep down, you say to yourself, "Fuck your war," I can tell from the look on your face. (*Grabs him*) How can you claim to be for the war, what's in it for you—admit it, you don't give a shit for this war.

SCHWEYK (*rudely*) I'm marching to Stalingrad, and so are you, because those are our orders, and because two lone stragglers would starve around here. I've said that before. (*They march on*)

CHAPLAIN On foot, war is depressing. (*Stops*) There, I see the hut, let's go in. Got your rifle off safety? (*A hut appears, they walk toward it*)

SCHWEYK But don't make a stink. They're people too, and you've had enough to drink.

CHAPLAIN Keep your rifle at the ready. They're heathen, and no backtalk! (*From the hut step an old peasant woman and a young woman with a small child*)

CHAPLAIN Look, they're going to run away. We've got to prevent them. Ask them where they've buried their vodka. And look at that shawl she's wearing, I'll take it, I'm frozen stiff.

SCHWEYK You're freezing because you're drunk, you've got two fur coats on already. (*To the young woman who stands motionless*) Good morning, which way to Stalingrad? (*The young woman points as in a trance*)

CHAPLAIN Does she admit they have vodka?

SCHWEYK You sit down, I'll do the talking, and then we'll move on, I don't want any trouble. (*To the woman, amiably*) Why are you standing here outside your house? Were you leaving? (*The woman nods*) Your shawl is so thin. Haven't you anything else to keep you warm? It's not really enough.

CHAPLAIN (*sitting on the ground*) Use your rifle butt. They're all gorillas, heathen.

SCHWEYK (*rudely*) You shut up. (*To the woman*) Vodka? The man is sick. (*Schweyk has accompanied all his questions with illustrative gestures. The woman shakes her head*)

CHAPLAIN (*viciously*) Shaking your head, huh? I'll show you. I'm freezing and you shake your head. (*He struggles to his feet and staggers toward the woman with raised fist. She withdraws into the hut, closing the door behind her. The chaplain kicks the door in and enters the hut)* I'll finish you off.

SCHWEYK *(trying in vain to hold him back)* You stay out here. It's not your house. *(He follows him in. The old woman also goes in. Then the woman's scream is heard, and sounds of struggle. Schweyk, from inside)* You better put your knife away, lady. Hold still, you bastard, or I'll break your arm. Get going, quick.

(From the hut steps the woman with the child. She is wearing one of the chaplain's coats. Behind her the old woman)

SCHWEYK *(coming out of the hut behind them)* He'll sleep it off. You'd better clear out.

THE OLD WOMAN *(bows low before Schweyk in the traditional manner)* God bless you, soldier, you're a good man. If we had some bread left, I'd give you a chunk. You could use it. Where are you going?

SCHWEYK To Stalingrad, babushka, to the battle. Can you tell me the way?

THE OLD WOMAN You're a Slav, you talk like us, you didn't come here to murder people, you're not with the Hitlers. God bless you. *(She blesses him with sweeping gestures)*

SCHWEYK *(without embarrassment)* No hard feelings, babushka. I'm a Slav all right, but don't waste your blessing on me, because I'm a satellite.

THE OLD WOMAN God protect you, son, your heart is pure, you've come to help us, you'll help us beat the Hitlers.

SCHWEYK *(firmly)* No offense but I've got to be moving on, it wasn't my idea. Say, babushka, I'm beginning to think you're deaf.

THE OLD WOMAN *(although her daughter keeps tugging at her sleeve)* You'll help us get rid of the robbers. Hurry, soldier, and God bless you.

(The young woman pulls the old woman away; they leave. Schweyk marches on, shaking his head. Night has come and the stars appear in the sky. Schweyk stops again at a road sign and shines his blacked-out flashlight on it. Surprised, he reads "Stalingrad—30 miles" and marches on.

Suddenly shots ring out. Schweyk immediately raises his rifle in surrender. But nobody appears and the shots stop. Schweyk keeps marching faster. When he appears again in his circular course, he is out of breath and sits down on a snowdrift

SCHWEYK (*sings*)

When we came marching to Kovno
It was pretty stinking.
For a slug of booze those dogs
Took our shoes and left us limping.

(*His pipe drops from his mouth, he falls asleep and dreams. Schweyk's table at the "Flagon" appears in a golden light. Around the table sit Mrs. Kopecka in her wedding dress, young Prochazka in his Sunday suit, Kati, Anna, and Baloun with a full plate in front of him*)

MRS. KOPECKA   And for the wedding banquet you're getting your smoked butt, Mr. Baloun. You took the oath without it, that does you honor, but to help you keep your oath, a little piece of meat once in a while can't do any harm.

BALOUN (*eating*)   I just love eating. God bless our food. God created everything, from the sun to caraway seeds. (*Pointing at the plate*) Can this be sin? The pigeons fly, the chickens pick seeds off the ground. The landlord of the "Hus" knew seventeen ways of cooking a chicken, five sweet, six sour, and four with stuffing. Wine grows from the earth for me, and so does bread, said the pastor in Budweis, that couldn't eat because of diabetes, and they're forbidden me. In Pilsen, in 1932, I ate a hare at the "Schlossbräu"—the cook has died in the meantime, so don't bother to go there any more—I tell you, I never tasted such a hare in all my life. It was served with gravy and dumplings. That's not unusual, but there was something in that gravy that made the dumplings go crazy like they didn't know themselves, like something got into those dumplings. It was really good, I've never seen the like of it since. The cook took the recipe with him to the grave. It's lost to mankind.

ANNA   Don't complain. What would dear Mr. Schweyk say—

he probably doesn't even know what fried potatoes look like any more.

BALOUN   That's true. There's always a way. In Pudonitz, when my sister was married, they did it with quantity: Thirty people at the Pudonitz tavern, men and women, and old people, too—they never weakened: soup, veal, pork, chicken, two calves and two fat pigs, from head to tail, plus dumplings and sauerkraut in kegs, and beer to start with, then schnapps. I only remember that my plate was never empty, and after every mouthful a bucket of beer and a waterglass of schnapps as a chaser. Once there was silence like in church when they brought in the pork. They were all good people when they sat there together, stuffing themselves. I'd have gone through fire for every one of them. And there were all sorts of characters, a judge from the district court in Pilsen, in private life he hounded thieves and workers. Eating takes the sting out of people.

MRS. KOPECKA   In honor of Mr. Baloun I will now sing the "Song of the Flagon."

(She sings)

Come, dear guest, and have a seat
Share with us our dishes
Have some soup and cabbage meat
Or some Moldau fishes.

   What you need is salt and bread
   And a roof above your head.
   As a man, these you deserve
   And we honor whom we serve
   For just eighty hellers.

No credentials, rank, and place
Ever need be cited.
If your face includes a nose
You will be invited.

   Just a little friendliness
   Wit and bragging count for less.
   Eat your cheese and drink your beer

And you will be welcome here—
You and eighty hellers.

One day, looking out to see
If the sky is clearing
We will find the earth to be
Friendly, warm, and cheering.

Everyone a man will be
Overlooked by nobody.
When it's cold we'll all keep warm
Have a roof 'gainst snow and storm.
With but eighty hellers!

(*All have joined in the chorus*)

BALOUN   When my grandfather who was auditor at the water department went to Pankratz hospital and they told him he'd have to cut down on his food or he'd lose his eyesight, he said, "I've seen enough, but I haven't eaten enough yet." (*Suddenly stops eating*) Christ, if only Schweyk doesn't freeze to death in the terrible cold out there!

ANNA   He mustn't lie down. It's when they feel warm and cozy, I hear, that they're closest to freezing to death.

(*The "Flagon" vanishes. It is daytime again. Driving snow. Schweyk stirs under a blanket of snow. The clanking of tank treads is heard*)

SCHWEYK (*sitting up*)   I almost fell asleep. But let's go now, on to Stalingrad!

(*He pulls himself up and starts marching again. A large armored car appears out of the driving snow, carrying German soldiers with chalky white or bluish faces under steel helmets, wrapped in all sorts of clothes, skins, even women's skirts*)

THE SOLDIERS   (*sing* "The German Miserere")

One fine day our generals handed down the order
To overrun Danzig by crossing the border.
With tanks and bomber squadrons Poland we invaded
And after two weeks' blitzing we had made it.
God have mercy and lead us back home again.

One fine day our generals handed down the order

To cross the Norwegian and then the French border.
With tanks and bombers France and Norway we invaded
And after five weeks' blitzing we had made it.
God have mercy and lead us back home again.

One fine day our generals handed down the order
To make war on Russia and trample its border.
With tanks and bomber squadrons Russia we invaded
And after two years we still haven't made it.
God have mercy and lead us back home again.

One fine day the order will come down from our dictator
To conquer the ocean's depths and the moon's deepest
    crater
But it is bad enough in Russia's landscape
Strong is the enemy, cold the winter, and there is no escape.
God have mercy and lead us back home again.

(*The armored car disappears in the driving snow. Schweyk
keeps on marching*)
(*A road sign appears, pointing at right angles. Schweyk
ignores it. But suddenly he stops and listens. Then he bends
down, whistles softly and snaps his fingers. From under the
snow-covered underbrush crawls a starving dog*)

SCHWEYK   Ha! I knew you were hiding in the brush, wondering whether to come out. You're a cross between a schnau-
zer and a German shepherd, with a little bulldog thrown in,
and I'll call you Ajax. Don't cringe, and stop that trembling,
I can't stand it. (*He marches on, followed by the dog*)
We're going to Stalingrad. You'll meet other dogs, it's a
busy place. If you want to survive in a war, stick to the
crowd and the regular routine, don't do anything original,
and keep quiet until you get a chance to bite. War doesn't
last forever, neither does peace, and when it's all over, I'll
take you back to the "Flagon." But we've got to watch
Baloun or he'll gobble you up, Ajax. People will be wanting
dogs again, and pedigrees will be faked because they want
purebreds, it's crazy, but that's what they want. Don't get
tangled up in my feet, or I'll give you a licking. On to
Stalingrad!
(*The snowstorm becomes more dense and hides them*)

Epilogue

The good Hitler-soldier Schweyk marches untiringly toward the ever-distant Stalingrad. Out of the driving snow wild music flares up and a larger-than-life-sized shape emerges: Adolf Hitler. The historic meeting between Schweyk and Hitler takes place.

HITLER

Halt. Friend or foe?

SCHWEYK (*with a routine salute*)

Heitler!

HITLER (*outshouting the storm*)

What? I can't hear what you say.

SCHWEYK (*louder*)

I said Heitler. Can you hear me now?

HITLER

Yes.

SCHWEYK

The wind carries everything away.

HITLER

True enough. Not to mention all this snow.

Do you know who you're speaking to?

SCHWEYK

Sorry, no.

HITLER

I am the Führer.

(*Schweyk, who has been standing with one arm upraised, is now frightened. He drops his rifle and raises the other arm as in surrender*)

SCHWEYK

Holy Saint Joseph!

HITLER

At ease. Who are you?

SCHWEYK

I'm Schweyk from Budweis at the bend of the Moldau. I've hurried here to help you at Stalingrad. Just tell me how to get there.

HITLER

How in all the devil's creation
Do I know that, with the rotten Bolshevik transportation!
From Rostov to Stalingrad, on the map
Seemed about the length of my little finger
Now it turns out to be a good deal longer.
What's more, the winter this year most unfairly
Started on the third of November instead of the fifth.
This is the second time it's started early.
This winter is a typically underhanded Bolshevik stunt
As a result I can't tell back from front.
I started on the assumption that the stronger side would
   prevail.

SCHWEYK

And so it has done.
(*Schweyk is very cold. He has been stamping his feet and
now beats his sides with his arms*)

HITLER

Herr Schweyk, if the Third Reich should fail
Nature will have played us a very dirty trick.

SCHWEYK

From all I hear, it's nature plus the Bolshevik.

HITLER   (*getting ready for a long explanation*)

Eastward or westward. That's the question, so history shows.
Let me start with Herman the Cheruscan . . .

SCHWEYK

We'd better keep moving while you talk, or we'll be froze.

HITLER

Very well. Move on.

SCHWEYK

But where do you want me to go?

HITLER

Let's try the north.
(*They push on a few steps toward the north*)

SCHWEYK

But this way we're up to our necks in the snow.

HITLER

Then the south.
(*They push a few steps toward the south*)

SCHWEYK
  This way there are mountains of dead men.
HITLER
  Then I'll push east.
  (*They push a few steps toward the east*)
SCHWEYK   (*stops, whistling him back*)
  That way there are armies of Red men.
HITLER
  True enough.
SCHWEYK
  Let's go home. Here we are nowhere.
HITLER
  There stand my German people. I cannot go there.
  (*Hitler starts in all directions one after the other. Schweyk
  whistles him back each time*)
HITLER
  To the east. To the west. To the north. To the south.
SCHWEYK
  You can't stay here and you can't get out.
  (*Hitler's movements in all directions are getting faster*)
SCHWEYK   (*starts to sing*)

  Yes, you cannot go back and you cannot move on
  You're all rotten on top and your bottom's gone
  And the east wind's too cold and the Reds are too red
  So I simply don't know whether to pump you with lead
  Or take down my pants and shit on your head.
  (*Hitler's desperate thrusts have become a wild dance*)
CHORUS OF ALL PLAYERS
  (*who take off their masks and step forward to the edge
  of the stage*)

  The times will be changing. The intricate plotting
  Of people in power must finally fail.
  Like bloodthirsty cocks though today they are strutting
  The times will be changing, force cannot prevail.

  The stones on the Moldau's bottom go shifting
  In Prague three emperors molder away.

The top won't stay top, for the bottom is lifting
The night has twelve hours and is followed by day.

HENRY SLEPT BESIDE HIS NEWLY-WEDDED*

Henry slept beside his newly wedded,
Heiress to a castle on the Rhine.
Snake bites, which tormented the false lover,
Would not let him peacefully recline.

At the stroke of twelve the curtain parted.
On the sill a pale cold hand appeared.
In a shroud he saw his Wilhelmina
And her mournful, ghostly voice he heard.

Do not tremble, said his Wilhelmina;
Faithless lover, do not be afraid.
I have not come here in hate or anger,
I've not come to curse your marriage bed.

Bitter grief my poor young life has shortened,
I have died because I loved you well,
But the Lord has fortified my spirit
Saved me from the headlong plunge to hell.

Why did I believe your protestations
That your love would always be the same,
Never dreaming that for you to vanquish
Maiden's heart was but a paltry game?

Do not weep. This world does not deserve it,
'Tis not worth a single tear or moan.
Live serene and happy with Eliza
Now that you have got her for your own.

Henry, you have treasure, ah, uncounted,
Use it now to give my soul repose.
Give your Wilhelmine the peace of spirit
You denied her living, heaven knows.

Sacrifice! cried Henry in his fever;

* [This street ballad is sung by Kati and Anna in scene 4—Translated by Ralph Manheim.]

That's what you have come to ask, he cried.
Whereupon the poor spurned woman vanished
And the churl committed suicide.

God had mercy on her, but the faithless
Lover was condemned beyond repair.
Still he lives, an evil spooky monster
Wand'ring in the dreary midnight air.

The Caucasian
Chalk Circle

Play

Collaborator: R. Berlau

Translator: Ralph Manheim

CHARACTERS

DELEGATES OF THE "GALINSK"
GOAT-BREEDING KOLKHOZ:
an old peasant, a peasant
woman, a young peasant,
a very young worker
MEMBERS OF THE "ROSA LUX-
EMBURG" FRUIT-GROWING
KOLKHOZ: an old peasant, a
peasant woman, the
woman agronomist, the
girl tractor driver, the
wounded soldier, and
other peasants and peasant
women
THE EXPERT FROM THE CAPITAL
ARKADI CHEIDZE, the singer
HIS MUSICIANS
GEORGI ABASHVILI, the governor
HIS WIFE NATELLA
THEIR SON MICHAEL
SHALVA, the aide-de-camp
ARSEN KAZBEKI, the fat prince
THE RIDER FROM THE CAPITAL
NIKO MIKADZE and MIKHA
LOLADZE, doctors
SIMON CHACHAVA, a soldier
GRUSHA VACHNADZE, a kitchen
maid
THREE ARCHITECTS
BROTHER ANASTASIUS, a monk

FOUR CHAMBERMAIDS: Assya,
Masha, Zulika, Fat Nina
THE NURSE
THE WOMAN COOK
THE MAN COOK
THE STABLE HAND
SERVANTS IN THE GOVERNOR'S
PALACE
IRONSHIRTS AND SOLDIERS OF
THE GOVERNOR AND THE FAT
PRINCE
BEGGARS AND PETITIONERS
THE OLD DAIRY MAN
TWO UPPER-CLASS LADIES
THE LANDLORD
THE HOUSE SERVANT
THE CORPORAL
BLOCKHEAD, a soldier
A PEASANT WOMAN AND HER
HUSBAND
THREE PEDDLERS
LAVRENTI VACHNADZE, Grusha's
brother
HIS WIFE ANIKO
THEIR HIRED HAND
THE PEASANT WOMAN, for a
time Grusha's mother-in-
law
HER SON YUSSUP
THE BLACKMAILER

WEDDING GUESTS
CHILDREN
AZDAK, the village scribe
SHAUVA, a policeman
A FUGITIVE, the grand duke
THE NEPHEW OF THE FAT
PRINCE
THE DOCTOR
THE INVALID
THE LAME MAN

LUDOVIKA, the landlord's
daughter-in-law
A POOR OLD PEASANT WOMAN
HER BROTHER-IN-LAW IRAKLI,
a bandit
THREE KULAKS
ILLO SHUBOLADZE and SANDRO
OBOLADZE, lawyers
THE VERY OLD COUPLE

reconstruction commission, I call on the two kolkhoz villages to decide between them whether the Galinsk kolkhoz should return here or not.

THE OLD PEASANT, RIGHT   First I wish to protest again against the restriction of discussion time. It has taken us delegates of the Galinsk kolkhoz three days and three nights to get here, and now we're told that only half a day has been set aside for discussion.

A WOUNDED SOLDIER, LEFT   Comrade, we haven't as many villages or as much manpower or as much time as we used to.

THE GIRL TRACTOR DRIVER   All pleasures have to be rationed. Tobacco and wine are rationed, and that goes for discussion too.

THE OLD PEASANT, RIGHT (*with a sigh*)   Death to the Fascists! Very well, I'll come straight to the point and explain why we want our valley back. There are many reasons, but I'll begin with the simplest. Makinä Abakidze, bring out the goat cheese.

(*A peasant woman, right, takes an enormous cheese wrapped in a cloth from a basket. Applause and laughter*)

THE OLD PEASANT, RIGHT   Help yourselves, comrades. Take some.

AN OLD PEASANT, LEFT (*distrustfully*)   Are you trying to influence us?

THE OLD PEASANT, RIGHT (*amid laughter*)   How can I expect to influence you, Surab, you valley-thief! Everybody knows you'll take the cheese and the valley too. (*Laughter*) All I want from you is an honest answer: do you like the taste of this cheese?

THE OLD PEASANT, LEFT   The answer is yes.

THE OLD PEASANT, RIGHT   You do, do you? (*Bitterly*) I ought to have known you wouldn't know anything about cheese.

THE OLD PEASANT, LEFT   Why not? I've told you I liked it.

THE OLD PEASANT, RIGHT   Because you can't like it. Because it's not the same as in the old days. And why isn't it the same? Because our goats don't like the new grass the way they liked the old grass. Cheese isn't cheese because grass isn't grass, that's the trouble. Kindly put that in your minutes.

THE OLD PEASANT, LEFT   But your cheese is perfect.

The Dispute over the Valley

Amid the ruins of a war-torn Caucasian village the members of two kolkhoz villages, for the most part women and old men, but also a few soldiers, are sitting in a circle, smoking and drinking wine. With them is an expert from the state reconstruction commission in the capital.

A PEASANT WOMAN, LEFT (*pointing*) Over there in the hills we stopped three Nazi tanks, but by that time the apple orchard was ruined.

AN OLD PEASANT, RIGHT Our beautiful dairy farm: nothing but rubble!

A GIRL TRACTOR DRIVER, LEFT I set that fire, comrade.

(*Pause*)

THE EXPERT Now listen to the minutes: Delegates of the Galinsk goat-breeding kolkhoz have come to Nukha. At the approach of Hitler's armies, the kolkhoz, by order of the authorities, drove its goats eastward. Its members are now contemplating a return to this valley. Their delegates have inspected the village and surroundings and found much destruction. (*The delegates, right, nod*) The adjoining Rosa Luxemburg kolkhoz grows fruit. (*Turning to those on the right*) Within the framework of the reconstruction program they have put in a petition that the former territory of the Galinsk kolkhoz, a valley where the grazing is poor, should be converted to orchards and vineyards. As expert for the

THE OLD PEASANT, RIGHT   It is not perfect, it's barely middling. The new pasture is no good, whatever the young folks may say. I say we can't live there. It doesn't even smell like morning in the morning.

(*Several laugh*)

THE EXPERT   Let them laugh, they know what you mean. Comrades, why does a man love his home country? Because the bread tastes better, the sky is higher, the air is spicier, voices ring out more clearly, the ground is softer to walk on. Am I right?

THE OLD PEASANT, RIGHT   The valley has always belonged to us.

THE SOLDIER   What do you mean "always"? Nothing has always belonged to anybody. When you were young, you didn't even belong to yourself, you belonged to the princes Kazbeki.

THE OLD PEASANT, RIGHT   The valley belongs to us by law.

THE GIRL TRACTOR DRIVER   The laws will have to be reexamined in any case to see if they still apply.

THE OLD PEASANT, RIGHT   Of course. I suppose it doesn't make any difference what kind of tree grows outside the house where you were born? Or who you've got for a neighbor? Doesn't that make any difference? Why, one of our reasons for wanting to come back is to have you near our kolkhoz, you valley-thieves. Now you can laugh again.

THE OLD PEASANT, LEFT (*laughs*)   Then why don't you listen quietly to what your "neighbor," Kato Vachtang our agronomist, has to say about your valley?

A PEASANT WOMAN, RIGHT   We haven't said half of what we've got to say about our valley. The houses aren't all gone, the foundations of the dairy are still intact.

THE EXPERT   You have a right to government aid in either place—you know that.

THE PEASANT WOMAN, RIGHT   Comrade expert, this isn't a matter for bargaining. I can't take your cap and give you another and say "this one is better." Maybe the other is better, but you like your own best.

THE GIRL TRACTOR DRIVER   It's not the same with a piece of land as with a cap. Not in our country, comrade.

THE EXPERT   Don't get excited. It's true we must regard a

piece of land largely as an implement for producing something useful, but it's equally true that we must recognize people's love for a particular piece of land. Before proceeding with the discussion, I propose that you tell the comrades from the Galinsk kolkhoz what you are planning to do with the disputed valley.

THE OLD PEASANT, RIGHT Agreed.

THE OLD PEASANT, LEFT Right, give Kato the floor.

THE EXPERT Comrade agronomist!

THE AGRONOMIST, LEFT (*stands up, she is in army uniform*) Comrades, last winter, when we were partisans fighting in these hills, we talked about the possibility of vastly increasing our fruit production once the Germans were driven out. I drew up an irrigation project. By damming our mountain lake we can irrigate three hundred acres of barren ground. That will enable our kolkhoz not only to plant more fruit trees, but to put in vineyards as well. However, the project will only be worthwhile if we can include the disputed valley, now belonging to the Galinsk kolkhoz. Here are my calculations. (*She hands the expert a portfolio*)

THE OLD PEASANT, RIGHT Put it down in the minutes that our kolkhoz is planning to start breeding horses.

THE GIRL TRACTOR DRIVER Comrades, the project was worked out in the days and nights when we were hiding in the mountains, half the time without cartridges for the few rifles we had. Even a pencil was hard to get.

(*Applause on both sides*)

THE OLD PEASANT, RIGHT Our thanks to the comrades of the Rosa Luxemburg kolkhoz and to all those who fought for our country!

(*They shake hands all around and embrace*)

THE PEASANT WOMAN, LEFT Our idea was that our soldiers, our men and yours, should come home to a still more fertile country.

THE GIRL TRACTOR DRIVER As the poet Mayakovski said, "The home of the Soviet people shall also be the home of reason!"

(*The delegates right, except for the old peasant, have stood up and are studying the agronomist's sketches with the expert. Exclamations such as "Why a twenty-three-yard* fall?"—"*The rock here will be blasted.*"—"*All they really need is concrete and dynamite!*"—"*They'll make the water come down here; mighty clever!*")

A VERY YOUNG WORKER, RIGHT (*to the old peasant, right*) They're going to irrigate all the fields between the hills. Look at that, Alleko.

THE OLD PEASANT, RIGHT I won't look. I knew their project would be good. I refuse to be forced at gunpoint.

THE SOLDIER, LEFT But they're only trying to force you at pencil point.

(*Laughter*)

THE OLD PEASANT, RIGHT (*stands up gloomily and goes to look at the drawings*) The trouble is these valley-thieves know perfectly well that nobody in this country can resist machines and projects.

THE PEASANT WOMAN, RIGHT Alleko Bereshvili, you're the worst sucker of all for new projects, everybody knows that.

THE EXPERT How about my minutes? Can I say that you'll go back to your kolkhoz and recommend that they relinquish their old valley in the interest of this project?

THE PEASANT WOMAN, RIGHT I'll recommend it. How about you, Alleko?

THE OLD PEASANT, RIGHT (*over the drawings*) I request copies of the plans to take back with us.

THE PEASANT WOMAN, RIGHT In that case we can sit down to eat. Once he has the plans and a chance to discuss them, the matter is settled. I know him. And the rest of our people are the same.

(*The delegates embrace each other again, laughing*)

THE OLD PEASANT, LEFT Three cheers for the Galinsk kolkhoz and good luck with your horses!

THE PEASANT WOMAN, LEFT Comrades, in honor of the delegates from the Galinsk kolkhoz and of the expert, we have arranged to put on a play related to our problem. Arkadi Cheidze, the singer, will take part.

(*Applause. The girl tractor driver has run off to get the singer*)

THE PEASANT WOMAN, RIGHT Comrades, your play had better be good, we're paying a valley for it.

THE PEASANT WOMAN, LEFT   Arkadi Cheidze knows 21,000 lines by heart.

THE OLD PEASANT, LEFT   We've worked up the play under his direction. He's a hard man to get. You people from the planning commission should arrange to have him come north more often, comrade.

THE EXPERT   Economics is more in our line.

THE OLD PEASANT, LEFT (*smiling*)   You organize the redistribution of vineyards and tractors, why not of songs?

(*Led by the girl tractor operator, Arkadi Cheidze, the singer, enters the circle. He is a powerfully built man of simple ways. He is accompanied by musicians with their instruments. The artists are greeted with applause*)

THE GIRL TRACTOR DRIVER   Arkadi, this is the comrade expert.

(*The singer greets those around him*)

THE PEASANT WOMAN, RIGHT   I am greatly honored to make your acquaintance. I heard about your songs when I was a little girl in school.

THE SINGER   This time it will be a play with songs, and almost everyone in the whole kolkhoz will take part.

THE OLD PEASANT, RIGHT   Will it be one of the old legends?

THE SINGER   A very old one. It is called *The Chalk Circle* and comes from the Chinese. We play it in different form, though. Shura, show them the masks. Comrades, it is an honor for us to entertain you after a difficult debate. We hope you will find that the old poet's voice still rings true, even in the shadow of the Soviet tractors. It may be wrong to mix different wines, but old and new wisdom make an excellent mixture. Well, I hope we shall all get something to eat before the play begins. That helps.

VOICES   Of course.—Everybody to the club house.

(*All go gaily to dinner. As they are leaving, the expert turns to the singer*)

THE EXPERT   How long will this story take, Arkadi? I've got to go back to Tiflis tonight.

THE SINGER (*offhand*)   Actually there are two stories. A couple of hours.

THE EXPERT (*confidentially*)   Can't you make it shorter?

THE SINGER   No.

2

The Noble Child

(*The singer is sitting on the ground in front of his musicians. A black sheepskin cloak over his shoulders, he leafs through a worn-out copybook with slips of paper inserted*)

In olden times, in bloody times
There ruled in this city, known as "the accursed city"
A governor by the name of Georgi Abashvili.
He was as rich as Croesus.
He had a beautiful wife.
He had a thriving child.
No other governor in Gruzinia had
So many horses in his stable
And so many beggars at his door
So many soldiers in his service
And so many petitioners in his courtyard.
How shall I tell you the kind of man Georgi Abashvili was?
He enjoyed his life.
One Easter Sunday morning
The governor and his family went
To church.

(*From the archway of a palace pour beggars and petitioners, holding up emaciated children, crutches and petitions. Behind them two Ironshirts, then, splendidly attired, the governor and his family*)

THE BEGGARS AND PETITIONERS   Mercy, your grace, the taxes are too high.—I lost my leg in the Persian War, where can I get . . .—My brother is innocent, your grace, a misunderstanding.—He's starving on me.—He's our last remaining son—please release him from military service.—Please, your grace, the water inspector has been bribed.

(*A servant collects the petitions, another hands out coins from a pouch. The soldiers push back the crowd, striking at them with heavy leather whips)*

A SOLDIER   Back! Clear the church door.

(Behind the governor, his wife, and an aide-de-camp, the governor's child is rolled out through the archway in a magnificent baby carriage. The crowd presses forward again to see him)

THE SINGER *(while the crowd is whipped back)*

That Easter the people saw the governor's heir for the first time.

Two doctors never stirred from the side of the Noble Child Apple of the governor's eye.

(Cries from the crowd: "The child!"—"I can't see him, don't push so." "God bless you, your grace.")

THE SINGER

Even the powerful Prince Kazbeki

Paid his respects to him at the church door.

(A fat prince steps forward and greets the family)

THE FAT PRINCE   Happy Easter, Natella Abashvili.

(A command is heard. A dust-covered rider dashes in and holds out a roll of papers to the governor. At a sign from the governor the aide-de-camp, a handsome young man, goes to the rider and holds him back. A brief pause while the fat prince looks distrustfully at the rider)

THE FAT PRINCE   What a beautiful day! When it rained last night, I thought to myself: gloomy holidays. But this morning, the sky was clear. I love clear skies, Natella Abashvili, and a simple heart. And little Michael, every inch a governor. Ti-ti-ti-ti. *(He tickles the child)* Happy Easter, little Michael, ti-ti-ti-ti.

THE GOVERNOR'S WIFE   What do you think, Arsen, Georgi has finally decided to start building the new east wing. The whole neighborhood with its wretched shacks is being torn down to make room for the garden.

THE FAT PRINCE   That is good news after so much bad news. What do you hear about the war, brother Georgi? *(The governor makes a gesture meaning that he doesn't wish to speak of it)* A strategic withdrawal, I hear? Oh well, there are always these little setbacks. Good days and bad days. The fortunes of war. Not very important, is it?

THE GOVERNOR'S WIFE He's coughing! Georgi, did you hear? (*Sharply to the two dignified doctors standing right behind the baby carriage*) He's coughing!

FIRST DOCTOR (*to the second*) Permit me to remind you, Niko Mikadze, that I was opposed to that lukewarm bath. A slight error in the temperature of the bath water, your grace.

SECOND DOCTOR (*also very polite*) I am unable to agree with you, Mikha Loladze. The temperature of the bath water was that prescribed by our great and beloved Mishiko Oboladze. More likely a draft during the night, your grace.

THE GOVERNOR'S WIFE But do something for him! He looks feverish, Georgi.

FIRST DOCTOR (*over the child*) No cause for alarm, your grace. We shall make his bath water a little warmer and it won't happen again.

SECOND DOCTOR (*with a venomous look at him*) I won't forget that, my dear Mikha Loladze. No cause for concern, your grace.

THE FAT PRINCE Ai, ai, ai, ai. I always say: If my liver pains me, give the doctor fifty strokes across the soles of his feet. And that's only because the times have gone soft; in the old days it was simply: Off with his head!

THE GOVERNOR'S WIFE Let's go inside, it's probably because of the draft out here.

(*The procession consisting of the family and their servants turns into the church door. The fat prince follows. The aide-de-camp steps out of the procession and indicates the rider*)

THE GOVERNOR Not *before* mass, Shalva.

THE AIDE-DE-CAMP (*to the rider*) The governor does not wish to be molested with reports before mass, especially if, as I presume, they are depressing. Go to the kitchen, my friend, and tell them to give you something to eat.

(*The aide-de-camp joins the procession while the rider with a curse enters the palace gate. A soldier comes out of the palace and stops in the archway*)

THE SINGER

The city is silent.

Pigeons are strutting on the square.

A soldier of the palace guard
Is joking with a kitchen maid
Who is coming up from the river with a bundle.
(*A kitchen maid with a bundle wrapped in large green
leaves tries to enter the archway*)

THE SOLDIER   What's this? Not in church? Playing hooky
from services, young lady?

GRUSHA   I was all dressed, but then they were missing a
goose for Easter dinner and they asked me to get one,
because I know about geese.

THE SOLDIER   A goose? (*With affected suspicion*) I'd like to
see that goose.

(*Grusha does not understand*)

THE SOLDIER   You've got to watch your step with women.
"I've only been getting a goose." That's what they say,
when actually it's something entirely different.

GRUSHA (*goes resolutely up to him and shows him the goose*)
Here it is. And if it isn't a good fifteen-pound goose
crammed full of corn, I'll eat the feathers.

THE SOLDIER   A queen of a goose. The governor himself will
eat it. So you've been down by the river again?

GRUSHA   Yes, at the poultry farm.

THE SOLDIER   Oh, at the poultry farm down by the river? Not
upstream in those willows?

GRUSHA   I only go to the willows when I wash clothes.

THE SOLDIER (*pointedly*)   Exactly.

GRUSHA   Exactly what?

THE SOLDIER (*winking*)   Exactly what I meant.

GRUSHA   Why shouldn't I wash clothes by the willows?

THE SOLDIER (*with exaggerated laughter*)   "Why shouldn't
I wash clothes by the willows?" That's good, really good.

GRUSHA   I don't understand you, soldier. What's good?

THE SOLDIER (*slyly*)   If someone finds out what I know, hot
and cold she's sure to grow.

GRUSHA   I fail to see what anybody can know about those
willows.

THE SOLDIER   Even if there were bushes nearby, where someone can sit and see everything? Everything that goes on
when a certain person "washes clothes"!

GRUSHA What goes on, soldier? Can't you just say what you mean and be done with it?

THE SOLDIER Something that someone can see.

GRUSHA Why, soldier, you wouldn't mean that on a hot day I sometimes put my toes in the water, because that's all there is to it.

THE SOLDIER There's more. Your toes and something more.

GRUSHA What more? Well, maybe my foot.

THE SOLDIER Your foot and a little more. (*He laughs loudly*)

GRUSHA (*angrily*) Simon Chachava, you ought to be ashamed. Sitting in the bushes on a hot day, waiting for someone to put her leg in the water. And probably with some other soldier at that! (*She runs away*)

THE SOLDIER (*calls after her*) Not with another soldier!

(*As the singer resumes his story, the soldier runs after Grusha*)

THE SINGER

The city lies silent, but why these men in arms?

The governor's palace is at peace.

Why then is it a fortress?

(*The fat prince comes quickly out of the church door, left. He stops and looks around. Two Ironshirts are waiting outside the archway to the right. The prince sees them and passes them slowly, making a sign to them; then he goes out quickly. One Ironshirt goes through the archway into the palace; the other stays behind on guard. Muffled cries are heard from various directions in the background. "Ready!" The palace is surrounded. Church bells are heard in the distance. Out of the church door comes the governor's family and the rest of the procession*)

THE SINGER

Then the governor returned to his palace

And the palace was a trap.

The goose was plucked and roasted

But the goose was not eaten

Noon was no longer a time for eating

Noon was a time for dying.

THE GOVERNOR'S WIFE (*passing by*) It's really impossible to live in this hovel, but of course Georgi builds only for his little Michael, not for me. Michael is everything, everything for Michael!

THE GOVERNOR Did you hear that? Brother Kazbeki wishing us a happy Easter! That's all very well, but as far as I know it didn't rain in Nukha last night. Where brother Kazbeki was, it rained. Where was brother Kazbeki?

THE AIDE-DE-CAMP We must investigate.

THE GOVERNOR Yes, immediately. Tomorrow.

(*The procession turns into the archway. The rider who has meanwhile come out of the palace steps up to the governor*)

THE AIDE-DE-CAMP Excellency, won't you listen to the rider from the capital? He arrived this morning with confidential papers.

THE GOVERNOR (*continuing on his way*) Not before dinner, Shalva!

THE AIDE-DE-CAMP (*while the procession disappears into the palace and only two soldiers of the palace guard remain at the gate; to the rider*) The governor does not wish to be molested with military reports before dinner, and his excellency is devoting the afternoon to a conference with eminent architects who have also been invited to dinner. Here they come. (*Three gentlemen have entered. While the rider goes off, the aide-de-camp welcomes the architects*) Gentlemen, his excellency is expecting you for dinner. He will devote the whole afternoon to you. And your great new plans! Come quickly!

ONE OF THE ARCHITECTS We are filled with admiration that his excellency should think of building despite the alarming reports about the Persian war.

THE AIDE-DE-CAMP "Because of them" would be more accurate. It's nothing. Persia is far away! The garrison here would let themselves be hacked to pieces for the governor. (*Noise from the palace. A woman's shrill scream. Cries of command. Aghast, the aide-de-camp goes toward the archway. An Ironshirt steps out and stops him with his pike*)

THE AIDE-DE-CAMP What's going on? Put down that pike, you dog! (*Furiously to the palace guard*) Disarm this man! Don't you see this is a plot against the governor's life?

(The soldiers of the guard do not obey. They look coldly and indifferently at the aide-de-camp and watch the following scene without interest. The aide-de-camp fights his way into the palace)

ONE OF THE ARCHITECTS   The princes! The princes met in the capital last night. They are opposed to the grand duke and his governors. Gentlemen, we'd better clear out.

(They go off quickly)

THE SINGER

O blindness of the great! They live like gods on high
Great over bended backs, trusting
In hired fists, confident
Of their power that has already endured so long.
But long is not forever.
O passage of time, o hope of the poor.
(Out through the archway comes the governor, in chains, between two soldiers armed to the teeth. His face is gray)
Forever good-bye, great lord. Deign to walk with head erect.
From your palace windows hostile eyes look down upon you.
You will need no more architects. A plain carpenter is all you'll need.
You will not be moving to a new palace, but to a small hole in the ground.
Look round you one last time, blind man.
(The arrested man looks around)
Are you pleased with what you had? Between Easter mass and Easter meal
You will go to the place whence no one returns.
(He is led away. The palace guard falls in behind. A horn sounds the alarm. Noise behind the archway)
When the house of the great man collapses
Many small folk will be crushed under the ruins.
Those who never shared the fortune of the mighty
Will often share their downfall. The
Swift-plunging wagon
Drags the sweating draft horses
Down to the abyss.

(*Panic-stricken servants come rushing out of the archway*)

THE SERVANTS (*all at once*) The baskets! All into the third courtyard! Provisions for five days.—The mistress has fainted.—Carry her downstairs, somebody, she can't stay here.—What about us?—They'll slaughter us like chickens. They always do.—Mother of God, what's going to happen? —They say there's been bloodshed in the city.—Nonsense, the governor has only been politely requested to attend a meeting of the princes. Everything will be settled peaceably, I have it from a reliable source.

(*The two doctors rush into the courtyard*)

FIRST DOCTOR (*trying to hold back the other*) Niko Mikadze, it is your duty as a physician to stay with Natella Abashvili.

SECOND DOCTOR My duty? Yours!

FIRST DOCTOR Whose turn is it with the child today, Niko Mikadze, yours or mine?

SECOND DOCTOR Mikha Loladze, do you really suppose I'm going to spend another minute in a plague-ridden house on account of that brat?

(*They start to fight. All that can be heard is: "You're neglecting your duty!" and "Duty be damned!" Then the second doctor strikes the first one down*)

SECOND DOCTOR Oh, go to hell! (*Out*)

THE SERVANTS Nothing to worry about until tonight, the soldiers won't be drunk before then.—Doesn't anybody know if they've mutinied?—The palace guard has ridden away.—Doesn't anybody know what's happened?

GRUSHA Meliva the fisherman says a comet with a red tail was seen over the capital; that means calamity.

THE SERVANTS They say news reached the capital yesterday that the Persian war has been completely lost.—The princes have all risen up. They say the grand duke has fled. All his governors are going to be executed.—They won't hurt the little people. I've got a brother in the Ironshirts. (*The soldier Simon Chachava appears, looking for Grusha in the crowd*)

THE AIDE-DE-CAMP (*appears in the archway*) Into the third courtyard, all of you! Everybody help with the packing! (*He drives the servants off*)

(*Simon finally finds Grusha*)

SIMON   There you are, Grusha. What are you going to do?

GRUSHA   Nothing. If the worst comes to the worst, I have a brother with a farm in the mountains. But what about you?

SIMON   Me? Nothing. (*Again with formality*) Grusha Vachnadze, your question about my plans gives me pleasure. I have received orders to escort Lady Natella Abashvili.

GRUSHA   But hasn't the palace guard mutinied?

SIMON   (*gravely*) It has.

GRUSHA   Isn't it dangerous to escort her?

SIMON   In Tiflis they say: Is stabbing dangerous for the knife?

GRUSHA   You're not a knife, Simon Chachava, you're only a man. What's the lady to you?

SIMON   The lady is nothing to me, but I've got orders and I'm going.

GRUSHA   Then you're just stubborn, soldier, running into danger for no reason at all. (*Someone calls her from the palace*) They want me in the third courtyard, I'm in a hurry.

SIMON   If you're in a hurry, let's not argue. A good argument takes time. May I ask whether the young lady still has her parents?

GRUSHA   No. Only my brother.

SIMON   Since the time is short, my second question is: Is the young lady as healthy as a fish in water?

GRUSHA   Maybe a stitch in my right shoulder now and then, but otherwise strong enough for every kind of work. No one has ever complained.

SIMON   That is common knowledge. When it's Easter Sunday and someone has to go for the goose nevertheless, she's the one. Third question: Is the young lady impatient? Does she want cherries in the winter?

GRUSHA   Not impatient, but when people go off to war for no reason and there's no news, it's bad.

SIMON   There will be news. (*Again Grusha is called from the palace*) And now the main question . . .

GRUSHA   Simon Chachava, I have to go to the third courtyard and I'm in a big hurry, so the answer is "Yes."

SIMON (*very much embarrassed*) They say that haste is the wind that blows the scaffolding down. But they also say that the rich are never in a hurry. I'm from . . .

GRUSHA Kutsk . . .

SIMON So the young lady has made inquiries? I'm healthy, I have no one to look out for, I get ten piasters a month, it'll be twenty when I'm paymaster, and with all my heart I ask for your hand.

GRUSHA Simon Chachava, it's all right with me.

SIMON (*takes from his neck a thin chain with a little cross on it*) The cross belonged to my mother, Grusha Vachnadze, the chain is silver; please wear it.

GRUSHA Many thanks, Simon.

  (*He puts it around her neck*)

SIMON I've got to harness the horses, the young lady must understand that. The young lady had better go to the third courtyard now, or there will be trouble.

GRUSHA Yes, Simon.

  (*They stand undecided*)

SIMON I'm only taking her to the troops who are still loyal. When the war is over, I'll be back. Two or three weeks. I hope the time won't hang heavy on my betrothed until I return.

GRUSHA

Simon Chachava, I will be waiting for you.

Never fear. Go off to war, soldier
The grim, bloody war, the hard bitter war
From which not every man returns.
But when you return I'll be there.
I will be waiting for you under the green elm tree
I will be waiting for you under the bare elm tree
I will be waiting till the last has come home again
And even more.
When you come back from the war
No boots will be standing at the door.
You will find no one in bed but me

And my mouth will be unkissed.
When you come back home
You'll be able to say everything's just the same.

SIMON   I thank you, Grusha Vachnadze. And good-bye!
(*He bows low to her. She bows just as low to him. Then
she runs away quickly without looking back. The aide-de-
camp steps out of the archway*)

THE AIDE-DE-CAMP   Harness the horses to the big carriage,
don't stand around, you stinker!
(*Simon Chachava comes to attention and goes off. Out the
archway creep two servants, bowed under the weight of
enormous trunks. Behind them stumbles Natella Abashvili
supported by her waiting-women. Following her, a woman
carrying the child*)

THE GOVERNOR'S WIFE   Nobody attends to anything. I'm at my
wits' end. Where is Michael? Don't hold him so clumsily.
Load the trunks on the carriage. Is there any news of the
governor, Shalva?

THE AIDE-DE-CAMP (*shakes his head*)   You must leave at once.

THE GOVERNOR'S WIFE   Any word from the city?

THE AIDE-DE-CAMP   No. It's been quiet so far, but there's no
time to be lost. There's no room in the carriage for the
trunks. Take out what you need. (*The aide-de-camp goes
out quickly*)

THE GOVERNOR'S WIFE   Just the barest necessities! Quick!
Open the trunks, I'll tell you what's needed.
(*The trunks are put down and opened*)

THE GOVERNOR'S WIFE (*pointing to some brocade dresses*)
The green one and of course the one with the fur trimming!
Where are the doctors? That terrible migraine is coming
on again, it always starts at the temples. The one with the
pearl buttons . . .
(*Enter Grusha*)

THE GOVERNOR'S WIFE   Taking your time, aren't you? Get the
hot water bottles.
(*Grusha runs out, comes back in a moment with the hot
water bottles, and is silently ordered about by the governor's
wife*)

THE GOVERNOR'S WIFE (*watching a young chambermaid*) Don't tear the sleeve!

THE YOUNG WOMAN But gracious lady, nothing has happened to the dress.

THE GOVERNOR'S WIFE Because I caught you. I've been watching you for a long time. All you're good for is making eyes at the aide-de-camp! I'll kill you, you bitch! (*Strikes her*)

THE AIDE-DE-CAMP (*comes back*) You must hurry, Natella Abashvili. There's fighting in the city. (*Off again*)

THE GOVERNOR'S WIFE (*lets the young woman go*) Good God! Do you think they'll dare lay hands on me? Why should they? (*All are silent. She begins to rummage in the trunks*) Find my brocade jacket! Help her! What's Michael doing? Is he asleep?

THE NURSE Yes, gracious lady.

THE GOVERNOR'S WIFE Then put him down a minute and bring me my red boots from the bedroom, I need them for my green dress. (*The nurse puts the child down and runs. To the young woman*) Don't stand around, you! (*The young woman runs away*) Stay right here or I'll have you whipped. (*Pause*) Look how these things have been packed! Without love, without understanding. If I'm not there standing over them . . . In times like these you see what kind of servants you've got. Masha! (*With an imperious gesture*) You know how to fill your bellies, but you never heard of gratitude. I'll remember this.

THE AIDE-DE-CAMP (*in great agitation*) Natella, you must come at once. The carpet weavers have revolted, they've just hanged Judge Orbeliani of the superior court.

THE GOVERNOR'S WIFE Why? I must take the silver one, it cost a thousand piasters. And this one and all the furs, and where's my wine-red dress?

THE AIDE-DE-CAMP (*trying to pull her away*) Riots have broken out in the slums. We've got to be going. (*A servant runs off*) Where is the child?

THE GOVERNOR'S WIFE (*calling the nurse*) Maro! Get the child ready! Where are you?

THE AIDE-DE-CAMP (*on his way out*) We may have to forget about the carriage and go on horseback.

(*The governor's wife rummages among the dresses, throws some on a pile that is to go along, then takes them off again. Sounds are heard. Drums. A red glow appears in the sky*)

THE GOVERNOR'S WIFE (*rummaging desperately*) My wine-red dress, I can't find it. (*Shrugging her shoulders, to the second woman*) Take the whole pile to the carriage. Why hasn't Maro come back? Have you all gone crazy? I knew it would be on the bottom.

THE AIDE-DE-CAMP (*returning*) Quick! Quick!

THE GOVERNOR'S WIFE (*to the second woman*) Run! Just throw them in the carriage!

THE AIDE-DE-CAMP We're not taking the carriage. Come now, or I'll go without you.

THE GOVERNOR'S WIFE Maro! Bring the child! (*to the second woman*) Look for her, Masha! No, first take the dresses to the carriage. Nonsense, I wouldn't dream of going on horseback! (*Turning around, sees the fiery glow and freezes with fright*) Fire! (*She rushes off; the aide-de-camp follows her. Shaking her head, the second woman follows her with the bundle of dresses*)

(*Servants come out from the archway*)

THE WOMAN COOK The east gate must be on fire.

THE MAN COOK They've gone. They've left the carriage and all the provisions. How are we going to get out of here?

A STABLE HAND Yes, this house won't be healthy for a while. (*To the third woman*) Zulika, I'll get a couple of blankets and we'll clear out.

THE NURSE (*coming out of the archway with a pair of boots*) Gracious lady!

A FAT WOMAN She's gone.

THE NURSE What about the child? (*She runs to the child and picks him up*) The beasts, they've left him. (*She hands the child to Grusha*) Hold him a second. (*Lying transparently*) I'm going to see about the carriage. (*She runs off after the governor's wife*)

GRUSHA What have they done to our master?

THE STABLE HAND (*drawing his finger across his throat*) Fft!

THE FAT WOMAN (*growing hysterical at his gesture*) Merciful heavens above! Georgi Abashvili, our master! Hale and

hearty at morning mass, and now . . . take me away.
We're lost! We'll die in sin. Like Georgi Abashvili our
master.

THE THIRD WOMAN (*trying to soothe her*) Calm down, Nina.
You're not in danger. You've never hurt anybody.

THE FAT WOMAN (*while she is being led away*) Merciful
heavens above, we must all get away before they come,
before they come.

THE THIRD WOMAN Nina takes it more to heart than his wife.
These people can't even do their own mourning! (*She
catches sight of the child that Grusha is still holding*) The
child! What are you doing with the child!

GRUSHA They left it behind.

THE THIRD WOMAN She left him? Michael, who was sheltered
from every draft!

(*The servants gather around the child*)

GRUSHA He's waking up.

THE STABLE HAND Better put him down! I don't like to think
what would happen to anybody they find with that child.
I'll get our stuff; wait here, all of you. (*Goes off into the
palace*)

THE WOMAN COOK He's right, once they start fighting each
other, they wipe out whole families. I'm getting my things.
(*All have gone out except for two maids and Grusha with
the child in her arms*)

THE THIRD WOMAN Didn't you hear? Put him down.

GRUSHA His nurse gave him to me to hold for a second.

THE WOMAN COOK You simple soul, she won't be back.

THE THIRD WOMAN Keep away from him.

THE WOMAN COOK They'll be hunting him more than his
mother. He's the governor's heir. Grusha, you're a good
soul, but you're not very bright. Take it from me, if he had
leprosy it couldn't be worse. Just save your skin.

(*The stable hand has come back with bundles which he
distributes among the women. All except Grusha prepare to
leave*)

GRUSHA (*obstinately*) He hasn't got leprosy. He's looking at
me. He's somebody.   people as people

THE WOMAN COOK Then stop looking at him. You're the

boneheaded kind that falls for anything. Go get the lettuce, they say, you have the longest legs; and you run. We're taking the oxcart, you can come with us if you hurry. Lord, the whole district must be on fire!

THE THIRD WOMAN   Haven't you packed anything? There isn't much time, the Ironshirts will be here any minute.

(*The two women and the stable hand go off*)

GRUSHA   I'm coming.

(*Grusha lays the child down, looks at it for a few moments, takes pieces of clothing from the trunks that are standing around, and covers the sleeping child. Then she runs into the palace to get her things. Hoofbeats and women's screams are heard. Enter the fat prince with some drunken Ironshirts. One is carrying the governor's head on a pike*)

THE FAT PRINCE   Here in the center! (*One of the soldiers climbs on the back of another, takes the head and holds it tentatively over the archway*) That's not the center, further to the right, that's it. When I give orders, I see to it that they're carried out properly. (*While the soldier, with hammer and a nail, fastens the head to the wall by the hair*) This morning at the church door I said to Georgi Abashvili: "I love clear skies," but to tell the truth I prefer the lightning that strikes out of a clear sky. Yes, indeed. The only trouble is they've taken the brat away. I need him badly. Search all Gruzinia for him. A thousand piasters.

(*While Grusha, looking cautiously around, comes to the portal, the fat prince goes off with the Ironshirts. Again the sound of hoofbeats is heard. Carrying a bundle, Grusha goes toward the archway. When she has almost reached it, she turns around to see if the child is still there. The singer starts singing. She stands motionless*)

THE SINGER

As she stood there between door and archway, she heard
Or thought she heard a faint cry: the child
Called out to her, he didn't whimper, but said quite reasonably
Or so at least it seemed to her.
"Woman," he said, "help me."

And he went on, not whimpering, but saying quite reason-
   ably
"Consider, woman, that one who does not hear a cry for
   help
But passes by with distracted ear will never
Hear again the hushed call of her lover nor
The blackbird in the dawn nor the contented
Sighs of the tired grape pickers at angelus."
Hearing this
(*Grusha takes a few steps toward the child and bends over
him*)
               she went back for one last look
At the child. Just to stay with him
For a few moments until someone should come—
His mother perhaps or someone else—
(*She sits down, leaning against a trunk and facing the child*)
Until she should have to go, for the danger was too great,
   the city was full
Of flames and lamentation.
(*The light dims as though evening were turning to night.
Grusha has gone into the palace and come back with a lamp
and some milk which she gives the child to drink*)

THE SINGER   (*in a loud voice*)
   Terrible is the temptation to do good!
(*All through the night, Grusha sits watching the child.
Once she lights the little lamp to look at the child, once she
throws a brocade mantle over him. From time to time she
listens and looks around to make sure no one is coming*)

THE SINGER
Long she sat with the child
Till evening came, till night came
Till the dawn came. Too long she sat
Too long she saw
The quiet breathing, the little fists
Until toward morning the temptation grew too great
And she stood up, bent down and with a sigh picked up the
   child
And carried him away.
(*She does as the singer says*)

Like something stolen she took him
Like a thief she crept away.

3

The Flight to the Northern Mountains

THE SINGER
    When Grusha Vachnadze left the city
    On the Gruzinian military highway
    On the way to the northern mountains
    She sang a song, she bought milk.

THE MUSICIANS
    How can she, so human, hope
    To escape the bloodhounds, the setters of snares?
    To the deserted mountains she plodded
    Along the Gruzinian military highway she plodded
    She sang a song, she bought milk.
    (*Grusha Vachnadze plodding along, carying the child in a
    sack on her back, in one hand a bundle, in the other a large
    stick*)

GRUSHA (*sings*)
    Four old commanders
    Set out for Iran.
    The first commander never fought
    The second's fighting came to naught
    The third one found the weather not right
    The fourth one found his soldiers would not fight.
    Four old commanders
    Away they ran.
    Sosso Robakidze
    Marched off to Iran.
    The war he fought was hard and tough
    He won the battle soon enough
    The weather was all right for him

His soldiers hacked away with vim.
Sosso Robakidze
Is our man.

(*A peasant hut appears*)

GRUSHA (*to the child*) Noon, time to eat. So we'll sit in the grass and wait impatiently while good old Grusha buys a cup of milk. (*She sets the child on the ground and knocks at the door of the hut; an old peasant opens*) Could you give me a cup of milk, grandfather, and a millet cake perhaps?

THE OLD MAN Milk? We haven't got any milk. The high and mighty soldiers from the city have taken our goats. Go to the high and mighty soldiers if you want milk.

GRUSHA But you must have a cup of milk left for a child, grandfather?

THE OLD MAN For a "God-reward-you," I suppose?

GRUSHA Who said anything about God rewarding you? (*Takes out her purse*) We pay like princes. Our heads in the clouds, our behinds in the water! (*Grumbling, the peasant brings milk*) And what is the price of this cup of milk?

THE OLD MAN Three piasters. Milk has gone up.

GRUSHA Three piasters? For a thimbleful? (*Without a word the old man slams the door in her face*) Michael, did you hear that? Three piasters! We can't afford it. (*She goes back and sits down and gives the child her breast*) We'll just have to try it again this way. Suck hard, think of those three piasters! There's nothing there, but you think you're drinking, and that's something. (*She sees that the child has stopped sucking, and shakes her head. She stands up, goes back to the door and knocks again*) Grandfather, open up, we'll pay! (*In an undertone*) I hope you drop dead. (*When the old man opens the door again*) I expected to pay half a piaster, but the child needs it. How about one piaster?

THE OLD MAN Two.

GRUSHA Don't close the door again. (*She rummages a long while in her purse*) Here are two piasters. But this milk had better be filling, we have a long way to go. It's highway robbery and a sin.

THE OLD MAN Kill the soldiers if you want milk.

GRUSHA (*giving the child milk to drink*) It's an expensive treat. Drink, Michael, it's half a week's wages. The people around here think we've made our money sitting on our asses. Michael, Michael, I've certainly let myself in for something. (*Looking at the brocade mantle in which the child is wrapped*) A brocade mantle worth a thousand piasters, and not one piaster for milk. (*She looks back*) Now there's a carriage full of rich refugees. Let's try and get a ride.

(*Outside a caravanserai*)
(*Grusha, wearing the brocade mantle, is seen approaching two fine ladies. She is holding the child in her arms*)

GRUSHA Oh, do the ladies wish to spend the night here too? It's so dreadfully crowded everywhere, and not a carriage to be had! My coachman simply took it into his head to go back. I've come at least half a mile on foot. Barefoot! My Persian shoes—you know those heels. But why doesn't somebody come?

OLDER LADY The landlord is taking his time. Ever since the events in the capital, the whole country has lost its manners. (*Out comes the landlord, a very dignified old man with a long beard, followed by his house servant*)

THE LANDLORD Forgive an old man for making you wait, my ladies. My little grandson was showing me a peach tree in blossom, over there on the slope, beyond the corn fields. We have a few fruit trees over there, a few cherry trees. Further west (*he points*) the ground is stonier, the peasants drive their sheep there to graze. You ought to see the peach blossoms, such an exquisite pink.

OLDER LADY You have a fertile region here.

THE LANDLORD God has blessed it. How are the fruit blossoms coming along further south, my ladies? You're from the south, aren't you?

YOUNGER LADY I must admit I didn't pay much attention to the landscape.

THE LANDLORD (*politely*) I understand. The dust. On our

highway it's best to proceed at a moderate pace, provided one isn't in too much of a hurry.

OLDER LADY Put your veil around your neck, dearest. The evening breezes here seem rather cool.

THE LANDLORD They come from the Yanga-Tau glaciers, my ladies.

GRUSHA Oh, I'm so afraid my son will catch cold.

OLDER LADY It's a good-sized caravanserai. Shall we go in?

THE LANDLORD Oh, the ladies desire rooms? But my caravanserai is overcrowded and the servants have run away. I'm dreadfuly sorry but I can't accommodate any more people, not even with references . . .

YOUNGER LADY But we can't spend the night on the road.

OLDER LADY (*dryly*) How much is it?

THE LANDLORD My ladies, surely you must understand that a landlord must be extremely careful in times like these with so many refugees looking for a place to stay. Perfectly respectable persons of course, but frowned on by the authorities. And so . . .

OLDER LADY My dear man, we are not refugees. We are on our way to our summer residence in the mountains, and that's all there is to it. It would never occur to us to ask your hospitality if we . . . if we needed it *that* badly.

THE LANDLORD (*nodding agreement*) Of course not. Still, I doubt whether the one tiny room I have available would suit the ladies. I am obliged to charge sixty piasters per person. Are the ladies together?

GRUSHA In a way. I, too, am in need of lodging.

YOUNGER LADY Sixty piasters! The man's a cutthroat!

THE LANDLORD (*coldly*) My ladies, I have no desire to cut anyone's throat, and so . . . (*Turns to go*)

OLDER LADY Must we talk about throats? Come along. (*Goes in, followed by the house servant*)

YOUNGER LADY (*in despair*) A hundred and eighty piasters for one room. (*Looking around at Grusha*) But not with a child! That's impossible! Suppose it cries!

THE LANDLORD The price of the room is a hundred and eighty piasters, for two persons or for three.

YOUNGER LADY (*changed on hearing this, to Grusha*) On the

other hand, my dear, I couldn't bear to think of you out on the road. Do come in.

(*They go into the caravanserai. On the other side of the stage the house servant enters from the rear with baggage. Behind him the elderly lady, then the second lady and Grusha with the child*)

YOUNGER LADY   A hundred and eighty piasters! I haven't been so upset since they brought poor Igor home.

OLDER LADY   Must you talk about Igor?

YOUNGER LADY   Actually there are four of us, the child is a person, isn't it? (*To Grusha*) Couldn't you pay at least half?

GRUSHA   That is impossible. You see, I had to leave in a great hurry and the aide-de-camp forgot to give me enough money.

OLDER LADY   Maybe you haven't even got the sixty?

GRUSHA   I will pay that.

YOUNGER LADY   Where are the beds?

THE HOUSE SERVANT   No beds. There are blankets and sacks. You'll just have to make do. Be glad you're not being lowered into the ground, like plenty of others. (*Goes out*)

YOUNGER LADY   Did you hear that? I'm going straight to the landlord. The man must be flogged.

OLDER LADY   Like your husband?

YOUNGER LADY   You're so cruel. (*She bursts into tears*)

OLDER LADY   How will we ever make anything resembling beds out of this?

GRUSHA   Leave it to me. (*She puts the child down*) It's always easier when there's more than one. And there's still your carriage. (*Sweeping the floor*) I was taken utterly by surprise! "My dear Anastasia Katarinovska," my husband said to me before dinner, "lie down a while, you know how those migraine headaches will come over you." (*She drags sacks into place, makes up beds; the ladies watch her at work and exchange glances*) "Georgi," I said to the governor, "with sixty guests for dinner I can't lie down, the servants aren't to be trusted, and Michael Georgivitch won't eat without me." (*To Michael*) You see, Michael, everything's going to be all right, didn't I tell you? (*She suddenly notices that the ladies are looking at her strangely and whispering*) There. At least we won't be lying on the bare ground. I've folded the blankets double.

OLDER LADY (*in a tone of command*) You're very clever at bedmaking, my dear. Show me your hands!

GRUSHA (*frightened*) What do you mean?

YOUNGER LADY You've been told to show your hands.
(*Grusha shows the ladies her hands*)

YOUNGER LADY (*triumphantly*) Cracks! A domestic!

OLDER LADY (*goes to the door, calls out*) Servants!

YOUNGER LADY We've caught you, you hussy. What have you been up to? Confess.

GRUSHA (*confused*) I haven't been up to anything. I thought maybe you'd take us with you in your carriage, just a little way. Please don't make a fuss. I'll go of my own accord.

YOUNGER LADY (*while the older lady continues to call for servants*) You'll go all right, but with the police. In the meantime stay here. Don't move!

GRUSHA But I was even going to pay the sixty piasters. Here. (*shows her purse*) See for yourself, I've got them. Four tens and a five, no it's a ten, that makes sixty. I only wanted the child to ride in the carriage, that's the truth.

YOUNGER LADY Oh, you wanted to ride in the carriage! Now it comes out.

GRUSHA Gracious lady, I confess, I'm of lowly descent, please don't call the police. The child is of high station, look at his linen, he's a refugee like yourselves.

YOUNGER LADY Of high station, we've heard that one. His father's a prince, isn't he?

GRUSHA (*wildly to the elderly lady*) Stop screaming! Haven't you any heart?

YOUNGER LADY (*to the elderly lady*) Be careful, she's going to attack you. She's dangerous! Help! Murder!

THE HOUSE SERVANT (*entering*) What's wrong?

ELDERLY LADY This person has wormed her way in here by playing the lady. Probably a thief.

YOUNGER LADY And dangerous too. She wanted to kill us. Call the police. I feel my migraine coming on, oh heavens!

THE HOUSE SERVANT There isn't any police right now. (*To*

Grusha) Pack up your belongings, sister, and make yourself
scarce.

GRUSHA (*angrily picking up the child*) You monsters!
At a time when they're nailing your heads to the walls!

THE HOUSE SERVANT (*pushing her out*) Shut your mouth. Or
the old man will come, and then I pity you.

OLDER LADY (*to the younger lady*) Look and see if she
hasn't stolen something!

(*While the ladies on the right search feverishly to see
whether something has been stolen, the house servant
steps out the door left with Grusha*)

THE HOUSE SERVANT I always say: Don't buy a pig in a poke.
Next time take a look at people before you trust them.

GRUSHA I thought they'd be decent if they thought I was
one of them.

THE HOUSE SERVANT That was silly of you. Believe me, nothing is harder than imitating lazy, useless people. Once they
suspect you of being able to wipe your own ass or of ever
in all your life working with your hands, you're done for.
Wait a second, I'll get you some millet bread and a few
apples.

GRUSHA Better not. I'd better go before the landlord comes.
If I walk all night, I'll be out of danger, I think. (*Goes*)

THE HOUSE SERVANT (*calls softly after her*) Keep to the
right at the next crossing.

(*She disappears*)

THE SINGER
   When Grusha Vachnadze went northward
   Prince Kazbeki's guards followed her.

THE MUSICIANS
   How can a barefoot girl escape from the Ironshirts?
   The bloodhounds, the setters of snares?
   Even at night they hunt. Pursuers
   Never get tired. Butchers
   Never sleep long.
   (*Two Ironshirts are trotting along the highway*)

THE CORPORAL Blockhead, you'll never amount to anything.
Your heart isn't in it. A superior can tell that by the little

things. When I laid that fat woman the other day, you carried out my orders, you held her husband, you kicked him in the stomach, but did you take pleasure in it like a good soldier, or did you just go through the motions? I watched you, Blockhead. You're dead wood, you're a tinkling cymbal, you'll never get a promotion. (*They go on a while in silence*) Don't think I won't remember that every move you make is a display of insubordination. I forbid you to limp. You only do it because I sold the horses because I'd never get such a good price again. By limping you wish to intimate that you don't care for hiking, I know you. It won't do you any good, it will make things worse for you. Sing!

THE TWO IRONSHIRTS (*sing*)
   To the war my weary way I'm wending
   While my sweetheart stays to mind the cattle.
   Loyal friends her honor are defending
   Till I come back from the bloody battle.
THE CORPORAL Louder!
THE TWO IRONSHIRTS
   As into my grave instead I travel
   See my sweetheart throwing in the gravel
   Hear her say: "There go the feet with which he chased me
   There the arms that many times embraced me."

   (*Again they walk for a while in silence*)
THE CORPORAL A good soldier has to put his heart and soul in it. He'll let himself be torn to pieces for a superior. With his dying glance he takes in his corporal's nod of approval. That's all the reward he wants. There won't be any nod for you, and you'll have to kick in all the same. Damnation, how am I going to find the governor's brat with a subordinate like you, just tell me that.
   (*They go on*)

THE SINGER
   When Grusha Vachnadze came to the Sirra River
   Her flight became too much for her, the helpless child too
      heavy.

THE MUSICIANS
   In the corn fields the rosy dawn
   Is merely cold to one who has not slept. To the fugitive
   The merry clatter of milk pails from the farm where the
      smoke rises
   Sounds menacing. Carrying the child, she
   Feels its weight and little else.
   (*Grusha stops outside a farm*)

GRUSHA Now you've wet yourself again and you know I
   have no diapers for you. Michael, I'll have to leave you
   now. We're far enough from the city. They can't care
   enough about a little nothing like you to follow you all
   this way. That peasant woman looks friendly, and get a
   whiff of the milk! So good-bye, Michael, I'll forget how
   you kicked me in the back all night to keep me on the
   move, and you forget the short rations. I did my best. I'd
   have liked to keep you longer because your nose is so little,
   but it can't be done. I'd have liked to show you your first
   bunny and—teach you to stop wetting yourself, but I've
   got to go back, because my sweetheart the soldier ought
   to be back soon, too, and what if he didn't find me? You
   can't ask that of me, Michael.
   (*A fat peasant woman carries a milk pail in through the
   door. Grusha waits until she is inside, then she goes
   cautiously toward the house. She steals up to the door
   and sets the child down in front of it. Then she hides behind
   a tree and waits until the peasant woman comes out again
   and finds the bundle*)

THE PEASANT WOMAN Heavens above, what's this? Husband!
THE PEASANT (*coming out*) Now what? Let me eat my soup.
THE PEASANT WOMAN (*to the child*) Where's your mother?
   Haven't you got one? It's a boy, I believe. And he's got
   fine linen, this is a noble child. And they just drop it on
   the doorstep. What terrible times!
THE PEASANT If they think we're going to feed him, they're
   mistaken. Take it to the priest in the village, and that's the
   end of it.
THE PEASANT WOMAN What would the priest do with him?
   He needs a mother. There, he's waking up. Don't you think
   we could keep him?

THE PEASANT (*shouting*) No!

THE PEASANT WOMAN If I bed him down in the corner beside the armchair, I'll only need a basket, and I'll take him out to the fields with me. Look, he's laughing. Husband, we have a roof over our heads, we can do it, I'm not listening.

(*She carries him in, the peasant follows protesting. Grusha comes out from behind the tree, laughs and hurries away in the direction from which she came*)

THE SINGER Why so happy, woman returning homeward?

THE MUSICIANS

Because with a smile, the helpless child has
Got himself new parents, I am happy. Because the dear child
Is off my hands, I am glad.

THE SINGER And why so sad?

THE MUSICIANS

Because I am free and unburdened, I am sad
As one who has been robbed
As one who has been made poor.

(*She has only gone a little way when she meets the two Ironshirts who bar the way with their pikes*)

THE CORPORAL Young lady, you have bumped into the armed forces. Where have you come from? And why? Have you illicit relations with the enemy? Where are they? What movements are they making in your rear? What about the hills, what about the valleys, how are your stockings fastened?

(*Grusha stands stock still in a fright*)

GRUSHA They are well-fortified, you'd better stop short.

THE CORPORAL I always stop short, you can count on me for that. Why are you gaping at my pike? "A soldier in the field never lets his pike out of his hand." That's the regulation, Blockhead, learn it by heart. Well, young lady, where are you going?

GRUSHA To meet my sweetheart, soldier, a certain Simon Chachava, of the palace guard in Nukha. If I write him a letter, he'll break every bone in your body.

THE CORPORAL Simon Chachava, of course, I know him. He

gave me the key, said to look in on you now and then.
Blockhead, we're getting unpopular. We'd better tell her
our intentions are honorable. Young lady, I may seem to
make jokes, but I'm serious underneath. So here you have
it officially: I want a child from you.

(*Grusha lets out a little scream*)

THE CORPORAL Blockhead, she catches our meaning. A sweet
shock, isn't it? "But first I must take the buns out of the
oven, lieutenant. First I must change my torn shirt, colonel!"
Joking aside, poking aside, young lady: we're combing the
region for a certain child. Have you heard anything about
such a child, that's turned up from the city, a noble child
in fine linen?

GRUSHA No, I haven't heard a thing.

THE SINGER

Run, kind-hearted girl, the killers are coming!
You who are helpless, help the helpless child! And so she
runs.

(*She turns suddenly and runs away in panic fear, toward
the peasant's house. The Ironshirts exchange glances and
follow her cursing*)

THE MUSICIANS

In the bloodiest times
There are kindly people.

(*In the peasant's house the fat peasant woman is bending
over the child in its basket when Grusha Vachnadze rushes
in*)

GRUSHA Hide him, quick. The Ironshirts are coming. I left
him on the doorstep, but he's not mine, he comes of a
noble family.

THE PEASANT WOMAN Who's coming? What Ironshirts?

GRUSHA Don't waste time. The Ironshirts that are looking for
him.

THE PEASANT WOMAN They've no business in my house. But
it looks like I'll want a word with you.

GRUSHA Take off his fine linen, it will give us away.

THE PEASANT WOMAN Don't bother me with linen. In my
house I give the orders. And don't throw up on my furniture. Why did you leave it? That's a sin.

GRUSHA (*looking out*) They'll be coming out from behind the trees any minute. I shouldn't have run away, that made them angry. Oh, what should I do?

THE PEASANT WOMAN (*also peers out and is suddenly scared stiff*) Mother of God, the Ironshirts!

GRUSHA They're looking for the child.

THE PEASANT WOMAN But what if they come in here?

GRUSHA You mustn't give it to them. Say it's yours.

THE PEASANT WOMAN Yes.

GRUSHA They'll run it through if you give it to them.

THE PEASANT WOMAN But suppose they ask me for it? I've got silver for the harvesters in the house.

GRUSHA If you give it to them, they'll run it through, right here in your house. You've got to tell them it's yours.

THE PEASANT WOMAN Yes. But suppose they don't believe me?

GRUSHA If you say it like you meant it . . .

THE PEASANT WOMAN They'll burn the roof over our heads.

GRUSHA That's why you've got to say it's yours. His name is Michael. I shouldn't have told you that.

(*The peasant woman nods*)

GRUSHA Don't nod your head like that. And don't tremble, they'll notice.

THE PEASANT WOMAN Yes.

GRUSHA Stop saying "yes." I can't stand it. (*Shakes her*) Haven't you one of your own?

THE PEASANT WOMAN (*mumbling*) Gone to war.

GRUSHA Then maybe he's an Ironshirt himself. Would you expect him to run babies through? Wouldn't *you* give him a piece of your mind! "Stop poking your pike into my house, is that how I raised you? Wash your neck before you talk to your mother."

THE PEASANT WOMAN That's a fact. I wouldn't let him do that.

GRUSHA Promise to tell them he's yours.

THE PEASANT WOMAN Yes.

GRUSHA They're coming now.

(*Knocking at the door. The women do not answer. Enter the Ironshirts. The peasant woman bows low*)

THE CORPORAL That's her all right. What did I tell you?

I've got a nose on me. I could smell her. I've got a question to ask you, young lady: Why did you run away? What did you think? That I wanted something from you? I bet it was something indecent. Admit it!

GRUSHA (*while the peasant woman keeps bowing*) I left milk on the stove. I suddenly remembered it.

THE CORPORAL I thought it was because you thought I was looking at you indecently. As if I had some idea about you and me. Kind of a sensual look, see what I mean?

GRUSHA I didn't see anything like that.

THE CORPORAL But it's possible, don't deny it. After all, I could be a swine. I'll be perfectly frank with you: I could get all sorts of ideas if we were alone. (*To the peasant woman*) Haven't you something to do in the yard? Feed the chickens?

THE PEASANT WOMAN (*falling suddenly on her knees*) Mr. Soldier, I didn't know a thing. Don't burn the roof over my head!

THE CORPORAL What are you talking about?

THE PEASANT WOMAN It's got nothing to do with me, Mr. Soldier. She left it on my doorstep, I swear it.

THE CORPORAL (*sees the child and whistles*) Oho, there's a little fellow in the basket, Blockhead, I smell a thousand piasters. Take the old woman outside and hold her fast. Seems to me I've got a little interrogation on my hands. (*Without a word the peasant woman lets the soldier lead her away*)

THE CORPORAL So here's the baby I wanted of you. (*He goes to the basket*)

GRUSHA Mr. Officer, it's mine. It's not the one you're looking for.

THE CORPORAL Let's have a look. (*He bends over the basket*) (*Grusha looks about in despair*)

GRUSHA It's mine, it's mine.

THE CORPORAL Fine linen.

(*Grusha rushes at him to pull him away. He flings her off and again bends down over the basket. She looks about desperately, sees a big log, lifts it and brings it down on the corporal's head from behind. He collapses. Quickly picking up the child, she runs out*)

THE SINGER

And fleeing from the Ironshirts
After twenty-two days of flight
At the foot of the Yanga-Tau glacier
Grusha Vachnadze adopted the child.

THE MUSICIANS

The helpless one adopted the helpless one.
(*Grusha leans over a half-frozen stream and scoops up water for the child in the hollow of her hand*)

GRUSHA (*sings*)

Since no one wants to take you, child
I shall have to take you.
Black the day as black can be
If you're satisfied with me
I will not forsake you.

I have carried you so far
Sore my feet and bleeding
Spent such fortunes buying milk
You've grown dear to me
(Fondness comes from feeding.)

I will throw your linen out
Swaddle you in tatters
I will wash you and baptize
You in glacier water.
(You'll just have to stand it.)

(*She has taken off the child's fine linen and wrapped him in a rag*)

THE SINGER

When Grusha Vachnadze, pursued by the Ironshirts
Came to the footbridge leading over the glacier to the
    village on the eastern slope
She sang the Song of the Shaky Bridge and risked two
    lives.
(*A wind has come up. The footbridge appears in the half-light. One cable is broken and the bridge is slanting over*

the abyss. Peddlers, two men and a woman, are standing undecided at the end of the bridge when Grusha arrives. One of the men is fishing with a pole for the dangling cable)

FIRST MAN Take your time, young lady, you won't get across the pass anyway.

GRUSHA But I have to take my baby to my brother's place on the east side.

THE WOMAN Have to! What do you mean have to! I have to get across because I have to buy two carpets in Atum, which a woman has to sell because her husband died. But can I do what I have to do; can *she?* Andrey has been fishing for the cable for two hours, but even if he catches it how are we going to make it fast? Tell me that.

FIRST MAN (*listening*) Sh-sh, I think I hear something.

GRUSHA (*in a loud voice*) The bridge isn't all that shaky. I think I'll try to cross it.

THE WOMAN I wouldn't try it if the devil himself were after me. Why, it's suicide.

FIRST MAN (*shouting*) Ho!

GRUSHA Don't shout! (*To the woman*) Tell him not to shout.

FIRST MAN But somebody's shouting down there. Maybe they've lost their way down there.

THE WOMAN Why shouldn't he shout? Is there something shady about you? Are they after you?

GRUSHA I guess I'd better tell you. The Ironshirts are after me. I hit one of them on the head.

SECOND MAN Hide the stuff.

(*The woman hides a sack behind a rock*)

FIRST MAN Why didn't you tell us right away? (*To the others*) If they catch her, they'll make hash out of her!

GRUSHA Get out of the way, I've got to cross that bridge.

SECOND MAN You can't! The chasm is two thousand feet deep!

FIRST MAN Even if we could catch the cable, there wouldn't be any sense in it. We could hold it in our hands, but the Ironshirts could cross the same way.

GRUSHA Out of my way!

(*Not very distant cries: "She's up there!"*)

THE WOMAN   They're coming close. But you can't take your child on the bridge. It's almost sure to collapse. And look down there.

(*Grusha looks into the chasm. More cries from the Iron-shirts below*)

SECOND MAN   Two thousand feet.

GRUSHA   But those men are worse.

FIRST MAN   You can't do it. Think of the child. Risk your own life if they're out to get you, but not the child's.

SECOND MAN   Besides, she'll be heavier with the child.

THE WOMAN   Maybe she really has to get across. Give it to me, I'll hide it, and you'll try the bridge by yourself.

GRUSHA   No. Where he goes, I go. (*To the child*) We're in this together, son. (*Sings*)

Deep is the chasm, son
See the bridge sway
Not of our choosing, son
Is our way.

You must go the way that
I have picked for you
You must eat the bread that
I have saved for you

Share the two, three morsels
Taking two of three.
How big or how little
Better not ask me.

I'll try it.

THE WOMAN   It's tempting God.

(*Cries from below*)

GRUSHA   I beg you, throw your pole away, or they'll fish up the cable and come after me.

(*She goes out on the swaying bridge. The peddler woman screams when the bridge threatens to break. But Grusha goes on and reaches the other side*)

FIRST MAN   She's across.

THE WOMAN   (*who had fallen on her knees and prayed,*

angrily) It was a sin all the same.

(*The Ironshirts appear from below. The corporal's head is bandaged*)

THE CORPORAL Have you seen a woman with a child?

FIRST MAN (*while the second man throws the pole into the chasm*) Yes. There she is. And the bridge won't carry you.

THE CORPORAL Blockhead, you're going to pay for this.

(*Grusha on the opposite side laughs and shows the Ironshirts the child. She goes on, the bridge stays behind. Wind*)

GRUSHA (*looking around at Michael*) Never be afraid of the wind, it's only a poor devil like us. His job is pushing the clouds and he gets colder than anybody.

(*Snow begins to fall*)

The snow isn't so bad either, Michael. Its job is covering the little fir trees so the winter won't kill them. And now I'll sing a song for you. Listen! (*Sings*)

Your father is a bandit
And your mother is a whore
Every noble man and honest
Will bow as you pass.

The tiger's son will
Feed the little foals his brothers
The child of the serpent
Bring milk to the mothers.

4

In the Northern Mountains

THE SINGER

The sister trudged for seven days.
Across the glacier, down the slopes she trudged.

When I come to my brother's house, she thought
He will stand up and embrace me.
"Is it you, sister?" he will say.
"I've long been expecting you. This is my beloved wife.
And this is my farm, mine by marriage.
With eleven horses and thirty-one cows. Be seated!
Sit down at our table with your child and eat."
Her brother's house was in a smiling valley.
When the sister came to the brother's house, she was ill
     from her journey.
The brother stood up from the table.

(*A stout peasant couple who have sat down to eat.
Lavrenti Vachnadze already has his napkin around his neck
when Grusha, supported by a hired hand and very pale,
enters with the child*)

LAVRENTI VACHNADZE   Where have you come from, Grusha?

GRUSHA (*feebly*)   I've come across the Yanga-Tau pass,
Lavrenti.

HIRED HAND   I found her outside the hay shed. She has a child
with her.

THE SISTER-IN-LAW   Go and curry the bay. (*The hired hand
goes out*)

LAVRENTI   This is my wife, Aniko.

THE SISTER-IN-LAW   We thought you were working in Nukha.

GRUSHA (*who can hardly stand up*)   Yes, I was.

THE SISTER-IN-LAW   Wasn't it a good position? We heard it
was.

GRUSHA   The governor has been killed.

LAVRENTI   Yes, we heard there was trouble. Your aunt told
us, don't you remember, Aniko?

THE SISTER-IN-LAW   It's perfectly quiet here. City people are
always looking for trouble. (*Goes to the door and calls*)
Sosso, Sosso, don't take the cake out of the oven yet, do
you hear? Where are you anyway? (*Goes out, calling*)

LAVRENTI (*quickly, in an undertone*)   Have you a father for
it? (*When she shakes her head*) Just as I thought. We've
got to think up something. She's very religious.

THE SISTER-IN-LAW (*coming back*)   Those servants! (*To
Grusha*) You have a child?

GRUSHA   It's mine. (*She slumps over. Lavrenti raises her up*)

THE SISTER-IN-LAW Saints alive, she's got some disease. What will we do?

(*Lavrenti starts leading Grusha to the bench by the stove. Aniko, horrified, gestures him to stop and points to a sack by the wall*)

LAVRENTI (*takes Grusha to the wall*) Sit down. Sit down. It's only weakness.

THE SISTER-IN-LAW What if it's scarlet fever!

LAVRENTI There would be spots. It's weakness, Aniko, nothing to worry about. (*To Grusha, who has sat down*) Are you feeling better now?

THE SISTER-IN-LAW Is the child hers?

GRUSHA Mine.

LAVRENTI She's going to join her husband.

THE SISTER-IN-LAW Oh. Your meat is geting cold. (*Lavrenti sits down and begins to eat*) It doesn't agree with you cold, the fat is no good when it's cold. You know you have a delicate stomach. (*To Grusha*) If your husband's not in the city, where on earth is he?

LAVRENTI He lives across the mountains, she says.

THE SISTER-IN-LAW Oh. Across the mountains.

(*Sits down to eat*)

GRUSHA I think you'll have to take me somewhere to lie down, Lavrenti.

THE SISTER-IN-LAW (*continues her interrogation*) If it's consumption, we'll all get it. Has your husband a farm?

GRUSHA He's a soldier.

LAVRENTI But he's inherited a farm from his father, a small farm.

THE SISTER-IN-LAW Hasn't he gone to war? Why not?

GRUSHA (*with difficulty*) Yes, he's gone to war.

THE SISTER-IN-LAW Then why are you going to the farm?

LAVRENTI When he comes back from the war, he'll go to the farm.

THE SISTER-IN-LAW But you're going there right away?

LAVRENTI Yes, to wait for him.

THE SISTER-IN-LAW (*screams*) Sosso, the cake!

GRUSHA (*mumbles feverishly*) A farm. Soldier. Wait. Sit down, eat.

THE SISTER-IN-LAW It's scarlet fever.

GRUSHA (*starting up*)   Yes, he has a farm.

LAVRENTI   I think it's weakness, Aniko. Don't you want to see about the cake, my love?

THE SISTER-IN-LAW   But when will he come back if what they're saying is true and the war has broken out again? (*Waddles out, calling*) Sosso, where are you? Sosso!

LAVRENTI (*stands up quickly, goes to Grusha*)   We'll put you to bed right away. She's a good soul, but not until after dinner.

GRUSHA (*holds out the child to him*)   Take it! (*He takes it, looking around*)

LAVRENTI   But you can't stay long. She's religious, you see. (*Grusha collapses. Her brother catches her*)

THE SINGER
     The sister was too sick.
     The cowardly brother had to take her in.
     The autumn went, the winter came.
     The winter was long
     The winter was short.
     The people mustn't find out.
     The rats mustn't bite.
     The spring mustn't come.

(*Grusha sitting at the loom in the storeroom. The child is huddled on the floor. They are wrapped in blankets*)

GRUSHA (*sings while weaving*)
     The loved one prepared to go
     And his betrothed ran after him pleading
     Pleading and in tears, tearfully admonishing:

     Dearest love, dearest love
     If you must go off to war
     If you must fight in the hard battle
     Don't run ahead of the war
     And don't lag behind the war
     Up in front there is red fire

In the rear there is red smoke.
Keep in the middle of the war
Stay close to the banner bearer.
The first are always sure to die
The last are sure to be struck down as well
Those in the middle come home again.

Michael, we must be very clever. If we make ourselves as
small as cockroaches, my sister-in-law will forget that we're
in the house. We'll be able to stay until the snow melts.
And don't cry because it's cold. If you're poor and suffer
from the cold besides, people won't like you.

(*Lavrenti comes in. He sits down beside his sister*)

LAVRENTI Why are you sitting here bundled up like coach-
men? Is the room too cold?

GRUSHA (*hastily removing her shawl*) It's not cold, Lavrenti.

LAVRENTI If it's too cold, you shouldn't be sitting here with
the child. Aniko would never forgive herself. (*Pause*) I
hope the priest didn't ask you questions about the child.

GRUSHA He asked, but I didn't tell him anything.

LAVRENTI That's good. I wanted to talk to you about Aniko.
She's a good soul, but she's so very, very sensitive. If
people say the least thing about the farm, she gets upset.
You see, she takes everything to heart. One time the
milkmaid had a hole in her stocking in church, and my
dear Aniko has been wearing two pairs of stockings to
church ever since. You won't believe it, but it's in the
family. (*He listens*) Are you sure there are no rats here?
You can't stay here if there are. (*A sound is heard as of
dripping from the roof*) What's that dripping?

GRUSHA It must be a leaky barrel.

LAVRENTI Yes, it must be a barrel.—You've been here for
six months now. Was I talking about Aniko? Of course I
didn't tell her about that Ironshirt, she has a weak heart.
So she doesn't know you can't look for work, and that's
why she spoke the way she did yesterday. (*They listen
again to the dripping of the melting snow*) You can't
imagine how worried she is about your soldier. "Suppose

he comes home and doesn't find her?" she says, and lies awake at night. "He can't be home before spring," I say. The good soul. (*The drops fall faster*) When do you suppose he'll come, what do you think? (*Grusha is silent*) Not before spring. Don't you agree? (*Grusha says nothing*) I see, you've given up expecting him. (*Grusha says nothing*) But when spring comes and the snow thaws here and on the passes, you can't stay here any longer, they're likely to come looking for you, and people are talking about an illegitimate child.

(*The glockenspiel of the falling drops has become loud and steady*)

LAVRENTI   Grusha, the snow is melting on the roof; it's spring.

GRUSHA   Yes.

LAVRENTI   (*with enthusiasm*)   I'll tell you what we'll do. You need a place to go, you've got a child (*he sighs*), so you need a husband to make people stop gossiping. I've been asking around—oh, very cautiously—about a husband for you. I've found one, Grusha. I've spoken to a woman who has a son just across the mountain, with a small farm, she's willing.

GRUSHA   But I can't marry anybody, I've got to wait for Simon Chachava.

LAVRENTI   Of course. I've thought of all that. You don't need a husband in bed, only on paper. I've found the right man. This woman I've made arrangements with—her son is dying. Isn't that perfect? He's at his last gasp. It will be just like we said: "A husband across the mountains." And when you got there, he breathed his last and you were a widow. What do you say?

GRUSHA   I could use an official document for Michael.

LAVRENTI   An official document makes all the difference in the world. Without an official document even the shah of Persia wouldn't dare to call himself the shah. And you'll have a roof over your head.

GRUSHA   What does the woman want for it?

LAVRENTI   Four hundred piasters.

GRUSHA   Where did you get them?

LAVRENTI   (*guiltily*)   Aniko's milk money.

GRUSHA Over there nobody will know us.—All right, I'll do it.

LAVRENTI (*stands up*) I'll let the woman know right away. (*Goes out quickly*)

GRUSHA Michael, you certainly mess things up. I came by you as a pear tree comes by sparrows. And because a Christian bends down and picks up a crust of bread to make sure that nothing is wasted. Michael, I ought to have left in a hurry that Easter Sunday in Nukha. Now I'm the ninny.

THE SINGER

The bridegroom lay on his deathbed when the bride appeared.

The bridegroom's mother was waiting at the door and pressed her to make haste.

The bride brought a child with her, the witness hid it during the wedding.

(*A room divided by a partition: on one side a bed. Under the mosquito netting a very sick man lies motionless. The mother-in-law comes running in on the other side, pulling Grusha by the hand. After them Lavrenti with the child*)

THE MOTHER-IN-LAW Hurry, hurry, or he'll kick in on us before the wedding. (*To Lavrenti*) You didn't tell me she had a child already.

LAVRENTI What difference does it make? (*With a gesture toward the dying man*) It can't matter to him, not in his condition.

MOTHER-IN-LAW Not to him! But I'll never outlive the disgrace. We're honest folk. (*She starts to cry*) My Yussup doesn't have to marry a woman that has a child already.

LAVRENTI All right. I'll throw in another two hundred piasters. You have it in writing that the farm goes to you, but she is entitled to live here for two years.

THE MOTHER-IN-LAW (*drying her tears*) That will hardly cover the funeral expenses. I hope she'll really give me a hand with the work. But where has the monk gone now? He must have crawled out the kitchen window. Now we'll have the whole village on our necks if they hear that Yussup is giving up the ghost. Oh my goodness! I'll go get him, but he mustn't see the child.

LAVRENTI I'll make sure he doesn't see it. But why a monk and not a priest?

THE MOTHER-IN-LAW It's just as good. Except I made the mistake of giving him half his fee before the ceremony, so now he's gone off to the tavern. I only hope . . . (*She runs off*)

LAVRENTI The priest was too expensive for her, the skinflint. She's hired a cheap monk.

GRUSHA Send Simon Chachava over here if he turns up.

LAVRENTI Yes. (*Indicating the sick man*) Don't you want to take a look at him?

(*Grusha, who has picked up Michael, shakes her head*)

LAVRENTI He doesn't even move. I hope we're not too late. (*They listen. On the other side neighbors enter, look around and line up along the walls. They begin to mumble prayers. The mother-in-law comes in with the monk*)

THE MOTHER-IN-LAW (*after a moment's surprise and irritation, to the monk*) There you have it. (*She bows to the guests*) Please be patient just a minute. My son's fiancée has just arrived from the city and there's to be an emergency marriage. (*Goes into the bedroom with the monk*) I knew you'd spread it far and wide. (*To Grusha*) The marriage can take place right away. Here's the contract. Me and the bride's brother . . . (*Lavrenti tries to hide in the background after quickly recovering Michael from Grusha. The mother-in-law waves him away*) Me and the bride's brother are the witnesses.

(*Grusha has bowed to the monk. They go to the bedside. The mother-in-law pushes back the mosquito netting. The monk begins to reel off his lines in Latin. Meanwhile Lavrenti tries to prevent the child from crying by showing him the ceremony and the mother-in-law keeps motioning him to put the child down. Once Grusha looks around toward the child and Lavrenti waves the child's hand at her*)

THE MONK Are you prepared to be a faithful, obedient, and

good wife to this man and to cleave to him until death you do part?

GRUSHA (*looking at the child*)   Yes.

THE MONK (*to the dying man*)   And are you prepared to be a good husband and provider to this woman until death you do part?

(*When the dying man does not answer, the monk repeats his question and looks around*)

THE MOTHER-IN-LAW   Of course he is. Didn't you hear him say yes?

THE MONK   All right, we declare the marriage concluded. But how about extreme unction?

THE MOTHER-IN-LAW   Nothing doing. The marriage cost enough. Now I've got to attend to the mourners. (*To Lavrenti*) Did we say seven hundred?

LAVRENTI   Six hundred. (*He gives her the money*) I won't sit down with the guests. I might make friends with somebody. So good-bye, Grusha, and if my widowed sister comes to see me one of these days, my wife will bid her welcome, or she'll hear from me.

(*He goes. The mourners look after him indifferently as he passes through*)

THE MONK   And may one ask who this child is?

THE MOTHER-IN-LAW   A child? I don't see any child. And you don't see one either. Understand? Or maybe I'll have seen certain goings-on behind the tavern. Come along now.

(*They go into the other room, after Grusha has set the child on the floor and told him to keep quiet. She is introduced to the neighbors*)

THE MOTHER-IN-LAW   This is my daughter-in-law. She was just in time to find our dear Yussup alive.

ONE OF THE WOMEN   He's been lying abed a whole year now, hasn't he? When my Vassili went off to the army, he came to the farewell party.

ANOTHER WOMAN   A thing like this is terrible for a farm, the corn ready to reap and the farmer in bed. A good thing for him if he doesn't have to suffer much longer is what I say.

FIRST WOMAN (*confidentially*)   At first we thought he took to his bed to keep out of the army. And now he's dying!

THE MOTHER-IN-LAW　Do sit down and have a few cakes.

(*The mother-in-law beckons to Grusha and they both go into the bedroom where they take pans of cake from the floor. The guests, including the monk, sit down on the floor and start a muffled conversation*)

A PEASANT (*the monk has taken a bottle from his cassock and passed it to him*)　There's a child, you say? How can that have happened to Yussup?

THIRD WOMAN　She was certainly lucky to swing it, with him so sick.

THE MOTHER-IN-LAW　Now they've started gossiping; and they'll be eating up the funeral cakes and if he doesn't die today, I'll have to bake more tomorrow.

GRUSHA　I'll bake them.

THE MOTHER-IN-LAW　Last night some men rode by and I went out to see who it was. When I came back he was lying there like a corpse. That's why I sent for you. He can't last long now. (*She listens*)

THE MONK　Dear wedding guests and mourners! Deeply moved, we stand before a death bed and a marriage bed, for a woman has been married and a man is soon to be buried. The groom has been washed and the bride is hot. For in the marriage bed there lies a last will, which arouses the lusts of the flesh. Dearly beloved, how various are the paths of humankind! One dies to get a roof over his head, another marries in order that flesh may return to the dust whence it was made. Amen.

THE MOTHER-IN-LAW (*who has listened*)　He's getting even. I shouldn't have taken such a cheap one, he's no better than I paid for. An expensive one behaves. In Sura there's a priest who's even said to be a saint, but naturally he costs a fortune. A fifty-piaster priest like this has no dignity, he's got just enough religion for fifty piasters, no more. When I went to get him out of the tavern, he was making a speech and yelling: "The war is over! Beware of peace!" We'd better go in.

GRUSHA (*gives Michael a cake*)　Here's a cake for you, be nice and quiet, Michael. We're respectable people now. (*They take the cake pans out to the guests. The dying man sits up under the mosquito net, sticks his head out, and looks after the two women. Then he sinks back. The monk has taken two bottles from his cassock and passed them to the peasant who is sitting beside him. Three musicians have entered; the monk grins and waves to them)*

THE MOTHER-IN-LAW (*to the musicians*)   What are you doing here with your instruments?

A MUSICIAN   Brother Anastasius here (*indicating the monk*) said there was a wedding.

THE MOTHER-IN-LAW   What's this? Three more people on my neck? Don't you know there's a dying man in there?

THE MONK   A fascinating problem for a musician. Shall it be a muffled wedding march or a dashing funeral dance?

THE MOTHER-IN-LAW   Play something at least, we know nothing can stop you from eating.

(*The musicians play a mixture of genres. The women pass cakes*)

THE MONK   The trumpet sounds like a whimpering baby, and you, little drum, what is your message to the world?

THE PEASANT (*beside the monk*)   Couldn't the bride give us a little dance?

THE MONK   With a skeleton?

THE PEASANT (*beside the monk, sings*)

Mistress Roundass thought it was time to wed
She took an elderly man to bed
To frolic and to dandle.
Next morning she had changed her mind:
I'd rather have a candle.

(*The mother-in-law throws the drunken man out. The music breaks off. The guests are embarrassed. Pause*)

THE GUESTS (*loudly*)   Did you hear that? The grand duke is back.—But the princes are against him.—Oh, it seems the shah of Persia has lent him a big army to restore order in Gruzinia.—How can that be? The shah of Persia hates the grand duke!—But he also hates disorder.—Anyway the war is over. Our soldiers are coming back. (*Grusha drops the cake pan*)

A WOMAN (*to Grusha*)   Aren't you feeling well? It's the excitement over our dear Yussup. Sit down and rest, my dear.

(*Grusha stands tottering*)

THE GUESTS Now everything will be the same as before.—Except there will be more taxes, because we'll have to pay for the war.

GRUSHA (*feebly*) Did someone say the soldiers are coming home?

A MAN I said so.

GRUSHA That can't be.

THE MAN (*to a woman*) Show her your shawl! We bought it from a soldier. It's from Persia.

GRUSHA (*looks at the shawl*) They're here.

(*A long pause. Grusha kneels down as though to pick up the cakes. She takes the silver cross and chain from her blouse, kisses the cross and begins to pray*)

THE MOTHER-IN-LAW (*seeing that the guests are silently looking at Grusha*) What's got into you? Can't you pay attention to our guests? What do we care about these fool rumors from the city?

THE GUESTS (*loudly resuming their conversation while Grusha kneels with her forehead to the floor*) You can buy Persian saddles from the soldiers, some are exchanging them for crutches.—Only the bigwigs on one side can win a war, the soldiers on both sides lose it.—At least the war's over. It's something if they can't drag you off to the army any more. (*The peasant in the bed has sat up. He is listening*)— What we need is two more weeks of good weather.—Our pear trees are hardly bearing at all this year.

THE MOTHER-IN-LAW (*passing the cake*) Have a little more cake. Help yourselves. There's more.

(*The mother-in-law goes into the bedroom with the empty cake pan. She does not see the sick man. She is bending over a full cake pan on the floor when he begins to speak in a hoarse voice*)

YUSSUP How much more cake are you going to stuff into their bellies? Do you think I shit money? (*The mother-in-law turns abruptly and stares at him aghast. He climbs out from behind the mosquito net*) Did they say the war was over?

THE FIRST WOMAN (*in the other room, amiably to Grusha*) Has the young lady someone in the army?

THE MAN It's good news that they're coming home, isn't it?

YUSSUP Stop goggling. Where is this woman you've saddled me with?

(Receiving no answer, he gets out of bed in his nightgown and staggers past the mother-in-law into the other room. She follows him trembling, with the cake pan)

THE GUESTS *(see him and exclaim)* Jesus, Mary and Joseph! Yussup!

(All spring up in alarm, the women rush toward the door. Grusha, still on her knees, turns her head and stares at Yussup)

YUSSUP A funeral supper. Wouldn't that suit you! Get out before I take a whip to you.

(The guests leave the house in haste)

YUSSUP *(grimly to Grusha)* Upsets your little game, eh?

(She says nothing; he takes a millet cake from the pan the mother-in-law is holding)

THE SINGER

Oh, confusion. The wife discovers she has a husband!
By day she has the child. At night she has the husband.
Day and night her beloved is on his way.
The couple look each other over. The room is small.

(Yussup sits naked in a tall wooden bathtub and the mother-in-law adds water out of a pitcher. In the bedroom Grusha is sitting huddled over with Michael who is playing at mending straw mats)

YUSSUP She should be doing this, not you. Where has she gone now?

THE MOTHER-IN-LAW *(calls)* Grusha! Yussup wants you.

GRUSHA *(to Michael)* Here are two more holes for you to mend.

YUSSUP *(as Grusha enters)* Scrub my back!

GRUSHA Can't the farmer do it himself?

YUSSUP "Can't the farmer do it himself?" Take the brush, damn it! Are you my wife or are you a stranger? *(To the mother-in-law)* Too cold!

THE MOTHER-IN-LAW I'll get some hot water right away.

GRUSHA Let me go.

YUSSUP You stay right here! (*The mother-in-law runs out*)
Rub harder. And don't put on airs like you'd never seen a
naked man before. Who made your kid? The Holy Ghost?

GRUSHA The child wasn't conceived in joy, if that's what the
farmer means.

YUSSUP (*looks around at her and grins*) I wouldn't say that,
to look at you. (*Grusha stops scrubbing him and shrinks
back. The mother-in-law enters*) Nice work. You've married me to a cold fish.

THE MOTHER-IN-LAW She just doesn't try.

YUSSUP Pour, but be careful. Ouch! Careful, I said. (*To
Grusha*) I wouldn't be surprised if you'd got yourself in
trouble in the city. Or what would you be doing here? But
I won't go into that. I haven't said anything about the bastard you've brought into my house, but with you my
patience is running out. It's not natural. (*To the mother-
in-law*) More! (*To Grusha*) Even if your soldier comes
back, remember, you're married.

GRUSHA Yes.

YUSSUP But your soldier won't come back any more, it's no
use thinking he will.

GRUSHA No.

YUSSUP You're cheating me. You're my wife and you're not
my wife. Where you lie, there's nothing, but nobody else
can lie there. When I go out to the fields in the morning,
I'm dead tired; when I lie down at night, I'm as spry as the
devil himself. God made you a woman, and what do you
do? My farm doesn't bring in enough for me to buy a
woman in the city, and besides, there's the trip to think of.
A woman hoes the fields and spreads her legs, that's what
it says in our almanac. Do you hear me?

GRUSHA Yes. (*Softly*) I'm sorry to be cheating you.

YUSSUP She's sorry! More water! (*The mother-in-law pours
more water*) Ouch!

THE SINGER
    As by the brook she sat washing the linen
    She saw his face in the water. And his face grew paler
    With each passing moon.

When she stood up to wring out the linen
She heard his voice from the murmuring maple and his voice
   grew softer
With each passing moon.
Sighs and excuses multiplied, salt tears and sweat were shed.
With each passing moon the child grew up.

(*Grusha is kneeling by a small brook, dipping clothes in the water. A little way off some children are standing. Grusha is talking to Michael*)

GRUSHA You may play with them, Michael, but don't let them order you around because you're the smallest.

(*Michael nods and goes to the other children. They start to play*)

THE BIGGEST BOY Today we're going to play Heads Off. (*To a fat boy*) You're the prince, you're supposed to laugh. (*To Michael*) You're the governor. (*To a little girl*) You're the governor's wife, you're supposed to cry when his head is chopped off. And I'm going to chop his head off. (*He shows his wooden sword*) With this. First the governor is brought into the yard. The prince leads the procession, the governor's wife comes last. (*The procession forms, the fat boy goes first, laughing. Then come Michael and the biggest boy, then the little girl who is crying*)

MICHAEL (*stops still*) Me chop head off too.

THE BIGGEST BOY That's my job. You're the littlest. Governor is easiest. Get down on your knees and let your head be chopped off. It's easy.

MICHAEL Want sword too.

THE BIGGEST BOY It's mine. (*Gives him a kick*)

THE LITTLE GIRL (*calls to Grusha*) He won't play right.

GRUSHA (*laughs*) They say the smallest duckling knows how to swim.

THE BIGGEST BOY You can be the prince if you can laugh.

(*Michael shakes his head*)

THE FAT BOY I laugh best. Let him chop your head off once, then you chop his off and then me.

(*Reluctantly the biggest boy gives Michael the wooden sword and kneels down. The fat boy has sat down, slapping his thighs and laughing loudly. The little girl is wailing. Michael swings the big sword and cuts the other boy's head off; he falls down in the process*)

THE BIGGEST BOY   Ouch! I'll show you the right way.

(*Michael runs off, the children after him. Grusha looks after them laughing. When she turns back, Simon Chachava, in a ragged uniform, is standing on the other side of the brook*)

GRUSHA   Simon!

SIMON   Am I addressing Grusha Vachnadze?

GRUSHA   Simon!

SIMON (*formally*)   God bless the young lady. I hope she is well.

GRUSHA (*stands up happily and bows low*)   God bless you, soldier. And thank heaven you have returned in good health.

SIMON   As the haddock said, they found better fishes, so they didn't eat me.

GRUSHA   Bravery, said the kitchen helper; luck, said the hero.

SIMON   How have things been? Was the winter bearable, were the neighbors kind?

GRUSHA   The winter was rather hard, Simon, and the neighbors as usual.

SIMON   May I ask whether a certain person is still in the habit of putting her legs in the water when she washes clothes?

GRUSHA   The answer is no because of the eyes in the bushes!

SIMON   The young lady is speaking about soldiers. A paymaster is standing before you.

GRUSHA   Doesn't that mean twenty piasters?

SIMON   And lodging.

GRUSHA (*tears coming to her eyes*)   Behind the barracks, under the date palms.

SIMON   Exactly. I see the young lady has taken a look around.

GRUSHA   So she has.

SIMON   And she hasn't forgotten. (*Grusha shakes her head*) Then the door is still on its hinges, as they say? (*Grusha looks at him in silence and shakes her head again*) What do you mean? Is something wrong?

GRUSHA   Simon Chachava, I can never go back to Nukha again. Something has happened.

SIMON   What has happened?

GRUSHA   It has happened that I hit an Ironshirt on the head.

SIMON   Grusha Vachnadze must have had good reason.

GRUSHA   Simon Chachava, my name isn't the same as before.

SIMON   (*after a pause*)   I don't understand.

GRUSHA   When do women change their names, Simon? Let me explain. Nothing has come between us, everything is the same, you've got to believe me.

SIMON   Nothing has come between us, but something has changed?

GRUSHA   How can I explain it so quickly with the brook between us? Can't you take the bridge and come over?

SIMON   Perhaps it's no longer necessary.

GRUSHA   It's very necessary. Come over, Simon. Hurry!

SIMON   Does the young lady mean the soldier has come too late?

(*Grusha looks at him despairingly, her face bathed in tears. Simon stares straight ahead. He has picked up a piece of wood and is whittling*)

THE SINGER

So many words are said, so many words are left unsaid.

The soldier has come. Where he has come from he does not say.

Hear what he thought and did not say:

The battle began at gray of dawn, blood flowed at noon.

The first fell before me, the second fell behind me, the third fell next to me.

On the first I trampled, the second I left behind, the third was run through by the captain.

My first brother perished by iron, my second brother perished by smoke.

They struck flame from my head, my hands were frozen in my gloves, my toes in my stockings.

To eat I had aspen buds, to drink I had maple broth, I slept at night on stones, or in water.

SIMON   I see a cap in the grass. Can there be a child so soon?

GRUSHA   Yes, Simon, there is. How could I hide it? But you mustn't fret, it's not mine.

SIMON   They say: Once the wind starts blowing, it blows through every crack and cranny. The lady need say no more.

(*Grusha bows her head and says nothing*)

THE SINGER

Yearning there was, but no waiting.
Broken the oath. The reason is not reported.
Hear what she thought and did not say:

Soldier, when you were fighting in the battle
The bloody battle, the bitter battle
I found a child who was helpless.
I hadn't the heart to leave it.
I had to care for what would have perished
I had to bend down for bread crumbs on the ground
I had to tear myself to pieces for what was not mine
A stranger.
Someone must help
For a sapling needs water.
The baby calf strays when the cowherd sleeps
And the cry goes unheard!

SIMON   Give me back the cross I gave you. No, throw it in the brook.

(*He turns to go*)

GRUSHA   Simon Chachava, don't go away, it's not mine, it's not mine! (*She hears the children calling*) What is it, children?

VOICES   Soldiers!—They're taking Michael away!

(*Grusha stands horrified. Two Ironshirts come toward her, leading Michael*)

IRONSHIRTS   Are you Grusha? (*She nods*) Is this your child?

GRUSHA   Yes. (*Simon goes away*) Simon!

IRONSHIRTS   We have a court order to take this child, found in your care, to the city. There is reason to believe that it is Michael Abashvili, son of Governor Georgi Abashvili and his wife Natella Abashvili. Here is the order, duly signed and sealed. (*They lead the child away*)

GRUSHA (*runs after them shouting*) Leave him, please, he's mine!

THE SINGER

The Ironshirts took the cherished child away. The unhappy woman followed them to the perilous city.

The mother who had borne him demanded the child's return. His foster-mother appeared in court.

Who will decide the case, to whom will the child be given?

Who will the judge be? A good one? A bad one?

The city was in flames. On the seat of justice sat Azdak.

5

The Story of the Judge

THE SINGER

Hear now the story of the judge:

How he became judge, how he passed judgment, what manner of judge he is.

That Easter Sunday when the great uprising took place and the grand duke was overthrown

And Abashvili, his governor, our child's father, lost his head

Azdak the village scribe found a fugitive in the thicket and hid him in his hut.

(*Ragged and tipsy, Azdak helps a fugitive disguised as a beggar into his hut*)

AZDAK Stop panting. You're not a horse. And running like snot in April won't save you from the police. Stop, I tell you. (*He catches the fugitive, who has kept going as though to run through the opposite wall of the hut*) Sit down and eat, here's a piece of cheese. (*He rummages through a chest full of rags and fishes out a cheese; the fugitive starts eating avidly*) Haven't eaten in some time, huh? (*The fugi-*

tive grumbles) What were you running for, you asshole? The policeman wouldn't even have seen you.

THE FUGITIVE Had to.

AZDAK Shits? (*The fugitive looks at him uncomprehendingly*) Jitters? Scared? Hm. Stop smacking your lips like a grand duke or a pig! I can't stand it. We've got to take blue-blooded stinkers the way God made them. Not you. I once heard of a chief justice who was so independent he farted at dinner. When I watch you eating, horrible thoughts come to me. Why don't you say something? (*Sharply*) Let's see your hand! Can't you hear me? I want to see your hand. (*Hesitantly the fugitive holds out his hand*) White. So you're not a beggar at all. A phony, a walking swindle! And me hiding you like you were a self-respecting citizen. What are you running for if you're a landowner? That's what you are, don't deny it, I can tell by your guilty look! (*Stands up*) Get out! (*The fugitive looks at him uncertainly*) What are you waiting for, you peasant-flogger?

THE FUGITIVE Looking for me. Request undivided attention, have proposition.

AZDAK What's that? A proposition? That's the height of insolence. He wants to make a proposition! The victim scratches till his fingers are bloody, and the leech makes a proposition. Get out, I say!

THE FUGITIVE Understand point of view, convictions. Pay hundred thousand piasters one night. Well?

AZDAK What? You think you can buy me? For a hundred thousand piasters? A rundown estate. Let's say a hundred and fifty thousand. Where are they?

THE FUGITIVE Not on me naturally. Will send. Hope no doubts.

AZDAK Deep doubts. Get out!

(*The fugitive stands up and trots to the door. A voice from outside*)

VOICE Azdak!

(*The fugitive turns around and trots to the opposite corner, where he stops still*)

AZDAK (*shouts*) I'm busy. (*Steps into the doorway*) Are you nosing around again, Shauva?

SHAUVA THE POLICEMAN (*outside, reproachfully*) You've caught another rabbit, Azdak. You promised it wouldn't happen again.

AZDAK (*sternly*) Don't talk about things you don't understand, Shauva. The rabbit is a dangerous and harmful animal that eats plants, especially the varieties known as weeds, and must therefore be exterminated.

SHAUVA Azdak, don't be so mean to me. I'll lose my job if I'm not severe with you. I know you've got a good heart.

AZDAK I haven't got a good heart. How often do I have to tell you I'm an intellectual?

SHAUVA (*slyly*) I know, Azdak. You're a superior man, you say so yourself. All right, I'm only an uneducated Christian and I ask you: If one of the prince's rabbits is stolen and I'm a policeman, what am I to do about the guilty party?

AZDAK Shauva, Shauva, you ought to be ashamed. There you stand asking me a question when a question is the worst of all temptations. Suppose you were a woman, Nunovna, for instance, the wicked slut, and you show me the upper reaches of your leg, Nunovna's I mean, and ask me: What should I do about my leg, it itches—is she innocent, behaving like that? No. I catch rabbits, but you catch men. A man is made in God's image, a rabbit isn't, you know that. I'm a rabbit-eater, but you're a cannibal, Shauva, and God will judge you. Go home, Shauva, and repent. No, wait a minute, maybe I've got something for you. (*He looks around at the fugitive who stands there trembling*) No, never mind. Go home and repent. (*He slams the door in his face. To the fugitive*) You're surprised, aren't you? That I didn't hand you over. But I couldn't even hand a bedbug over to that dumb-ox policeman, it goes against my grain. Never be afraid of a policeman. So old and such a coward. Eat up your cheese like a poor man, or they're sure to catch you. Do I have to show you how a poor man behaves? (*He pushes him down in his chair and puts the piece of cheese back in his hand*) This chest is the table. Put your elbows on the table, surround the cheese on the plate as if it might be snatched away at any moment, can you ever be sure? Hold your knife like a small sickle and don't look at the cheese so greedily, your expression should be more on the sorrowful side, because it's already vanishing, like all beauty. (*Watches him*) They're looking for you, that's in your favor, but how can I know they're not mistaken about you? In Tiflis one time they hanged a landowner, a Turk. He was able to prove that he didn't just cut his peasants in half the usual way, but quartered them. He gouged out twice as much taxes as anybody else, his zeal was above suspicion, but they hanged him as a criminal all the same, just because he was a Turk, which he couldn't help. That was an injustice. He found himself on the gallows the way Pontius Pilate found himself in the Creed. To make a long story short, I don't trust you.

THE SINGER
  And so Azdak lodged the old beggar for the night.
  When he found out that he was the grand duke in person, the butcher
  He was ashamed. He denounced himself, he ordered the policeman
  To take him to Nukha, to court, to be tried.
  (*In the courthouse yard three Ironshirts are sitting drinking. From a column hangs a man in a judge's robe. Enter Azdak bound, dragging Shauva behind him*)
AZDAK (*cries out*) I helped the grand duke, the grand thief, the grand butcher, to escape. In the name of justice I demand a public trial and a severe sentence!
THE FIRST IRONSHIRT Who's this bird?
SHAUVA It's Azdak, our scribe.
AZDAK I'm a contemptible traitor, a marked man! Report, flatfoot, how I insisted on being taken to the capital in chains because I sheltered the grand duke, grand scoundrel, by mistake, which was only made clear to me later by this document that I found in my hut. (*The Ironshirts study the document. To Shauva*) They can't read. See, the marked man denounces himself! Tell them how I made you run with me half the night to clear everything up.
SHAUVA By threatening me. That wasn't nice of you, Azdak.

AZDAK Shut up, Shauva, you don't understand. A new era has dawned, it will rumble over you like thunder, you're through, policemen will be exterminated, pfft. Everything will be investigated, brought to light. A man with any sense will turn himself in, he can't escape from the people. Report how I yelled all the way down Shoemaker Lane. (*He acts it out with sweeping gestures, squinting at the Ironshirts*) "I let the grand scoundrel escape out of ignorance. Tear me to pieces, brothers!" To forestall any questions.

THE FIRST IRONSHIRT And what was their answer?

SHAUVA They comforted him on Butcher Lane and laughed themselves sick on Shoemaker Lane, that's all.

AZDAK But you're different, I know that, you're men of iron. Where's the judge, brothers, I want to be questioned.

THE FIRST IRONSHIRT (*points to the hanged man*) There's the judge. And stop bothering us. We're touchy about that kind of thing right now.

AZDAK "There's the judge." Such an answer has never been heard in Gruzinia. Townspeople, where is his excellency the governor? (*He points to the gallows*) There's his excellency, stranger. Where is the chief tax collector? The chief recruiting officer? The patriarch? The chief of police? Here, here, here, all here. Brothers, that's what I was expecting of you.

THE SECOND IRONSHIRT That's enough! What did you expect, you clown?

AZDAK What happened in Persia, brothers, what happened in Persia?

THE SECOND IRONSHIRT What happened in Persia?

AZDAK Forty years ago. Hanged, the whole lot of them. Viziers, tax collectors. My grandfather, a remarkable man, saw it. Three whole days, all over the country.

THE SECOND IRONSHIRT But who governed if the vizier was hanged?

AZDAK A peasant.

THE SECOND IRONSHIRT And who commanded the army?

AZDAK A soldier, soldier.

THE SECOND IRONSHIRT And who gave them their pay?

AZDAK A dyer, a dyer gave them their pay.

THE SECOND IRONSHIRT   Are you sure it wasn't a carpet weaver?

THE FIRST IRONSHIRT   But why did all that happen, you Persian?

AZDAK   Why it all happened? Do you need a special reason? Why do you scratch yourself, brother? War! Too much war! And no justice! My grandfather brought back a song that tells the way it was. My friend the policeman and I will sing it for you. (*To Shauva*) And keep a good hold on the rope, that goes with it. (*He sings, while Shauva holds the rope*)

Why are our sons not bleeding any more, and our daughters weep no more?
Why is it that only the calves in the slaughterhouse have any blood left?
Why is it that only the willows on Lake Urmi are shedding tears?

The emperor stands in need of a new province, the peasant must hand over his savings.
So that the roof of the world may be conquered, the roofs of all the huts are carted off.
Our men are taken away, scattered to all four winds so that the noble lords at home may feast and revel.
And the soldiers kill one another, the generals salute one another.
They bite the widow's tax farthing to see if it is real.
The lances are broken.
The battle has been lost. But the helmets have been paid for.
Is it so? Is it so?

SHAUVA   Yes, yes, yes, yes, it is so.

AZDAK   Do you want to hear the rest?
(*The first Ironshirt nods*)

THE SECOND IRONSHIRT (*to the policeman*)   Didn't he teach you the song?

SHAUVA   Oh yes, but my voice is no good.

THE SECOND IRONSHIRT No. (*To Azdak*) Go on, go on.

AZDAK The second stanza is about the peace. (*Sings*)
Public offices overcrowded, officials sitting all the way out
  to the street.
Rivers overflow the banks and devastate the fields
Men who can't take their own pants down are ruling
  empires.
They can't count to four but they eat eight courses.
The corn growers look round for buyers, find only starve-
  lings
The weavers go home from their looms in rags.
Is it so? Is it so?
SHAUVA Yes, yes, yes, yes, it is so.

AZDAK
That's why our sons are not bleeding any more, and our
  daughters weep no more
Why only the calves in the slaughterhouse have any blood
  left.
Why it is that only the willows on Lake Urmi are shedding
  tears.

THE FIRST IRONSHIRT (*after a pause*) Are you going to sing
that song here in town?
AZDAK What's wrong with it?
THE FIRST IRONSHIRT Do you see that red glow over there?
(*Azdak looks around. There is a fiery glow in the sky*)
That's out in the slums. When Prince Kazbeki had Governor Abashvili beheaded this morning, our carpet weavers
caught the "Persian disease" too and asked if Prince Kazbeki
didn't eat too many courses. And at noon today they strung
up the city judge. But we took care of them for two
piasters a weaver. See what I mean?
AZDAK (*after a pause*) I see. (*He looks around fearfully,
slinks off to one side and sits down on the ground with his
head in his hands*)
THE FIRST IRONSHIRT (*after all have taken a drink, to the third*)

Now we're going to have a little fun.

(*The first and second Ironshirt go toward Azdak, blocking his retreat*)

SHAUVA   I don't think he's really bad, gentlemen. Steals a few chickens, maybe a rabbit now and then.

THE SECOND IRONSHIRT (*stepping up to Azdak*)   You came here to fish in troubled waters, didn't you?

AZDAK (*looking up at him*)   I don't know why I came here.

THE SECOND IRONSHIRT   Are you the kind that sides with the carpet weavers? (*Azdak shakes his head*) What about that song?

AZDAK   Got it from my grandfather. A stupid, ignorant man.

THE SECOND IRONSHIRT   Right. And what about the dyer that handed out the pay?

AZDAK   That was in Persia.

THE FIRST IRONSHIRT   And what about your denouncing yourself for not hanging the grand duke with your own hands?

AZDAK   Didn't I tell you I let him go?

SHAUVA   I'll vouch for that. He let him go.

(*The Ironshirts drag the screaming Azdak to the gallows. Then they let him go and laugh uproariously. Azdak joins in the laughter and laughs loudest. Then he is untied. All begin to drink. Enter the fat prince with a young man*)

THE FIRST IRONSHIRT (*to Azdak*)   Here comes your new era. (*More laughter*)

THE FAT PRINCE   And what might there be to laugh about, my friends? Permit me to put in a serious word. Yesterday morning the princes of Gruzinia overthrew the grand duke's bellicose government and liquidated his governors. Unfortunately the grand duke himself escaped. In this fateful hour our carpet weavers, those eternal agitators, have had the audacity to revolt and hang the city judge, a man whom everyone loved, our dear Illo Orbeliani. Ts, ts, ts. My friends, what we need in Gruzinia is peace, peace, peace. And justice! Here I've brought you my dear nephew, Bizergan Kazbeki, an able man, to be the new judge. I say: The decision rests with the people.

THE FIRST IRONSHIRT   You mean we're to elect the judge?

THE FAT PRINCE   Exactly. The people will elect an able man.

Talk it over, my friends. (*While the Ironshirts put their heads together*) Don't worry, duckling, the job is yours. And once they nab the grand duke, we can stop sucking up to the rabble.

THE IRONSHIRTS (*among themselves*) They're scared shitless because they haven't caught the grand duke.—We can thank this village scribe for letting him go.—They're not sure of themselves yet, that's why they're saying "my friends" and "the decision rests with the people."—Now he's even talking about justice for Gruzinia.—But fun is fun, and this is going to be fun.—We'll ask the village scribe, he knows all about justice. Hey, stinko . . .

AZDAK Do you mean me?

THE FIRST IRONSHIRT (*continues*) . . . would you want this nephew for a judge?

AZDAK Are you asking me? You're not asking me, are you?

THE SECOND IRONSHIRT Why not? Anything for a laugh.

AZDAK The way I see it, you want to put him to the test. Am I right? Haven't you got some criminal handy, so the candidate can show his ability? One who knows the ropes.

THE THIRD IRONSHIRT Let's see. We've got the governor's bitch's two doctors down in the cellar. Let's take them.

AZDAK No, that's no good. You can't take real criminals when the judge hasn't been confirmed in office. It's all right for him to be a jackass, but he's got to be confirmed in office, or it's an offense against the law, which is a very sensitive organ, something like the spleen, which must never be punched or death sets in. You can hang them both, that won't be an offense against the law, because no judge was present. The law must be administered with perfect gravity, because it's so stupid. For instance if a judge jails a woman for stealing a piece of millet bread for her child, and he hasn't got his robe on or he scratches himself while handing down the sentence, so that more than a third of him is naked, I mean, suppose he has to scratch the upper part of his leg, then his judgment is a scandal and the law has been flouted. A judge's robe and a judge's hat can hand down a better sentence than a man without them. Justice goes up in smoke if you're not very careful. You wouldn't test a jug of wine by giving it to a dog to drink, hell, your wine would be gone.

THE FIRST IRONSHIRT   So what do you suggest, you hair-splitter?

AZDAK   I'll play the defendant for you. I already know who he'll be. (*He whispers something in their ears*)

THE FIRST IRONSHIRT   You?

(*All laugh uproariously*)

THE FAT PRINCE   What have you decided?

THE FIRST IRONSHIRT   We've decided to give it a try. Our good friend here will play the accused, and here's a seat of justice for the candidate.

THE FAT PRINCE   It's unusual, but why not? (*To his nephew*) A mere formality, duckling. What have you learned? Who won the race, the slow runner or the fast one?

THE NEPHEW   The stealthy runner, Uncle Arsen.

(*The nephew sits down on the seat of justice, the fat prince stands behind him. The Ironshirts sit down on the steps. Azdak enters with the unmistakable gait of the grand duke*)

AZDAK   Is there anybody here who knows me? I am the grand duke.

THE FAT PRINCE   What is he?

THE SECOND IRONSHIRT   The grand duke. He really knows him.

THE FAT PRINCE   Good.

THE FIRST IRONSHIRT   Start the trial.

AZDAK   Hear I'm accused inciting war. Ridiculous. Repeat: ridiculous! Sufficient? If not sufficient, brought lawyers, believe five hundred. (*He motions behind him, as though there were many lawyers around him*) Need all available seats for lawyers.

(*The Ironshirts laugh; the fat prince joins in*)

THE NEPHEW (*to the Ironshirts*)   Do you wish me to try the case? I must say it seems rather unusual, in poor taste I mean.

THE FIRST IRONSHIRT   Get started.

THE FAT PRINCE (*smiling*)   Throw the book at him, duckling.

THE NEPHEW   Very well. People of Gruzinia versus grand duke. Accused, what have you to say for yourself?

AZDAK   Plenty. Naturally read war lost. Declared war only on advice patriots like Uncle Kazbeki. Demand Uncle Kazbeki as witness. (*The Ironshirts laugh*)

THE FAT PRINCE   (*good-naturedly to the Ironshirts*)   Quite a character, isn't he?

THE NEPHEW   Motion overruled. Obviously you can't be prosecuted for declaring war, every ruler has to do that now and then, but only for conducting it incompetently.

AZDAK   Nonsense. Didn't conduct it at all. Had it conducted. Had it conducted by princes. Naturally fouled it up.

THE NEPHEW   Do you mean to deny that you were in supreme command?

AZDAK   Certainly not. Always in supreme command. When born, bellowed at nurse. Raised to drop shit in privy. Accustomed to command. Always commanded officials to rob my treasury. Officers flog soldiers, only my command; landowners sleep with peasants' wives only my strict command. Uncle Kazbeki here has big belly only by my command.

THE IRONSHIRTS   (*applauding*)   He's rich. Hurrah for the grand duke!

THE FAT PRINCE   Answer him, duckling! I'm with you.

THE NEPHEW   I will answer him as befits the dignity of the court. Accused, respect the dignity of the court.

AZDAK   Right. Command you proceed with trial.

THE NEPHEW   Not taking commands from you. You claim forced by princes declare war. How then can you claim princes fouled up war?

AZDAK   Not sending enough men, embezzling funds, delivering sick horses, drinking in whorehouse during attack. Move call Uncle Kaz witness.

(*The Ironshirts laugh*)

THE NEPHEW   Do you mean to make the monstrous assertion that the princes of this country did not fight?

AZDAK   No. Princes fought. Fought for war contracts.

THE FAT PRINCE   This is too much. The man talks like a carpet weaver.

AZDAK   Indeed? Only tell truth!

THE FAT PRINCE   Hang him! Hang him!

THE FIRST IRONSHIRT Take it easy. Go on, excellency!

THE NEPHEW Silence! Pronounce sentence: must be hanged. By neck. Lost war. Sentence pronounced. Irrevocable. Take him away.

THE FAT PRINCE (*hysterically*) Take him away! Take him away!

AZDAK Young man, earnestly advise not fall into clipped, military delivery in public. Can't be employed watchdog if howl like wolf. Get me?

THE FAT PRINCE Hang him!

AZDAK If people notice princes talk same as grand duke, they will hang grand duke and princes. Moreover annul sentence. Reason: war lost, but not for princes. Princes won their war. Collected three million eight hundred sixty-three piasters for horses not delivered.

THE FAT PRINCE Hang him!

AZDAK Eight million two hundred forty thousand piasters for army provisions not supplied.

THE FAT PRINCE Hang him!

AZDAK Therefore victorious. War only lost for Gruzinia, not present in this court.

THE FAT PRINCE I think that will do, my friends. (*To Azdak*) You can step down, gallowsbird. (*To the Ironshirts*) My friends, I think you can now confirm the new judge.

THE FIRST IRONSHIRT I guess we can. Bring down the judge's robe. (*One of them climbs on another's back and takes off the hanged man's robe*) And now (*to the nephew*) beat it, so the right ass can sit in the right seat. (*To Azdak*) Step forward, take the seat. (*Azdak hesitates*) Sit down on it, man. (*Azdak is forced onto the seat of justice by the Ironshirts*) The judge was always a blackguard, so now let a blackguard be judge. (*The robe is put on him, a basket is set on his head*) Look at our judge!

THE SINGER

There was civil war, the ruler was insecure.

Azdak was made judge by the Ironshirts.

For two years Azdak was judge.

THE SINGER AND HIS MUSICIANS

When with flame the skies were glowing and with blood the gutters flowing

Bugs and roaches rose from every crack.
Lances were replaced by cleavers, sermons made by unbelievers
And upon the seat of justice sat Azdak.

(*Azdak is sitting on the seat of justice, peeling an apple. Shauva is sweeping the courtroom. On one side an invalid in a wheelchair, a doctor who is the defendant, and a lame man in rags. On the other side a young man accused of blackmail. An Ironshirt bearing the banner of the Ironshirts corps, stands at the door*)

AZDAK   Today, in view of the large number of cases pending, the court will hear two cases at once. Before I begin, a brief announcement: I take. (*He holds out his hand. Only the blackmailer takes out money and gives it to him*) I reserve the right to punish one of the parties here present (*He looks at the invalid*) for contempt of court. (*To the doctor*) You are a doctor, and you (*To the invalid*) are the plaintiff. Is the doctor to blame for your condition?

THE INVALID   He is. I had a stroke on account of him.

AZDAK   That would be professional negligence.

THE INVALID   Worse than negligence. I loaned him money for his studies. He's never repaid a cent, so when I heard he was treating patients for nothing, I had a stroke.

AZDAK   You had every right. (*To the lame man*) And what are you doing here?

THE LAME MAN   I'm the patient, your worship.

AZDAK   I gather he treated your leg?

THE LAME MAN   Not the right one. My rheumatism was in my left leg, he operated on the right leg, that's why I limp.

AZDAK   And he did it for nothing?

THE INVALID   A five-hundred-piaster operation for nothing! Gratis! For a mere thank you. And I staked him to his studies! (*To the doctor*) Did your professors teach you to operate for nothing?

THE DOCTOR   Your worship, it is indeed customary to ask for the fee before operating, because the patient pays more willingly before an operation than afterward. In the present case I believed at the moment of operating that my assistant had already collected my fee. I was mistaken.

THE INVALID He was mistaken! A good doctor doesn't make mistakes! He examines the patient before operating.

AZDAK That is correct. (*To Shauva*) What's the other case, Mr. Public Prosecutor?

SHAUVA (*zealously sweeping*) Blackmail.

THE BLACKMAILER Your worship, I'm innocent. I simply wanted to ask a certain landowner whether he had really raped his niece. He informed me most amiably that he had not; if he gave me money, it was only because my uncle wishes to take music lessons.

AZDAK Aha! (*To the doctor*) Whereas you, doctor, can cite no extenuating circumstance for your offense?

THE DOCTOR The most I can say is that to err is human.

AZDAK Don't you realize that a good doctor must have a sense of financial responsibility? I once heard of a doctor who made a thousand piasters out of a sprained finger by discovering that it had something to do with the circulation, which an incompetent doctor might have overlooked, and another time by careful treatment, he turned a gall bladder into a gold mine. There's no excuse for you, doctor. Uxu, the grain dealer, had his son study medicine to learn business methods, which gives you an idea of the high standards of our medical schools. (*To the blackmailer*) What's this landowner's name?

SHAUVA He doesn't wish to be named.

AZDAK Then I'll hand down the verdicts. The court holds that blackmail has been proved, and you (*to the invalid*) are fined one thousand piasters. If you have another stroke, the doctor is ordered to treat you free of charge and amputate if necessary. (*To the lame man*) You are accorded a bottle of cognac in lieu of damages. (*To the blackmailer*) You will assign half your fee to the public prosecutor inasmuch as the court does not divulge the landowner's name, furthermore you are advised to study medicine because you're cut out for that profession. And you, doctor, for unpardonable professional error, you are acquitted. Next cases!

THE SINGER WITH HIS MUSICIANS
  Every pleasure costs full measure, funds are rarely come by squarely

Justice has no eyes in front or back.
That is why we ask a genius to decide and judge between us
Which is done for half a penny by Azdak.

(From a caravanserai on the Gruzinian military highway comes Azdak, followed by the landlord, the old man with the long beard. Behind them the hired hand and Shauva carry the seat of justice. An Ironshirt takes his stance with the banner of the Ironshirts corps)

ADZAK Put it here. Here at least we get some air and a bit of a breeze from that lemon grove over there. It's a good thing for justice to be conducted in the open. The wind picks up her skirts and you can see what she's got on underneath. Shauva, we've had too much to eat. These inspection trips are strenuous. *(To the landlord)* It's about your daughter-in-law?

THE LANDLORD Your worship, it's about the honor of my family. I wish to make a complaint on behalf of my son who has gone across the mountains on business. Here is the guilty hired hand, and here is my unfortunate daughter-in-law. *(Enter the daughter-in-law, a voluptuous type. She is veiled)*

AZDAK *(sits down)* I take. *(With a sigh the landlord gives him money)* Good. So much for the formalities. A case of rape?

THE LANDLORD Your worship, I caught the fellow in the stable, pushing our Ludovika into the straw.

AZDAK Yes, yes, the stable. Splendid horses. That little bay struck my fancy.

THE LANDLORD Naturally, on behalf of my son, I raked Ludovika over the coals.

AZDAK *(gravely)* I said it struck my fancy.

THE LANDLORD *(coldly)* Really?—Ludovika confessed that the hired man had taken her against her will.

AZDAK Remove your veil, Ludovika. *(She does so)* Ludovika, the court has taken a fancy to you. Tell us what happened.

LUDOVIKA *(who has learned her part by rote)* When I entered the stable to look at the new foal, the hired hand said to me without provocation: "Warm weather we're having," and placed his hand on my left breast. I said to him: "Stop that," but he continued to touch me in an immoral manner, which aroused my anger. Before I could discern his sinful intentions, he had overstepped the bounds. The deed was done when my father-in-law entered and kicked me by mistake.

THE LANDLORD (*explaining*)   On my son's behalf.

AZDAK (*to the hired hand*)   Do you admit that you started it?

HIRED HAND   Yes, sir.

AZDAK   Ludovika, do you like sweets?

LUDOVIKA   Yes, sunflower seeds.

AZDAK   Do you like to sit a long time in the bathtub?

LUDOVIKA   Half an hour or so.

AZDAK   Mr. Public Prosecutor, put your knife on the ground over there. (*Shauva does so*) Ludovika, go pick up the public prosecutor's knife.

(*Swaying her hips, Ludovika goes over to the knife and picks it up*)

AZDAK (*pointing at her*)   Did you see that? The wiggle on her. The guilty party is discovered. Rape is proved. By eating too much, especially sweet things, by prolonged sitting in warm water, by indolence and a soft skin, you have raped that poor man. Do you think you can display a rear end like that in court and get away with it? It's premeditated assault with a dangerous weapon. You are sentenced to assign to the court the little bay that your father-in-law rides on his son's behalf. And now, Ludovika, you will accompany me to the stable, because the court wishes to inspect the scene of the crime.

(*Over the Gruzinian military highway Azdak on his seat of justice is carried from place to place by his Ironshirts. Behind him Shauva carrying the gallows and the hired hand leading the little bay*)

THE SINGER WITH HIS MUSICIANS

Times when master fights with master for the poor are no disaster

Chaos gets the tax collector off their back.

Bearing weights and measures phony, leading someone else's pony

Through the country rode the poor man's judge, Azdak.

And he took away from Croesus and distributed gold pieces
To their rightful owners gave them back.
By a bodyguard protected of the humble and neglected
Rode Gruzinia's good-bad judge, Azdak.

(*The little procession moves off*)

When you go to judge your neighbors leave at home your
 legal papers
Take a good sharp ax and you'll be on the track.
Never mind about God's thunders, axes often will do
 wonders.
Such a wonder worker is the judge Azdak.

(*Azdak's seat of justice is set up in a tavern. Three kulaks
are standing before Azdak, to whom Shauva brings wine.
In the corner stands an old peasant woman. In the open
doorway and outside, the audience of villagers. An Ironshirt
stands at the entrance with the banner of the Ironshirts
corps.*)

AZDAK The public prosecutor has the floor.

SHAUVA It's about a cow. For five weeks the defendant has
 had in her barn a cow belonging to the kulak Suru. She has
 also been found in the possession of a stolen ham, and some
 cows belonging to the kulak Shutev were killed after he had
 asked the defendant to pay the rent on a field.

THE KULAKS It's my ham, your worship.—It's my cow, your
 worship.—It's my field, your worship.

AZDAK What have you to say to all this, little mother?

THE OLD WOMAN Your worship, one night five weeks ago,
 just before morning, somebody knocked on my door, and
 outside there was a man with a beard, holding a cow. "Dear
 lady," he said to me, "I am St. Banditus, the worker of
 miracles, and because your son was killed in the war I'm
 bringing you this cow as a souvenir. Take good care of
 her."

THE KULAKS Irakli, the bandit, your worship.—Her brother-
 in-law, your worship! The cow-thief, the firebug!—He
 should have his head cut off!

(*A woman's scream is heard from outside. The crowd grows uneasy and moves back. Enter Irakli the bandit with an enormous ax*)

THE KULAKS Irakli! (*They cross themselves*)

THE BANDIT A very good evening to you, dear friends! A glass of wine!

AZDAK Public prosecutor, a jug of wine for our guest. Who are you?

THE BANDIT I'm a wandering hermit, your worship, and thank you for the charitable gift. (*He drains the glass that Shauva has brought him*) Another.

AZDAK I'm Azdak. (*He stands up and bows; the bandit bows likewise*) The court bids the visiting hermit welcome. Continue, little mother.

THE OLD WOMAN Your worship, the first night I didn't know St. Banditus could perform miracles; it was only a cow. But a few days later the kulak's hired men came and wanted to take the cow away. Outside my door they turned around and went home without my cow and great big bumps sprouted on their heads. Then I knew St. Banditus had moved their hearts and changed them into kindly men. (*The bandit laughs loudly*)

THE FIRST KULAK I know what changed them.

AZDAK That's fine. You'll tell us later. Continue!

THE OLD WOMAN Your worship, the next to be changed into a good man was the kulak Shutev, a devil as everyone knows. But St. Banditus got him to remit the rent on my little field.

THE SECOND KULAK Because somebody cut my cows' throats in the field.

(*The bandit laughs*)

THE OLD WOMAN (*at a sign from Azdak*) And then one morning the ham came flying through the window. It hit me in the small of my back, I'm still lame, see, your worship. (*She takes a few steps. The bandit laughs*) I ask you, your worship: When did a poor woman ever get a whole ham without a miracle?

(*The bandit begins to sob*)

AZDAK (*coming down from his seat*) Little mother, that

question goes straight to the heart of this court. Kindly be seated. (*Hesitantly the old woman sits down on the judge's chair. Azdak sits on the floor with his glass of wine*)

AZDAK   Little mother, I almost called you Mother Gruzinia, the Sorrowful

The Bereft, whose sons are in the war

Beaten with fists, hopeful

Weeping when she gets a cow.

Surprised when she is not beaten.

Little mother, deign to sit in merciful judgment upon us, the damned.

(*Bellows at the kulaks*) Admit you don't believe in miracles, you godless scum! Each of you is fined five hundred piasters for godlessness. Get out!

(*The kulaks slink out*)

AZDAK   And you, little mother, and you, pious man, share a jug of wine with the public prosecutor and Azdak.

THE SINGER AND HIS MUSICIANS

So he bent the regulations to his own interpretations

And he took the law and stretched it on a rack.

And they found out with a shock, it's men with nothing in their pockets

Who alone are able to corrupt Azdak.

Seven hundred days and twenty, he dealt justice to the gentry

And he dealt them every joker in the pack.

On the woolsack you could find him with the gallows close behind him

Passing judgments worthy of Azdak.

THE SINGER

Then the days of disorder were over, the grand duke returned.

The governor's wife returned, vengeance was taken.

Many died, again the slums were in flames, Azdak was seized with fear.

(*Azdak's seat of justice in the courthouse yard. Azdak is*

*sitting on the ground, mending his shoe and talking with
Shauva. Noise from outside. Behind the wall the fat prince's
head is carried past on a pike)*

AZDAK Shauva, the days of your bondage are numbered, the
minutes for all I know. For a long time now I've led you by
the iron bit of reason till you bled at the mouth, spurred
you on with syllogisms and abused you with logic. You're
weak by nature; if an argument is slyly tossed your way,
you gobble it up, you can't control yourself. It is your nature to lick the hand of a higher being, but there are very
different kinds of higher beings. Now you are going to be
set free, and soon you'll be able to follow your bent, which
is low, and your unerring instinct which teaches you to
plant your heavy boot in human faces. For the days of confusion and disorder are past and it's too soon for the great
day that I find described in the Song of Chaos, which we
shall now sing one last time in memory of those glorious
times. Sit down and don't tangle with the tune. Don't be
afraid, let it be heard, the refrain is loved by all. (*Sings*)

Sister, veil your face, brother, go get your knife, the times
  are out of joint.
The masters are filled with lamentation and the little men
  with joy.
The city says: Let us drive the powerful from our midst.
The offices are invaded, the lists of serfs are destroyed.
The masters are harnessed to the millstones. Those who have
  never seen daylight come out.
The ebony poor-boxes are shattered, the sesnem wood is cut
  up for beds.
Those who had no bread have granaries now, those who
  begged for grain, now distribute grain.

SHAUVA Oh, oh, oh, oh.

AZDAK Where are you, general? Please, please, please make
order.

The son of the respected lord can no longer be known. The
  child of the mistress becomes the son of the slave-girl.
Rich aldermen look for refuge in cold barns, and the pau-

pers who could scarcely find ditches to sleep in loll in soft beds.

The former boatman now owns many ships. When the owner looks for them, they are no longer his.

Five men are sent out by their masters. They say: Go yourselves, we have already arrived.

SHAUVA Oh, oh, oh, oh.

AZDAK Where are you, general? Please, please, please make order!

Yes, that's what our country might have come to if law and order had been neglected any longer. But now the grand duke, whose life I saved like a dumb ox, has returned to the capital and the Persians have lent him an army to restore order with. Already the slums are in flames. Bring me the thick book I always sit on. (*Shauva takes the book from the seat of justice and Azdak opens it*) This is the book of the law, I've always used it, you can testify to that.

SHAUVA Yes, to sit on.

AZDAK Now I'd better look and see what they can pin on me. I've connived with paupers, that will cost me dearly. I've helped poverty up on its rickety legs, they'll hang me for drunkenness; I've looked into rich men's pockets, they'll get me for blasphemy. And there's nowhere I can hide, everybody knows me, because I've helped everybody.

SHAUVA Someone's coming.

AZDAK (*stands up in a fright, then goes trembling to the chair*) Finished! But I won't do anybody the favor of behaving like a great man. I beg you on my knees for mercy, don't go away, I'm drooling at the mouth. I'm afraid of death. (*Enter Natella Abashvili, the governor's wife, with the aide-de-camp and an Ironshirt*)

THE GOVERNOR'S WIFE Who is this fellow, Shalva?

AZDAK A fellow who knows his place, your excellency, and yours to command.

THE AIDE-DE-CAMP Natella Abashvili, the late governor's wife, has just returned. She is looking for her two-year-old son, Michael Abashvili. She has received word that the child was carried off to the mountains by a former servant.

AZDAK   The child will be brought back, your highness. Yours to command.

THE AIDE-DE-CAMP   They say the woman calls the child her own.

AZDAK   She will be beheaded, your highness. Yours to command.

THE AIDE-DE-CAMP   That will be all.

THE GOVERNOR'S WIFE *(on her way out)* I don't like that man.

AZDAK *(follows her to the door, bowing low)* It will all be taken care of, your highness. Yours to command.

those who have more productive ideas are entitled to more.

The Chalk Circle

definition of a mother. —
corollary to land belongs to those who cares for it

THE SINGER

Hear now the story of the lawsuit over Governor Abashvili's child

And how the true mother was identified

By the famous test of the chalk circle.

*(In the yard of the courthouse in Nukha. Ironshirts bring in
Michael, lead him across the courtyard and out behind. An
Ironshirt holds Grusha back in the archway with his pike
until the child has been led away. Then she is admitted.
With her is the woman cook from the former governor's
household. Tumult and fiery glow in the distance)*

GRUSHA   He's a brave boy, he can already wash himself.

THE COOK   You're in luck, it's not a real judge, it's Azdak. He
drinks like a fish and he doesn't know a thing, the biggest
thieves have got off free. He gets everything mixed up and
the rich people never bribe him enough, that makes it better
for our kind of people.

GRUSHA   I need luck today.

THE COOK   Don't say it! *(She crosses herself)* I'd better say
another rosary for the judge to be drunk. *(She moves her
lips in silent prayer while Grusha tries in vain to get a*

glimpse of the child) The only thing I don't understand is why you're so intent on keeping him if he isn't yours. In times like these.

GRUSHA He's mine, I've brought him up.

THE COOK Didn't you ever stop to think what would happen if she came back?

GRUSHA At first I thought I'd give him back, and then I thought she wouldn't come after him any more.

THE COOK And even a borrowed coat keeps a body warm, is that it? (*Grusha nods*) I'll swear to anything you say, because you're a good girl. (*Refreshes her memory*) I was boarding the child for five piasters and then on Easter Sunday evening when the trouble broke out, Grusha came and took him. (*She sees the soldier Chachava approaching*) But you haven't done right by Simon, I've talked with him, he doesn't understand.

GRUSHA (*who doesn't see him*) I can't worry my head about him now if he doesn't understand.

THE COOK He understands that the child isn't yours, but your being married and not free till death you do part is too much for him to understand.

(*Grusha sees Simon and greets him*)

SIMON (*gloomily*) I wish to inform the lady that I am ready to swear. I am the father of the child.

GRUSHA (*softly*) That's all right, Simon.

SIMON At the same time I wish to state that this obligates me in no way. Nor the lady either.

THE COOK You didn't have to say that. You know she's married.

SIMON That's her affair, no need to rub it in.

(*Two Ironshirts come in*)

THE IRONSHIRTS Where's the judge?—Has anyone seen the judge?

GRUSHA (*who has turned away and covered her face*) Stand in front of me. I shouldn't have come to Nukha. If I run into the Ironshirt I hit on the head . . .

ONE OF THE IRONSHIRTS (*who have brought the child steps forward*) The judge isn't here.

(*The two Ironshirts go on looking*)

THE COOK I hope nothing has happened to him. With another

you won't stand any more chance than a snowball in hell.
(*Another Ironshirt enters*)

THE IRONSHIRT (*who has inquired about the judge, reports*)
Nobody there but two old people and a child. The judge
has taken a powder.

THE OTHER IRONSHIRT   Keep looking!
(*The first two Ironshirts go out quickly, the third stops still.
Grusha lets out a scream. The Ironshirt turns around. It is
the corporal, he has a scar across his whole face*)

THE IRONSHIRT IN THE ARCHWAY   What's the matter, Shotta?
Do you know her?

THE CORPORAL (*after staring at her at length*)   No.

THE IRONSHIRT IN THE ARCHWAY   They say she kidnapped the
Abashvili child. If you know anything about it, you can
make a pile of money, Shotta.
(*The corporal goes off cursing*)

THE COOK   Is he the one? (*Grusha nods*) He'll button up if
you ask me. Or he'll have to admit he was after the child.

GRUSHA (*relieved*)   I'd almost forgotten I saved the child from
them . . .
(*The governor's wife comes in with the aide-de-camp and
two lawyers*)

THE GOVERNOR'S WIFE   Thank goodness the populace haven't
come. I can't stand the smell. It gives me migraine.

THE FIRST LAWYER   Please, gracious lady, be careful what you
say until we get another judge.

THE GOVERNOR'S WIFE   I haven't said a thing, Illo Shuboladze.
I love the common people and their simple, straightforward
ways, it's only the smell that gives me migraine.

THE SECOND LAWYER   There won't be much of an audience.
Most of the people have shut themselves up in their houses
on account of the fighting in the slums.

THE GOVERNOR'S WIFE   Is that the creature?

THE FIRST LAWYER   My dear Natella Abashvili, please refrain
from invective until it's definite that the grand duke has
appointed a new judge and we're rid of the present judge
who is just about the lowest individual ever seen in a judge's
robe. Look, things seem to be moving.
(*Ironshirts enter the yard*)

THE COOK The mistress would be tearing your hair out if she didn't know that Azdak is the friend of the poor. One look at a face is enough for him.

(*Two Ironshirts have started fastening a rope to a column. Azdak is brought in in chains. Behind him, also in chains, Shauva. After him come the three kulaks*)

AN IRONSHIRT Thought you'd make a getaway, did you? (*He strikes Azdak*)

A KULAK Take off his robe before you string him up!

(*Ironshirts and kulaks pull the judge's robe off Azdak. His ragged underwear becomes visible. One gives him a push*)

AN IRONSHIRT (*pushing him to another*) Want a lump of justice? Here it is!

(*Amid cries of "You take it!" and "I don't need it!" they push Azdak from one to the other until he collapses. Then he is pulled to his feet and dragged under the noose*)

THE GOVERNOR'S WIFE (*who has been clapping hysterically during the "ball game"*) I disliked that man the moment I laid eyes on him.

AZDAK (*covered with blood, panting*) I can't see. Give me a rag.

THE OTHER IRONSHIRT What do you want to see?

AZDAK You, you dogs. (*He wipes the blood from his eyes with his shirt sleeve*) Greetings, dogs! How are you, dogs? How's the dog pack, stinking nicely? Licking the old boot again? Back at each other's throats, dogs? (*A dust-covered rider has entered with the corporal. He has taken papers from a leather pouch and looked through them. Now he intervenes*)

THE DUST-COVERED RIDER Stop! Here's the grand duke's decree concerning the new appointments.

THE CORPORAL (*roaring*) Attention! (*All come to attention*)

THE DUST-COVERED RIDER Here's what it says about the new judge: We hereby appoint a man who distinguished himself by saving a life that is of the utmost importance to our country—a certain Azdak of Nukha. Who's he?

SHAUVA (*pointing to Azdak*) The one under the gallows, your excellency.

THE CORPORAL (*bellowing*) What's going on here?

THE IRONSHIRT Beg leave to report that his worship was already his worship and was denounced by these kulaks as an enemy of the grand duke.

THE CORPORAL (*indicating the kulaks*) Take them away! (*They are led off, bowing without interruption*) See to it that his worship suffers no further annoyance. (*Goes out with the dust-covered rider*)

THE COOK (*to Shauva*) She clapped before. I hope he saw her.

THE FIRST LAWYER This is disastrous.

(*Azdak has fainted. He is brought down, revives, and is again clothed in the robe of justice. He staggers out of the group of Ironshirts*)

THE IRONSHIRTS No offense, your worship!—What does your worship wish?

AZDAK Nothing, fellow dogs. An occasional boot to lick. (*To Shauva*) You're pardoned. (*He is unbound*) Get me some red wine, sweet. (*Shauva goes out*) Beat it, I've got a case to try. (*The Ironshirts go off. Shauva comes back with a jug of wine. Azdak drinks copiously*) Something for my ass! (*Shauva brings the law book and puts it on the seat of justice. Azdak sits down*) I take!

(*The plaintiffs who have been holding a worried conference smile with relief. They whisper among themselves*)

THE COOK Oh dear!

SIMON They say "You can't fill a well with dew."

THE LAWYERS (*approach Azdak, who looks up expectantly*) A perfectly ridiculous case, your worship.—The defendant has abducted the child and refuses to return it.

AZDAK (*holds out his open hand, looking at Grusha*) A very attractive young lady. (*They give him more*) I open the proceedings and demand the strict truth. (*To Grusha*) Especially from you.

THE FIRST LAWYER High court of justice! As the people say, "Blood is thicker than water." This venerable wisdom . . .

AZDAK The court wishes to know what counsel's fee is.

THE FIRST LAWYER (*astonished*) I beg your pardon? (*Azdak amiably rubs his thumb and forefinger together*) Oh! Five hundred piasters, your worship, to answer the high court's unusual question.

AZDAK   Did you hear that? The question is unusual. I ask you because I listen with a very different ear if I know you're good.

THE FIRST LAWYER (*bows*)   Thank you, your worship. High court of justice! Of all human ties the ties of blood are the strongest. Mother and child: can there be any closer relationship? May a child be taken from its mother? High court of justice! She conceived it in the sacred ecstasies of love, she carried it in her womb, fed it with her blood, bore it in pain. High court of justice! It is common knowledge that even the ferocious tigress, robbed of her cubs, goes ranging through the mountains without rest, shrunk to a shadow. Nature itself . . .

AZDAK (*interrupting, to Grusha*)   What's your answer to that and all the rest of what counsel is going to say?

GRUSHA   It's mine.

AZDAK   Is that all? I hope you can prove it. In any case, I suggest that you tell me why you think I should award you the child.

GRUSHA   I brought him up the best I knew how, I always found him something to eat. He had a roof over his head most of the time, I let myself in for all kinds of trouble for his sake, and expenses too. I didn't worry about my own convenience. I taught the child to be friendly to everyone and right from the start to work as best he could, he's still so little.

THE FIRST LAWYER   Your worship, it is significant that the defendant herself alleges no blood tie between the child and herself.

AZDAK   The court takes note.

THE FIRST LAWYER   Thank you, your worship. Permit a sorely bereaved woman, who has lost her husband and must now fear to lose her child, to address a few words to you. Gracious Natella Abashvili . . .

THE GOVERNOR'S WIFE (*softly*)   A cruel fate, sir, compels me to plead with you to return my beloved child. It is not for me to describe the torments of a bereaved mother, the sleepless nights, the . . .

THE SECOND LAWYER (*erupting*)   It is unspeakable how this

woman has been treated. She is barred from entering her husband's palace, the income from his estates is withheld from her. Without an iota of feeling they tell her the income is entailed to the legal heir, she can't do a thing without the child, she can't pay her lawyers! (*To the first lawyer who, in despair over this outburst, is motioning him frantically to keep quiet*) My dear Illo Shuboladze, why should it not be made known that the Abashvili estates are at stake?

THE FIRST LAWYER　Honored Sandro Oboladze, please! We agreed we . . . (*To Azdak*) It is true, of course, that the outcome of this trial will also determine whether our noble client obtains possession of the sizable Abashvili estates; "also," I say, and by design, for the paramount consideration, as Natella Abashvili justly pointed out in the first words of her moving plea, is the tragedy of a mother. Even if Michael Abashvili were not heir to the estates, he would still be my client's dearly beloved child.

AZDAK　Enough! The court looks upon your mention of the estates as proof that we're all human.

THE SECOND LAWYER　Thank you, your worship. My dear Illo Shuboladze, we can prove in any event that the woman who seized the child is not the child's mother! Allow me to set the hard facts before the court. By an unfortunate concatenation of circumstances, this child, Michael Abashvili, was left behind when his mother fled the city. Grusha, a kitchen maid in the palace, was present that Easter Sunday and was seen busying herself with the child . . .

THE COOK　While the lady was busy worrying which dresses to take with her!

THE SECOND LAWYER (*impassive*)　Almost a year later Grusha appeared with the child in a mountain village and concluded a marriage with . . .

AZDAK　How did you get to this mountain village?

GRUSHA　On my feet, your worship, and he was mine.

SIMON　I am the father, your worship.

THE COOK　He was boarding with me, your worship, for five piasters.

THE SECOND LAWYER　This man is Grusha's betrothed, your worship, his testimony is therefore untrustworthy.

AZDAK Are you the man she married in the mountain village?

SIMON No, your worship. She married a peasant.

AZDAK (*motions Grusha over to him*) Why? (*Indicating Simon*) No good in bed? I want the truth.

GRUSHA We didn't get that far. I married on account of the child. To give him a roof over his head. (*Indicating Simon*) He was in the war, your worship.

AZDAK And now he wants to get back with you, is that it?

SIMON I wish to state . . .

GRUSHA (*angrily*) I'm no longer free, your worship.

AZDAK And the child, you claim, comes from whoring? (*When Grusha does not answer*) Let me ask you one question: What kind of a child is it? A ragged little bastard off the streets or the child of a noble, well-to-do family?

GRUSHA (*angrily*) An ordinary child.

AZDAK I mean: did he show refined features at an early age?

GRUSHA He showed a nose in his face.

AZDAK He showed a nose in his face. I regard that as a significant answer. There's a story they tell about me; it seems that once before pronouncing a verdict I went out and sniffed at a rosebush. Little tricks like that are necessary nowadays. Now I'm going to make it short, I'm not going to listen to any more of you people's lies—(*to Grusha*) especially yours. I can imagine how you (*to the group around the defendant*) cooked this all up to pull the wool over my eyes. I know you, you're crooks.

GRUSHA (*suddenly*) I can imagine you'd want to make it short, I saw what you took.

AZDAK Shut up! Did I take anything from you?

GRUSHA (*in spite of the cook who is trying to restrain her*) Because I haven't got anything.

AZDAK Perfectly right. I don't get a thing from you down-and-outers, I could starve. You want justice, but you don't want to pay. When you go to the butcher's, you know you'll have to pay, but you go to the judge like you'd go to a wake.

SIMON (*in a loud voice*) "When the horse was to be shod, the horse fly held out his legs." As the saying goes.

AZDAK (*takes up the challenge with enthusiasm*) "Better a

treasure from the manure pile than a pebble from a mountain spring."

SIMON   "A fine day, let's go fishing, said the angler to the worm."

AZDAK   "I'm my own master, said the hired man and cut off his foot."

SIMON   "I love you like a father, said the tsar to the peasants and chopped the tsarevitch's head off."

AZDAK   "A fool's worst enemy is himself."

SIMON   But "a fart has no nose!"

AZDAK   You're fined ten piasters for indecent language in court, that'll teach you what justice is.

GRUSHA   Some justice! You throw the book at us because we don't talk refined like her with her lawyers.

AZDAK   Right. You're too dumb. You deserve to be sat on.

GRUSHA   Because you want to hand the child over to that woman who's so refined she wouldn't know how to change its diapers! You don't know any more about justice than I do, put that in your pipe!

AZDAK   You've got something there. I'm ignorant, the pants under my robe are full of holes, see for yourself. With me it all goes into eating and drinking, I was raised in a monastery. Come to think of it, I'm fining you ten piasters too, for contempt of court. What's more, you're stupid, antagonizing me instead of making eyes at me and wiggling your ass a little to put me in a good humor. Twenty piasters.

GRUSHA   You can make it thirty and I'll still tell you what I think of your justice, you drunken turnip. How dare you talk to me like the cracked Isaiah on the church window—big shot! When they pulled you out of your mother, they didn't expect you to rap her knuckles if she stole a cup of millet some place, and aren't you ashamed of yourself to see me trembling like this on account of you? You serve these people so their houses won't be taken away—because they stole them; since when do houses belong to bedbugs? But you take care of them, or they couldn't drag our men off to their wars, you flunky!

(Azdak has stood up. He is beaming. Halfheartedly he strikes the table with his little gavel as though to obtain

order, but when Grusha goes on reviling him, he merely beats time for her)

GRUSHA I have no respect for you. No more than I have for a thief and murderer with a knife, he does what he pleases. It's a hundred to one you can take the child away from me, but I'll tell you one thing: for a job like yours they should only pick rapists and usurers, to punish them by making them sit in judgment over their fellow men, which is worse than hanging on the gallows.

AZDAK That makes it thirty, and I'm not going to wrangle with you any more, this isn't a tavern. I'm a judge and I've got my dignity to think of. To tell you the truth, I've lost interest in your case. Where are those two who wanted a divorce? *(To Shauva)* Bring them in. I'm adjourning this case for fifteen minutes.

THE FIRST LAWYER *(as Shauva leaves)* We can rest our case, gracious lady, it's in the bag.

THE COOK *(to Grusha)* You've rubbed him the wrong way. Now he'll take the child away from you.

(Enter a very aged couple)

THE GOVERNOR'S WIFE Shalva, my smelling salts.

AZDAK I take. *(The old people do not understand)* I hear you want a divorce. How long have you been together?

THE OLD MAN Forty years, your worship.

AZDAK Why do you want a divorce?

THE OLD MAN We don't like each other, your worship.

AZDAK Since when?

THE OLD WOMAN The whole time, your worship.

AZDAK I will take your request under deliberation and give you my decision when I'm through with the other case. *(Shauva leads them to the rear)* I need the child. *(Motions Grusha to come over to him and bends down to her in a not unfriendly manner)* Woman, I've seen you have a soft spot for justice. I don't believe he's your child, but supposing he were, wouldn't you want him to be rich? You'd only have to say he's not yours. One two three he'd have a palace, and plenty of horses in his stable and plenty of beggars on his doorstep, plenty of soldiers in his service and plenty of petitioners in his courtyard. See? What's your answer to that? Don't you want him to be rich? (*Grusha is silent*)

THE SINGER   Hear now what the angry woman thought and did not say: (*Sings*)

If he walked in golden shoes
Cold his heart would be and stony.
Humble folk he would abuse
He wouldn't know me.

Oh, it's hard to be hard-hearted
All day long from morn to night.
To be mean and high and mighty
Is a hard and cruel plight.

Let him be afraid of hunger
Not of the hungry man's spite
Let him be afraid of darkness
But not fear the light.

AZDAK   Woman, I think I understand you.

GRUSHA   I won't give him up. I've raised him and he knows me.

(*Shauva brings the child in*)

THE GOVERNOR'S WIFE   He's in rags!

GRUSHA   That's not true. They didn't give me time to put on his good shirt.

THE GOVERNOR'S WIFE   He's been in a pigsty!

GRUSHA (*furious*)   I'm not a pig but I know someone who is. Where did you leave your child?

THE GOVERNOR'S WIFE   I'll show you, you vulgar slut. (*She is about to fling herself on Grusha but is restrained by the lawyers*) She's a criminal! She ought to be flogged! This minute!

THE SECOND LAWYER (*stops her mouth*)   Gracious Natella Abashvili! You promised . . . Your worship, the plaintiff's nerves . . .

AZDAK   Plaintiff and defendant: the court has heard your case, but has not yet ascertained who this child's real mother is. It is my duty as judge to pick a mother for the child. I'm going to give you a test. Shauva, take a piece of chalk. Draw a circle on the floor. (*Shauva draws a chalk circle on the floor*) Put the child in the circle! (*Shauva places Michael, who is smiling at Grusha, in the circle*) Plaintiff and defendant, stand just outside the circle, both of you! (*The governor's wife and Grusha step close to the circle*) Each of you take the child by one hand. The true mother will have the strength to pull the child out of the circle.

THE SECOND LAWYER (*quickly*)   High court of justice, I object to making the fate of the large Abashvili estates, which are entailed to the child as heir, hinge on the outcome of so dubious a contest. Furthermore, my client is not as strong as this person who is accustomed to physical labor.

AZDAK   She looks well fed to me. Pull!

(*The governor's wife pulls the child out of the circle. Grusha has let go, she stands aghast*)

THE FIRST LAWYER (*congratulates the governor's wife*)   What did I say? The ties of blood.

AZDAK (*to Grusha*)   What's the matter with you? You didn't pull.

GRUSHA   I didn't hold on to him. (*She runs to Azdak*) Your worship, I take back what I said against you, I beg your forgiveness. If only I could keep him until he knows all his words. He knows just a few.

AZDAK   Don't try to influence the court! I bet you don't know more than twenty yourself. All right, I'll repeat the test to make sure.

(*Again the two women take their places*)

AZDAK   Pull!

(*Again Grusha lets the child go*)

GRUSHA   I raised him! Do you want me to tear him to pieces? I can't.

AZDAK (*stands up*)   The court has now ascertained who the true mother is. (*To Grusha*) Take your child and clear out. I advise you not to stay in the city with him. (*To the governor's wife*) And you get out of here before I convict you of fraud. The estates devolve to the city, they will be turned into a park for the children, they need it, and the park shall be named "Azdak Park" after me.

(*The governor's wife has fainted and is led away by the aide-de-camp; the lawyers have already gone*)

(*Grusha stands motionless. Shauva brings her the child*)

AZDAK Because I'm taking off the robe of justice, it's got too hot for me. I'm nobody's hero. But I invite you all to a little farewell dance out there in the meadow. Oh, I almost forgot something, too much wine. The divorce. (*Using the seat of justice as a table, he writes something on a piece of paper and starts to leave*)

(*The dance music has started up*)

SHAUVA (*has read the paper*) But this is all wrong. You haven't divorced the two old people, you've divorced Grusha from her husband.

AZDAK Divorced the wrong people? That's too bad, but it sticks, I retract nothing, the law's the law. (*To the very old couple*) I invite you to my celebration instead, I'll bet you still like each other enough to dance together. (*To Grusha and Simon*) And from you two I want forty piasters.

SIMON (*takes out his purse*) Fair enough, your worship. And many thanks.

AZDAK (*putting the money away*) I'm going to need it.

GRUSHA We'd better leave the city tonight, hadn't we, Michael? (*Starts to lift the child on her back. To Simon*) Do you like him?

SIMON (*lifts the child on his back*) Beg to report: I like him.

GRUSHA Now I can tell you: I took him because I betrothed myself to you that Easter Sunday. So it's a child of love. Michael, let's dance.

(*She dances with Michael. Simon dances with the cook. The old couple dance too. Azdak stands in thought. Soon the dancing couples hide him. He is seen from time to time, more and more seldom as more couples come in and dance*)

THE SINGER

And that night Azdak disappeared and was never seen again.

But the people of Gruzinia did not forget him, they long remembered

The days of his judging as a brief

Golden Age when there was almost justice.
(*The dancers dance off the stage. Azdak has vanished*)

And you who have heard the story of the chalk circle
Bear in mind the wisdom of our fathers:
Things should belong to those who do well by them
Children to motherly women that they may thrive
Wagons to good drivers that they may be well driven
And the valley to those who water it, that it may bear fruit.

Notes and Variants

THE VISIONS OF
SIMONE MACHARD

Texts by Brecht

The Visions of Simone Machard

Little Simone Machard works for the hostelry at a small town called Saint-Martin in central France. She is there to help out, primarily in connection with the hotel gas pump; the hotel also runs a trucking business. It is June 1940; the Nazis have taken Paris; streams of refugees are pouring across central France and passing through Saint-Martin.

Simone's seventeen-year-old brother is at the front; she loves him dearly and is sure that he is involved in the fighting. Meanwhile in the village and in the hotel she finds that at this point, in the middle of a great national disaster, high and low alike can think of nothing but themselves. It is now that she reads a book given her by her teacher, which contains the story of the Maid of Orleans, greatest of all French patriots.

During those feverish nights, with the Germans already at the Loire, she is moved by the course of events to dream that she is herself Saint Joan. An angel appears to her from the garage roof and tells her that she has been chosen to save France. He has the features of her soldier brother André. In her dream the legend of the book mingles with the reality of the little hotel. The hotel's owner is suddenly a constable of the royal court; the hotel staff, the truck drivers, and the old night porter, wear armor and form a little unit of feudal soldiery who escort her to the king; while in the king himself she recognizes the spineless local mayor.

Thereafter Simone at the hostelry undergoes a miniature

version of the terrible and uplifting fate of Joan of Arc, and again and again in her dreams she turns into the saint.

She dreams that the angel gives her an invisible drum. He tells her that this drum is the soil of France, and that in an emergency the soil of France—her drum—will resound, summoning the people to resist France's enemies. In her role as a great popular leader she then in her dream goes to the king, holds confidential talks with the king-mayor and warns him not to spend his time playing cards with his nobles, the owner-constable and the other luminaries of Saint-Martin, but instead to attend to the arming and feeding of the people. The people, for their part, are called on to fight wholeheartedly. In this way she manages to unite king, people, and nobles and to crown the king-mayor in Rheims.

In the real world of the hotel, when its owner and his drivers simply wish to run away from the Germans, she fetches the mayor and has the hotel forced to hand over its stocks of food to the municipality rather than remove them to the rear, while the drivers and their trucks are made to evacuate the refugees who are blocking the French army from using the roads. (The owner allows the child to have her way because at least this stops his hostelry from being looted, and the drivers help her because they sympathize with her anxiety for her brother at the front.)

But when she calls for the hostelry's secret stocks of gasoline to be destroyed to prevent them from falling into enemy hands she is going too far, and the owner's mother dismisses her.

That night she dreams the chapter in her book in which the Maid, following her initial victories, encounters the first problems in her own ranks. Although Paris is still in enemy hands she is not given command of a fresh army. The king-mayor and the owner-constable ennoble her, admittedly, but they take away her sword. Once more the angel appears on the garage roof and she has to tell him that she has been dismissed. Severely the angel recommends her to stick to her course and not, for instance, to let the gas fall into the hands of the Germans, or else their murderous tanks will be able to keep on thrusting ahead.

A few days later the Germans enter Saint-Martin. The

owner has fled. His mother and old Captain Beleire, a Laval supporter and vineyard owner, wish to come to terms with the victorious Germans at any price. To prove that they mean to collaborate they tell the German commandant that the gasoline is hidden in the brickyard. But the brickyard is already ablaze when the Germans get there. Simone has set fire to it. This act of sabotage threatens the new and promising Franco-German collaboration. Wanted: the incendiary.

In a disturbing dream Simone once again encounters the heroic Joan of the legend, now deserted by her own side, because the queen mother Isabeau and the duke of Burgundy have asserted themselves at court and are trying to arrange an armistice with the enemy. The queen mother looks just like the mother of the owner, while the duke of Burgundy is like the constable. Only Simone, now wide awake, cannot believe this dream. And when on the owner's return he feels sorry for her, and he and the drivers want to take her away, she insists on staying. How is her brother to find her if and when he returns? So she is denounced to the Germans and arrested.

In a final vision Simone dreams that she, Joan, has been taken captive and handed over by the enemy to an ecclesiastical court which has to decide whether the voices which she heard summoning her to resist the enemy came in fact from God or from the devil. She is tragically shocked to find that the noble judges who condemn her to the stake for having spoken with the devil's voice are all people whom she knows: the mayor, the captain, the owner, with the owner's mother putting the case for the prosecution.

Simone dreams this last dream in prison, and the following morning the Germans hand her back to the French. Her friends among the hotel staff are hopeful for her. They feel that a French official inquiry into the fire must be bound to admit the patriotic nature of her motives. But there are good reasons why the German attitude should be so generous. The Germans think it undesirable that there should have been an act of sabotage which might serve as a precedent for others. And shooting a child would jeopardize the collaboration they so badly need. So they have agreed with their French friends that the case should be sidetracked.

Simone has to hear the owner and his mother, her employers, giving evidence against her, while the mayor leaves her to her fate. Numb with shock, she learns that a French court finds that her action was not undertaken for patriotic reasons, but that she caused the fire for purely personal motives, as a mischievous act of revenge for her dismissal. She is sent to a home for delinquent children.

The people, however, are not fooled. When the owner returns to the hostelry he finds that his staff have left. And as Simone is being led away after the verdict Saint-Martin is shaken by a bombing attack. English planes are carrying on the struggle.

For Simone these explosions have a special meaning. Did her dream angel not tell her that the soil of France was her invisible drum, whose sound would bring the sons of France hurrying to defend it? And here is French soil reverberating. It is the angel, her brother André, who has sent her the planes.

N.B. Interwoven with the play is the delicate story of little Simone's relations with a wounded soldier, one of her brother's friends.

> [GW *Schriften zum Theater* 3, pp. 1181–85. This plan for the play, which may have been conceived as a film treatment, differs from our text, particularly in its ending, which is unlike that in any other version. Nowhere else is the captain specifically described as being old, while the identification of the drum with the soil of France is also unusually clearly made. Note that there is no mention of the refugees in the schoolhouse.]

Working Plan

1. *the germans invade france. at the hostelry "au relais" it is business as usual, but simone machard is reading a book of legends.*

    (a)   two drivers see bombs, an old man mends tires, a soldier licks his wounds, a child reads a book.

    (b)   the colonel does not wish to be greeted.

(c) conversation about the treachery of the top people, about visions, hordes of refugees, headaches, teachers and wine.

(d) soldiers get their stew pot half-filled with lentils. simone's brother is unknown.

(e) the owner defends his stocks and tells simone to give the colonel his bill.

(f) the hotel has a star, the staff remain cool.

(g) the mayor is bawled out by the colonel because the roads are blocked.

(h) the mayor wants trucks for the refugees, the owner has no gasoline, the staff confirm it, the captain needs the trucks for his wine barrels, the war is lost.

(i) only a miracle can save france, in the mayor's view; the staff say "simone thinks one will take place."

2. *joan of arc, summoned by divine voices, crowns the king in rheims and unites all frenchmen against the hereditary foe.*

(a) the angel calls joan and gives her the task.

(b) she gets helmet and bayonet.

(c) the ajaxes escort her, and battles are won.

(d) she recognizes the king.

(e) her argument with the king.

(f) she crowns him.

3. *simone gets a hearing for the mayor, and the hotel is saved.*

(a) the germans have crossed the loire, the staff has breakfast, the owner has certain wishes, the staff has breakfast, simone disappears.

(b) the owner is horrified to find that he is not liked. simone is looked for by her parents.

(c) the mayor arrives with soldiers, having been fetched by simone. the trucks are requisitioned but the mayor weakens.

(d) simone supports him and arranges everything, aided by madame mère. the soldiers are given wine, and leave for the front. the village is given the food stocks, and simone's parents are the first.

(e) the wave of patriotism infects the owner. handshake and toast. the gasoline must be saved, as simone said.

(f)   the owner has departed. madame mère fires simone. the mayor admires the tip.

4. *joan, rewarded by the court but dismissed in her native village, is encouraged by her voices to continue the struggle.*
   (a)   although the enemy is still in her country, joan can get no more troops.
   (b)   instead she is thanked for her services. she is knighted with her own sword.
   (c)   but her sword is not returned to her; the king gives it to the constable as a mark of gratitude.
   (d)   the angel appears and tells her to carry on the struggle.

5. *the germans occupy the village. simone sets fire to the gasoline.*
   (a)   madame mère receives the german commandant. "he's human like the rest of us."
   (b)   the captain harangues the staff. in future discipline will prevail.
   (c)   simone hears the captain warning the mayor not to conceal the existence of the gas in the brickyard.
   (d)   simone tells the mayor of her plan to set fire to the brickyard. he seems to approve.
   (e)   the opponents also get on at a low level. the commandant's batman talks with the wounded soldier.
   (f)   the gentry enter the yard to inspect the brickyard. a good understanding prevails.
   (g)   the brickyard is ablaze.

6. *simone is surrendered by the top people.*
   (a)   simone's parents come to thank her: as a result of her generous action her father has got the beadle's job.
   (b)   the owner returns. he is embarrassed by the parents' tributes: "your hotel is france in miniature." père gustave accompanies him inside.

daydream
   (a)   the maid's messenger is kept from the king. why?
   (b)   because the english are within. and what is being talked about?

(c) the maid. and what else?

(d) the fact that she is to blame for the war.

(e) so she isn't relieved, but her troops are thrown in again and so she is captured.

(f) but the angel appears once more and assures her that everything she did was right, and warns her to stick to her mission.

6. *simone is surrendered by the top people*, continued.

(c) the drivers urge simone to flee. she stands by her faith in the owner.

(d) then the owner comes out too and urges her to flee.

(e) simone is seized by panic, and does flee.

(f) the german commandant and the french gentry enter the courtyard and a search is made for simone. she is not there. the commandant is angry and goes back indoors.

(g) sigh of relief from the gentry. simone is standing in the courtyard. she has come back. they implore her. she refuses to flee. the commandant arrives. simone: it's me.

7. *the english hand joan over to an ecclesiastical court consisting of frenchmen, which interrogates her about the angel.*

(a) the english bring joan before the ecclesiastical court. they ask for a report as to whether the voices come from god or from the devil.

(b) the constable, the burgundian, and the renegade colonel don their ecclesiastical robes.

(c) the ecclesiastical court discusses the voices' origin with joan and finds them devilish.

8. *trial of simone machard by the authorities of her village. she is found not guilty of the crime of sabotage but is sent to the pious sisters' corrective institution on the grounds of incendiarism and vindictiveness.*

(a) the germans hand simone back.

(b) the commission goes out of its way to whitewash her of any accusation of sabotaging the germans.

(c) the staff welcome this attitude on the court's part and hope for her release.

(d) the remainder of the interrogation is devoted to

simone's attitude to her employers, particularly on the day of the great panic.

(e)   questioned about her motives for incendiarism she continues to insist that she did it for france's sake.

(f)   she is forced however to admit that she really wanted to save the gasoline from its owners.

(g)   she is therefore handed over to the pious sisters of sainte-madeleine for correction.

(h)   while she says good-bye in the yard to the staff and to her parents the commission goes off to report to the german commandant.

> [BBA 1204/1–3. This is one of the most elaborately worked-out of all Brecht's characteristic structural plans. It is mounted on a card, with scenes 1 to 8 (and their sub-headings) forming eight parallel columns. There are penciled figures by Brecht giving (apparently) the estimated duration of each subscene, and it seems altogether probable that the collaborators used it as a basis for their first script.]

The Dreams

The dreams in which Simone relives the St. Joan legend can be made intelligible to audiences unaware of the legend by the large-scale projection of individual pages from the book, possibly including woodcut illustrations.

For the *first dream:* "Summoned by an angel to save France, Joan unites the French by crowning Charles VII king in the city of Rheims."

For the *second dream:* "Following some brilliant victories, Joan is ennobled. However, she has powerful enemies at court who would like to see an armistice."

For the *third dream:* "Betrayed into enemy hands, Joan is handed over to an ecclesiastical court which condemns her to death."

> [GW *Schriften zum Theater* 3, p. 1185. These captions can be compared with those in the plans quoted in the

editorial note, below. Illustrations reproduced from old illuminated manuscripts are gummed into one or two of Brecht's typescripts of the play.]

First Dream of Simone Machard (during the night of June 14)

I was addressed from the garage roof in a loud voice as "Joan!", went immediately out into the yard and saw *the angel* on the roof of the garage. He waved to me in friendly fashion and told me that I had been called to defeat France's enemies. He ordered me to go straightway to Châlons and crown the king, as I had read in the book. After the angel had disappeared once more the soldier came out of the garage towards me and handed me sword and helmet. The former looked like a bayonet. I asked whether I should clean it for him but he answered that it was against the enemies of France. Thereupon I felt as if I were standing in green countryside. A strong wind was blowing and the sky was like it is between four and five in the morning when you go to mass. Then I saw how the earth, together with all the meadows and poplars upon it, curved as if it were a ball, and how the enemy loomed up in a mighty procession without end. In front rode the drummer with a voice like a wolf and his drum was made of a Jew's skin; a vulture perched on his shoulder with the features of Farouche the banker from Lyons. Close behind him came the field marshal firebug. He went on foot, a fat clown, in seven uniforms and in none of them did he look human. Above these two devils was a canopy of newspapers, so it was easy for me to recognize them. Behind them rode the remaining executioners and marshals, with countenances for the most part like the backsides of plucked chickens, and behind them drove an endless procession of guns and tanks and railroad trains, also cars on which were altars or torture chambers, for everything was on wheels.

[BBA 118–19. More than anything else, this draft of the first dream, part of which was taken into the play (p.

19), links the "Visions" of the play's title with the series of poetic "Visions" written by Brecht from 1938 on. See the notes to the *Poems*, the section dealing with the Steffin Collection/Visions (1938–40). The drummer is Hitler, the field marshal Hermann Goering, whom the Communists held responsible for the Reichstag fire of 1933.]

Two Characters

Scene 1

SIMONE

All this being ordered hither and thither remains characteristic of the little maid-of-all-work so long as the hither and the thither are still undefined, and the hither and thither is not contrasted with something else. This would be the case were she, for instance, to be rent apart between the wishes of those above her and the needs of those below—for she is exploited from on top and from underneath—and if, to form the contrast, there were something at some particularly rending moment to be observed about TANKS that was of special worry and concern to her.

Scene 6 [*our scene 3b*]

THE OWNER

The owner can only develop into a character if he acquires an evolution of his own in this scene. His confrontation with the staff becomes manly as a result of the invasion. The invasion offers him the opportunity to score a "victory," but he shouldn't be too eager to pick up this particular laurel wreath. It is essential that he should fall into a rage on hearing that his brickyard has been destroyed; this is not the kind of war he wants to wage. Waging it in this way destroys the point of war. Patriotic feelings raise their head later, as inhibitions. How is it going to look if he hands a French citizen over to the Germans? That would be setting a bad example.

[BBA 1190/50. For the renumbering of scenes, see the editorial note.]

Editorial Note

1. General

When Brecht and Feuchtwanger discussed collaborating on a play at the end of October 1942 they considered various possibilities before settling on a St. Joan story:

A confused person has dreams in which the characters of the patriotic legend take on features of her superiors, and she learns how and why those superiors are waging their war, and how long for.

Thus the note in Brecht's journal, which calls the project *Saint Joan of Vitry* (*The Voices*). According to Feuchtwanger's recollection many years later the heroine was originally to be called Odette, but in what must be one of the earliest plans she is Jeanne Gotard. This was for a play of eleven scenes, starting:

1. the germans attack france. jeanne gotard is given an old book with the story of joan of arc.
2. joan of arc calls on the king.
3. jeanne gotard hides the gasoline stocks from the advancing german tanks.

—and finishing:

7. incendiarism of jeanne gotard.
8. respectable frenchmen talk to respectable englishmen.
9. arrest of jeanne gotard.
10. initiation of proceedings against joan of arc.
11. condemnation of jeanne gotard by a french court.

What seems like the beginning of a treatment in Brecht's typing is headed *Saint Joan of Vitry* and goes as follows:

In Vitry, a small town in Champagne, during the German invasion of 1940, a young girl by the name of Jeanne Gotard dreamt a strange dream lasting five consecutive nights. By day she worked her father's gasoline pump, he being a soldier serving in the Maginot Line. The schoolmaster across the way had lent her an old book with the illustrated story of Joan of Arc, and so at night she dreamt she was Joan. In her dreams however the historical events reported in the book were intermingled with memories of certain incidents at the gas station, so that the story of the saint displayed strange variations which not only made a profound impression on those listeners to whom she recounted her nightly experiences but would also certainly have interested an historian, if such a person had been present. In her dreams she appeared armed with bayonet and steel helmet, but the rest of her clothes were those that she wore every day, while the historical personalities with whom she had to deal—king, marshals, cardinals, and ordinary people—bore the faces of familiar personalities of the town of Vitry, such as visited the gas station in the daytime. Coulonge the banker merely wore a plumed hat, the mayor of the town simply a flowing cloak over his grey suit. . . .

A nine-scene version of the plan eliminates the missing scenes 4–6 of the scheme given above, and renames the heroine Michèle. Thus:

1. the germans attack france, michèle gotard reads a patriotic legend.
2. joan of arc, summoned by divine voices, crowns the king in rheims and unites all frenchmen against the hereditary foe.

3. michèle saves stocks from the advancing german tanks.
4. joan of arc, rewarded by the mighty and dismissed in her native village, is moved by the divine voices to continue the struggle.
5. michèle's incendiarism.
6. highly-placed frenchmen talk to highly-placed englishmen.
7. michèle is betrayed and is arrested by the germans; however, certain circles arrange for her to come before a french court.
8. joan is perturbed by the angel's failure to appear. the high court meets and questions her about the voices.
9. condemnation of michèle gotard by a french court.

With the much more elaborately worked-out plan given above on pp. 236–40 Michèle Gotard finally turned into Simone Machard, but the English decision to hand Joan of Arc over for trial by her own people—which Feuchtwanger saw as the pivotal point of the play—became swallowed in the next scene. Nonetheless this eight-scene version seems to have served as the basis for the actual writing of the play.

Brecht's first typescript is in eight scenes, bearing the dates December 28, 1942, at scene 5 and January 1943 near the end; a note in his handwriting calls it "first script, written in California." An almost entirely rewritten script follows, which is not in Brecht's typing and bears corrections by his and other hands; it was among his collaborator Ruth Berlau's papers and is headed "a play in two acts by Bertolt Brecht and Lion Feuchtwanger" with three suggested English titles: *Simone Hears Voices*, *St. Joan in Vichy* and *The Nights of St. Joan*. Feuchtwanger seems to have used a copy of this, lacking Brecht's last revisions, for a third, slightly modified version which he headed "a play in eight scenes by Bertolt Brecht and Lion Feuchtwanger" and sent to Elisabeth Hauptmann in Berlin a year before Brecht's death; it bears no marks by Brecht. The fourth and final script derives likewise from the rewritten version; it dates from 1946 and contains none of Feuchtwanger's modifications, but is heavily corrected by Brecht, who at some points went back to the first version. This is the script which was used for the German collected edition and accordingly is the basis of our own text. We shall refer to them respectively as the first version, the Berlau script, the Feuchtwanger script, and the 1946 or final version.

For Brecht there were two principal points of uncertainty in the writing of it. The first was the question of Simone's age; he found himself wanting to make her younger and younger ("mainly because i cannot give a motive for her patriotism," he noted in his journal), yet by doing so he destroyed her interest as a character. "The difficulty is," he noted on December 8, 1942, of his struggle with the Handshake scene,

> i'm writing the scene with no picture of the principal part, simone. originally i saw her as a somewhat ungainly, mentally retarded, and inhibited person; then it seemed more practical to use a child, so i'm left with the bare functions and nothing to offset them with in the way of individuality.

The other problem was the actual ending of the play, which is unresolved in the first script and may well have been left in some confusion when Brecht went off to New York on February 8. As will be seen from the detailed analysis that follows, he envisaged two alternative endings, arguing (in the journal entry for January 5) that

> the correct version is unperformable. in reality of course the wendells [i.e. the De Wendels of the Schneider arms firm] and pétains made use of the defeat and the foreign occupation to put down their social opponents. simone accordingly would need to be released by the germans (following false evidence by the staff of the hostelry) then handed over to the corrective institution by madame mère and captain fétain for subversive activities. in the performable version this would have to be blurred over; condemning simone for incendiarism due to her hatred of the owner means at the same time saving her from execution by the germans.

It was only in the final version that he seems finally to have settled for the less blurred alternative.

But besides these a number of other important variables can be observed in the scripts, though Brecht himself had nothing to say about them. To summarize these, they are:

(a) the identification of the angel with Simone's brother. At the beginning of the first version it is the Archangel Michael, while there is also a note saying "the angel's voice is [? the voice] of the people."

(b) the characters of Maurice and Robert, who in the first version are brothers. There they are shown shirking the call-up, and Maurice has evidently refused to help move the refugees (as is made explicit in the Berlau script). However, at the end of the Berlau (ii) and Feuchtwanger scripts they turn against the owner. Not so in the final script.

(c) the character of Père Gustave. He seems much more unpleasant in the earlier versions, bootlicking the owner and giving evidence against Simone.

(d) the rôle of the mayor, who compromises at a different stage in each version. Thus in the Feuchtwanger and Berlau (ii) versions of the fourth dream (i.e. our scene 4a) he is still defending Simone, whereas in the final text he is one of her judges.

(e) the owner's journey with the two truck drivers. In our version it is not explained how they came back, nor why they brought back the china and not the wines (initially the captain's) nor what happened to such refugees as they found room for. In the other texts the party runs into the Germans and/or breaks down, but again it is far from clear what is really supposed to have happened.

(f) the rôle of the refugees is heavily stressed in the final text, which brings in the notion of their being a "mob" quartered in the schoolhouse.

(g) Simone's escape is exclusive to the last version, though she half-tries in the Berlau and Feuchtwanger scripts.

(h) the placing of the daydream varies. This section of the play, Feuchtwanger told Brecht in a letter of March 27, 1943, had displeased all with whom he had discussed it (William Dieterle, Hanns Eisler, Oscar Homolka, and Berthold Viertel) and should therefore be cut.

Such points reflect a good deal of uncertainty in the authors' minds, and the effect is visible even in the final version, where the definition of the characters is further smudged by the occasional reallocation of lines. Besides this there is not only the altering of names—thus in the first script the mayor was Phillip (sic) Duclos, the owner Henri Champon, his mother "madame mère," and the captain Captain Bellair—but a basic insecurity about places and dates. In the earlier scripts the scope of the action embraced Saint-Nazaire, Tours, and Lyons —places several hundred kilometers apart and all of them far from the Champagne country where the previous scheme of the play was laid. Again, where the final text puts Simone's village on one of the main roads from Paris to the south, the Berlau script puts it on the Paris-Bordeaux road. The cumulative effect of all these hesitations and improbabilities helps to weaken the play.

2. Scene-by-Scene Account

The following is an account of the main changes. It uses the numbering of the final text with, in brackets, the numbers and titles of the corresponding eight-scene arrangement.

1. The Book [1]

The first version had Simone on stage from the start, reading her book; her present moves and business come from the Berlau script, which also changes the provenance of the book from "the nuns" (first version) to "the schoolmistress" and then, in Brecht's hand, to "the owner," as now. The soldier Georges's dialogue with Simone about the beauties of France was reworked more than once, and is altogether missing in the Feuchtwanger script. An addition to the Berlau script reads, in lieu of the lines from "Is that what it says in the book?" to "To the schoolhouse again today?" (p. 6):

(*Simone nods*)
GEORGES Perhaps they mean the cafés with their orange awnings or the food markets in the early morning, full of meat and vegetables.
SIMONE What do you like best?

GEORGES   They say one's own fish, bread, and wine are best.

SIMONE   What's the most beautiful thing you've seen?

GEORGES   I don't know. In Saint-Malo, for instance, I saw the launching of the *Intrépide*, a big blue box for catching cod. We went to a bistro and drank so much framboise that my cousin Jean fell out of his swing-boat.

SIMONE   Was he hurt?

GEORGES   No, he fell on the fat proprietress. What do you like best?

SIMONE   When they give us milk rolls at school.

GEORGES   Yes, that's something that could stay the way it is. Same with playing bowls in the shade outside the town hall, wouldn't you say? And the women would be all right, particularly the girls in Lyons or Arles, say, pleasant ways they've got, but then you're not interested in that. Yes, there's quite a lot one could put up with.

SIMONE   And our hostelry?

GEORGES   Just like France. Certain people spoil the whole picture so to speak.

The reference to the engineers which follows (with the mention of Simone's brother), derives from the same script, as does also the dialogue between Père Gustave and the owner (up to the latter's exit on p. 8) and most of the ensuing detail about "the gentleman with the trout" and his meal. Only part of this is in the Feuchtwanger script, while the first script goes almost straight from Georges's attempt to take away Simone's book (p. 7) to the engineers' actual entry on p. 8 (though it does make the point that Simone is holding down her brother's job while he is at the front). The fact that the brother is Saint-Martin's only volunteer comes from the Berlau script; the phrase "And the people are the enemy" (p. 9) is from an addition to the 1946 version. Virtually everything from the colonel's exit (p. 10) to the mayor's entry (p. 12) is new in the Berlau script; in the first version the mayor arrives before the colonel leaves, and is bawled out for permitting the confusion on the roads, the colonel threatening to report him to the préfecture at Lyons.

Thereafter the first version moves straight from the mayor's request for the trucks to his formal confiscation of them (p.

12). It is at this point that the owner states his prior obligation to the captain and his wines, provoking the mayor to speak of his duty to France.

> MONSIEUR SOUPEAU Don't talk about France. You're just using an opportunity to score off the captain because he cut your wife at the préfet's ball in return for your taking Simone out of his service so she might go to school. . . .

This leads quickly into the mayor's demand for the gasoline too. From there down to Maurice's statement (p. 14) that they never heard of any gas the first version is like a draft of the final text. Thereafter:

> MAYOR So that's your answer? I see. Only a miracle can save France; it's rotten from top to bottom. (*To Simone*) You've got a brother at the front; in the south, isn't he? Do you imagine he'll have any gas for his tank? Jammed in the endless stream of refugees, he's no doubt waiting for a mortal attack by enemy dive-bombers. But I don't suppose you're any more likely than the others to tell me where I can get him some gas, eh, Simone?
> (*Simone stands motionless, then gives a dry sob and rushes away. Sighing, the mayor turns and leaves*)

Neither the Berlau nor the Feuchtwanger script has any mention of the gasoline in this scene or the dream which follows. The former has the final text from the mayor's entry to Monsieur Soupeau's "I want to talk to you in private" (p. 13); whereupon the mayor replies:

> No, Henri, we will no longer talk in private. I may be a bad mayor, I suppose, and have done wrong to shut an eye so often. But unless I can organize those twenty trucks for the refugees I don't know how I'll be able to look my son in the face when he gets back from the front. (*He notices Simone*) Sending some of your food parcels to the schoolhouse? You only filled the soldiers' pot half full. I ought to have confiscated your stocks long ago.
>
> MONSIEUR SOUPEAU (*threateningly*) Try it and see.

MAYOR How can the refugees get anywhere if they're robbed of their last sou all along the line?

MONSIEUR SOUPEAU This is a restaurant, not a charitable institution. You can go, Simone.

(*Simone starts to go*)

MAYOR (*stops her. Calmly*) Any news from your brother?

(*Simone shakes her head*)

MAYOR I've not heard from my son either. (*Quietly and bitterly to the others*) At this moment her brother can see the German tanks advancing towards him, Stukas above him, blocked roads behind him so that no reinforcements can get through to him; and here she is being expected to help exploit Frenchmen who are in trouble.

The owner claims that this is undermining her respect for her employer, to which the mayor replies "I see," and so on to the end as in the final version.

Simone Machard's First Dream [2]

The angel's opening speech in verse is in the first version, but not the brief dialogue between him and Simone which follows and identifies him with her brother André; a preliminary version of this is in the Berlau script. Simone's song, which had Saint-Nazaire in the first version, had Saint-Omer in the Berlau script and Rocamer in both the Feuchtwanger and the final scripts till Brecht restored Saint-Nazaire once again on the latter. The three "dream language" phrases on p. 15 ("Leftit cribble clump"), p. 17 ("Workers gobbie girl, belie!"), and p. 20 ("Clidder dunk frim, Klemp!") are pen additions by Brecht to the final script, which had already contained "Ockal grisht burlap" (p. 20). Two other nonsense remarks referred to in the stage directions were spelled out in the Berlau script: Simone's unintelligible reply on p. 17 ("Allekiwist, Maurice") and Robert's remark (p. 17) ("Wihilirichi"). In the first version the whole scene is shorter. Thus after Simone's offer to clean Père Gustave's guns for him the owner enters and Simone almost instantly beats her drum to summon the king with a version of her long speech on pp. 19–20. He thereupon enters, asks after her brother, confiscates the trucks and inquires about the gasoline (which is not mentioned in the Berlau script). Why are the drivers lying, he asks.

> SIMONE   They have to lie, or else they'll be called up, see? because Monsieur Soupeau will give up certifying that they're essential workers.

Then the engineers appear as on p. 20 and beat their stew pots like bells, and the scene ends much as in the final text.

2. The Handshake [3]

There is some characteristic geographical confusion in the first version, where the owner's wines and china were to go to Saint-Nazaire and the refugees to Lyons (several hundred kilometers apart); then Lyons was changed to "Vermillon," a place apparently invented by Brecht. The mayor arrives in this version not with the town police but with the sergeant from scene 1 and his two soldiers. Simone's ensuing explanation (to her mother and the owner) is not included; it was worked out on the Berlau script. Then from where the mayor weakens (p. 24) to the entry of Madame Soupeau everything is different, the drivers in particular being more uncooperative and the refugees not making an appearance:

> MAYOR (*weaker*)   Monsieur Soupeau, I'm only doing my duty. All I asked was for you to put your trucks at my disposal.
> MONSIEUR SOUPEAU (*yells*)   What do you want my trucks for?
> MAYOR   I told you. I'm going to shift the refugees.
> SIMONE   The old people and children anyhow, so as to clear Route 74 for the troops in Lyons to move up.
> MONSIEUR SOUPEAU (*stares at her, then to the mayor, nastily*)   Have you got the drivers? I'm told my men won't drive.
> MAYOR (*to the drivers*)   Are you really refusing to evacuate the refugees?
> SIMONE   No, they'll drive them. Maurice, Robert, will you drive?

MAURICE (*ironically*) If monsieur le maire orders . . .

MONSIEUR SOUPEAU Certain officials seem to be using this disastrous war as a pretext for laying down the law to the business community. But very well, then, I bow to force. My drivers can take the refugees to Vermillon.

MAYOR Not to Vermillon; that would mean using Route 74. First to Saint-Nazaire.

MONSIEUR SOUPEAU What can I have my trucks do in Saint-Nazaire? But very well, you're hiding behind your orders and the army. I'm asking the army to do something for me in return: pack up my wine reserves and the china, because that must go too.

MAYOR Why can't your men do that?

MONSIEUR SOUPEAU Because my men are on strike. I'd be within my rights if I put them up against the wall for refusing to remove French property to safety in face of the enemy. But there's no discipline left.

MAYOR (*to the sergeant*) Is that something you can put to your men, do you think? I've nothing against giving Monsieur Soupeau a hand to save his property.

MADAME MACHARD (*sees that her daughter wants to say something*) Quiet, Simone.

SIMONE But aren't the soldiers supposed to be bringing up the equipment for blowing the bridges?

MAURICE No. [illegible]

SIMONE To hold up the tanks till reinforcements come; you know. They ought to go right away.

SERGEANT We'd have been there by now if we hadn't had to wait for the field kitchen on account of their not giving us a meal. I don't see why I should fall over myself to help this gentleman and his hotel; he's the one refused to feed us.

SIMONE You'll get fed, won't he, Monsieur Henri? There'll be no room for provisions on the trucks if you're to be able to carry a proper number of refugees, will there, Maurice? I'll just get the key of the cellar.

MADAME MACHARD Simone!

MONSIEUR SOUPEAU What's got into you, Simone? I was amazed to see you bring in the mayor against me. Go indoors at once and wash your neck, you shameless ungrateful creature.

MADAME MACHARD Please excuse our daughter, Monsieur Soupeau; she has lost her head.

Monsieur Soupeau's mother, here called Madame Mère, then enters and gives Simone the key, telling her to get wine for the soldiers. There is no mention of feeding the refugees or of the danger of looting, and it is the soldiers who then help themselves to the provisions. Simone returns with the bottles and persuades Maurice and Robert to load up. German planes dive, prompting M. Soupeau to say that he must get away, as on p. 25, but his mother is also on stage and she replies contemptuously that she is staying:

> Thanks to Simone's very sensible arrangements you will get to Saint-Nazaire as planned, and Maurice and Robert will take the china and the refugees south to Lyons. Is that right, Simone?

She proposes to give the town such food stocks as cannot be moved, saying (in a line later given to the mayor) "This is a time for making sacrifices, Henri. We must let our hearts speak" (p. 29). Then they all drink as on p. 30, and the owner makes his conciliatory speech (p. 30). The drivers are told to load up with Monsieur Machard, and leave. It is then the owner himself who asks about the gasoline in the brickyard, saying:

> The Germans mustn't get it. Georges, Gustave, run down to the brickyard. Smash the pump and seal up the tank, right?
>
> MAYOR   Better set fire to it, Henri. There's an army order says all stocks of gasoline have got to be burnt. The Germans must not find a single canful in any village.
>
> MONSIEUR SOUPEAU   Burn it? Rubbish. We'll need it. How are our forces to replenish their tanks when they attack? Simone, tell the mayor that France isn't lost yet.
>
> SIMONE   That's a fact, monsieur le maire.
>
> MAYOR   But so many people are in the know, Simone.
>
> MONSIEUR SOUPEAU   No Frenchman could give away the secret. If I didn't realize that before I do now. Georges, Gustave, get moving.
>
> SIMONE   (to Gustave)   I cleaned the garage out for you, Père Gustave.
>
> PÈRE GUSTAVE   Right. Patriotism seems to have become all the fashion around here.

Then the owner says good-bye to his mother (p. 31), and kisses her and Simone. The radio is heard saying that the French will counterattack and not a foot of ground is to be given up. There is no more reference to the gasoline, and madame says that she is closing the hotel. Simone is not specifically dismissed, but the last exchange between her and the mayor is as in the final text, and she picks up the owner's suitcases and slowly leaves with lowered head.

The Berlau script is approximately the same as the final version as far as the appearance of the representatives of the refugees (p. 25). Then, from the mayor's "What is it?":

ONE OF THE REFUGEES (*excitedly*) Monsieur le maire, we've heard the hotel is selling off its trucks. We insist you do something about it.

WOMAN There are sick people in the schoolhouse. We can't take our children to Bordeaux on foot.

The mayor replies "Madame, messieurs" etc. as in the final text, and is answered by the woman. Then this script cuts straight to the long stage direction on p. 26, with the difference that the main crowd of refugees does not appear. In the simultaneous dialogue which follows, the left hand column is that of the final version. In the right hand column, however, when Simone asks Robert and Maurice to take the refugees, Maurice refuses, saying "I'm not a nurse" and telling Robert "You've got no influence at the mairie. The mayor and M. Soupeau are birds of a feather; it's always us who pay the bill in the end . . . " The argument is interrupted by the announcement that the German tanks are nearly at Tours, causing the owner to complain "And my Sèvres and my vintage wines haven't yet been loaded." An approximate version of the dialogue from "SIMONE (*angrily*)" to "VOICES (*from outside*)" then follows (in the final version it comes earlier on pp. 25–26), with the difference that Simone's anger is initially against Maurice for wanting to clear out and abandon the refugees. Here madame enters and gives Simone the key (p. 27), and the ensuing dialogue down to her "Will somebody load them for us?" (p. 28) is more or less that of the final text. Thereafter:

> SIMONE   Of course, madame. Right, Maurice?
>
> MAURICE   Go to hell. Pack china, with the Germans arriving? High time we were off.
>
> MADAME MÈRE (*sharply*)   Nobody but the children seems to realize that French property cannot be allowed to fall into the hands of the Germans.
>
> MAURICE (*to Robert*)   All right, we can help carry out the cases. (*Goes out with Robert into the storehouse*)

It continues approximately as in the final text from "ONE OF THE REFUGEES" (p. 28) to the general dispersal on p. 30. Here Maurice, Robert, and Georges also leave; Maurice poses the question about the brickyard as he goes, after which the dialogue is a blend of the first and final versions until M. Soupeau takes his leave. Asked yet again about the gasoline (this time by the mayor) he says to ask his mother. In the Feuchtwanger script Simone then suggests getting Georges and Père Gustave and blowing it up, but in the Berlau script this is changed to a mere inquiry what should be done.

> MADAME MÈRE   Didn't you hear what M. Soupeau said? He asked us not to do anything precipitate. We can leave the problem of whether to destroy the gasoline till the last minute. After all, it's still my son's property we're dealing with.
>
> SIMONE   But it would be terrible if the Germans used our gasoline to fill up, like they did in Abbeville. Wouldn't it, monsieur le maire?
>
> MAYOR   It hasn't come to that yet by a long shot.

The rest of the scene is virtually as in the final text.

Simone Machard's Second Dream [4]

The first version and the Berlau script both have Père Gustave in lieu of the soldier Georges as a member of Simone's bodyguard; neither establishes the identification of the owner's

mother as Queen Isabeau. When Simone calls on the angel
(p. 34) both versions have her sitting on the ground and
beating her drum, crying "Come here, you Frenchmen, the
enemy has arrived." In the Berlau script there is no reaction;
she calls Georges and drums harder, then calls on the angel.
The first version makes the angel St. Michael. Also it has no
mention of the mayor's dream language (pp. 33–34). The
angel's song "When the conqueror" (p. 35) is slightly different
in the first version, which omits the previous recitative ("Maid
of France," etc., pp. 34–35) and the dialogue with Simone after
that.

3. The Fire

In the first version subscene (a) bears this title and is scene
5, while subscene (b) is scene 6, The Betrayal, and is followed
by the Daydream of Simone Machard. In the Berlau and
Feuchtwanger scripts the Daydream is incorporated in the
second of these two scenes (instead of, as now, in the first).

(a)   [5. The Fire]

At the beginning of the scene the exchange where Georges
suspects that Simone has been fired, the mention by Père
Gustave of the "mob from the schoolhouse" (p. 37) and
Simone's wondering if seeing a person in a dream means that
he is dead (p. 37), are none of them in the first version,
while the actual entry of the refugees (p. 38) occurs only
in the final script. Thereafter there are extensive differences.
In the first script the captain enters at this point, saying that
the mayor will come. "And another thing. I've been told
there were cases of looting and blackmail in these parts
yesterday. Order and discipline are herewith reestablished:
you get me, friends?" He is followed instantly by Père
Gustave. The captain thereupon delivers a version of the
speech which now comes just before the Daydream:

> CAPTAIN   Ah, monsieur le maire, I trust your wife is in good
> health. I just wanted to tell you, Duclos, that France's
> one hope of avoiding total disaster is to collaborate as

honorably as she can with the gentlemen of the German
general staff. Paris is overrun with communists, and here
too all kinds of things occurred yesterday without the
authorities lifting a finger. To put it in a nutshell, the
commandant is fully aware of this hotel's connection
with a certain brickyard. You might like to take action
accordingly, Duclos. Wait a moment before you follow
me out, or it'll look as if I had to have you dragged down
here. (*Goes in*)

This is much the same in the Berlau script. Then Simone and
the mayor conduct their dialogue about the brickyard, from
his (present) entry (p. 39) to his exit, which in the final version becomes *He starts to go in* (p. 40), allowing the captain
to reenter with his speech roughly as above. All the present
dialogue from Madame Soupeau's entry (p. 38) to the entry
of the mayor is an addition to the final script.

In the earlier versions the dialogue with Georges and Père
Gustave which now follows the Daydream runs straight on
from the mayor's exit, with slight differences. Thereafter
from the entry of the German soldier to the end of (a) everything else is the same except that the German captain (or
commandant in the first version) says nothing. The Berlau
script however inserts the following dialogue before "So
you won't come?" (p. 43):

SOLDIER [i.e. GEORGES] What are you after? Oh, the gaso-
line, is it? Don't you touch it. You keep out.
SIMONE But M. Soupeau said it was up to us.
SOLDIER M. Soupeau's gone, but you're here. They'll shoot
you down like a mad dog. (*He draws her downstage.
Urgently*) Simone, promise me you'll be sensible.
SIMONE But you said yourself that they're bringing up
whole new regiments. They broke through against the
132nd, you said.
SOLDIER But not against the 7th [her brother's unit, in
this version].
SIMONE (*quietly*) That's not true, Monsieur Georges.
PÈRE GUSTAVE Don't you get mixed up with the Germans.
Sabotage can cost you your neck.
SOLDIER It all comes from that damned book of yours.

You've been reading it all day again, then you go and imagine you're God knows who, isn't that it?

Apart from the first sentence this is not in the Feuchtwanger script. But from then on to the end of (a) both are practically identical with the final text.

(b)   (6. The Betrayal)
The first version specifies that this occurs three days after (a). In all three of the early scripts the scene starts with Georges reading the paper as the German captain saunters across the stage and into the hotel. Simone brings a hot-water bottle for the owner's mother, who is unwell. Then Simone wonders about the significance of seeing a person in a dream (the passage now near the beginning of [a]) and her parents enter, delighted that M. Machard has got the job of bailiff. It appears that the owner has returned; the Berlau and Feuchtwanger scripts add that he and Maurice were held up by German tanks. In all three versions he comes in with Robert, looking pale and sleepless. All this is prior to the beginning of the present subscene (b), but from then on the dialogue continues much as in the final text up to where Simone says that she will confess to the Germans to save the owner (p. 46). The main differences are (1) that the Machard parents are present up to the firing of Georges; (2) that there is no mention of the refugees in the schoolhouse; (3) that in lieu of Père Gustave's remark about the hotel's sudden popularity (p. 46) Robert tells Simone that the Peugeot has been stolen, that one of the trucks has broken down and that Maurice is bringing back the other. Thereafter, however, the scene ends differently.

In the first version it ends quickly, with the owner assuring Simone that since she no doubt meant well he will stand by her, then going into the hotel without saying whether she is really fired or not. Robert asks if he will betray her, and Georges says, "He can't do that. After all he is a Frenchman." The mayor and the captain walk across the stage into the hotel; Simone bows to the mayor, who pays no attention. That is the end of the scene, and the Daydream follows.

Daydream of Simone Machard

In the first version there is no game of cards. The owner is present, and the captain enters later, bringing the German captain as an "unknown knight" with whom the French are invited to collaborate. He offers the mayor a cigar, but the drumming starts again and the mayor refuses. There are no references to "the mob"; madame boxes the owner's ears, not the mayor's, and the dream ends with the German captain saying, "Of course the Maid must be got rid of."

In the Berlau and Feuchtwanger scripts, after Simone has said that she will confess to the Germans (as above) Madame Machard reappears to say that the mayor has given the bailiff's job to "old Frossart" instead of to her husband, who has been "dropped like a hot potato." "The mayor," comments Georges, "is scared of his own courage." This leads straight into the Daydream. Mayor, captain, and the owner sit playing cards, and neither madame nor the German captain appears. After "So I can sell my wines" (p. 42), the owner says "Have you really decided to support her, King Charles the Seventh? And given her father the bailiff's job?" The mayor announces his determination much as in the final version, then sits down. The dream ends with the captain pointing this out to the owner and saying "There you are, Henri; France doesn't support her any more."

A quite different concluding section follows in both these scripts. After the dream Simone says she must leave, then Maurice arrives, having heard about the explosion:

MAURICE   Are you crazy, Simone? How could you?
SIMONE   He won't give me away.
MAURICE   Get your things on at once, you must get out of here. I'll drive you. Pack up whatever she needs most, Madame Machard.
MADAME MACHARD   I don't understand you people. You aren't expecting her to throw up her job?
GEORGES (*to Maurice*)   You really think he might . . . ?
MAURICE (*shrugs his shoulders*)   If he cares about saving his wretched hotel he'll have to. They might have used

the gasoline as a way of showing how ready they are to collaborate. She's put a spoke in that. There's only one thing left for them to do: turn her in. (*With emphasis*) At this moment she's got no more vindictive enemies in the world than Madame Mère and her respected son.

ROBERT   You're exaggerating. After all, they are French.

MAURICE   Didn't you get what they were saying on the radio?

GEORGES   Wasn't listening. What was it?

MAURICE   The marshal has dissolved the government and taken over all its powers. That means open collaboration. Meantime *she's* still at war.

ROBERT   M. Soupeau said he'd stand by her.

MAURICE   He hadn't been told about the radio announcement. Get your things on, Simone.

SIMONE   (*still absent-mindedly*) I can't leave, Maurice.

GEORGES   Ten minutes back you were saying you must.

SIMONE   That was only because I was imagining things. But M. Soupeau won't give me away.

MADAME MACHARD   But, messieurs, don't give the girl crazy ideas. She can't possibly give up her job now, when the rent's due. What with our André being away as well.

MONSIEUR SOUPEAU   (*comes out of the hotel, very excitedly*) Simone! You've got to disappear! At once! Maurice, get her out of here! Doesn't matter where. Got that?

MAURICE   Yes sir.

MONSIEUR SOUPEAU   It's a matter of minutes. (*Goes back into the hotel*)

ROBERT   So he *isn't* going to give you away.

MAURICE   He's given her away already. Did you see how he'd been sweating? Get a move on, Simone!

SIMONE   No, no, no. I don't want to leave. He's not going to touch me. He only came out to help me.

MAURICE   He's got a bad conscience, that's all.

(*Simone obstinately stays put*)

GEORGES   What have you got against leaving?

SIMONE   I can't. Suppose my brother comes back. I promised him I'd be here and keep his job for him.

MAURICE   That's enough. (*He seizes her, picks her up and carries her struggling into the garage over his shoulder*) Go outside the hotel, Georges, and whistle if the coast is clear. (*Goes out with Simone*)

(*Georges goes out into the road. During what follows he is heard whistling*)

MADAME MACHARD   I knew it would come to this. Her brother's to blame, and all that book-reading.

SIMONE'S VOICE (*from outside*)   I'm not going. I can't. You don't understand.

MADAME MACHARD   What have I done to deserve it?

ROBERT   Oh, do shut up. Don't you realize that she'll be shot if they catch her?

MADAME MACHARD   Simone? Holy mother of God! (*Sits distraught at the foot of the gasoline pump*)
    (*Robert goes out into the garage*)
    (*Enter from the hotel Monsieur Soupeau and the captain*)

MONSIEUR SOUPEAU   Simone! Père Gustave! (*To the captain*) Actually she was discharged some days ago. But went on hanging around my yard, so I've been told.

CAPTAIN (*notices Madame Machard*)   Isn't that her mother?

MONSIEUR SOUPEAU (*embarrassed*)   Ah, Madame Machard. Have you by any chance seen Simone?

MADAME MACHARD   No, Monsieur Henri, I'm looking for her myself. That girl's always doing errands for the hotel, monsieur le capitaine.
    (*Père Gustave enters from the storehouse*)

MONSIEUR SOUPEAU   Oh, there you are, Père Gustave. Go and get Simone, would you?
    (*Père Gustave goes obediently up the road. The whistling stops*)

MONSIEUR SOUPEAU (*to the captain*)   I just can't imagine what put the idea in her head.

CAPTAIN   It's not as hard as all that, Monsieur Soupeau. But it'll all be sorted out.

PÈRE GUSTAVE (*coming back, as Georges's whistling is heard once more*)   I can't find her, Monsieur Henri. Georges says she left half an hour ago.

CAPTAIN (*skeptically*)   Too bad that you people "can't find her," Monsieur Soupeau. (*Turns and goes into the hotel*)

MONSIEUR SOUPEAU (*mopping his perspiration*)   Thank God for that.

MADAME MACHARD   In the nick of time. The things we have to go through for our children!
    (*Maurice appears at the garage door*)

MONSIEUR SOUPEAU   Why are you still here, Maurice? Shouldn't you be . . .

MAURICE Did she come out this way? She broke away from me.

(*Simone comes in from the street, with Georges behind her*)

MONSIEUR SOUPEAU Are you out of your mind? Quick, quick . . .

SIMONE You aren't going to give me away, are you, Monsieur Henri?

MONSIEUR SOUPEAU I told you to disappear. And now— (*furious gesture of helplessness*) First you set fire to my brickyard. I don't say a word, though it's *I* who have to answer for it with the Germans. And now you're being pigheaded just so as to make things harder for me. They can shoot you for all I care; I wash my hands of it.

(*The German captain comes out of the hotel in helmet and greatcoat, with the captain behind him*)

CAPTAIN But we'll do everything we can, sir. Give us two hours.

(*Simone has instinctively tried to hide behind M. Soupeau. He steps to one side so that she is seen*)

CAPTAIN Why, here she is. Here's our arsonist, sir.

THE GERMAN CAPTAIN A child like that?

(*Pause*)

MONSIEUR SOUPEAU Simone, this is a pretty kettle of fish.

All this is omitted from the final version, where the dialogue about the German poster ("It all depends on whether" p. 46 to Père Gustave's "I told you nothing of the kind" p. 47) has been brought forward from the beginning of scene 8 in the earlier versions, and the rest is new.

4. *The Trial*

   (a) *Simone Machard's Fourth Dream* [7]
In the first version this takes place "during the night of June 18" (i.e. three days earlier than in the final text). All three earlier scripts specify that the confused music is to "continue the motifs of the third dream." In the first version there is only one soldier with the German captain.

Down to the entry of the judges all three are more or less

the same as the final text, and the first version continues so as far as the point where they put their heads together (p. 50). In the Berlau and Feuchtwanger scripts, however, there are at first only three judges, the mayor suddenly appearing beside them "in the capacity of a defense counsel"; nor does Simone identify them one by one as they come in but all at once when they uncover their faces. Otherwise these two scripts continue close to the final version down to the end of the scene, the main later additions being the reference to the refugees in the schoolhouse and Madame Soupeau's concluding line. In the first version a number of the lines were differently allotted, though their wording remains the same: thus Père Gustave's call for accusers from the public (p. 51) and his challenge to the angel (p. 53) were given to Simone's father, while it was the mayor who called for a chair for Queen Isabeau and asked Simone "Where is God? . . ." (p. 53).

(b)   [8. The trial]

The first version gives two alternative scenes, one of them incomplete and each differing widely from the other. The Berlau script also gives two texts, the first of which peters out in a series of shorthand notes, while the second is identical with that of the Feuchtwanger script. Altogether therefore there are four main variants of this scene: the first version (i) and (ii), the Feuchtwanger version (which seems to have been worked out from Berlau (i) and possibly copied in Berlau (ii)), and the final 1946 text.

In the first version (i) there is no flag visible, and the mayor, the owner, his mother, and the captain are on stage at the start, as well as the four of the final version. A German soldier marches Simone in, hands the mayor a document, salutes and leaves. The document gives the responsibility of dealing with Simone to the local authorities.

CAPTAIN   The tone of the document is severe, but the contents are very decent. The commandant is leaving it to the local authority to interrogate the incendiary. Monsieur le maire, do your duty by the township of Saint-Martin.
MAYOR (*sighing*)   Simone, the Germans have handed you

back to your own authorities. You are strongly suspected
of sabotage, a crime for which one can be shot. However, the authorities have been able to raise some doubt as
to the deliberateness of your intention to commit sabotage. Do you understand the purpose of this inquiry?

SIMONE Yes, monsieur le maire.

MAYOR Luckily the question is easily settled. Now listen
carefully. If you caused the fire *before* the Germans put
up their poster forbidding the destruction of essential
stocks then it was not sabotage. Suppose you had done
it after the poster, it would have been sabotage and we
couldn't save you. Do you understand that? Did you
see the poster?

The dialogue follows as on p. 46 (which is where it was
shifted to in the final text), except that there it is Monsieur
Soupeau, not the mayor, who asks the questions. After Père
Gustave's "I told you nothing of the kind" (p. 47) it goes on:

MAYOR Père Gustave, you have offered to give evidence to
the effect that Simone set fire to the brickyard. But you
insist that she did it before the German order?

PÈRE GUSTAVE (*avoiding Simone's eye*) Yes.

ROBERT Oh, you've volunteered to give evidence, have
you?

MADAME MÈRE Quiet, Robert.

MAYOR It's all quite clear. (*To Simone*) Will you show
us where the red poster was displayed? Come along, it'll
still be there.

SIMONE But I saw it before that, monsieur le maire.

MAYOR Don't be difficult. This is official.
(*Mayor, Monsieur Soupeau and captain leave with Simone
through the gateway*)

PÈRE GUSTAVE I had to, because of what I let out when
Monsieur Soupeau drove off.

MAURICE Shut up.

GEORGES The mayor's a decent man. He's whitewashing
her to the Germans, and they'll let her off.

MAURICE They're a lot of crooks. All they're doing is
clearing Saint-Martin of any suspicion that it has Frenchmen in it [p. 59 in our text]. They're set on collaborating

with the Germans. Simone's right. It's as though she knew what tune they were going to play.

ROBERT   We won't have heard the last of it. You wait.

Then the party returns with Simone, and the mayor says he thinks the Germans will agree that it was not sabotage. The captain differs, and M. Soupeau's mother says "It was a base act of revenge against my son and myself."

MAYOR   Revenge? What for?

MADAME MÈRE   Because we dismissed her. It's quite simple.

MAYOR   Henri, do you believe that?

MONSIEUR SOUPEAU (*forcefully*)   I refuse to stand up for this creature any longer. I offered her a chance to get away; she insisted on staying. I'm through with her. I've had enough to worry about.

Then Madame sends Maurice, Robert, Père Gustave, and Georges back to their work, and they leave. She starts cross-examining Simone, approximately as from where she *turns to Simone* (p. 57) to Simone's "I did it because of the enemy" (p. 58). Then she tells Thérèse to "fetch the sister" and delivers a speech that is partly the captain's "The least our guests can expect . . ." (p. 58) and partly her own "The child is insubordinate" etc. (p. 60) of the final text. Thérèse returns with an Ursuline nun.

MADAME MÈRE   Sister Michèle is being so good as to take this unfortunate child into the educational establishment run by the strict sisters of St. Ursula.

SIMONE (*trembling*)   No, no! Not to St. Ursula's! I did it because of the Germans. I want to stay.

(*The sister takes her arm and leads her to the gateway*)

SIMONE   André! André!

There it breaks off at the foot of a page.

The first version (ii), headed in Brecht's hand "Second version, January 43," likewise breaks off at the foot of a page, this time towards the end of madame's interrogation of Simone. It starts with Maurice, Robert, Georges, and Père

Gustave on stage, as in the final version, but with two German sentries. They are discussing Simone's examination by the mayor, which has taken place off stage and in the German captain's presence, but evidently went much as in (i). Georges says "I don't see why he doesn't do the interrogating himself, Maurice."

> MAURICE Well, you saw how angry it made him yesterday when he heard it was a child. Shooting children doesn't go all that well with their policy of dishing out soup on the square in front of the mairie. The captain had supper with him last night. I can tell you exactly how the conversation will have gone. (*He mimics the German captain and the French captain in turn*) "Bad show. I'll have to shoot her." "That'll put the kybosh on peaceful collaboration for the next couple of years, sir."—"What's the answer?" "Collaboration, my dear captain. Leave the case to us."—"Then tomorrow up goes the water tower, eh, monsieur? Here's our radio announcing every hour that the French population is receiving us with open arms, wants nothing but peace."—"My dear captain, but whoever says the person responsible was acting against the Germans?"—"Aha . . . I see. You mean you can prove that she did it *before* . . ." So that now she did it *before* the proclamation, d'you see?

Then the owner enters and tells Père Gustave that his evidence won't be needed: "A child! What do they expect?" etc. (as on p. 55). Georges's ensuing remarks finish with him saying that someone betrayed her.

> MONSIEUR SOUPEAU You dare to say that to me after I've stood here and told her she must get away?

He seizes the wounded Georges by the arm, and there is a struggle in which Robert joins till it is interrupted by the entry of the German captain. The captain tells the two sentries to follow him and leaves.

> PÈRE GUSTAVE He's taking his men away. Does that mean that Simone's been let free?

MAURICE   I'd be extremely surprised.

GEORGES   Anyhow that boche with the monocle realizes that Captain Bellaire isn't the only person around here. Monsieur le capitaine has had his innings. They couldn't conceal the fact that there are still some Frenchmen in France. Ow! Even kids of thirteen can show them, eh, Maurice?

But the mayor's two policemen appear at the gate, then madame leads in Simone from the hotel, with the mayor and the captain following, and they all go into the storehouse. Maurice makes his remark about clearing Saint-Martin, and M. Soupeau angrily orders the policemen to clear the yard.

MAURICE   Let's go. There's nothing we can do here for the moment. They've got their police and they've got the Germans. (*Draws Robert and Georges away*) Poor Simone. Too many enemies.

GEORGES   (*hoarsely*) Look out, Monsieur Henri, other times are coming. And when they come we'll be asking you about Simone. (*All three go out*)

The party then emerges from the storehouse, and madame conducts her interrogation of Simone on lines rather closer to the final text, including a mention of "the mob from the schoolhouse." This version breaks off with madame's "Who told you the Germans would ever . . ." (p. 58).

Finally the Feuchtwanger script (identical with Berlau ii) starts with much the same stage direction as our text, but without Georges and with the addition of the two German sentries. It opens with Maurice's remark about the marshal; Simone, however, has not got away but is being interrogated as in the first version (ii). Georges, who has been giving evidence, comes out of the hotel to report that they are all behaving very decently, even madame and the captain. The German captain has said "that these are tragic days and he has no desire to hurt Frenchmen's feelings." He is allowing the others to establish Simone's ignorance of the poster because, as Maurice puts it, "I don't imagine they want to start off their armistice and their formal collaboration by shooting our children for us."

GEORGES (*scratching his head*) Do you think nothing's going to happen to her?

MAURICE That's another question.

ROBERT If they do anything to Simone I'm coming to Algiers with you, Maurice. (*To Georges*) The radio says the old government's going to carry on the fight from there.

GEORGES (*moving his arm thoughtfully*) That's what one ought to do.

PÈRE GUSTAVE They talk a lot on the radio.

Then M. Soupeau enters as in the first version (ii), leading on to the struggle and a version of the ensuing dialogue as far as Madame Soupeau's entry with Simone (but no policemen) and disappearance into the storehouse.

MONSIEUR SOUPEAU (*complainingly, as he dusts down his suit*) I gave her an opportunity to disappear. She insisted on staying. She's caused me nothing but troubles from the very first. A hundred thousand francs, she's cost me. As for the cost to my nerves, I can't count it. And now she's causing bad blood between me and my old employees. That's what comes of trying to protect her. Well, the time for sentimentality is over. I shan't interfere any more. Not that I bear you people a grudge. She upset all of us. Back to work, Maurice and Robert! (*Maurice and Robert stay put*)

MONSIEUR SOUPEAU Didn't you hear me?

MAURICE Robert and I will just wait and see what's happening to Simone.

The party leaves the storehouse, and this time madame's interrogation of Simone is witnessed and occasionally interrupted by Robert, Maurice, and Georges. It is longer than in the final version, though largely coinciding with it, and ends with an admission by Simone that she was acting on her own, not on the mayor's orders.

MADAME SOUPEAU   To settle a score with the hotel.
MONSIEUR SOUPEAU   And to think maman told lies to the
Germans to make them set you free!

The two policemen enter, and thereafter the script stays close
to the final text, except that there are no nuns and the institution is the "house of correction at Tours"; (an addition to the
Berlau (ii) script in Brecht's hand introduced the "brutish
lady" and the comments indicating that this was a place for
the mentally handicapped). However, instead of fetching her
things from the storehouse, as in the final text, she says good-
bye to Georges, Maurice, and Robert until she is dragged off
calling "André! André!" There is no appearance of the angel,
and after M. Soupeau's order to resume work the ending is
different.

MAURICE   What, us? You'll find it difficult to get anyone in
Saint-Martin to work for you after this. Come on.
(*Maurice, Robert, and Georges turn to leave.*)
MONSIEUR SOUPEAU (*running after them*)   But Maurice! I
haven't done anything to you, have I?—Five years we've
been together—It was for the hotel's sake—It was for the
sake of your jobs, for that matter—Maurice! Robert!
GEORGES (*at the gateway, turns around, hoarsely*)   You
look out. Other times are coming. When they come we'll
be asking you about Simone. (*Curtain*)

In the 1946 script, which our text follows, the date is given
as "Morning of June 19" (later changed to June 22). The
mayor's order to M. Machard to clear the schoolhouse is a
typed addition. The nuns are mainly handwritten amendments
(as in Berlau ii); the "brutish lady" remains in one stage direction (the published text makes her plural) but elsewhere is
amended to "the nuns" or "one of the nuns." The house of
correction is struck out, together with all references but one
to Tours (the mayor offers to give evidence there). References to St. Ursula come from the first version, those to the
mentally handicapped from the additions to the Berlau script,
reinforced by Simone's new comment "They tie you up!"
(p. 59).

3. Feuchtwanger's Novel

Simone, a novel by Lion Feuchtwanger, was published in 1944 by the Viking Press in a translation by G. A. Herrmann. It is less "the book of the play" than an independent reworking of the ideas discussed in the course of the author's collaboration with Brecht, who, as far as we know, was not involved in its composition, and it differs in various important respects. Thus out of twenty-one chapters only two contain visions (as against the much more even alternation in the play) though there are three others where Simone is shown reading the books (plural) which she has been given by an old bookbinder friend. The town of Saint-Martin in this account is a fair-sized place, a Burgundian chef-lieu d'arrondissement (i.e. of the importance, say, of Châlons-sur-Saône) where the stepuncle who corresponds to the hotel owner runs a largish trucking business, not a hotel. The refugees are in the Palais de Justice; the sous-préfet corresponds to the mayor, and the local Marquis de Saint-Brisson to the captain who wants his wines evacuated. Simone Planchard is "a tall, lanky fifteen-year-old":

> Her bony, tanned face framed with dark blond [*sic*] hair was tense; her dark, deep-set eyes under a low but broad and well-shaped forehead eagerly absorbed all that moved before her. . . . She could scarcely be called beautiful, but her intelligent, thoughtful, somewhat stubborn face with its strong chin and prominent Burgundian nose was good to look at.

Moreover, her father had been a local left-wing hero who had died in the Congo two years previously while investigating native working conditions. Madame, who corresponds to the hotel owner's mother (and like her appears as Queen Isabeau) was evidently the father's stepmother. Thanks to her, Simone's rôle in the household (the Villa Monrepos) is that of an unpaid servant.

This Simone has no brother. She has a confidant in the

secretary of the sous-préfecture and two friends of her own age—her schoolmate Henriette and Henriette's brother Étienne —though neither figures very largely in the story. Of her uncle's employees in the loading yard Maurice (there is no Robert, and Georges is a nonentity) is at first cruelly and gratuitously offensive to her; it looks as if he is meant to stand for the French communists, skeptical of the bourgeoisie and their war, and uninvolved until after the German victory. In the dream episodes he figures as the monstrous Gilles de Rais. From the first Simone seems attracted to him, and once she has set fire to the yard (trucks, gasoline, and all)—which occurs about halfway through the book, as against two-thirds of the way through the play—he starts behaving more amicably, though still in a rather condescending way. He offers to get her away on his motorcycle; but by the time she decides to accept his offer it is too late and he has already gone. She escapes by herself, but is arrested in Nevers and brought back.

Though madame and the other villains (such as the lawyer Maître Levautour) seem heavily caricatured, the stepuncle's actions are generally credible and within the bounds of reason. For much of the story he even behaves kindly. "Don't you understand," he asks her, "that I can't live without my business? I am a business man. I can't help that." And again, in explanation of his actions, "Some people are born to be artists, others to be engineers; I was born to be a business man, a promoter." To save his business and at the same time prevent the Germans from punishing the entire town he arranges with the French authorities that Simone shall confess to having caused the fire for personal reasons. This she formally does on the understanding that no proceedings will be taken against her. However, the marquis and madame see to it that she is sent away to the Grey House, the reformatory at "Francheville," the departmental capital, and "an uncouth woman" escorts her away. As she is driven off the crowd in the street makes signs to her—

Arms were raised waving to her, women and girls wept, the gendarme had come to attention, shouts sounded in her direction: "Good-bye, Simone—good-bye, Simone Planchard—take care of yourself, Simone—so long, Simone —we won't forget you, Simone Planchard—we'll come and get you, Simone."

And she rides away confident "that she would survive the Grey House."

SCHWEYK IN THE SECOND WORLD WAR

Texts by Brecht

The Story

The Good Soldier Schweyk, after surviving the First World War, is still alive. Our story shows his successful efforts to survive the Second as well. The new rulers have even more grandiose and all-embracing plans than the old, which makes it even harder for today's Little Man to remain more or less alive.

The play begins with a

Prelude in the Higher Regions

wherein a preternaturally large Hitler with a preternaturally large voice talks to his preternaturally large police chief Himmler about the putative loyalty, reliability, self-denial, enthusiasm, geopolitical consciousness, and so on and so forth of the European "Little Man." The reason why he is demanding such virtues of the Little Man is that he has made up his mind to conquer the world. His police chief assures him that the European Little Man bears him the same love as does the Little Man in Germany. The Gestapo will see to that. The Führer has nothing to fear, and need have no hesitation about conquering the world.

1

There has been an attempt on Hitler's life. Hearty applause
from the "Flagon" in Prague, where the good dog hustler
Josef Schweyk and his friend Baloun are sitting over their
morning drinks and discussing politics with the "Flagon's"
landlady, the young widow Anna Kopecka. Fat Baloun, whose
exceptional appetite presents him with special problems in
these days of Nazi rationing, quickly lapses into his normal
gloom. He has learned from reliable sources that the German
field kitchens will dish out sizable helpings of meat. How
much longer is he going to be able to hold out against the
temptation simply to go and join up in the German army?
Mrs. Kopecka and Schweyk are greatly disturbed by his situation. A soul in torment! Schweyk, ever the realist, suggests
making Baloun swear an oath never under any circumstances
to have anything to do with the Germans. Baloun reminds
them that it is six months since he last had a square meal. In
exchange for a square meal, he says, he would be prepared to
do *anything*. Mrs. Kopecka thinks something might be arranged. She is a blazing patriot, and the idea of Baloun in the
German army is more than she can bear. When her young admirer turns up, the butcher's son Prochazka, they hold a
touching conversation in which she poses Cleopatra's age-old
question: "If it truly is love, then tell me how much?" She
wants to know if his love, for instance, would run to the
scrounging of two pounds of smoked butt for the under-
nourished Baloun. He could take it from the paternal shop,
only the Nazis have established heavy penalties for black-
marketeering. Nonetheless, seeing the way to the widow's
heart open before him for the first time, young Prochazka
agrees in a positive tornado of emotion to bring round the
meat. Meanwhile the "Flagon" has been filling up and Schweyk
has started letting all and sundry know what he thinks of the
Munich plot against Hitler. Inspired by the announcements
on the German radio, he plunges with foolhardy innocence
into a mortally dangerous conversation with Brettschneider,
who is known to all the regular customers as a Gestapo agent.

His classic driveling fails to deceive the Gestapo man. Without any more ado Herr Brettschneider arrests the amazed but obliging Schweyk.

2

Introduced to Gestapo headquarters at the Petschek Bank by Herr Brettschneider, Schweyk flings up his right hand, bawls out "Hurrah for our Führer Adolf Hitler! We're going to win this war!" and is discharged as chronically half-witted.

Hearing that Schweyk is a dog hustler, the interrogating SS officer Ludwig Bullinger asks about a pedigreed dog he has seen in the Salmgasse. "Beg to report, sir, I am professionally acquainted with the animal," says Schweyk cheerfully, and goes on to expatiate on the racial question. That spitz is the apple of Undersecretary Voyta's eye, and not to be had for love or money. Schweyk and the SS officer discuss how best to have the undersecretary arrested and expropriated as an enemy of the state; however, it turns out that he is "no yid" but a quisling. So Schweyk gets the honorable job of stealing the pedigreed spitz and showing himself to be a good collaborationist.

3

Returning in triumph to the "Flagon," Schweyk finds that a tense situation has developed. Fat Baloun is waiting for his meal like a cat on hot bricks, fully prepared at the first glimpse of the pork to abjure all intention of ever joining Hitler's army. It is now ten past twelve, and young Prochazka has not yet shown up. Schweyk has been so considerate as to bring along SS Man Müller 2 from Gestapo headquarters, with the promise that widow Kopecka will tell his future by reading his hand. At first the landlady refuses on the grounds that she has had unfortunate experiences with her predictions. Young Prochazka now finally appears, and everyone looks nervously at his music case—he is a student at the music academy—be-

cause of course the SS man must not see the meat. To get him
out of the way Mrs. Kopecka sits down and reads his hand.
It seems that he is destined to perform heroic deeds, and has
been picked out finally for a hero's death. Depressed and de-
moralized, the SS man lurches out and Baloun flings himself
on the music case round which he has been longingly circling
for some time. The case is empty. Young Prochazka makes his
miserable confession: he didn't dare steal the smoked butt because the sight of Schweyk's arrest gave him such a fear of the
Gestapo. Angrily the widow Kopecka spurns him with a
Biblical gesture, for he has failed the test as a man and a Czech.
Despondently he leaves, but no sooner does the bitterly
frustrated fat man speak slightingly of her suitor than she
snaps back that the Nazis are to blame for it all. So Baloun's
wrath is diverted to the oppressors of his once beautiful
country, and when Herr Brettschneider the Gestapo agent
comes in he starts singing the subversive song of the black
radish, which must "get on out" and be "cut up and salted"
till "he sweats," all of which strikes Herr Brettschneider as
suspicious, but offers him no pretext to intervene.

First Schweyk Finale:
Interlude in the Upper Regions

The mighty Hitler, having encountered obstacles in his attempt to conquer the world, needs more bombers, tanks, and
guns, and inquires of the mighty Göring whether the European Little Man is prepared to work for him. Göring assures
him that the European Little Man will work for him just like
the Little Man in Germany. The Gestapo will see to that.
The Führer has nothing to fear and need have no hesitation
about carrying on conquering the world.

4

Schweyk's operation against the germanophile Undersecretary
Voyta's spitz takes place in the park along the Moldau,

which is where Voyta's maidservant and her friend Paula are
accustomed to take the pedigreed hound for his walkies every
evening. Schweyk and Baloun come up to the bench where the
two girls are sitting, and pretend to have erotic aims in view.
Schweyk warns the girls in all honesty that SS leader Bullinger
wants to annex the spitz for the sake of its racial purity and
have it sent to his lady wife in Cologne; he has had this on
impeccable authority. Thereupon he goes off "to meet someone at the Metropole." Baloun exchanges pleasantries with the
girls, and they are moved by the Moldau's majestic flow to
start singing a folk song. By the end of the song the dog has
gone. Schweyk has underhandedly lured it away as they were
singing. The girls rush off to the police station, and Schweyk
has just returned with the spitz to tell his friend that they
mustn't let the SS leader have it till he has put down the
money, when a sinister-looking individual appears on the
scene. Schweyk the dog-catcher has a man-catcher on his
track; the individual identifies himself as a functionary of the
Nazi labor organization whose job it is to recruit idlers and
loafers into the "voluntary labor service." Concerned for the
spitz, Schweyk and Baloun are led off for registration.

5

Noon break at the Prague freight station. Schweyk and Baloun have become railroad workers for Hitler and are waiting
under the eyes of a heavily-armed German soldier for their
cabbage soup to be sent up from the "Flagon." Today it is
widow Kopecka in person who brings their enamel dishes.
The stolen spitz left in her care by Schweyk is becoming the
focus of some intense political activity, and must be got off
the premises. The controlled press is saying that the dog's
disappearance is due to an act of vengeance by the population
against a pro-German official. Schweyk promises to come and
collect it. He is listening with only half an ear, since he is
troubled by Baloun's condition. The sentry's dinner has arrived—goulash! Trembling from head to foot, Baloun has
gone sniffing after the cauldron as it was borne past him. Now

he is excitedly asking the sentry whether the helpings in the German army are always as big as that, etc., etc., and scarcely pays attention to the imploring glances of his friends. The soldier is plunged in thought as he munches his goulash, all the while silently moving his lips between bites. He has been told to memorize the number 4268, being that of a freight car with harvesting machines for Lower Bavaria, and this is something he finds difficult. Always ready to help, Schweyk sets out to teach him a mnemonic technique which he learned from a water-board statistician who is one of the regulars at the "Flagon." By the time Schweyk has finished explaining it, the poor sentry's brain is in such a tangle that when they eventually ask him for the freight car he helplessly points to the first car he sees. Schweyk is afraid that this may mean that a carload of machine guns for Stalingrad may get sent to Bavaria in lieu. "But who knows?" he remarks consolingly to Baloun and Mrs. Kopecka. "Maybe by that time they'll need harvesting machines in Stalingrad and machine guns in Bavaria. Why not?"

6

Saturday night at the "Flagon." Dance. A morose Baloun takes the floor with the undersecretary's maidservant, who is there with her friend. The police are still interviewing the two girls about the spitz. Yesterday, however, they dropped a hint to Herr Brettschneider as to its whereabouts: at SS leader Bullinger's, possibly already in Cologne. Baloun hints that this may be his last evening at the "Flagon": he is fed up with feeling hungry. And it incidentally emerges that the noisy fun of the dance floor serves a higher purpose: covering up the sound of the news from London, which Kopecka is listening to and passing on to the guests. Enter then Schweyk, cheerfully, with a parcel under his arm: meat for Baloun's goulash. The fat man can hardly believe it; the two friends embrace most movingly. Baloun's enthusiasm is such, however, that Schweyk asks Mrs. Kopecka to put extra paprika in the goulash, since it's only horsemeat. The landlady looks quizzically at him, and he confesses that it is Mr. Voyta's spitz. A police car draws up. SS leader Bullinger enters the "Flagon," with SS men at his heels. Hue and cry for the Voyta spitz. Asked by Bullinger whether he knows the dog's whereabouts, Schweyk innocently replies that he hasn't got it. "Didn't you see in the papers, Herr SS Leader, where it said it had been stolen?" Bullinger's patience gives way. He bellows that the "Flagon" is the source of all subversive Czech subversiveness and will have to be smoked out. Moreover, the dog can only be there. The SS is starting to search the place when Herr Brettschneider arrives. Herr Brettschneider, who has long pictured himself in the rôle of protector (this is, after all, a protectorate) to the charming Mrs. Kopecka, forcefully stands up to the fuming Bullinger and invites him to Gestapo headquarters, where he has some rather revealing information about the present location of the missing dog. Mrs. Kopecka's house is above suspicion; he would go to the stake for that. Unfortunately at this very moment the gentlemen's attention is drawn to a parcel reposing on one of the tables. The wretched Baloun has been unable to keep his fingers off Schweyk's gift. A triumphant Bullinger discloses the contents of the parcel: meat. So the "Flagon" is a center of the black-market! At that Schweyk feels forced to admit that he put the parcel there. He claims that a gentleman with a black beard gave it to him "to hold." All those present affirm having seen the man, while Herr Brettschneider, after going to the stake on the "Flagon's" behalf, thinks it very possible that the criminal spotted the SS a hundred yards off and accordingly ran away. Nonetheless Bullinger insists on arresting Schweyk, and the gentlemen escort him out of the "Flagon"—Bullinger, with the parcel under his arm, prophesying that he will find that dog yet. Cold-shouldered by the widow, young Prochazka has spent the entire evening sitting in a corner; now he slinks guiltily out, followed by the widow's icy stare. Baloun bursts into tears. Thanks to his weakness the loving couple has been parted and his friend landed in mortal danger. The "Flagon's" landlady consoles him. In a big song she foretells that just as the Moldau washes away all the dirt, so her oppressed people's love of their country will wash away the cruelties of their invaders.

Second Schweyk Finale:
Interlude in the Upper Regions

The anxious Hitler, having been caught by the Russian winter, needs more soldiers. He inquires of the anxious Goebbels whether the European Little Man is prepared to fight for him. Goebbels assures him that the European Little Man will fight for him just like the Little Man in Germany. The Gestapo will see to that.

7

As a result of disagreements between Bullinger the crocodile and Brettschneider the tiger, and what with Hitler's screaming for fresh soldiers, the good soldier Schweyk has moved from the cellars of the Gestapo to the recruiting bureau for the German army. Among those whom he encounters there is Undersecretary Voyta, who is being sent to the front because his spitz was stolen. All the inmates are discussing what loathsome diseases they can report to the doctors at their medical inspection. Schweyk for his part feels another bout of rheumatism coming, since he has no time to travel to Russia for Hitler when "nothing's been settled in Prague." Hearing that young Prochazka is standing outside the barracks with an important message for him, he fears the worst. Happily Prochazka manages to bribe an SS man to smuggle in a note to him, and it is an encouraging one. The "Flagon" landlady's suitor writes that, having been deeply moved by Schweyk's self-sacrifice and ghastly fate, he will now supply "the desired article." At that Schweyk feels prepared to devote himself with an untroubled mind to Hitler's Russian affairs, which are said to be going none too well. Outside is heard the Nazis' notorious "Horst Wessel" song; a battalion is moving off to the East. The inmates begin singing their own version of the Nazi anthem, where "The butcher calls" and "The sheep march on," and an NCO comes in who is mistaken enough to praise them for joining in so cheerfully, then informs them that they are all undoubtedly fit to enlist and are accordingly accepted into the army. They are to be divided among different units to prevent them from getting up to any filthy tricks, so Schweyk bids a touching farewell to the undersecretary and goes off to Hitler's war.

8†

Weeks have elapsed. Deep in the wintry plains of the Russian empire Hitler's good soldier Schweyk is marching to join his unit near Stalingrad, where it is supposed to combine with other sections of the Nazi army in holding back the Red army's terrible assaults. As a result of one of his numerous misadventures he has lost contact with the rest of his draft. Untroubled by geographical preconceptions, however, and in his usual blithely trusting frame of mind, he is marching towards his allotted destination wrapped in a great bundle of assorted articles of clothing to keep out the cold. A semi-demolished signpost says that Stalingrad is 100 miles off.

While he is thus marching to Stalingrad the "Flagon" keeps looming up in a rosy light before our good Schweyk's eyes. He pictures to himself how young Prochazka lives up to his promises. The man's love of the landlady has overcome his fear of the Gestapo, and to her agreeable surprise he hands Mrs. Kopecka two pounds of smoked butt for Schweyk's unfortunate friend Baloun.

As he battles courageously against the icy blasts of the steppes, the indefatigable and utterly well-intentioned Schweyk becomes uncomfortably aware that he is getting no closer to his goal. The farther he marches, the greater the distances shown on the signposts to Stalingrad, where Hitler so urgently needs him. A thousand miles away Anna Kopecka may at this moment be singing her "Song of the Flagon," that homely and hospitable place. The voracious Baloun's long-awaited meal will have developed into a wedding feast for the landlady and young Prochazka.

Schweyk marches on. The blizzards on those interminable eastern steppes, where the distance to Stalingrad always re-

† The stage is divided in two.

mains about the same, cloak the sun by day and the moon by night from the view of the good soldier Schweyk, who set out to give the great Hitler a helping hand.

Epilogue

It is likewise deep in the eastern steppes that the good soldier Schweyk personally encounters his Führer Hitler. Their conversation in the driving snow is brief and almost entirely swallowed by the storm. The gist of this historic conversation is that Hitler is asking Schweyk whether he knows the way back.

> [GW *Schriften zum Theater* 3, pp. 1186–96. Dated New York City, May 1943. This preliminary summary of the story was made for Kurt Weill, and it contains some differences from the final text. Thus the interludes balance more neatly; there is no interlude after scene 2; and Goebbels appears instead of von Bock. This is the only version which makes Prochazka a music student (scene 3) and has Schweyk preparing for an attack of rheumatism (scene 7). It omits the army chaplain and the singing of "The German Miserere," and the ending is unlike that of any of the scripts.]

Staging

The "Flagon" bar in Prague forms the center of the set. Black oak paneling, bar with brass fitting, electric piano with a transparent top in which the moon and the flowing Moldau can appear. In the third act only a part of the "Flagon" appears to Schweyk in his thoughts and dream: his own table. Schweyk's Anabasis" shown in this act; move in a circle around this part of the "Flagon." The length of his march can be indicated by such devices as having the peasants' hut roll forward or backward, growing larger or smaller in the process. —The interludes should be played in the style of a grisly fairy tale. The whole Nazi hierarchy (Hitler, Göring, Goebbels) can appear in all of them (plus Himmler and von Bock as the case may be). The satraps can accentuate the verses with shouts of "Heil!"

[Note "Zur Inszenierung" appended to the text of the play in GW5, p. 1995.—Tr. Ralph Manheim.]

Editorial Note

1. General

Brecht's Schweyk play derives from Jaroslav Hašek's novel *The Adventures of the Good Soldier Švejk* [or Schweik] *in the World War*, or more precisely from its German translation by Grete Reiner, which was first published in 1926 and from then on remained one of Brecht's favorite books. It was promptly dramatized by Max Brod, the Prague German writer who was responsible also for the publication of Kafka's posthumous novels, and by the German humorist Hans Reimann. The resulting play was one of those chosen by Erwin Piscator for his first season with his own company in Berlin in 1927–28, when Brecht was one of his team of dramaturges, and because it seemed far too conventional and static for the form of production which Piscator had in mind, which was to make use of a treadmill stage and George Grosz projections, it was radically overhauled by this team. In Brecht's own mind, he himself was the main author of the Piscator version of this play; thus according to *The Messingkauf Dialogues* "he did Schweik for him entirely." However, all other accounts give Piscator's principal dramaturge Felix Gasbarra an equal or even greater share in the new adaptation, and there is nothing in Brecht's papers to bear him out, beyond his penciled title page to the script (the rest of which is not typed by him): "Adventures of the Good Soldier Schweik./Brecht, Gasbarra,

Piscator, G. Grosz." Nor, as far as we know, did either he or his editors subsequently consider publishing it among his own works, though these contain a number of his adaptations, notably those for the Berliner Ensemble.

This script differs from the Brod-Reimann version above all in its attempt to match the "epic" and picaresque form of Hašek's unfinished masterpiece. In his journal Brecht termed it "a pure montage from the novel." Briefly, its first part, corresponding to the novel's part I, is divided into the following short scenes (the numbers of the relevant chapters in the book being given in brackets): 1. [1] At Schweik's./ 2. [1] At the "Flagon."/3. [7] At Schweik's (where he determines to volunteer)./4. [7] Street scene (with Schweik in the wheelchair shouting "To Belgrade!")./5. [8] Recruiting office (medical inspection)./6. [8] Military hospital./7. [8] Streets in Prague (with Schweik under arrest)./8. [9] Transformation scene: detention room, chapel, and sacristy./9. [14] Lieutenant Lukaš's rooms (Katz, the chaplain, loses to Schweik at cards)./10. [14] The same (where Schweik fulfills the lady's wishes)./11. [14] The same (preparatory to the stealing of the dog)./12. Street in Prague (Schweik and sapper Voditchka as dog thieves)./13. [3 of part II] The same (Voditchka making anti-Hungarian gestures)./14. [15] Barrack square (the colonel recognizes his dog and packs Schweik and Lukaš off to the front).

The second part, drawn from parts II and III of the novel, is in a slightly confused order (e.g., the numbering of the second scene) and differs from the staged version in its ending. (Piscator himself recounts that his team suggested various alternatives, but that he finally settled for Gasbarra's idea, based on Cadet Biegler's dream in part III, chapter 1, of a scene in heaven with Schweik and war wounded parading before God; when this proved under-rehearsed, however, it was changed for the parting scene between Schweik and Voditchka, who agree to meet "at six o'clock after the war".) Again, the scenes are as follows: 1. [II/1] Transformation scene: in the train, changing to the station police office at Tábor./5. [II/2] Film, with Schweik marching (the start of Schweik's "Anabasis") and episode with the herdsman./2.

[II/2] Transformation scene: country road, then Putim police station, then film./3a. In a troop train (about Baloun and his hunger)./3b. Schweik rejoins his unit./3c. [III/2] In the train (where Baloun has eaten the sardines)./3d. [III/3] Beside the railway track (with Baloun doing physical jerks)./3e. [III/2] Other side of the train (with Schweik made to do the same). Schweik here tells the 4268 episode as a story./4. [III/4] Battlefield. (He gets lost, puts on Russian uniform and is taken prisoner by a Hungarian unit of his own army. A shell bursts, and he is killed.)

In returning to this material with a view to reworking it for the Second World War, Brecht found little that he could incorporate as it stood. Discussing his plan with his son on his return from New York at the end of May 1943, he realized that he was changing Schweik's character by allowing him to risk frequenting so dangerous a tavern as the "Flagon" (which figures little in the book), and to sacrifice himself for the sake of Baloun. "That indeed is where the situation is sharper than in 1914," he noted in his journal for May 27, where he reports that he has been re-reading the novel in the train on the way back:

> once again i was overwhelmed by hašek's vast panorama and the authentically un-positive point of view which it attributes to the people, they being themselves the one positive element and accordingly incapable of reacting "positively" to anything else. whatever happens schweik mustn't turn into a cunning underhanded saboteur. he is merely an opportunist exploiting the tiny openings left him.

He had already written the "Story" for Kurt Weill before leaving New York, and it seems that he soon showed this to Eisler, who commented that Schweik could not be seen as a typical "Little Man" and suggested that Brecht's play ought to end with him leading Hitler to Stalingrad, not back home. Another diary entry, of the 29th, shows that he also discussed it with Peter Lorre, whom he evidently had in mind for the title part, while again on July 12, when the first rough version was already complete, he noted that the language of the play differs substantially from that of the german hašek translation. south german elements have been worked in, and in various ways the gest is different. so it would be wrong, e.g., to speak bohemian dialect in this play; in other words the vocal inflections shouldn't be bohemian german.

Scene 2 of the first part of the Piscator adaptation is the only one to have survived in recognizable form, and even there Brecht changed the sex of the landlord Palivec, turning him (doubtless for Lotte Lenya's sake) first into Mrs. Natonek, then changing her name to Kopecka. Most of Hašek's characters, too, he abandoned, so that aside from a brief glimpse of Father Lacina (the less interesting of Hašek's two disgraceful chaplains) only Baloun and the police agent Brettschneider appear with Schweik in the play; all other characters are Brecht's or belong to history. But the basic concept and a number of subsidiary situations or elements were transplanted into the new terms: the stealing of the dog, for instance, Baloun's embarrassing appetite, the incident of freight car 4268, the notion of an "Anabasis" with its semiconscious loss of orientation, and above all the whole Schweikian approach to authority, patriotism, and war. Though the songs were mainly Brecht's, three of Schweik's chants are taken from the book— "Standing behind the gun" (p. 114) from II/2; "Onward to Jaromersh hoofing" (pp. 118–19) from III/4 (Piscator II/5); and "Thought that in the service" (p. 120) from I/8 (Piscator I/7)—while Baloun's "Beseda Song" (p. 102) can be found in III/4, where it is described as "the song the Czech regiments sang when they marched and bled for Austria at Solferino." And despite what Brecht says, Schweik's whole way of speaking derives from the novel. If at times it resembles that of Mother Courage, or Matti (in *Puntila*), or even Galy Gay (in *A Man's a Man*, another part which Brecht identified with Lorre), this is only because they too in some measure reflect the same source.

The new play was at first simply called *Schweyk*, the phrase "in the Second World War" making its appearance as an addition on the title page of what seems to be the latest of the four versions in the Brecht Archive. The other three of these all date from 1943 and consist of a bound copy in Brecht's typing, dated Santa Monica, July 1943; a largely identical Brecht typescript (but divided into acts and with a different ending) which he gave to Peter Lorre; and a fair copy not typed by Brecht. In summarizing their slight differences scene by scene we will refer to them respectively as the first script, the Lorre script, the fair copy, and the old Berliner Ensemble script (it bears that company's stamp). The first printed text appeared in volume X of the collected *Stücke* (1958), though a duplicated stage script was available from Henschel-Verlag in East Berlin in 1956.

2. Scene-by-Scene Account

Prelude in the Higher Regions

Our text is identical with the first script. The fair copy has a different version of the first three lines:

HITLER
> My dear Himmler, forty-eight is the age I've now got to.
> And so henceforward "now or never" must be my motto.
> Accordingly I've just decided [to conquer the whole world, etc.]

This version ends, after "Where does the humble Little Man in Europe stand?":

HIMMLER
> My Führer, he loves you—or that's how it's been planned
> —much as the Little Man in Germany loves you too.
> The Gestapo arrange all that.

HITLER
> It's just as well they do.

—thus matching the last lines of the subsequent Interludes between scenes 3 and 4, and between scenes 6 and 7.

Scene 1

Virtually unchanged from the first script.

Scene 2

Virtually unchanged. The report about the banker Krusha and Bullinger's reaction to it were additions to the first script.

Interlude in the Nether Regions

Is in the first script but not in the fair copy, the old Berliner Ensemble script, or the duplicated stage script.

Scene 3

The fat lady shopkeeper is an addition by Brecht on the first script, which remained virtually unchanged.

Interlude in the Higher Regions

Unchanged. In the Lorre script this ends Act 1.

Scene 4

One or two cuts have been made since the first script, notably a characteristic Schweyk story following after "Ah yes, the Moldau" on p. 95. The *Moritat* "Henry Slept beside his Newly-wedded," unattributed by Brecht, who gives it as an appendix in the printed version, is by J. F. A. Kazner (1779); according to Dr. Sammy McLean it is also known as "Heinrich und Wilhelmine," "Die Geisterstimme von Mitternacht," and "Der ungetreue Liebhaber."

In the first script this scene was originally followed by a

second "Interlude in the Nether Regions," which Brecht cut there.

Scene 5

A speech by Schweyk about sabotage, added as an after-thought to the first script, was dropped in the fair copy.

Scene 6

All through this scene the references were to the London, not the Moscow Radio. The amendment was made on the first script, but not on the other three, nor on the duplicated stage script. Kati's remark about Schweyk's hat (p. 109) was an addition to the first script, which also lacks the "Song of the Moldau" at the end, presumably because Brecht was still re-writing it; (besides those in the other scripts, there are seven separate versions of this song).

In the Lorre script Act 2 ends here.

Interlude in the Higher Regions

Stalingrad replaced Rostov on the first script, and similarly with the numerous references that follow up to the end of the play.

Scene 7

Virtually unchanged.

Scene 8

The drunken chaplain was originally not Bullinger's brother but the Reverend Matz from Rosenberg. The relevant amendments were made on the first script, but the fair copy and the duplicated stage script still have him as Matz. A reference to the torture chambers was also added, and taken over into the fair copy; presumably it was dropped so that Schweyk should remain innocent of such things. The price specified in Mrs. Kopecka's song "Come, dear guest, and have a seat" (which was accompanied by a melody in Brecht's characteristic notation) was 80 Kreuzers in the first script; the final cry "On to Stalingrad!" was missing; and there were a number of other even smaller changes.

Epilogue

All four scripts and the duplicated stage script originally had Schweyk saying of the south (p. 132):

> But there are piles of corpses there.
> HITLER
>   Then I'll push east.
> SCHWEYK
>   Then we'll have the British in our hair.

(We have omitted the stage directions.) This is changed to the present reading on the first script alone; hence it seems likely (as with the references to the London Radio) that Brecht used the bound script for his final amendments in the 1950s. In the Lorre script the ending is different from mid-scene on; thus after "And so it has done" (p. 131) there is no examination of the prospects north, south, east, and west, and instead Hitler finishes by returning to his opening theme:

> HITLER
>   The average German's useless without my grip to keep
>   him steady.
> SCHWEYK
>   You kicked him too hard when he was down; he's a
>   master race already.

HITLER
When I took over I found his international reputation
was sinking.
But now you're fighting side by side with him.

SCHWEYK

I'd much

rather we were drinking.

*(Schweyk picks up his rifle and shoves Hitler in front of
him. They stop at the signpost, and Schweyk turns his
torch on it. He reads "Stalingrad—30 miles," and marches
on in that direction with Hitler before him. The darkness
and the storm swallow them up)*

The final chorus is not in the fair copy.

THE CAUCASIAN CHALK CIRCLE

Texts by Brecht

Notes to *The Caucasian Chalk Circle*

1. REALISM AND STYLIZATION

Actors, stage designers, and directors normally achieve stylization at the cost of realism. They create a style by creating "the" peasant, "the" wedding, "the" battlefield; in other words by removing whatever is unique, special, contradictory, accidental, and by providing hackneyed or hackneyable stereotypes, the bulk of which represent no mastery of reality but are just drawings of drawings—simple to provide since the originals already have elements of style in them. Such stylists have no style of their own, nor any wish to grasp that of reality; all they do is to imitate methods of stylization. Plainly all art embellishes (which is not the same as glossing over). If for no other reason, it must do so because it has to link reality with enjoyment. But this kind of embellishment, formulation, stylization, must not involve phoniness or loss of substance. Any actress who plays Grusha needs to study the beauty of Brueghel's *Dulle Griet*.

2. TENSION

The play was written in America after ten years of exile, and its structure is partly conditioned by a revulsion against the commercialized dramaturgy of Broadway. At the same time it makes use of certain elements of that older American theater whose forte lay in burlesques and "shows." In those highly imaginative manifestations, which recall the films of that splendid man Chaplin, the tension focused not merely on the progress of the plot (or only in a much cruder and larger sense than now), but more on the question "How?". Nowadays when we are "offered an amusing trifle" it is simply the feverish efforts of a rapidly aging whore who hopes that her graceless tricks will serve to postpone or annul the moment when her painful and frequently-operated vagina has once again to be handed over to a client. The pleasure of telling a story is hamstrung by fear that it will fall flat. Unleashing this pleasure, however, does not mean freeing it from all control. Detail will be of the greatest importance, but that does not mean that economy won't be of great importance too. Imagination can be applied to the achievement of brevity. The point is not to abandon something rich. The worst enemy of true playing is playing about; meandering is the sign of a bad story-teller, while cosiness is just self-satisfaction and to be despised as such. Direct statement is among the most important methods of epic art, and it is as fair to [speak] of epic restlessness as of epic repose.

3. THE CHALK CIRCLE

The test of the chalk circle in the old Chinese novel and play, like their Biblical counterpart, Solomon's test of the sword, still remains a valuable test of motherhood (by ascertaining motherliness) even if motherhood today has to be socially rather than biologically defined. The Caucasian Chalk Circle is not a parable. Possibly the prologue may create confusion on this point, since it looks superficially as if the whole story is being told in order to clear up the argument about who owns the valley. On closer inspection, however, the story is seen to be a true narrative which of itself proves nothing but merely displays a particular kind of wisdom, a potentially model attitude for the argument in question. Seen this way, the prologue becomes a background which locates the practicability and also the evolution of such wisdom in an historic setting. And so the theater must not use the kind of technique developed by it for plays of the parable type.

4. BACKGROUND AND FOREGROUND

In the English language there is an American term "sucker," and this is exactly what Grusha is being when she takes over the child. The Austrian term "die Wurzen" means something of the same sort, while in High German one would have to say "der Dumme," "the fool" (as in the context "they've managed to find somebody fool enough to . . ."). Her maternal instincts lay Grusha open to troubles and tribulations which prove very nearly fatal. All she wants of Azdak is permission to go on producing, in other words to keep on paying. She loves the child; her claim to it is based on the fact that she is willing and able to be productive. She is no longer a sucker after the trial.

5. [SETTING OF THE PLAY]

The play's setting needs to be very simple. The varying backgrounds can be indicated by some form of projection; at the same time the projections must be artistically valid. The bit players can in some cases play several parts at once. The five musicians sit onstage with the singer and join in the action.

6. INCIDENTAL MUSIC FOR *THE CHALK CIRCLE*

Aside from the few songs which can take personal expression, the story-teller's music need only display a cold beauty, but it should not be unduly difficult. Though I think it is possible to make particularly effective use of a certain kind of monotony, the musical basis of the five acts needs to be clearly varied. The opening song of Act 1 should have something barbaric about it, and the underlying rhythm should be a preparation and accompaniment for the entry of the governor's family and the soldiers beating back the crowd. The mimed song at the end of the act should be cold, so that the girl Grusha can play against the grain of it.

For Act 2 (The Flight to the Northern Mountains) the theater calls for thrustful music to hold this extremely epic act together; nonetheless it must be thin and delicate.

Act 3 has the melting snow music (poetical) and, for its main scene, funeral and wedding music in contrast with one another. The song in the scene by the river has the same theme as the Act 1 song in which Grusha promises the soldier to wait for him.

In Act 4 the thrustful, scurrilous ballad about Azdak (which would best be sung *piano*) must be interrupted twice by Azdak's two songs (which definitely have to be simple to sing, since Azdak must be played by the most powerful actor rather than by the best singer). The last (lawsuit) act demands a good dance at the end.

7. BEHAVIOR OF THE SINGER IN THE LAST SCENE OF ACT 1

The playwright's suggestion that the general principle of having the scenes embody specific passages of the singer's song in such a way that their performance never overshadows the singer's solo performance to the villagers ought to be deliberately abandoned in production.

8. CASTING OF AZDAK

It is essential to have an actor who can portray an utterly genuine man. Azdak is utterly genuine, a disappointed revolutionary posing as a human wreck, like Shakespeare's wise men who act the fool. Without this the judgment of the chalk circle would lose all its authority.

9. PALACE REVOLUTION

The curt orders given offstage inside the palace (sporadically and in some cases quietly so as to imply the palace's vast size) must be cut once they have served to help the actors at rehearsal. What is going on onstage is not supposed to be a slice of some larger occurrence, just the part of it to be seen at this precise spot outside the palace gate. It is the entire occurrence, and the gate is *the* gate. (Nor is the size of the palace to be conveyed in spatial terms.) What we have to do is replace our extras with good actors. One good actor is worth a whole battalion of extras. I.e., he is more.

> [Sections 1–6, 8, and 9 are from GW *Schriften zum Theater* 3, pp. 1204–08. The typescripts suggest that sections 1–4 belong together, and we have put them in their original, possibly accidental, but still logical order. They and section 6 are thought to date from 1944. Sections 5 and 7 are notes accompanying the first version of the script that year, 7 being taken from BBA 192/178. The last two were written nearly ten years later, 8 being assigned to about 1953 by BBA while 9 relates to a rehearsal held on December 4 of that year in preparation for Brecht's Berliner Ensemble production.]

Dance of the Grand Duke with his Bow

Oh, the green fields of Samara!
Oh, the bent backs of a warlike race!
O sun, o domination!

I am your prince. This bow they are bringing
Is elm tipped with bronze, strung with flexible sinew.
This arrow is mine, which I mean to send winging
To plunge itself deep, o my enemy, in you.

Oh, the green fields of Samara!
Oh, the bent backs of a warlike race!
O sun, o domination!

Off, off to the fight, bowstring taut. Aren't you frightened
To feel how much deeper the bronze will go worming
Its way through your flesh as the bowstring is tightened?
Fly, arrow, and cut up that enemy vermin!

So I tug, tug and tug at the bow that they made me.
How strong are my shoulders! A fraction more. Steady . . .
Why, it's broken! All lies! Elm and bronze have be-
    trayed me.
Help, help! God have mercy: my soul's so unready.

Oh, the cattle-stocked fields of Samara!
Oh, the bent backs of a warlike race!
Oh, the cutting up of the enemy!

> [BBA 28/23-4. A penciled note by Elisabeth Hauptmann,
> dating probably from the 1950s or later, identifies this as
> material discarded from the play.]

Concerning the Prologue

Your dislike of the prologue puzzles me somewhat; it was the
first bit of the play to be written by me in the States. You
see, the problem posed by this parable-like play has got to
be derived from real-life needs, and in my view this was
achieved in a light and cheerful manner. Take away the prologue, and it's impossible to understand on the one hand why
it wasn't left as the Chinese chalk circle, and on the other why
it should be called Caucasian. I first of all wrote the little story
which was published in *Tales from the Calendar*. But on coming to dramatize it I felt just this lack of elucidatory historical
background.

> [From Werner Hecht (ed.): *Materialien zu Brecht's
> "Der kaukasische Kreidekreis,"* Frankfurt, Suhrkamp-Ver-
> lag, 1966, p. 28. This passage is taken from a letter to

Brecht's publisher Peter Suhrkamp, and reflects a common attitude among West German critics and theater directors. The "little story" was "The Augsburg Chalk Circle," for which see p. 309.]

Contradictions in *The Caucasian Chalk Circle*

1. Main contradictions

The more Grusha does to save the child's life, the more she endangers her own; her productivity leads to her own destruction. That is how things are, given the conditions of war, the law as it is, and her isolation and poverty. In the law's eyes the rescuer is a thief. Her poverty is a threat to the child, and the child adds to it. For the child's sake she needs a husband, but she is in danger of losing one on its account. And so forth.

Bit by bit, by making sacrifices, not least of herself, Grusha becomes transformed into a mother for the child; and finally, having risked or suffered so many losses, fears no loss more than that of the child itself. Azdak's judgment makes the rescue of the child absolute. He is free to award the child to her because there is no longer any difference between the child's interests and hers.

Azdak is the disappointed man who is not going to cause disappointment in others.

2. Other contradictions

The petitioners prostrate themselves before the governor as he goes to Easter mass. Beaten back by the Ironshirts, they fight wildly among themselves for a place in the front row.

The same peasant who overcharges Grusha for his milk is then kindly enough to help her pick up the child. He isn't mean; he's poor.

The architects make utterly servile obeisances to the governor's aide-de-camp, but one of them has to watch the other two to see how they do it. They are not just natural boot-lickers; they need the job.

Grusha's spineless brother is reluctant to take in his sister, but furious with his kulak of a wife on account of his dependence on her.

This spineless brother cannot say boo to his kulak of a wife, but is overbearing with the peasant woman with whom he fixes up the marriage contract.

The motherly instincts of the peasant woman who takes in the foundling against her husband's wishes are limited and provisional; she betrays it to the police. (Likewise Grusha's motherly instincts, though they are so much greater, so very great, are limited and provisional: she wants to see the child into safety, then give it away.)

The maid Grusha is against war because it has torn her beloved from her; she recommends him always to stay in the middle in order to survive. However, on her flight into the mountains she sings of the popular hero Sosso Robakidze who conquered Iran, in order to keep her courage up.

[GW *Schriften zum Theater* 17, pp. 1208–10. Assigned by BBA to 1954. However, Brecht's concept of main and subsidiary contradictions (i.e., conflicting elements in a situation) derives from Mao Tse-tung, whose pamphlet *On Contradiction* he seems to have read in 1955.]

A Detour

P: The people at X want to cut "the way to the northern mountains." The play is a long one, and they argue that this whole act is really no more than a detour. One sees how the maid wants to get rid of the child as soon as she has got it away from the immediate danger zone; but then she keeps it after all, and that, they say, is what counts.

B: Such detours in modern plays have to be studied carefully before one makes up one's mind to take a short cut. It might prove to seem longer. Certain theaters cut one of

Macheath's two arrests in the *Threepenny Opera* on the grounds that both might have occurred because he twice went to the brothel instead of clearing out. They made him come to grief because he went to the brothel, not because he went to it too often, was careless. In short, they hoped to liven things up and finished by getting tedious.

P: They say it weakens the maid's claim to the child in the trial scene if her feeling for him is shown as subject to limitations.

B: To start with, the trial scene isn't about the maid's claim to the child but about the child's claim to the better mother. And the maid's suitability for being a mother, her usefulness and reliability are shown precisely by her level-headed reservations about taking the child on.

R: Even her reservations strike me as beautiful. Friendliness is not unlimited, it is subject to measure. A person has just so much friendliness—no more, no less—and it is furthermore dependent on the situation at the time. It can be exhausted, can be replenished, and so on and so forth.

W: I'd call that a realistic view.

B: It's too mechanical a one for me: unfriendly. Why not look at it this way? Evil times make humane feelings a danger to those who have them. Inside the maid Grusha the child's interests and her own are at loggerheads with one another. She must acknowledge both interests and do her best to promote them both. This way of looking at it, I think, must lead to a richer and more flexible portrayal of the Grusha part. It's true.

> [From "Die Dialektik auf dem Theater" in *Versuche 15*, Suhrkamp and Aufbau Verlags, 1957. As with other dialogues in that collection, Brecht shows himself as B, talking with some of his young collaborators: in this case P for Peter Palitzsch, R for Käthe Rülicke, and W for Manfred Wekwerth. They were not literal transcriptions.]

Editorial Note

1. General

The Caucasian Chalk Circle brings together two threads that had been twining their way gently through Brecht's mind for several years before Luise Rainer asked him to write the play. They are of course the old Chinese story of the chalk circle, with its strong resemblance to the judgment of Solomon, and the story of the eccentric, paradoxical judge which (though one can never be certain of this) Brecht appears to have devised for himself. Of these the former probably has the longer ancestry—in Brecht's mind, that is—for Klabund's modern German dramatization was staged by Max Reinhardt at the Deutsches Theater, where Brecht had just spent a year as a junior dramaturge, on October 20, 1925. Brecht knew Klabund, or Alfred Henschke (as he was really called), from Munich as a writer and singer of ballads faintly akin to his own—he had actually replaced Brecht in the second performance of the *Red Raisin* program that followed *Drums in the Night* there—and Klabund's wife, the actress Carola Neher, was to become one of his best-loved performers. Moreover, his still earlier friend, her unrelated namesake Caspar Neher, was designer for the new play, while Elisabeth Bergner, then coming to the peak of her fame in Germany, played its leading part. "We all saw it," said Hanns Eisler later.

Described as "*The Chalk Circle*. A play in five acts from the Chinese, by Klabund," the text was published the same year (by J. M. Spaeth Verlag, Berlin). In fact it and its heroine, the prostitute Haitang, have a good deal more in common with *The Good Person of Szechwan* than with *The Caucasian Chalk Circle*, and almost certainly helped also to inspire the former play, which was already written by the time of Brecht's arrival in the U.S. Even the basic situation of the chalk circle differs from Brecht's version, in that the heroine (who naturally wins the test) is the biological mother and the false claimant a stepmother, while the symbolism of the circle is already underlined by Haitang's princely lover in the first act, as he draws one in white on a black wall, to represent the vaulted sky and the uniting of two hearts:

HAITANG Whatever lies outside this circle is nothing. Whatever lies inside this circle is everything. How are everything and nothing linked? In the circle that turns and moves (*drawing spokes in the circle*)—in the wheel that rolls . . .

The test is conducted twice, first by the corrupt judge Tschutschu in Act 3, when Haitang loses, then again by her old lover, now become emperor, in Act 5. "Take a piece of chalk," says the emperor to his master of ceremonies:

draw a circle here on the ground before my throne, put the boy in the circle.

MASTER OF CEREMONIES It has been done.

EMPEROR And now, both you women,
Try to draw the boy out of the circle
At the same time. One of you take his left arm,
The other his right. It is certain
The right mother will have the right strength
To draw the boy out of the circle to herself.
(*The women do as he says. Haitang grips the boy gently; Mrs. Ma tugs him brutally to her side*) It is clear that this person (*indicating Haitang*) cannot be the mother. Otherwise she would have managed to draw the boy out of the circle. Let the women repeat the experiment. (*Mrs. Ma once again pulls the boy to her side*) Haitang, I see that you do not make the slightest effort to draw the boy out of the circle to you. What's the meaning of that?

Haitang explains that, having brought the child up, she knows that his arms are too delicate to stand tugging:

If the only way I can get my child is by pulling off his arms, then let somebody who has never known a mother's suffering for her child pull him out of the circle.

EMPEROR (*standing up*)   Behold the mighty power locked in the chalk circle! This woman (*indicating Mrs. Ma*) aimed to get control of all Mr. Ma's fortune and to that end seized the child. Now that the real mother has been acknowledged it will be possible to find the real murderer . . .

for Mrs. Ma had murdered their joint husband and accused Haitang of the crime. She now confesses, and together with the judge is pardoned by Haitang, who is left alone with her son and her imperial lover as the curtain falls.

At the time this slightly sugary play provoked Brecht to parody it, making Jackie Pall in *The Elephant Calf* of 1926 (volume 2 of the *Collected Plays*) pull his mother out of a "doubtless most incompetently drawn circle" in order to prove contrariwise that he, the elephant child, is her son or alternatively her daughter. Roughly twelve years later, however, when Brecht was living in Svendborg, he took up the theme again and must have wondered whether to give it a Chinese or a European setting. The title *The Odense Chalk Circle* (Odense being the principal city of Fünen Island, where Svendborg is situated) seems to suggest the latter, but only a few fragmentary notes under this heading are left, e.g.:

the governor who has to act like a poor man. he pretends to eat too crudely and is sharply rebuked.

—and:

the gentry are scared because the governor has been driven out. they flee, fully expecting the peasantry to institute a bloodbath.

but the peasants don't come and there is no bloodbath.

by an oversight the judge appointed by the rebels is confirmed by the governor.

he pronounces judgment in the case of the two mothers.

There was to be a character called Hieronymus Dan, while another note suggests accompaniment by "old and austere music (fifes, drums, organs)." There is also, however, a more coherent scheme headed simply *The Chalk Circle*, and this is full of Chinese names. It appears to go thus:

I

how schao-fan gets to be a judge. he hides a hunted man. this upsets his wedding. the bride's family withdraws.

the peasants propose schao-fan for the judge's post. laughter all round.

the governor returns to power and sends a messenger appointing a judge: schao-fan.

the wedding takes place. ([what] was taken out is brought back in before the scene starts, silently or to a song: love is an irresistible force, etc.) the new judge gives judgment in a long lawsuit between the village and the bride's family. the judge finds for the village by sticking to the letter of the law.

II

the judge's pranks. he gets drunk in a case involving property and makes everything depend on what shape one of the litigants' nose is, etc.

he is put in gaol. his house is destroyed as if by a tornado.

the maid's wanderings with the child. through the dangers of the blizzard, through the worse dangers of the slums.

she rejects good food for the child and exposes it to hunger.

III

the mother denies the child. by acknowledging him she would be acknowledging that she is the judge's wife.

the maid adopts it, mutely, behind her own back, like a jackdaw whose thieving is hereditary.

IV

the judge gets his post back by mistake.

he bribes witnesses, he fails to examine them once bribed, he muddles everything, proposes marriage to a lady witness in open court and so on.

Section III was later shifted to precede Section I.

A single sample of the dialogue (BBA 128/05–06) shows how Brecht's interest was already centering on the disreputable judge, and goes on to outline a "second part" in which the heroine is again called Haitang:

PEOPLE   he's a very bad judge. he breaks the law—no, he's never read it—aye, it was pure accident he got the job. he used to be a rice planter. one night an old man broke into his paddy-fields and begged him to have mercy: soldiers were after him. tao-schun was sorry for him and hid him in his hut under some old baskets. that old man was the governor of the province, and after the foiling of the plot against him that night thanks to his flight and the planter's sympathy he quickly smote down his enemies. he had the planter trained and made him a judge. but tao-schun was a great disappointment to him. he said quite openly in a bar that it just hadn't occurred to him to ask the old man what level of society he came from. and so he had treated him as a fugitive not as a governor. but for that he'd no doubt have handed him over to the soldiers. he regretted having saved one of the oppressors.—for some time they've only been giving cases to tao-schun when the senior judge is ill, like today.

PARTY WAITING (*jump up appalled*)   is it really tao-schun on the bench today? if so we must have an adjournment. (*to one another*) he won't accept a penny. we're sunk.

PARTY OPPOSITE   tao-schun's in charge! hear that? it's all up, then. he won't accept a penny.

PARTY OF THE FIRST PART   hey, you! we've just been told one of our family's seriously ill. so we'd like to go home. would it make any difference to you if we held the case some other day? (*in an undertone*) you dirty lot of vultures!

PARTY OF THE SECOND PART   it's all the same to us so long as the truth comes out.

THE FIRST FAMILY   you're right there. better lose our field tomorrow than today. let's go (*exeunt*)

THE FAMILY OPPOSITE *(as they leave)* those crooks! wait
 till judge tai's recovered, that'll put an end to their claims
 even if it costs us 50 taels.
THE JUDGE, TAO-SCHUN *(sings)*
 the judge is unwell, his thumb's feeling sore
 (he pretends to count money)
 so today there's a healthier look to the law.
 but what d'you imagine a verdict is for?
 eat your fill; then you'll stink all the more.

The few notes headed "second part" follow:

 haitang is caught in the civil war. together with the
 child, she is forced to take risks for the sake of the cause.
 she exposes the child to many dangers. their journey
 through the blizzard. cheerful song. their journey through
 the slums. (more dangerous.)

 in face of a snowstorm
 i once was full of courage
 but in face of people
 i now am cowardly.
 the snowstorm will not destroy us.
 the earthquake is not avid for us.
 but the coal merchant wants money
 and the shipowner must be paid for the voyage.

Even before leaving Denmark, however, Brecht had begun
work on *The Good Person of Szechwan*, for which this last
"aria" could easily have been written, and around the same
time he seems to have set aside the oriental version of the
story and started to see the judge figure in German garb.
Thus Mother Courage, in the 1939 script of that play, re-
calls a corrupt judge in Franconia who sounds very like him
(*Collected Plays*, vol. 5, p. 399), and the following year
Brecht wrote the short story "The Augsburg Chalk Circle"
which appeared in the June 1941 issue of the Moscow *Inter-
nationale Litérature* and later in *Tales from the Calendar*. This
develops the theme a lot further in the direction of our play,
but at the same time shifts it bodily to Brecht's own home-
town and the period of the Thirty Years' War. Here the

child's mother, fleeing before the invading Catholics, spends too long packing her clothes and runs off without it. Instead Anna the maid takes charge, watching by it much as does Grusha at the end of scene 2:

> When she had spent some time, an hour perhaps, watching how the child breathed and sucked at its little fist, she realized that she had sat too long and seen too much to be able to leave without the child. Clumsily she stood up, wrapped it in its linen coverlet, took it on her arm and went out of the courtyard with it, looking shyly around like someone with a bad conscience, a thief. [pp. 160-61]

She takes it off to her brother's in the country, where he makes her marry a dying cottager with the same results as in the eventual play. When the child's mother arrives "several years" later and removes it, she sues for her boy's return. The judge is one Ignaz Dollinger, who is described as "a short but extremely meaty old man," famous for "his homely cross-examinations, with their cutting remarks and proverbs" and accordingly "praised by the lower orders in a lengthy ballad." "Is he yours?" he bellows at her, accusing her of being after the dead father's property. "Yes," she replies, ". . . If I can just keep him till he knows all the words. He only knows seven" (p. 227). So he hears the case, concludes that both mothers are lying, and makes the test of the chalk circle, in which Anna lets the boy go, so that he is jerked to his mother's side.

> Old Dollinger got to his feet.
> "And that shows us," he announced in a loud voice, "who the right mother is. Take the child away from that slut. She'd tear him cold-bloodedly in two."

Three or four years later, when Jules Leventhal commissioned him to write the play for Broadway (which may seem inconsistent with his professed "revulsion" but was not wholly so), the main structure and principal characters were ready in Brecht's mind, and the only remaining problems were setting and framework: what period and country to pick for it and how to relate it to the present day. The choice of medieval Georgia and of a contemporary Soviet framework must already have been made before he left New York in mid-March 1944 to return to Santa Monica and work on the script, for there is no sign of hesitation. Certainly the resulting first script is written with great sureness and an unusual scarcity of amendments and afterthoughts, while there are far fewer drafts and alternative versions than for some of the less complex or elaborately developed plays. The dating of the framework was to change; in the first script the prologue is set in 1934, without reference to the war. So were most of the names of the characters, which started by being mainly Russian and were Georgianized later; thus Grusha Vachnadze was originally Katya Grusha (or at one point Katya Kirshon), her soldier Volodya Surki, her brother Piotr, and the lesser characters Petrov Petrovitch, Maxim Maximovitch, and the like, while the princes were boyars and Gruzinia Georgia throughout.

Just when the various alterations were made is impossible to say. A journal entry of May 8 shows that Brecht was held up for a fortnight while he evolved social reasons for the judge's shabby eccentricities, grounding these ultimately in

> his disappointment that the fall of the old rulers had not introduced a new era but merely an era of new ones. hence he goes on practicing bourgeois justice, but in a disreputable, sabotaged version which has been made to serve the total self-interest of the judge. this explanation of course mustn't modify what i had previously, and is for instance to be no excuse for azdak.

But this hitch is not reflected in the script. Nor, other than very marginally, is the remodeling of the heroine, which another entry of August 8 says has taken him three weeks; he may have found Katya in the first script "nicer" and not enough like Brueghel's *Dulle Griet* (who is glued on the title pages of the three earliest scripts), but he does not seem to have altered her much, or provided those practical motives for her goodness which Feuchtwanger (who found her "too holy") had asked for. Altogether the changes to his first conception were surprisingly slight.

The first script bears a note by Brecht, "first version" and is dated "Santa Monica June 5, 1944," the day when he posted it off to Luise Rainer. The second, which contains the new version of the prologue and an ad lib epilogue, is similarly called "second version"; it must have been finished early in September, and consists very largely of carbons of the first, with some retyped pages. Its title page gives the names of Eisler and Winge as "collaborators" as well as (Ruth) Berlau who figures alone in the published version; (John Hans Winge was an Austrian who had been working in a Los Angeles factory). Both scripts were bound for Brecht, and he seems to have made his amendments, e.g., of names, indifferently in one or the other. These were then taken into a third, undated script of 1944. Like the first two, this version was typed by Brecht, but this time more conventionally, using upper- and lower-case letters. The play was first actually published in English, Eric and Maja Bentley's translation appearing as one of *Two Parables for the Theater* in 1948; the first German publication being in the special Brecht issue of *Sinn und Form* (Potsdam) the following year. This in turn was amended by Brecht for publication in the *Versuche* series in 1954.

2. Scene-by-Scene Account

The following are scene-by-scene notes on the main differences:

1. The Dispute over the Valley

In all three scripts and the *Sinn und Form* version this was called "Prologue," and perhaps as a result many critics and directors have taken it as not forming an integral part of the play. However, as Brecht pointed out in his letter to his publisher Suhrkamp (p. 300), it forms the beginning of the first script and, though altered, was never thereafter omitted. In that first version, which sets the episode on Sunday, June 7, 1934, there are no references to the war damage and the scene is nearly two pages shorter. We reproduce it in full on pp. 323–27.

Another early note, which may even have preceded it, specifies:

> *scene:* in the background a school with posters and a soviet flag. a few dusty trees.

> *meeting:* the folklore not to be overdone. those present are in their sunday best, no traditional costumes. among them a soldier on leave. a woman has a child on her lap. some of the men have very short haircuts.

> *the singer* wears european garb. very comfortable; like all suits, his is somewhat crumpled. his musicians wear russian shirts; one of them has a georgian cap.

> *the tone* of the discussion is very relaxed; a general delight in argument is evident. now and again one of the young people shoots a paper dart at a girl opposite and is told to shut up.

Within three months the scene had been rewritten virtually in its final form. Only its ending was different, being taken from the first version, from its last stage direction ("As they are leaving," etc.) to the Voice's closing announcement. This was altered in 1954, after the *Sinn und Form* publication. Another minor point involved the switching of the names of the two collective farms, which was done on the second script but inadvertently overlooked in the *Sinn und Form* version. Here Hanns Eisler performed what he ironically called "one of my great services to German literature" by telling Brecht that he must not identify a goat farm with the name of Rosa Luxemburg in view of the insulting use of the term "goat" for a woman in Germany (as the English "cow").

2. The Noble Child

The scripts all amplify the opening stage direction by the words "his manner of performing shows that he has done it a hundred times before; he turns the pages mechanically, casting an occasional glance at them. By slight movements he tells the musicians when to come in." In the first script this ran on . . . "and prefixes each entry of the actors by striking the ground with a wooden mallet." See the note in Brecht's journal for July 3, 1944, which argues that the play's successive episodes are "embodiments of the main incidents in his tale" and pictures him striking the ground thus and behaving like a director at a performance. "This is necessary to avoid illusion and its intoxicating effects." This idea is abandoned in number 7 of Brecht's notes above (p. 298).

Aside from the subsequent change of names, which has already been mentioned and which gives a much more Georgian flavor, the amendments to the first script are generally minor ones. The dust-covered rider originally entered just before the governor's "Not *before* mass, Shalva," which was followed by the exchange "Did you hear that?" etc., p. 150; this was altered only in the 1950s. The references to geese in the dialogue between Grusha (Katya) and Simon (Volodya/Surki) were originally to fish, but appear in the second script. Katya's answer to the query "Is the young lady as healthy as a fish in water?" is

> Why as a fish in water, soldier? Why not like a horse at a horse market? Can it pull two carts? Can it stand out in the snow while the coachman gets drunk? Being healthy depends on not being made ill.
>
> SURKI   That won't happen.

—while when he asks if she is impatient and wants apples (not cherries) in winter she retorts "Why not say 'does she want a man before she's too old?'" This and the new stress on her aptitude for the role of "sucker" ("you simple soul," "you're a good soul," "you're the boneheaded kind," pp. 158–59) represent the main differences between Grusha and the Katya of the first script.

Her song "When you come back home I'll be there" (pp.

154–55) was a response to Konstantin Simonov's war poem "Wait for Me," whose translation, by Nathalie Rene, Brecht had cut out of *Moscow News* and gummed in his journal at the time of the first work on *Simone Machard:*

> Wait for me and I will come.
> Wait, and wait again.
> Wait where you feel sad and numb
> And dreary in the rain.
> Wait, when snows fall more and more,
> Wait when days are hot . . .

etc., the "I" of course here being a soldier. The remainder of the verse in this scene is virtually unchanged from the first version, though the "temptation to do good" there was "great" and not "terrible." It is interesting perhaps that the whole line in its present form should have been very firmly written in by Brecht on the second script; he clearly felt it to be important.

3. The Flight to the Northern Mountains

Much of the unrhymed verse (which was originally not broken into lines but divided by oblique strokes) differs in the first script, where it is mainly struck out without having yet been replaced by the new versions; maybe these became detached from the script. In the second script it is all there, virtually as now. According to Rudolf Vápeník the song "To the war my weary way" of the two Ironshirts on p. 168 is translated from a Moravian folk song set (as one of his Slovak Folk Songs) by Bartók.

The first episode (Grusha getting milk from the old peasant) is one of those which Brecht retyped entirely for the second script, but despite some rewording it was not substantially changed. As revised, it ended with the words "Michael, Michael, I've certainly let myself in for something" (p. 163), followed by the stage direction:

> (*She stands up, worried, takes the child on her back and marches on. Grumbling, the old man collects his cup and looks expressionlessly after her*)

The next episode (Outside a Caravanserai), which figures in
the first script, was then cut, not to be restored till the collected edition; it was not performed in Brecht's production.
The brief appearance of the two Ironshirts which follows
was slightly bowdlerized in the 1950s; before "He'll let himself be torn to pieces for a superior" (p. 168) it read "When
he hears an order he gets a stand; when he sticks his lance into
the enemy's guts he comes." The short scene with the two
peasants is virtually unchanged from the first script, but once
Grusha runs into the Ironshirts there are a fair number of
alterations, the central part of the episode being among the
passages retyped by Brecht for the second script. The gist of
his changes here is to make Grusha more evidently frightened
of the soldiers than was Katya in the first version, and also
to make it seem less likely that she is handing the child over
to the peasants for good. Thus Katya was not "*in a fright*"
(p. 170) and did not "*let out a little scream*" (p. 171)—these
directions appearing only from the third script on—while
instead the first script made her laugh and say:

> Corporal, if you're going to question me so severely I'll
> have to tell you the truth: that I'd like to be on my
> way. How about lowering your pike?

The episode of the bridge is once again almost as in the first
script, though there is one possibly significant detail: the first
man originally greeted Katya's feat in exactly the words the
first soldier uses of Kattrin in the drum scene of *Mother
Courage* (*Collected Plays*, vol. 5, p. 208): "She's done it."
Brecht changed this in the 1950s to "She's across," presumably in order not to stress the connection between the
two characters, both of whom were then being played by the
same actress.

4. In the Northern Mountains

Originally entitled "Katya Grusha's sojourn at her spineless brother's: her strange marriage and the return of the
soldier." A number of passages here were retyped and re-

written for the second script, for instance the episode of the melting snow, starting with the singer's introduction (p. 180):

THE SINGER
> The sister was too sick. The cowardly brother had to let her stay / She lay in the storeroom. Through the thin wall she heard him talking to his wife: / "She'll / soon be gone," he said. "When she's well. How soft your breasts are. . . ." / The sister was sick till winter came. The cowardly brother had to let her stay./The storeroom grew cold and she heard him talk to his wife. / "When spring comes she'll be gone," he said. "How firm your thighs are. . . ." / The room was cold. The road was colder. The winter was long, the winter was short./ The rats mustn't bite, the child mustn't cry, the spring mustn't come. / Where to go when the snow melts? (*Still weak, Katya squats at the loom in the storeroom. She and the child, who is squatting on the ground, are wrapped in rugs and rags against the cold. The child cries. Katya tries to comfort it*) [At this point there is a photograph of a Mongolian-looking woman at a spinning-wheel gummed into the script.]

KATYA Don't cry, or do it quietly. Otherwise my sister-in-law will hear us and we'll have to go. Cockroaches aren't supposed to make any noise, are they? If we keep as quiet as cockroaches they'll forget we're in the house. Remember the cockroaches. (*The child cries again*) Hush. The cold doesn't have to make you cry. Being poor's one thing, freezing's another. It doesn't get you liked. You keep quiet and I'll let you see the horses; remember the horses. (*The child cries again*) Michael, we have to be clever, we've no wedding lines for my sister-in-law. If we make ourselves small we can stay till the snow melts. (*She draws the child to her and looks, appalled, at one particular point*) Michael, Michael, you've got no sense. If it's on account of the rats you don't need to cry. Rats are quite human. They have families. They store up food for 500 years.

PIOTR (*slips in*) What's up? Why are you looking over at that corner, Katya? Is he frightened?

KATYA What's he to be frightened of? There's nothing there.

PIOTR   I thought I heard scuffling in the straw. I hope it isn't rats. You wouldn't be able to stay with the child here.

KATYA   There aren't any rats. It'd be impossible to get a job anywhere with him.

PIOTR   (*sits by her*)   I wanted to talk to you about Lisaveta . . .

Piotr is Lavrenti, and Lisaveta his wife Aniko, and the conversation continues much as in our text from "She's a good soul" (p. 181) to "Was I talking about Aniko?" (p. 181), then:

You can't think how it upsets her not to be able to offer you anything better than this room. The big room above is too hard to heat. "My sister will understand": I've told her that a thousand times, but does she believe me? She even blames herself in private for not being able to stand children. That's because she hasn't any of her own. Her heart's not strong enough, you see.

Grusha's song "The loved one prepared to go" (pp. 180–81) then comes after the second "Grusha is silent" (p. 182). After the *glockenspiel of the falling drops* (p. 182) Piotr makes his proposal about the marriage, much as in our text except that Katya is to come back to live in his house again as soon as her bridegroom dies; the provision about her being entitled to live on the latter's farm for two years (p. 183) only appearing in the third script. The wedding ceremony itself was hardly changed except in this respect, thus on leaving (p. 185) Piotr/Lavrenti says "I'll wait for you by the poplar at the entrance to the village, Katya."

KATYA   Suppose it takes longer?
MOTHER-IN-LAW   It won't take longer.

The conversation among the guests (p. 187) was retyped virtually as now for the second script; in the first it ran:

THE GUESTS   (*noisily*)   There've been more disturbances in the city, have you heard?—Ay, the boyar Rajok's besieged in the palace, they say.—The grand duke is back and it's all going to be like it used to be.—Lots of them coming back all the time from the Persian war.—They even say the old governor's wife's come back, and all the palace guard with her. (*Katya drops the cake pan. People help her to pick up the cakes*)

A WOMAN (*to Katya*)   You not feeling well? Too much excitement, that's it. Sit down and have a rest. (*Katya sits down*)

THE GUESTS   Here today, gone tomorrow. Gone tomorrow, here today. But we still have to pay taxes.

KATYA (*feebly*)   Did someone say the palace guard had come back?

A MAN   That's what I heard.

ANOTHER   They say, though, that boyar Rajok's green flag is still flying over the palace. But the palace is being besieged. The old governor's wife is supposed to be living in one of the houses opposite.

KATYA   Who told you that?

THE MAN (*to a woman*)   Show her your shawl! . . .

Thenceforward to the end of the scene the first version has been altered very little, the one significant addition (on the second script) being Grusha's explanation that she can never go back to Nukha (originally Kachezia) because she had knocked down an Ironshirt.

5. The Story of the Judge

Most of the amendments to this scene are minor ones, and a good few date from 1954; the three scripts are thus close to one another, only the episode with the fat prince's nephew having been to some extent rewritten after the first script. Already there the singer, who up to that point had only figured as such, began from the beginning of the Azdak ballad on (p. 206) to be "*the singer and his musicians,*" and this is oddly enough the only hint anywhere in the play or Brecht's notes that he may be required to perform Azdak's part, though Brecht seems to have taken this for granted in the production.

The Ironshirts' action in dragging Azdak to the gallows was added in 1954; previously they had been slapping him and Shauva genially on the shoulder. The fat prince's (the boyar Rajok's) first speech was altered and expanded in the rewriting for the second script; at the same time the chatter of the Ironshirts (p. 203) emphasizing their awareness of their (momentary) political importance was also added. Some small changes were made to heighten the dialogue where the nephew pronounces his verdict (p. 206), both in the rewriting and in 1954. After the first two of Azdak's cases (respectively the doctor and Ludovika) the stage direction showing Azdak on his travels (p. 210) along the military highway and the two accompanying verses of the Azdak ballad were introduced in 1954. The presence of Ironshirts behind Azdak's throne each time, with their flag as a tangible sign of support for him, was an addition on the first script, as was also the appearance of the fat prince's head on one of their pikes (p. 214).

6. The Chalk Circle

In the first script there is a song near the beginning of the scene (after the cook starts praying, p. 216) which was thereafter omitted:

> The people say: the poor need luck
> They won't get far by using their heads.
> They won't grow fat by the work of their hands.
> Therefore, it is said
> God has devised for them games of chance
> And the dog races. Likewise God
> In his unremitting care for his poor folk
> Sees to it that the tax inspectors sometimes slip.
> For the poor need luck.

All through there are two elements missing from this version —the threat which the wounded corporal represents to Grusha (p. 218) and Simon's confession that he is the father of the child (p. 217). Instead Simon alleges that it was the son of one of his comrades. Then after the entry of the governor's wife the first lawyer go   on from his condemnation of the

judge as "just about the lowest individual ever seen" (p. 218)
to say

> I insist you settle this matter out of court.
>
> GOVERNOR'S WIFE   As you wish.
>
> FIRST LAWYER   In view of the size of the estate which the
> child is inheriting, what do a few piasters count here and
> there? (*On a nod from her he strolls over to Katya*) A
> thousand piasters. (*Seeing Katya's look of uncertainty*) I
> am authorized to offer you a thousand piasters if the case
> can be kept from coming to court.
>
> THE COOK   Holy Mary, a thousand piasters!
>
> FIRST LAWYER (*strutting off*)   You see what your friends
> think.
>
> KATYA   Are they trying to offer me money for Michael?
>
> THE COOK   And they'd certainly go higher.
>
> VOLODYA (*darkly*)   A meal that doesn't fill you makes you
> hungry, they say.
>
> FIRST LAWYER (*coming back*)   Well, what about that thou-
> sand?
>
> GOVERNOR'S WIFE   Is she being brazen enough to think it
> over? (*Crosses to Katya*) You shameless person, don't
> you know you've to bow when I speak to you?
>
> KATYA (*bows deeply, then*)   I can't sell him, milady.
>
> GOVERNOR'S WIFE   What? You call that selling, when you've
> got to return what you stole? You thief, you know it's
> not yours!
>
> VOLODYA (*sees Katya hesitating; at attention*)   I attest that
> this is the child of my comrade Illo Toboridze, Mrs.
> Anastasia Sashvili, sir.
>
> GOVERNOR'S WIFE   Aren't you one of the palace guard? How
> dare you lie to me, you swine?
>
> VOLODYA   Straight from the horse's mouth, sir, as the saying
> goes. (*The governor's wife is speechless. Ironshirts have
> entered the courtyard and the aide-de-camp has been
> whispering to one of them. The second lawyer tugs the
> governor's wife's sleeve and whispers something to her*)
>
> THE COOK   They wouldn't be offering money if they
> weren't frightened of Azdak's favoring you. He goes by
> faces.

All this was dropped in the second script, which contained
the present short bridge passage to cover the cut.

The first part of the actual trial, up to Simon's testimony, was retyped after the first script, everything between Grusha's "It's mine" (p. 221) and the middle of the second lawyer's speech beginning "Thank you, your worship" (p. 222) being new. Originally Grusha was followed by the second lawyer saying

> Excuse me, Maxim Maximovitch, but the court wants facts. My lord . . .
>
> FIRST LAWYER   My dear Pavlov Pavlovitch, I would have thought my address . . .
>
> SECOND LAWYER   Is dispensable, my dear Maxim Maximovitch. My lord, by an unfortunate concatenation of circumstances, this child, etc.

This means that all reference to the Abashvili (Sashvili) estates was lacking from the original scene, since the same is true of their mention in the second lawyer's speech later on p. 227. Much of the backchat between Azdak and Grusha likewise comes from the second script, which first introduced Grusha's long diatribe starting "You drunken turnip" (p. 224) and ending "than hanging on the gallows" (p. 225). Her passage too with the governor's wife (p. 226) is a product of that script, but from then on till the final dance the first version has survived very largely intact. It ends with the singer's final verses in a slightly different line arrangement and without the ironic qualifying word "almost," which was an addition to the second script. An epilogue follows, but was evidently written later; its use was to be optional, and it is not included in the third script or any of the published versions other than the *Materialien zu Brechts "Der kaukasische Kreidekreis"* (Frankfurt, Suhrkamp-Verlag, 1966), from which the following translation has been drawn:

Epilogue
(ad libitum)

The ring of spectators from the two collective farms becomes visible. There is polite applause.

PEASANT WOMAN RIGHT   Arkadi Cheidze, you slyboots, in league with those who stole our valley, how dare you compare us members of the Rosa Luxemburg kolkhoz with people like that Natella Abashvili of yours, just because we think twice about giving up our valley?

SOLDIER LEFT (*to the old man right, who has stood up*) What are you looking over there for, comrade?

THE OLD MAN RIGHT   Just let me look at what I'm to give up. I won't be able to see it again.

THE PEASANT WOMAN LEFT   Why not? You'll be coming to call on us.

THE OLD MAN RIGHT   If I do I mayn't be able to recognize it.

KATO THE AGRONOMIST   You'll see a garden.

THE OLD MAN RIGHT (*beginning to smile*)   May God forgive you if it's not one.

(*They all get up and surround him, cheering*)

3. Prologue from the First Script (1944)

Public square of a Caucasian market town, with peasants and tractor drivers of two kolkhoz villages seated in a circle, smoking and drinking wine; among them a delegate from the planning commission in the capital, a man in a leather jacket. There is much laughter.

THE DELEGATE (*in an effort to get their attention*)   Let's draw up an agreed statement, comrades.

AN OLD PEASANT (*standing*)   It's too soon for that, I'm against it; we haven't thrashed things out; I object on scientific grounds.

WOMAN'S VOICE (*from the right*)   Not thrashed it out? We've been arguing ten hours.

THE OLD PEASANT   And what about it, Tamara Oboladze? We've still got four hours left.

A SOLDIER   Correct. I'm surprised at you, Tamara. Who's going to get up from table when there's still a quarter of a calf left in the dish? Who's going to be satisfied with ten hours of argument if he can have fourteen?

A GIRL   We've done Cain and Abel, but nobody's even mentioned Adam and Eve yet. (*Laughter*)

THE DELEGATE   Comrades, my head's in a whirl. (*Groaning*) All this elaborate business about scientifically based goat breeding, all those examples to back it, all those subtle allusions, and then great masses of goat's cheese and endless jugs of wine to top it off! I suggest we draw up a concluding statement, comrades.

A TRACTOR DRIVER (*decisively*)   Even the best things must come to an end. Hands up those who want the discussion closed! (*The majority raise their hands*)

THE TRACTOR DRIVER   The closure's carried. Now for the statement!

THE DELEGATE   The point at issue then (*he begins writing in his notebook*) is a difference between two kolkhoz villages, the Rosa Luxemburg and Galinsk, concerning a valley which lies between them and is not much good for grazing. It belongs to the Rosa Luxemburg kolkhoz (*addressing those at his left*) and is being claimed by the Galinsk kolkhoz, that's (*to those on his right*) you people.

THE OLD MAN   Put down that we have to have the valley for raising our goats, just like we have to have other valleys, and it's always belonged to our village. (*Applause left*)

A PEASANT RIGHT   What d'you mean, "always"? Nothing's "always" belonged to anybody. You haven't even always belonged to yourself. Twenty-five years ago, Chachava, you still belonged to the grand duke. (*Applause left*)

THE DELEGATE   Why don't we say the valley belongs to you now?

THE PEASANT RIGHT   And when you say you have to have it for your goats, better put in that you've got all the pasture land you need not more than half an hour from there.

A WOMAN LEFT   Put this down. If goats are driven half an hour every day they give less milk.

THE DELEGATE   Please don't let's go through all that again. You could have government aid to build stables on the spot.

THE OLD MAN LEFT   I'd like to ask you (*addressing the peasant right*) a small personal question. Did you or did you not enjoy our goat's-milk cheese? (*On his not immediately replying*) Did you or did you not enjoy those four or five pounds you were tucking away? I'd like an answer, if you don't mind.

THE PEASANT RIGHT   The answer's yes. So what?

THE OLD MAN (*triumphantly*)   I wonder if the comrade knows why he enjoyed our goat's-milk cheese? (*Pause for effect*) Because our goats enjoyed the grass in that particular valley. Why isn't cheese just any old cheese? Eh? Because grass isn't just any old grass. (*To the delegate*) Put that in your book.

(*Laughter and applause right*)

THE DELEGATE   Comrades, this isn't getting us anywhere.

THE PEASANT RIGHT   Just write down why we think the valley ought to be made over to us. Mention our expert's report on the irrigation scheme, then let the planning commission make up its mind.

THE DELEGATE   The comrade agronomist!

(*A girl stands up right*)

NATASHA   Put me down as Nina Meladze, agronomist and engineer, comrade.

THE DELEGATE   Your native village of Galinsk sent you to technical school in Tiflis to study, is that right? (*She nods*) And on getting back you worked out a project for the kolkhoz?

NATASHA   An irrigation scheme. We've a lake up in the mountains that can be dammed so as to irrigate 2,000 versts of barren soil. Then our kolkhoz can plant vines and fruit trees there. It's a project which can only be economic if the contested valley is included. The yield of the land will go up 6,000 percent. (*Applause right*) It's all worked out here, comrade. (*She hands him a file*)

THE OLD MAN LEFT (*uneasily*)   Put in a word to say that our kolkhoz thinks of going in for horse breeding, will you?

THE DELEGATE   Gladly. I think I've got it all now. There's just one more suggestion I'd like to make if I may, comrades. It would please me very much if I could add a footnote to my report saying that the two villages have come to an agreement after having heard all the arguments put forward this day, Sunday, June 7, 1934.

(*General silence*)

THE OLD MAN LEFT (*tentatively*)   The question is, who does the valley belong to? Why don't we have another drink or two and talk it over? There are still some hours to go. . . .

THE PEASANT RIGHT   All right, let's take our time over the footnote, but do let's close the discussion as decided, specially as it gets in the way of our drinking, eh, comrades?

(*Laughter*)

VOICES   Yes, close the discussion. How about a bit of music?

A WOMAN   The idea was to round off this visit by the planning commission's delegate by listening to the singer Arkadi Cheidze. We've been into it with him. (*While she is speaking a girl runs off to fetch the singer*)

THE DELEGATE   That sounds interesting. Thank you very much, comrades.

THE OLD MAN LEFT   But this is off the point, comrades.

THE WOMAN RIGHT   Not really. He got in this morning, and promised he'd perform something which had a bearing on our discussion.

THE OLD MAN LEFT   That'd be different. They say he's not at all bad.

THE PEASANT RIGHT (*to the delegate*)   We had to telegraph to Tiflis three times to get him. It nearly fell through at the last minute because his chauffeur caught a cold.

THE WOMAN RIGHT   He knows 21,000 verses.

THE PEASANT RIGHT   It's very difficult to book him. You people in the planning commission ought to see he comes north more often, comrade.

THE DELEGATE   I'm afraid we're mainly involved with economics.

THE PEASANT RIGHT (*with a smile*)   You sort out the distribution of grapes and tractors; why not songs too? Anyhow here he is.

(*Led by the girl, the singer Arkadi Cheidze enters the circle, a thickset man with simple manners. He is accompanied by four musicians with their instruments. Applause greets the artists*)

THE GIRL (*introducing them*)   This is the comrade delegate, Arkadi.

THE DELEGATE (*shakes his hand*)   It is a great honor to meet you. I heard about your songs way back as a schoolboy in Moscow. Are you going to give us one of the old legends?

THE SINGER   An extremely old one. It's called "The Chalk Circle" and comes from the Chinese. We perform it in a somewhat altered version of course. Comrades, it's a great honor for me to entertain you at the end of your day of strenuous debates. We hope that you'll find the old

poet's voice doesn't sound too badly under the shadow of
Soviet tractors. Mixing one's wines may be a mistake, but
old and new wisdom mix very well. I take it we're all
having something to eat before the performance begins?
It's a help, you know.

VOICES Of course. Everyone into the club.

(*As they disperse the delegate turns to the girl*)

THE DELEGATE I hope it won't finish too late. I have to go
home tonight, comrade.

THE GIRL (*to the singer*) How long will it take, Arkadi?
The comrade delegate has got to get back to Tiflis tonight.

THE SINGER (*offhandedly*) A matter of a few hours.

THE GIRL (*very confidentially*) Couldn't you make it
shorter?

THE SINGER (*seriously*) No.

VOICE When you've finished eating, Arkadi Cheidze will
give his performance out here on the square.

(*All go off to eat*)

> [From Werner Hecht (ed.): *Materialien zu Brechts "Der
> kaukasische Kreidekreis,"* Frankfurt, Suhrkamp-Verlag,
> 1966. This comes from the first script of the play, which
> was finished by June 1944. The inconsistency in the girl
> agronomist's name (which is Kato in the final version)
> is due to its being Georgianized from Natasha Borodin in
> course of many similar amendments to this script.]

APPENDIX
The Duchess of Malfi

Edited, with notes

by A. R. Braunmuller

Introductory Note

Nearly every aspect of Brecht's adaptation of John Webster's *Duchess of Malfi*— the text, the collaborators' shares, the dates of composition and revision, even the spelling of the title itself—offers puzzles and confusions almost impossible of certain solution. The text printed on pp. 335–417 approaches as nearly as possible what can be reconstructed of Brecht's version of the play, or rather, the version over which he seems to have exercised the most influence and on which he expended the most care.

Both the origin of the project to adapt the play and the process of that adaptation helped ensure that the result would be neither a full-scale reworking (on the order of *Edward II* or *Coriolanus*) nor a purely Brechtian enterprise. Elisabeth Bergner, the actress, and her husband, the producer Paul Czinner, suggested the play as suitable material for Brecht's attention and Miss Bergner's talents. Around April or May 1943, work on the project began in New York. H. R. Hays, Brecht's early translator, also worked on the adaptation at this time. From this period dates *The Duchess of Malfy . . . An Adaptation for the Modern Stage* copyrighted June 26, 1943, by Brecht and Hays, and a variety of drafts in the Brecht Archive in Berlin. Many sheets from this copyrighted version became the basis for Brecht's further work.

Late in 1943, W. H. Auden joined the effort, and shortly thereafter Hays withdrew. Bergner and Czinner seem to have suggested about this time that an effort be made to incorporate material from Webster's other tragedy, *The White Devil*, into the new adaptation, and some subsequent drafts show an increasing use of scenes and lines from this play (see the editorial notes to Act 1, scene 2 and Act 2, scene 4). The *Duchess* appears in Brecht's journal as a finished work on July 21, 1943, probably a reference to the Brecht-Hays copyrighted version. Brecht continued to work on it, however, for another journal entry covering his next New York visit (November 1943 to March 1944) describes it as "not completely finished," while as late as June–July 1945 it is only described as finished "in the rough."

Although Brecht continued to write, Auden's name alone appears on a text, copyrighted October 24, 1945, which is largely reworked Webster with an excellently concise first act (apparently by Auden, but following Webster's text closely). Brecht reappears with Auden in a version copyrighted on April 4, 1946, and continued his association wit' the project at least through the trial performances in Prov idence, Rhode Island (September 20, 1946) and in Bostor The play opened on Broadway October 15, 1946. Althoug the programs and advertisements for the trial productior mention "Bertold [*sic*] Brecht" along with Auden, Brecht name appears nowhere in the New York program or in tl generally condemnatory reviews. The final Broadway version had returned to Webster's original with some revisions and modernization; it even includes part of the "Julia" subplot which had been excised from all but one of the now surviving versions.

It is not easy to make a precise statement of Brecht's practical contribution to adapting the *Duchess*. Certainly, he made important decisions about restructuring the play and rearranging large units of Webster's original. These decisions led him to write new scenes, such as the battlefield scene (2,1) and the Cardinal's murder (3,1), and to rewrite the play's conclusion. At one point, his interest in a conversation between Bosola and the old woman (2,2) nearly reverses the general reduction which he makes in Bosola's part. Brecht made many smaller and more detailed contributions as well. He understood Webster's English well enough to rearrange the play without having always to pass through a German version first. For example, having decided to increase the economic motive for Ferdinand's murder of his sister, Brecht adds (in English) some lines from Webster's IV.ii to his own 1,2. For longer passages, sometimes sandwiched between pieces of Webster or of translated Brecht, he often used German. In the version of 2,6 which we follow, for instance, the Duchess' reading of Ferdinand's letter appears in German in the text with two marginal translations, one quite literal and another, a replacement, more fluent and in near-blank verse. At another point, opposite an English speech near the end of the echo scene, appears the note, "Brecht's rough translation" (see the editorial notes on 3,2), suggesting that Brecht may have occasionally translated his own German. In one of the drafts for Ferdinand's concluding speech to 3,3 (see the notes), some of the English spellings suggest Brecht's mental translation from German cognates or his use of similar sounds. H. R. Hays also testifies to Brecht's ability to read and write English, when he wished. Thus, while it might be accurate to say that Brecht's chief contribution lies in his wholly original scenes, the rearrangement of Webster's original, and some very clear-sighted choices of omissions and new emphases, it must be added that he often dipped into the minutiae of the play. He had the ability and the interest to work over single lines and short speeches.

The text which follows has been constructed from the following Brecht Archive sources: "Dramatis Personae" (1174/02); "Prologue" (1174/68–69); 1,1 (1419/06–13 and 1174/03–07); 1,2 (1174/08–13); 1,3 (1419/25–26, 1174/154–157, and 1174/18–20); 1,4 (1174/21–23); 2,1 (1174/25–28); 2,2 (1174/29–30 and 1174/162); 2,3 and 2,4 (1174/31–44); 2,5 and 2,6 (1419/64–74); 3,1 (1174/185–187); 3,2 through 3,5 (1174/45–63); 3,6 (1174/64 and 1419/107–108); "Epilogue" (1176/109). Manuscript corrections and changes have been incorporated into the text; obvious typographical errors and misspellings have been silently corrected. Brecht Archive sources for material in the editorial notes are cited in the appropriate places.

(The editor of this text gratefully acknowledges the help of Lee Bliss and Edward Mendelson, and the financial support of the University of California Research Committee.)

The Duchess of Malfi

(After John Webster)

CHARACTERS

(In order of their appearance)

DELIO BOLOGNA

ANTONIO BOLOGNA

BOSOLA

CARDINAL OF ANCONA

DUKE FERDINAND

CASTRUCHIO

CARIOLA

ATTENDANT

DUCHESS OF MALFI

FIRST OFFICER

SECOND OFFICER

FIRST SERVANT

SECOND SERVANT

NEGRO PAGE

MONK

THIRD OFFICER

FOURTH OFFICER

COURTIERS, GENTLEMEN, MEN AT ARMS, STANDARD BEARERS, LADIES

Prologue

Friar's Cell.

Friar and Duke Ferdinand.

FRIAR (*cries out in horror*)
  No more, young man, no more! I dare not hear it!
FERDINAND
  Gentle father,
  To you I have unclasped my burdened soul,
  Emptied the storehouse of my thoughts and heart
  That I might have the comfort, now to ask you:
  Must I not do what all men else may,—love?
FRIAR
  Why, foolish madman—
FERDINAND
  Shall, then, for that I am her brother born,
  My joys be ever banished from her bed?
FRIAR
  Have done, unhappy man! For thou art lost!
FERDINAND
  So tell me, holy man,
  What cure shall give me ease in these extremes?
FRIAR
  Art thou, my son, that miracle of wit,
  Who once, within these three years, wert esteem'd
  A wonder of thine age, throughout the world?
  How did the [people (?)] of Italy applaud

Thy government, behavior, learning, speech, and all that
    could make up a man!
O Ferdinand, why hast thou left the school
Of knowledge, to converse with lust and death?
For death waits on thy lust. Look through the world,
And thou shalt see a thousand faces shine
More glorious than this idol thou ador'st:
Leave her and take thy choice.

FERDINAND

It were more easy to stop the ocean
From floats and ebbs, than to dissuade my vows.

FRIAR

Thou must.

FERDINAND

       I can not, holy father.

FRIAR

Then I have done, and in thy wilful flames
Already see thy ruin; Heaven is just.—
Yet hear my counsel.
Hie to thy house, and lock thee fast
Alone within thy chamber; then fall down
On both thy knees, and grovel on the ground;
Cry to thy heart; wash every word thou utter'st
In tears (and if't be possible) of blood:
Beg heaven to cleanse the leprosy of lust
That rots thy soul; acknowledge what thou art,
A wretch, a worm, a nothing; weep, sigh, pray
Three times a day and three times every night.

FERDINAND

That I have done to no avail.
If you can not absolve me, holy father,
Then I am lost. Therefore I am determined
I'll to the war in Cyprus.
And may that conflict drown the earth in blood,
I'll be content if I do not return.

FRIAR

Pray for thyself, abroad,
Whilst I pray for thee here—away!
My blessing with thee! We have need to pray!

1

Presence Chamber in the Palace of the Duchess of Malfi.

Delio and Antonio are on. Bosola lurks in the background.

ANTONIO
    In these unruly times you are welcome, cousin Delio.
    I fear my letter drew you rudely
    Out of sweet France. How did you like it there?

DELIO
    'Tis still a land of sunshine. You will spend
    In a fortnight what you may scarcely win there
    In a twelve-month. The French are exceeding skillful
    In the arts, not those of love alone
    But likewise martial stratagem. In Paris
    I have studied their new fashion of gunnery.

ANTONIO
    New come from Paris, how doth Malfi please you?

DELIO
    So well that I am sorry I shall straightway
    Be leaving it. I thank you, dear Antonio,
    For my preferment with Lord Ferdinand.
    'Tis agreed I follow him to the wars.
    (Indicating Bosola)
    What doth this fellow seek here?

ANTONIO
    I know not. One of those parasites

That breed in princes' palaces. Here comes
The Cardinal.

(*Enter the Cardinal of Ancona with a monk who is his
chaplain and secretary and several other gentlemen. Bosola
immediately crosses to the Cardinal*)

BOSOLA

I do haunt you still.

CARDINAL   So.

BOSOLA   I have done you better service than to be slighted
thus. Miserable age where the only reward of doing well is
the doing of it.

CARDINAL   You enforce your merit too much.

BOSOLA   I fell into the galleys in your service, where for two
years together I wore two towels instead of a shirt with a
knot on the shoulder after the fashion of a Roman mantle.
Slighted thus? I will thrive some way.

CARDINAL   Would you become honest!

BOSOLA   With all your divinity do but direct me the way to it.
I have known many travel far for it yet return as arrant
knaves as they went forth because they carried themselves
always along with them.

(*The Cardinal moves away brusquely and begins to talk to
his secretary*)

Are you gone? Some fellows, they say, are possessed with
the devil but this great fellow were able to possess the greatest devil and make him worse. Could I be one of their flattering panders, I would hang on their ears like a horse leech,
'til I were full and then drop off.

DELIO (*to Antonio*)   He hath denied him some suit. I knew
this fellow seven years in the galleys for a notorious mur-
derer and 'twas thought
In the Cardinal's pay. He was released
By the French general, Gaston de Foux
When he recovered Naples.

ANTONIO

Here comes the great Calabrian Duke.

(*The Duke Ferdinand enters with Castruchio, courtiers,
men at arms, standard bearers, all the appurtenances of a
princely train. He is in armor*)

FERDINAND
  Are the galleys come about yet?

CASTRUCHIO   They are, my lord. But methinks you should not
  desire to go to war in person.

FERDINAND   Now for some weighty reason. Why not?

CASTRUCHIO   It is fitting a soldier should rise to be a prince
  but not necessary that a prince should descend to be a captain.

FERDINAND   No?

CASTRUCHIO   No, lord, he were far better do it by deputy.

FERDINAND   This war too nearly touches mine honor. Since
  the old Duke of Malfi fell, I have sworn to defend my sister
  Duchess in his stead. While I live she need fear no foe.

CASTRUCHIO   Believe my experience. That realm is never long
  quiet where the ruler is a soldier.

FERDINAND   Who was it tamed the Arab stallion and broke
  him to his paces?

CASTRUCHIO   Antonio Bologna.
  (*Ferdinand crosses to Antonio*)

FERDINAND
  Matchless Antonio, great master of our sister
  Duchess' household!
  (*He nods to Delio*)
                        Your cousin pleases me.
  His skill in this new science of gunnery
  From France we'll soon know how to use in Cyprus.
  (*Crowd noises without*)

CASTRUCHIO   My lord, the people line the streets awaiting your
  progress to the haven. You may hear their lusty shouts.
  (*Ferdinand moves off toward the window to observe the
  crowd*)

DELIO (*To Antonio*)
  The presence begins to fill. You promised me
  To make me partaker of the natures
  Of some of your great courtiers.

ANTONIO   Well, there's the cardinal—

DELIO   What's his temper? They say he's a great scoundrel.

ANTONIO   He should have been pope but did bestow bribes too
  impudently. Some good he hath done.

DELIO   What's his brother, my new master?

ANTONIO   The Duke, there? A most perverse and turbulent
nature.

DELIO   Twins?

ANTONIO   In quality. The Cardinal and his brother, the Duke,
are like plum trees that grow crooked over standing pools.
They are rich and o'erladen with fruit but none grows; pies
and caterpillars feed on them.

DELIO
What of their sister, the fair Duchess?

ANTONIO
You never fixed your eye on three fair medals
Cast in one figure of so different temper.
For her discourse it is so full of rapture
You will only begin then to be sorry
When she doth end her speech and wish, in wonder,
She held it less vainglory to talk much.
She throws upon a man so sweet a look
That it were able to raise one that lay
Dead in a palsy but in that look
There speaketh so divine a continence
As cuts off all lascivious and vain hope.
Her days are practiced in such noble virtue
That sure her nights, nay more her very sleeps,
Are more in heaven than other ladies' shrifts.
Let all sweet ladies break their flattering glasses
And dress themselves in her.

DELIO
                              Fie, Antonio,
Have you turned scholar studying of her virtues?

ANTONIO
I'll case the picture up. Only this much—
All her particular worth grows to this sum.
She stains time past, lights the time to come.

FERDINAND (*as the Cardinal joins him*)   A word with you,
brother. Have you bethought you concerning the protection
of our widowed sister in mine absence at the wars? How
like you my proposal that she dwell with thee at Ancona?

CARDINAL   I like it not. If you think my palace is a cloister
you are deceived. She shall abide at Malfi. You worry more

than is a brother's duty. And are you doubtful of her virtue,
though I think she hath given thee no cause, hire an intelligencer.

FERDINAND (*silent*)

CARDINAL There is a fellow plagues me, one Daniel de Bosola,
who hath had practice in this trade.

FERDINAND Would not Antonio, the master of her household,
be far fitter?

CARDINAL His nature is too honest for such business. I'll send
Bosola to thee.

(*Cariola, waiting woman to the Duchess, and attendant
enter*)

ATTENDANT (*announcing*) Her grace the Duchess of Malfi
will be here anon.

CARIOLA (*crosses to Antonio*) You must attend my lady in
her chamber half an hour hence. She hath business with thee.
(*She exits*)

DELIO (*to Antonio*) What's this, you blush?

ANTONIO Nay, 'tis surely the matter of my accounts. I'll go
fetch my books.
(*He exits*)

BOSOLA (*approaching Ferdinand*) I was lured to you.

FERDINAND My brother, here, the Cardinal, could never abide
you.

BOSOLA Never since he was in my debt.

FERDINAND Maybe some oblique character in your face made
him suspect you?

BOSOLA He did suspect me wrongfully.

FERDINAND (*giving money*) There's gold.

BOSOLA What follows? Whose throat must I cut?

FERDINAND
I give you that
To live i' the court here and observe the Duchess,
To note all particulars of her behavior,
What suitors do solicit her for marriage
And whom she best affects. She's a young widow.
I would not have her marry again.

BOSOLA
No, sir?

FERDINAND

Do not you ask the reason but be satisfied.
I say I would not.

BOSOLA

It seems you would create me
One of your familiars.

FERDINAND

Familiar? What's that?

BOSOLA

Why,
An intelligencer.

FERDINAND

Such a kind of thriving thing
I would wish thee and ere long thou mayest arrive
At a higher place by 't.

BOSOLA (*offers to give back money*)

Take your devils
Which hell calls angels. These cursed gifts would make
You a corrupter, me an impudent traitor
And should I take these they'll take me to hell.

FERDINAND (*imperiously*)

Sir, I'll take nothing from you I have given.
There is a place I shall procure for you,
The provisorship o' th' horse.

BOSOLA

The provisorship
O' the horse? Say then my corruption
Grew out of horse dung. I am your creature.

ATTENDANT

Her grace, the noble Duchess of Malfi.
(*Enter the Duchess with her ladies. Her brothers greet her
formally*)

FERDINAND

Sister, I have a suit to you.

DUCHESS

To me, sir?

FERDINAND

A gentleman here, Daniel de Bosola,
A worthy fellow, pray let me entreat for him
The provisorship of your horse.

DUCHESS

Your knowledge of him
Commends him and prefers him.

CARDINAL

We are now to part from you and your own discretion
Must be your director.
(*The court withdraws*)

FERDINAND

You are a widow;
You know already what man is and therefore
Let not youth, high promotion, eloquence—

CARDINAL

No, nor anything without the addition, honor,
Sway your high blood.

FERDINAND

Marry? They are most lascivious
Will wed twice.

CARDINAL

O fie!

FERDINAND

Their livers are more spotted
Than Laban's sheep.

DUCHESS

Diamonds are of most value,
They say, that have passed through most jewelers' hands.

FERDINAND

Whores, by that rule, are precious.

DUCHESS

Will you hear me?
I'll never marry.

CARDINAL

So most widows say,
But commonly that motion lasts no longer
Than the turning of an hourglass, the funeral sermon
And it end both together.

FERDINAND

Now hear me:
You live in a rank pasture here in the court.
There is a kind of honeydew that's deadly.
'Twill poison your fame; look to it; be not cunning.

Nor they whose faces do belie their hearts
Are witches, ere they arrive at twenty years,
Aye, and give the devil suck.

DUCHESS

This is terribly good counsel.

FERDINAND

Hypocrisy is woven of a fine small threat,
Subtler than Vulcan's engine; yet believe it
Your darkest actions, nay your privatest thoughts,
Will come to light.

CARDINAL

You may flatter yourself
And take your own choice privately to be married
Under the eyes of night.

FERDINAND

Think it the best voyage
That e'er you made, like the irregular crab,
Which though it goes backward, thinks it goes right
Because it goes its own way, but observe;
Such weddings may more properly be said
To be executed than celebrated.

CARDINAL

The marriage night
Is the entrance into some prison.

FERDINAND

And those joys,
Those lustful pleasures are like heavy sleeps
Which do forerun man's mischief.

CARDINAL

Wisdom begins at the end. Remember it.
(*Cardinal exits*)

DUCHESS

I think this speech between you both was studied.
It came so roundly off.

FERDINAND

You are my sister,
This was my father's poignard, do you see?
I'd be loath to see't look rusty 'cause 'twas his.
I would have you give over these costly balls.
A visor and a mask are whispering rooms

That were never built for goodness. Fare ye well.
And women like that part which, like the lamprey,
Hath never a bone in't.

DUCHESS

                          Fie, sir.

FERDINAND

                                    Nay,
I meant the tongue, variety of courtship.
What can not a neat knave with a smooth tale
Make a woman believe? Farewell, lusty widow.
(*He exits*)

DUCHESS

Shall this move me? If all my royal kindred
Lay in my way unto this marriage,
I'd make them my low footsteps. And even now,
Even in this hate, as men in some great battles
By apprehending danger have achieved
Almost impossible actions (I have heard soldiers say so)
So I, through frights and threatenings will assay
This dangerous venture. Let old wives report
I winked and chose a husband, Cariola,
To thy known secrecy I have given up
More than my life, my fame.

CARIOLA

                                    Both shall be safe
For I'll conceal this secret from the world
As warily as those that trade in poison
Keep poison from their children.

DUCHESS

Have you spoke with Antonio?

CARIOLA

                                    He attends you.

DUCHESS

Good, dear soul, now leave me. But go
And place yourself behind the arras of my chamber
Where thou mayest overhear it. Wish me godspeed.
For I am going into a wilderness.
(*Cariola exits*)
Oh the misery of us that are born great, for thus
We are forced to woo because none dare woo us.

2

Boudoir of the Duchess of Malfi.

Duchess on stage.

DUCHESS (*enter Antonio*)
  I sent for you; sit down;
  Take pen and ink and write: are you ready?
ANTONIO
                                          Yes.
DUCHESS
  What did I say?
ANTONIO
                  That I should write somewhat.
DUCHESS
  Oh, I remember:
  After this farewell and this large expense,
  It's fit (like thrifty husbands) we inquire
  What's laid up for tomorrow.
ANTONIO
  So please your beauteous excellence.
DUCHESS
                          Beauteous?
  Indeed I thank you: I look young for your sake.
  As my steward you have taken my cares upon you.
ANTONIO
  I'll fetch your grace the particulars,
  Of all your revenues and your expenses.
DUCHESS
  Oh, you are an upright treasurer; but you mistook
  For when I said I meant to make inquiry
  What's laid up for tomorrow, I did mean
  What's laid up yonder for me.
ANTONIO
                    Where?

DUCHESS

                              In heaven,
I am making my will (as 'tis fit princes should
In perfect memory), and I pray, sir, tell me
Were it not better to make it smiling, thus,
Than in deep groans and terrible ghastly looks
As if the gifts we parted with procured
That violent distraction?

ANTONIO

                              Oh, much better.

DUCHESS

If I had a husband now this care were quit:
But I intend to make you overseer.
Lend me a hand!
What virtue shall I claim in my account with heaven?

ANTONIO

If you want me to write down
Now all your virtues, I must beg your pardon
For having not provided enough material.

DUCHESS

Thank you.
But I was thinking of but one:—obedience.
I practiced that one when my forceful brothers
Picked my husband for me. Do write down obedience.
Hold! Now I do not know for certain, if it's to be written
To my credit or to my debit, sir.

ANTONIO

Who knows how they are reading accounts up there?

DUCHESS

Down here I'd put it on the debit side.
What do you think of marriage?

ANTONIO

I take it as those that deny purgatory,
It locally contains or heaven or hell;
There's no third place in it.

DUCHESS

                              How do you like it?

ANTONIO

My loneliness, feeding on my melancholy,

Could often reason thus—

DUCHESS

                    Pray let's hear it.

ANTONIO

Say a man never marry, nor have children,
What takes that from him? Only the bare name
Of being a father, or the weak delight
To see the little wanton ride a cock-horse
Upon a painted stick or hear him chatter
Like a taught starling.

DUCHESS

                    Fie, fie, what's all this?
One of your eyes is bloodshot. Use my ring to it.
They say 'tis a good remedy. 'Twas my wedding ring
And I did vow never to part with it
But to my second husband.

ANTONIO

                    You have parted with it now.

DUCHESS

Yes, to help your eyesight.

ANTONIO

                    You have made me stark blind.

DUCHESS

How?

ANTONIO

        There is a saucy and ambitious devil
Is dancing in the circle.

DUCHESS

                    Remove him.

ANTONIO

How?

DUCHESS

        There needs small conjuration when your finger
May do it; thus, is it fit?

ANTONIO

                    What said you?

  (*He kneels*)

DUCHESS

                                        Sir,

This goodly roof of yours is too low built;
I cannot stand upright in't, nor discourse
Without I raise it higher: raise yourself,
Or if you please, my hand to help you: so.

ANTONIO

Ambition, madam, is a great man's madness.
Conceive not I am so stupid but I guess
Whereto your favors tend: but he's a fool
That, being acold, would thrust his hands in the fire
To warm them.

DUCHESS

                      So, now the ground's broke,
You may discover what a wealthy mine
I make you lord of.

ANTONIO

                      O my unworthiness!

DUCHESS

You were ill to sell yourself.
This darkening of your worth is not like that
Which tradesmen use i' the city; their false lights
Are to rid bad ware: and I must tell you
If you will know where breathes a complete man
(I speak it without flattery), turn your eyes
And progress through yourself.

ANTONIO

Be it so.
I have long served virtue
And never taken wages of her.

DUCHESS

                      Now she pays it.
And as a tyrant doubles with his words
And fearfully equivocates, so we highborn ladies
Are forced to express our violent passions
In riddles and in dreams and leave the path
Of simple virtue which was never made
To seem the thing it is not. Go, go, brag
You have left me heartless; mine is in your bosom.
I hope 'twill multiply love there. You do tremble.
Make not your heart so dead a piece of flesh

To fear more than to love me. Sir, be confident.
What is it distracts you? This is flesh and blood, sir;
'Tis not the figure cut in alabaster
Kneels at my husband's tomb. Awake, awake, man,
I do here put off all vain ceremony
And only do appear to you a young widow
That claims you for her husband, and like a widow,
I use but half a blush in it.
(*Antonio remains silent*)
And now that you shall not come to me in debt
(Being now my steward), here upon your lips
I sign your quittance. This you should have begged now:
I have seen children oft eat sweetmeats thus
As fearful to devour them too soon.

ANTONIO
But for your brothers?

DUCHESS
                 Do not think of them:
All discord without this circumference
Is only to be pitied and not feared!
It's true, they had a hope
Had I continued widow to have gain'd
An infinite mass of treasure by my death.
Yet could they know it, time will easily
Scatter the tempest.

ANTONIO
            These words should be mine,
And all the parts you have spoken, had not my tongue
Been too long used to servitude.

DUCHESS
               Kneel.
(*Both kneel*)
(*Enter Cariola*)

ANTONIO
               Hah!

DUCHESS
Be not amazed, this woman's of my counsel:
I have heard lawyers say a contract in a chamber,
Per verba presenti, is absolute marriage.
Bless, heaven, this sacred knot, which no violence

Ever untwine!
What can the church force more?

ANTONIO

May fortune know no accident
Either of joy or sorrow to divide
Our fixed wishes!

DUCHESS

              How can the church build faster?
We now are man and wife and 'tis the church
That must but echo this. Maid, stand apart;
I now am blind!

ANTONIO

            What do you mean by this?

DUCHESS

I would have you lead your fortune by the hand
Unto your marriage bed:
(You speak in me in this, for we now are one)
We'll only lie and talk together and plot
To appease my passionate kindred: and if you please,
Lay a naked sword between us, keep us chaste.
Oh let me shroud my blushes in your bosom,
Since 'tis the treasury o' all my secrets!
(*Duchess and Antonio exit*)

CARIOLA

Whether the spirit of greatness or of woman
Reign in her most, I know not, but it shows
A fearful madness. I owe her much of pity.

3

A Room in the Duchess' Palace. Some Months Later.

Enter Bosola with a book. He encounters an old woman.

BOSOLA   And who would you be?

OLD WOMAN   It's not your business, young man.

BOSOLA So you do not know that I make it my business to note down address, name and color of hair of all beauties? I did it from the cradle, lest I run out of opportunities.

OLD WOMAN Put me on your last page, young man. I am the last stage of all opportunities. See you at the end, young man, see you at the end.

(*Exit*)

BOSOLA

I hope not. A mountain of ugliness! And covered in mystery.
We account it ominous
If nature do produce a colt or lamb,
A fawn or goat in any limb resembling
A man and fly from it as a prodigy.
Man stands amazed to see his own deformity
In any other creature but himself.
But in our own flesh, though we bear diseases
Which have their true names only taken from beasts
And the most ulcerous wolf and swinish measle;
Though we are eaten up of lice and worms
And though continually we bear about us
A rotten and dead body, we delight
To hide it with rich tissue. All our fear,
Nay all our terror is lest our physician
Should put us in the ground to be made sweet.
But I have work on foot: I observe our Duchess
Is sick a days, she pukes, her stomach seethes,
The fins of her eyelids look most teeming blue,
She wanes in the cheek and waxes fat in the flank
And, contrary to our Italian fashion,
Wears a loose-bodied gown; there's somewhat in it.
I have a trick may chance discover it—
A pretty one—I have bought some apricots,
The first our spring yields.

(*Enter Antonio*)

ANTONIO (*pointing to book*) You are studying to become a great wise fellow?

BOSOLA Let me be simply honest.

ANTONIO Who would not be so?

BOSOLA Oh sir, I look no higher than I can reach. You are lord of the ascendant, chief man with the Duchess. Search the heads of the greatest rivers of the world, you shall find them but bubbles of water. Some would think the souls of princes were brought forth by some more weighty cause than those of meaner persons. They are deceived, there's the same hand to them, the like passions sway them; the same reason that makes a vicar go to law for a tithe-pig and undo his neighbors makes them spoil a whole province and batter down goodly cities with the cannon.

(*Enter Duchess and ladies of her court*)

DUCHESS

Your arm, Antonio: do I now grow fat?
I am exceeding short-winded. Bosola,
I would have you, sir, provide for me a litter,
Such a one as the Duchess of Florence rode in.

BOSOLA

The Duchess used one when she was great with child.

DUCHESS

I think she did.
(*To lady*)
                Come hither, mend my ruff,
Here, when? Thou art such a tedious lady
And thy breath smells of lemon peels—would thou hadst
    done!
Shall I swoon under thy fingers? I am
So troubled with the vapors!

BOSOLA (*aside*)
                I fear too much.

DUCHESS

I have heard you say the French courtiers
Wear their hats on fore the king.

ANTONIO

I have seen it.

DUCHESS

                In the presence.

ANTONIO

                                Yes.

DUCHESS

Why should we not bring up that fashion?
'Tis ceremony more than duty that consists
In the removing of a piece of felt.

Be you the example to the rest o' th' court.
Put on your hat first.

ANTONIO

                You must pardon me.
I have seen in colder countries than in France
Nobles stand bare to the prince: and the distinction
Methought showed reverently.

BOSOLA

I have a present for your grace.

DUCHESS

                      For me, sir?

BOSOLA

Apricots, madam.

DUCHESS

O sir, where are they?
I have heard of none to year.

BOSOLA (*aside*)

                  Good, her color rises.

DUCHESS (*as they are brought on*)
Indeed I thank you; they are wondrous fair ones.
What an unskilful fellow is our gardener!
We shall none this month.

BOSOLA (*as she bites into one*)

              Will not your grace pare them?

DUCHESS

No, they taste of musk methinks; indeed they do.

BOSOLA

I know not; yet I wish your grace had pared them.

DUCHESS

Why?

BOSOLA

I forgot to tell you the knave gardener,
Only to raise his profit by them sooner,
Did ripen them in horse dung.

DUCHESS

                O you jest.
You shall judge. Pray taste one.

ANTONIO

                Indeed, madam,
I do not love the fruit.

DUCHESS

                  Sir, you are loath
To rob us of our dainties. 'Tis a delicate fruit;
They say they are restorative.

BOSOLA

                      'Tis a pretty
Art, this grafting.

DUCHESS

             'Tis so; a bettering of nature.

BOSOLA

To make a pippin grow upon a crab,
A damson on a blackthorn—
(*Aside*)

                  How greedily she eats them!
A whirlwind strike off these bawd-farthingales!
For, but for that and the loose-bodied gown,
I should have discovered apparently
The young springball cutting a caper in her belly.

DUCHESS

I thank you, Bosola, they were right good ones,
If they do not make me sick.

ANTONIO

                  How now, madam?

DUCHESS

This green fruit and my stomach are not friends—
How they swell me!

BOSOLA (*aside*)

             Nay, you are too much swollen already!

DUCHESS

Oh, I am in an extreme cold sweat!

BOSOLA

                I am very sorry.

DUCHESS

Lights to my chamber! O, good Antonio,
I fear I am undone!
(*Exit with her ladies except Cariola. Bosola follows her*)

ANTONIO

             We are lost, Cariola,
We are lost. I fear me she has fallen in labor.
And there is no time for her remove.

CARIOLA
    I had prepared those ladies to attend her.
    Let us give out that Bosola had poisoned
    Her with those apricots. That will give color
    For her keeping close.
ANTONIO
                                    No, no, the physicians
    Will then flock to her. I am lost in amazement.
    I know not what to think on't. Oh we must
    Straightway hit upon some stratagem.
    (*Exeunt*)

    (*Re-enter Bosola*)
BOSOLA   So, so. There's no question but her tetchiness and
    most vulturous eating of the apricots are apparent signs of
    breeding. The experiment worked.
    (*Enter Old Woman with linen over her arm*)
    Now!
OLD WOMAN   Nay, I am in haste.
BOSOLA   Nay, nay, methinks you are in time. Yes, go, give
    your foster daughters good counsel. Tell them the devil
    takes delight to hang at a woman's girdle, like a false and
    rusty watch that she cannot discern how the time passes.
    (*She exits. Enter Antonio and two palace officers*)
ANTONIO
    Shut up the court gates.
FIRST OFFICER
                                    Why, sir? What's the danger?
ANTONIO
    Shut up the posterns presently and call
    All the officers of the court.
FIRST OFFICER
                                    I shall instantly.
    (*He exits*)
ANTONIO
    Who keeps the keys o' the park gate?
SECOND OFFICER
                                    Forobosco.

ANTONIO
Let him bring it presently.
(*Exit*)
(*Enter first officer with servants*)

FIRST SERVANT
Oh, gentlemen o' th' court, the foulest treason!

BOSOLA (*aside*)
If that these apricots should be poisoned now,
Without my knowledge?

FIRST SERVANT   There was taken even now a Switzer in the
Duchess' bed-chamber.

SECOND SERVANT   A Switzer?

FIRST SERVANT   With a pistol in his great codpiece.

BOSOLA   Ha, ha, ha!

FIRST SERVANT   The codpiece was the case for't.

SECOND SERVANT   There was a cunning traitor. Who would
have searched his codpiece?

FIRST SERVANT   True, if he had kept out of the ladies' chambers. And all the moulds of his buttons were leaden bullets.

SECOND SERVANT   Oh wicked cannibal! A firelock in's codpiece!

FIRST SERVANT   'Twas a French plot upon my life.

SECOND SERVANT   To see what the devil can do!
(*Enter Antonio*)

ANTONIO
All the officers here?

SERVANTS
                    We are.

ANTONIO
                    Gentlemen,
We have lost much plate, you know, and but this evening
Jewels to the value of four thousand ducats
Are missing in the Duchess' cabinet.
Are the gates shut?

FIRST SERVANT
                    Yes.

ANTONIO
                    'Tis the Duchess' pleasure
Each officer be locked into his chamber

Till the sunrising and to send the keys
Of all their chests and of their outward doors
Into her bedchamber. She is very sick.

SECOND OFFICER

At her pleasure.

ANTONIO

She entreats you take it not ill. The innocent
Shall be the more approved by it.

BOSOLA (*to servants*)

Gentlemen o' th' woodyard, where's your Switzer now?
(*All exit except Antonio*)

ANTONIO

Fear presents me somewhat that looks like danger.
How superstitiously we mind our evils!
The throwing down salt or crossing of a hare,
Bleeding at the nose, the stumbling of a horse,
Or singing of a cricket are of a power
To daunt the whole man in us.

CARIOLA (*enters with linens over her arm*)

Sir, you are the happy father of a son.
Your wife commends him to you.

ANTONIO

Blessed comfort!
For heaven's sake tend her well. I'll presently
Go set a figure for his nativities.

4

The Court of the Palace.

Enter Bosola with a dark lantern.

BOSOLA

Sure I did hear a woman shriek

And the sound came, if I received it right,
From the Duchess' lodgings. There's some stratagem
In the confining all our courtiers
To their several wards. I must have part of it;
My intelligence will freeze else.
It may be 'twas the melancholy bird,
Best friend of silence and of solitariness,
The owl that screamed so. Hah! Antonio?

ANTONIO (*enters with a candle and his sword drawn*)
I heard some noise. Who's there? What art thou? Speak.

BOSOLA
Antonio? Put not your face nor body
To such a forced expression of fear.
I am Bosola, your friend.

ANTONIO
     Bosola?

(*Aside*)
This mole does undermine me—Heard you not
A noise even now?

BOSOLA
    From whence?

ANTONIO
From the Duchess' lodging.

BOSOLA
     Not I. Did you?

ANTONIO
I did or else I dreamed.

BOSOLA
Let's walk towards it.

ANTONIO
    No; it may be 'twas
But the rising of the wind.

BOSOLA
     Very likely.
Methinks 'tis very cold and yet you sweat.
You look wildly.

ANTONIO
    I have been setting a figure
For the Duchess' jewels. They are stolen.

BOSOLA
  And what have you discovered?
ANTONIO
                        What's that to you?
  'Tis rather to be questioned what design,
  When all men are commanded to their lodgings,
  Makes you a night walker?
BOSOLA
                  In sooth I'll tell you.
  Now all the court's asleep, I thought the devil
  Had least to do here. I came to say my prayers.
ANTONIO (*aside*)
  I fear this fellow will undo me.
  (*To Bosola*)
  You gave the Duchess apricots today.
  Pray heaven they were not poisoned.
BOSOLA
  Poisoned? A Spanish fig
  For the imputation.
ANTONIO
          Traitors are ever confident
  Till they are discovered. There were jewels stolen, too.
  In my belief none are to be suspected
  More than yourself.
BOSOLA
            You are a false steward.
ANTONIO
  Saucy slave! I'll pull thee up by the roots.
  You are an impudent snake indeed, sir.
  Are you scarce warm and do you show your sting?
  You libel well, sir!
BOSOLA
          Now, sir, copy it out
  And I will set my hand to it.
ANTONIO
  My nose bleeds.
  (*Takes out handkerchief and drops paper as he does so*)
  One that were superstitious would count
  This ominous, when it merely comes by chance.

Two letters that are wrought here for my name
Are drowned in blood. Mere accident. For you, sir,
I'll take order. This door you pass not.
I do not hold it fit that you come near
The Duchess' lodgings till you have quit yourself.
(*Exits*)

BOSOLA

Antonio here did drop a paper—
(*Raises lantern*)
Some of your help, false friend—Oh, here it is. What's here?
A child's nativity calculated?

"The Duchess was delivered of a son 'tween the hours
twelve and one in the night, Anno Dom. 1504."

That's this year—
"decimo nono Decembris,"
That's this night—
"Taken according to the meridian of Malfi."
That's our Duchess. Happy discovery!

"The lord of the first house being in the ascendant signi-
fies short life; and Mars being in a human sign joined
to the tail of the Dragon, in the eighth house, doth
threaten a violent death. Caetera non scrutantur."

Why, now 'tis most apparent this precise fellow
Is the Duchess' pimp. I have it to my wish.
This is news indeed.
Our courtiers were cased up for it. It needs must follow
That I must be committed on pretense
Of poisoning her which I'll endure and laugh at.
If one could find the father now! But that
Time will discover. Let me be dismissed.
I'll bear intelligence of this to the Duke
Shall make his gall overflow his liver.
Though lust do mask in ne'er so strange disguise,
She's oft found witty but is never wise.

CURTAIN

ACT TWO

1

The Duke of Calabria's Tent.

Ferdinand attended by a Negro page who hands him his armor onstage. Offstage a soldier sings.

SOLDIER (*sings song offstage*)
  I wrote my love a letter
  When we entered fair Milan:
  Oh the war will soon be over
  For the cook has lost his coppers
  And the captain's lost his head
  And we've shot away our lead.

FERDINAND
  Methinks this war, like a long winter, hath no end
  And spring, frost-bitten, waits on victory.
  (*To page*)
  My corselet.
  (*Page begins to buckle it on*)
  How now, boy? How fares it with your love?

PAGE She is well save for the stripes she hath earned from my rival. She hath an eye like a dark lantern for its light is securely hidden.

FERDINAND 'Tis time you rid her of the scurvy knave.

PAGE How can I? I am so small a thing she cannot see me. 'Tis e'en the same to her an' I had not been born.

FERDINAND And you born for her!

PAGE   She hath received no intelligence of it. Or mayhap she puts no credence i' th' stars.

FERDINAND   A tragedy.

PAGE   If she but knew it.

SOLDIER *(entering)*
A gentleman would see the Duke.

FERDINAND
His name?

SOLDIER
Bosola.

FERDINAND
Bosola here? I'll see him.
(To page)
Now my beaver.

(Soldier exits and Bosola enters)

BOSOLA *(travel-stained and ragged)*   Your Grace.

FERDINAND   How fares the Duchess?

BOSOLA   Sir, I am worn out in your service. 'Tis two years since I left Malfi. There are rewards for horses and dogs but for a faithful servant only a sore breech from riding, these several scars, and scarce enough rags to cover my flesh.

FERDINAND   How fares the Duchess?

BOSOLA   Your Grace, I was pitifully misdirected. I have been robbed, lain in prison, took sick of the plague and like to have died only to bring you intelligence shall earn your ingratitude. I am like a raven of ill omen that endures a score of tempests, twoscore snowstorms, eludes the hawk and the fowler, to croak a message against which all would stop their ears. Thus I am very industrious to work my own ruin.

FERDINAND
I said: how fares the Duchess?

BOSOLA
Excellently. She hath a son.
(Ferdinand stands amazed)
I said she hath a son.
(Ferdinand half draws his sword)

BOSOLA *(quickly hands him a paper)*
Read this nativity. It speaks for me.
(While Ferdinand reads the paper the soldier sings offstage)

SOLDIER
But when we left the city
A second war began
Though the first was scarcely over
And I'll drink a thousand beakers
With a whore upon my knee
Till my love again I see.

FERDINAND (*reads*)
The Duchess was delivered of a son . . .
(*Reads on, then speaks slowly*)
Mars joined to the dragon's tail doth prophesy
Short life, a violent death.—Although ere now
I put but little faith i' the stars, this forecast
I'd believe—could I believe thee, lying knave!
(*Suddenly*)
Who is the man?

BOSOLA
     I know not.

FERDINAND (*violently*)
        Uncase me, slave!
Unmarried then!
(*He begins to tear off his armor. Outside alarms and sounds of battle*)
Ho, send me Delio. He shall command for me. I am off for Malfi.
(*Delio enters. He is bleeding*)

DELIO Your Highness, the enemy hath surprised us. They fall upon us mightily with a great body of fresh horse. The Duchess' great standard hath been taken.

FERDINAND
No matter.
We give you our command. I am for Malfi.
You shall lead our troops.

DELIO
      Alas, I can not.
(*He falls*)

FERDINAND
What's this? Delio's hurt? We are undone!
(*A soldier rushes in*)

SOLDIER

Sir, you are sorely needed.

(*Ferdinand snatches up his armor and rushes out buckling it on. The sound of battle grows. Ferdinand turns back suddenly and speaks to Bosola*)

FERDINAND

Thou villain, 'tis false! Thy paper is counterfeit.
Yet I'll come in a fortnight, depend upon it—
I'll come shortly. Late or soon I'll come
And should this bloody war endure ten years
Or e'en a score of years I'll come thereafter
And should I fall my vengeful ghost will come
To set our house in order. Breathe no word of this.
Meanwhile do you return and this I charge you:
Find out the father!

(*He exits clapping his visor shut. All during the end of this scene a monotonous trumpet call has been playing outside*)

BOSOLA   What's the matter with him? Why should she not bear a son? Her brother steals enough land for five sons. Yet the Duke's eyes did start from his head to hear it. 'Twas as if a Calabrian knight in Turkey should hear his betrothed lies with another and be denied a furlough. Yet all this is but policy for a gentleman like him was never in such a sweat over less than a dukedom.

2

A Room in the Duchess' Palace. Music.

Enter Antonio and Delio.

ANTONIO

Beloved Delio! The god of war
Has taken his time to give me back my friend!

DELIO
    Let me behold your face: it's somewhat leaner.
    Lord Ferdinand has been most eager
    To revisit Malfi and twice made ready
    To return and twice he could not. In the end
    The victory was greater. But how fares
    Your noble Duchess?

ANTONIO
                        She is well.

DELIO
                                I think
    You hold your tongue in check. Speak freely.
    I'd say, you look pale.

ANTONIO
    Oh cousin Delio, I fear some great
    Misfortune threatens. Since you saw the Duchess,
    She has had three children, two sons and a daughter.

DELIO
    How? Is she married?

ANTONIO
                        No, 'tis all in secret.

DELIO
    But is't known?

ANTONIO
                        The rumor spreads apace.

DELIO
    What say the common people?

ANTONIO
                                The rabble
    Do directly say she is a strumpet.

DELIO
    And your graver heads; what is their opinion?

ANTONIO
    They are politic and say nothing.

DELIO
    But who, then, is the father?

ANTONIO
    Oh Delio, cousin, I've almost forgotten
    How 't is to have a confidant. My mouth

Has long been locked.
I am the father of her children.

DELIO
    Antonio!

ANTONIO
                Tell me, Delio, swiftly,
    Hath not this gossip yet arrived to the ear
    Of the Lord Ferdinand? For you must know
    Both brothers, for reasons best known to themselves,
    Will not allow their sister to remarry.

DELIO
    You stun me with your news, Antonio.
    How very great must be your passion
    To dwarf your reason thus. Lord Ferdinand? His bearing
    Altered while he tarried in the field. He grew
    So quiet towards the end, he seemed to sleep
    The tempest out as dormice do in winter.
    I could now believe some rumor reached him
    For houses that are haunted are most still.

ANTONIO   The banquet is over. Here come the Duchess and
    her brother.

3

The Bedchamber of the Duchess.

Enter Duchess, Antonio, Cariola.

DUCHESS
    Bring me the casket hither and the glass.
    You get no lodging here tonight, my lord.

ANTONIO
    Indeed I must persuade one.

DUCHESS
                        Very good.
    I hope in time 'twill grow into a custom

That husbands shall come with cap and knee
To purchase a night's lodging of their wives.

ANTONIO

  I must lie here.

DUCHESS

             Must? You are lord of misrule.

ANTONIO

  Indeed my rule is only in the night.

DUCHESS

  To what use will you put me?

ANTONIO

                  We'll sleep together.

DUCHESS

  Alas, what pleasure can two lovers find in sleep?

CARIOLA

  Good sir, I lie with her often and I know
She'll much disquiet you.

ANTONIO

              See, you are complained of.

CARIOLA

  For she's the sprawlingest bedfellow.

ANTONIO

  I shall like her the better for that.

CARIOLA

  Sir, shall I ask you a question?

ANTONIO

  I pray thee, Cariola.

CARIOLA

  Wherefore still when you lie with my lady
Do you rise so early?

ANTONIO

            Laboring men
Count the clock oftenest, Cariola,
Are glad when their task's ended.

DUCHESS

               I'll stop your mouth.

  (*Kisses him*)

ANTONIO

  Nay, that's but one, Venus had two soft doves

To draw her chariot. I must have another.
(*Kisses her again*)
When wilt thou marry, Cariola?

CARIOLA

I wouldn't know. I pray you tell me,
If there were proposed me wisdom, riches and beauty
In three several young men which should I choose?

ANTONIO

'Tis a hard question. This was Paris' case
And he was blind in it and there was great cause
For how was it possible he could judge right,
Having three amorous goddesses in view
And they stark naked?

DUCHESS

If I were to choose 'tween wisdom, riches and beauty,
I'd choose love. Even so, you shall not sleep here.

CARIOLA

'Tis well, for the silkworm is accustomed
To fast every third day and the next following
Spins the better for it.
(*They laugh*)

DUCHESS

                    I pray thee tell me
When were we so merry? My hair tangles.

ANTONIO (*takes Cariola aside*)

Pray thee, Cariola, let's steal forth the room
And let her talk to herself. I have diverse times
Served her the like when she hath chafed extremely.
I love to see her angry. Softly, Cariola!
(*They tiptoe out*)

DUCHESS

Doth not the color of my hair 'gin to change?
When I wax gray, I shall have all the court
Powder their hair with orris to be like me.
You have cause to love me, I entered you into my heart
(*Enter Ferdinand unseen*)
Before you would vouchsafe to call for the keys.
We shall one day have my brothers take you napping.
Methinks his presence, being now in court,
Should make you keep your own bed. But you'll say

Love mixed with fear is sweetest. I'll assure you
You shall get no more children till my brothers
Consent to be godfathers. Have you lost your tongue?
Or have I angered you? Forgive me, husband,
You shall sleep here. In truth I fear nothing
For I have tasted so much joy that now,
Whether I am doomed to live or die,
I can do both.
(*Ferdinand discloses himself and gives her a poignard*)

FERDINAND

        Die then, quickly.
Virtue, where art thou hid? What hideous thing
Is it that doth eclipse thee?
(*Duchess stands transfixed*)
Or is it true thou art but a bare name
And no essential thing?

DUCHESS

        Sir—

FERDINAND

        Do not speak.

DUCHESS

        No sir.

FERDINAND

Oh most imperfect light of human reason
That mak'st us so unhappy to foresee
What we can least prevent! Pursue thy wishes
And glory in them. There's in shame no comfort
But to be past all bounds and sense of shame.

DUCHESS

I pray, sir, hear me. I am married.

FERDINAND

        So!

DUCHESS

Perhaps not to your liking but for that,
Alas, your shears do come untimely now
To clip the bird's wings that's already flown.
Will you see my husband?

FERDINAND

        Yes, if I could change
Eyes with a basilisk.

DUCHESS

                      Sure, you came hither
By his confederacy?

FERDINAND

                     The howling of a wolf
Is music to thee, screech owl—prithee peace.
Whatever thou art that hast enjoyed my sister,
For I am sure you hear me, for thine own sake
Let me not know thee. I came hither prepared
To work thy discovery yet am now persuaded
It would beget such violent effects
As would damn us both. I would not for ten millions
I had beheld thee. Therefore use all means
I never may have knowledge of thy name;
And for thee, vile woman,
If thou do wish thy lecher may grow old
In thy embracements, I would have thee build
Such a room for him as our hermits
To holier use inhabit. Let not the sun
Shine on him till he's dead. Let dogs and monkeys
Only converse with him and such dumb things
To whom nature denies use to sound his name.
If thou do love him, cut out thine own tongue
Lest it betray him.

DUCHESS

                   Why might not I marry?
I have not gone about, in this, to create
Any new world or custom.

FERDINAND

                   Thou art undone.
Thou has ta'en that massy sheet of lead
That hid thy husband's bones and folded it
About my heart.

DUCHESS

              Mine bleeds for it.

FERDINAND

Thine? Thy heart?
What should I name it unless a hollow bullet
Filled with unquenchable wildfire?

DUCHESS

You are in this
Too strict and, were you not my princely brother,
I would say too wilful. My reputation
Is safe.

FERDINAND

Dost thou know what reputation is?
I'd tell thee—but to no avail since th' instruction
Comes now too late. And so for you I say
You have shook hands with reputation,
He's left you for good. So fare you well.
I will never see you more.

DUCHESS

Why should I,
Of all the other princes of the world
Be cased up like a holy relic? I have youth
And a little beauty.

FERDINAND

So you have some virgins
That are witches. I will never see thee more.
(*Exits*)
(*Enter Antonio with a pistol and Cariola*)

ANTONIO

We are betrayed.
(*To Cariola*)
I should turn
To thee for that.

CARIOLA

But I am innocent.

ANTONIO

How came he hither?

CARIOLA

That gallery gave him entrance.

ANTONIO

I would this terrible thing would come again
That, standing on my guard, I might relate
My warrantable love.
(*Duchess silent*)
There is a weapon, little used but mighty

Even against the mightiest. Let us employ it:
Let us oppose your brother. And against his frenzy
Hold up the Gorgon-head of reason, and make him see:
He strives 'gainst nature who opposes love.

DUCHESS

You must leave me.
I stand as if a mine beneath my feet
Had been blown up.

ANTONIO

Methinks some strange enchantment, sprung
From ties of blood hath bewitch'd thee. You seem
Transfixed and can hear your husband's voice no more.
The great Lord Ferdinand is a mighty warrior, but
I have heard soldiers speak of a brave captain
Who cried: I'm powerless to defend myself, so I'll
Attack. This is my counsel: Let's call the officers
Of your palace, bid them renew their oaths
Of loyalty and attend you closely to prevent
All dark designs upon your person. Having armed
Our arguments with these precautions,
We'll speak with your too hasty brother and unfold
The history of our honorable marriage.
(*Knocking within*)
How now? Who knocks? More earthquakes?

CARIOLA

It is Bosola.

DUCHESS (*to Antonio*)
                    Away! You must instantly part hence.
I have fashioned it already.

ANTONIO (*sadly*)

I would you had given me leave to defend you
As any fishmonger would strike a blow
To shield his dear ones. But do not spare me.
Great adversaries now do menace you,
Let's put an end to strife between us two.
(*Exit Antonio. Enter Bosola*)

BOSOLA

The Duke, your brother, is ta'en up in a whirlwind,
Hath took horse an's rid post to Rome.

DUCHESS

So late?

BOSOLA

He told me, as he mounted into the saddle,
You were undone.

DUCHESS

Indeed I am very near it.

BOSOLA

What's the matter?

DUCHESS

Antonio, master of our household,
Hath dealt so falsely with me in's accounts:
My brother stood engaged with me for money
Ta'en up of certain Neapolitan bankers
And Antonio let the bonds be forfeit.

BOSOLA

Strange! This is cunning.

DUCHESS

And hereupon
My brother's bills at Naples are protested
Against. Call up our officers.

BOSOLA

I shall.

(*He exits*)
(*Antonio enters*)

DUCHESS

The place that you must fly to is Ancona.
'Tis the diocese of my brother, the Lord
Cardinal. Surely he will be merciful
And give us shelter, and even sanctify
Our marriage for we may bribe him.
He is covetous. I'll feign a pilgrimage
To Our Lady of Loretto. We shall meet there.
Hire a house and I'll send after you
My treasure and my jewels. Our weak safety
Runs upon ingenious wheels. Short syllables
Must stand for periods. I must now accuse you
Of such a feigned crime as is a noble lie
Cause it must shield our honors. I'll give out

You have dealt falsely with me in your accounts.

ANTONIO

'Tis a good stratagem. But if I do so—
At your request not fight for you—I fear
That you yourself may learn to scorn me
When I am gone for you'll have many teachers.
Say what you will but stop your ears with wax.

DUCHESS

Dear friend, I'll love no one that hates thee.
Lacking your sweet presence, I'll gaze upon
Your portrait oftener than my looking glass.
Hark, they are coming.

(*Enter Bosola and gentlemen*)

ANTONIO

                            Will your grace hear me?

DUCHESS

I have got well by you, you have yielded me
A million of loss. I am like to inherit
The people's curses for your stewardship.
You had the trick in audit time to be sick
Till I had signed your quietus and that cured you
Without the help of a doctor. Gentlemen,
I would have this man be an example to you all
So you shall hold my favor. Pray observe him,
For he has done that, alas, you would not think of
And, because I intend to be rid of him,
I mean not to publish. Use your fortune elsewhere.

ANTONIO

I am strongly armed to brook my overthrow
As commonly men bear with a hard year.
I will not blame the cause on it but do think
The necessity of my malevolent star
Procures this not her humor. O the inconstant
And rotten ground of service! You may see
'Tis even like him that in a winter night
Takes a long slumber o'er a dying fire,
As loath to part from it, yet parts thence as cold
As when he first sat down.

DUCHESS

                            We do confiscate,

Toward the satisfying of your accounts,
All that you have.

ANTONIO

I am all yours and 'tis very fit
All mine should be so.

DUCHESS

So, sir, you have your pass.

ANTONIO

You may see, gentlemen, what it is to serve
A prince with body and soul.
(*Exits*)

BOSOLA Here's an example for extortion; what moisture is
drawn out of the sea, when foul weather comes, pours down
and runs into the sea again.

DUCHESS I would know what are your opinions of this Antonio.

SECOND OFFICER He could not abide to see a pig's head gaping. I thought your grace would find him a Jew.

THIRD OFFICER I would you had been his officer for your own
sake.

FOURTH OFFICER You would have had more money.

FIRST OFFICER He stopped his ears with black wool and to
those that came to him for money said he was thick of
hearing.

SECOND OFFICER Some said he was a hermaphrodite for he
could not abide a woman.

FOURTH OFFICER And how scurvy proud he would look when
the treasury was full! Well, let him go.

FIRST OFFICER Yes, and the chippings of the buttery fly after
him to scour his golden chain.

DUCHESS Thank you, gentlemen; you may leave now.
(*Exeunt officers. Bosola remains*)
What do you think of these?

BOSOLA

These are rogues that in his prosperity
Would have prostituted their daughters to his lust,
Made their first-born intelligencers; and do these lice
Drop off now!—Alas, poor gentleman!

DUCHESS

Poor! He has amply filled his coffers!

BOSOLA

Sure he was too honest.

DUCHESS

I did not know you were his friend.

BOSOLA

Let me show you what a most unvalued jewel
You have in a wanton humor thrown away,
To bless the man shall find him. He was an excellent
Courtier and most faithful; a soldier that thought it
As beastly to know his own value too little
As devilish to acknowledge it too much.
Hath his virtue and his form deserved a far better fortune;
His breast was filled with all perfection,
And yet it seemed a private whispering room,
It made so little noise of it.

DUCHESS

But he was basely descended.

BOSOLA

Will you make yourself a mercenary herald
Rather to examine men's pedigrees than virtues?
You shall miss him;
For know an honest statesman to a prince
Is like a cedar planted by a spring;
The spring bathes the tree's root, the grateful tree
Rewards it with his shadow. You have not done so.
I would sooner swim to the Bermudas on two politicians'
Rotten bladders, tied together with an intelligencer's heart-
    string
Than depend upon so changeable a prince's favor.
Fare thee well, Antonio! Since the malice of the world
Would needs down with thee, it can not be said yet
That any ill thing happened to thee, considering thy fall
Was accompanied with virtue.

DUCHESS

Oh you render me excellent music!

BOSOLA

Say you?

DUCHESS

This good one that you can speak of is my husband.

BOSOLA

Do I not dream? Can this ambitious age
Have so much goodness in it as to prefer
A man merely for worth, without those shadows
Of wealth and painted honors? Possible?

DUCHESS

I have had three children by him.

BOSOLA

Fortunate lady!
For you have made your private nuptial bed
The humble and fair seminary of peace.
And the neglected poets of your time
In honor of this trophy of a man
Raised by that curious engine your white hand
Shall thank you in your grave for it; and make that
More reverend than all the cabinets
Of living princes. For Antonio,
His fame shall likewise flow from many a pen
When heralds shall want coats to sell to men.

DUCHESS

As I taste comfort in this friendly speech,
So I would find concealment.

BOSOLA

Oh, the secret of my prince,
I'll wear it on the inside of my heart!

DUCHESS

You shall take charge of all my coin and jewels
And follow him for he retires himself to Ancona—

BOSOLA

So?

DUCHESS

      Whither within a few days I mean to follow him.
   (*Duchess exits*)

BOSOLA

What rests but I reveal all to my lord?
Now for this act I am certain to be raised
And men that paint weeds to the life are praised.

4

A Room in the Cardinal's Palace.

On stage Cardinal and Ferdinand with a letter.

FERDINAND
  She's loose in the hilts;
  Grown a notorious strumpet.
CARDINAL
                          Speak lower.
FERDINAND
                                  Lower?
  Read here what's written by my intelligencer.
  A servant, her own steward!
CARDINAL (*reads letter*)
                          Can this be certain?
FERDINAND
  Rhubarb, oh for rhubarb
  To purge this choler! Here's the cursed day
  To prompt my memory and here it shall stick
  Till of her bleeding heart I make a sponge
  To wipe it out.
CARDINAL
              Why do you make yourself
  So wild a tempest?
FERDINAND
                  Would I could be one
  That I might toss her palace 'bout her ears,
  Root up her goodly forests, blast her
  And lay her general territory as waste
  As she hath done her honor.
CARDINAL
                      Shall our blood,

The royal blood of Aragon and Castile
Be thus attained?

FERDINAND

Apply desperate physic,
We must not now use balsamum but fire,
The smarting cupping glass for that's the means
To purge infected blood, such blood as hers.
There is a kind of pity in mine eye—
I'll give it to my handkerchief and now 'tis here.
I'll bequeath this to her bastards.

CARDINAL

What to do?

FERDINAND

Why to make soft lint for their mother's wounds
When I have hewed her to pieces.

CARDINAL

Cursed creature.

FERDINAND

Methinks I see her laughing,
Excellent hyena! Talk to me somewhat quickly,
Or my imagination will carry me
To see her in the shameful act of sin
With everyone! With some strong-thighed bargeman!
Or one o' the woodyard that can quoit the sledge
Or toss the bar, or else some lowly squire
That carries coal up to her private lodging!

CARDINAL

You fly beyond your reason.

FERDINAND

Go to, mistress!
'Tis not your whore's milk that shall quench my wildfire,
But your whore's blood.

CARDINAL

How idly shows this rage, which carries you
As men conveyed by witches through the air
In violent whirlwinds! This intemperate noise
Fitly resembles deaf men's shrill discourse,
Who talk aloud, thinking all other men
To have their imperfection.

FERDINAND

                        Have you not
My palsy?

CARDINAL

               Yes, but I can be angry
Without this rupture.
(*Looks at letter*)

                    She will visit Ancona.

FERDINAND
  You shall not receive her!

CARDINAL

                  I will think upon it.

FERDINAND
  I could kill her now,
In you or in myself, for I do think
It is some sin in us heaven doth revenge
By her.

CARDINAL
       Are you stark mad?

FERDINAND

                     I would have their bodies
Burnt in a coal pit with the ventages topped
That their cursed smoke might not ascend to heaven;
Or dip the sheets they lie on in pitch of sulphur,
Wrap them in it and then light them like a match;
Or else boil their bastards to a cullice
And give it to their lecherous father to renew
The sin of his back.

CARDINAL (*coldly*)
              I'll leave you.

FERDINAND

                   Nay, I have done.
I am confident that had I been damned in hell
And should have heard of this, it would have put me
Into a cold sweat. In, in! I'll go sleep.
Now that I know who leaps my sister
I'll find scorpions to string my whips
And fix her in a general eclipse!
(*Ferdinand exits*)

5

The Shrine of Our Lady of Loretto in Ancona.

Enter two pilgrims.

FIRST PILGRIM
　We are fortunate our pilgrimage brings us
　Here today. The Cardinal himself conducts
　The service for his sister, the Duchess
　Who hath arrived from Malfi to pay her vow
　At the shrine of Our Lady of Loretto.

SECOND PILGRIM
　She hath much need to pray. 'Tis whispered
　Through all Ancona that she came seeking shelter
　For her steward lover and her bastards.

FIRST PILGRIM
　Is not this a grievous sin in the eyes of the church?

SECOND PILGRIM
　Not if it be performed in the bedchamber
　Of a palace.

FIRST PILGRIM
　　　　　　Who would have thought
　So great a lady would have matched herself
　Unto so mean a person.

SECOND PILGRIM
　　　　　　　　　Nay, lechery
　Is a great equalizer. 'Tis blind to rank.

FIRST PILGRIM
　The ceremony begins.
　(*Sound of organ music and chanting*)

SECOND PILGRIM
　'Tis strange so many monks in yon procession.

FIRST PILGRIM
　Who is that woman, clad like a penitent;
　It seems she hath a man and three small children by her side.

SECOND PILGRIM
  'Tis the Duchess, I saw her
  As she drove along the streets of fair Ancona.

FIRST PILGRIM
  Meseems she's very pale.

SECOND PILGRIM
                              Here comes the Cardinal
  From out the sacristy. What is that parchment
  He carries in his hand?

VOICE OF CARDINAL   Herefore, through the authority of the
  Almighty God, Father of Heaven, and His Son, Our Savior,
  I, Cardinal of Ancona, denounce, proclaim and declare
  Angelica Teresa, Duchess of Malfi, and her paramour, Antonio Bologna, together with their children, anathema by
  the avise and assistance of our Holy Father, the pope, and
  all bishops, abbots, priors, and other prelates and ministers
  of our Holy Church, for her open lechery and sins of the
  flesh.

FIRST PILGRIM   He hath excommunicated her!

VOICE OF CARDINAL   I curse her head and the hairs of her head,
  her eyes, her mouth, her nose, her tongue, her teeth, her
  neck, her shoulders, her breast, her heart, her arms, her
  legs, her back, her stomach, her womb, and every part of
  her body from the top of her head to the soles of her feet.

SECOND PILGRIM   There hath been no rumor she was to be
  judged.

FIRST PILGRIM   And to think 'twas said she came here for
  sanctuary!

VOICE OF CARDINAL   I dissever and part them from the church
  of God and likewise from contracts and oaths of law. I forbid all Christian men to have any company with them and
  all her earthly goods I seize in the name of the Holy
  Church. And as their candles go from our sight so may their
  souls go from the visage of God and their good fame from
  the world.

SECOND PILGRIM
  Then she is no longer Duchess of Malfi!

FIRST PILGRIM
  By what justice hath her brother
  Seized her estates?

SECOND PILGRIM

                    Sure I think by none.

FIRST PILGRIM

  I have not seen a goodlier ceremony than this
  Though I have visited many.

SECOND PILGRIM

  What was it with such violence he took
  From off her finger?

FIRST PILGRIM

                 'Twas her wedding ring.

6

A Road Near Loretto.

Enter Antonio, Duchess, children, Cariola, servants.

DUCHESS

  Banished from Ancona!

ANTONIO

                 And what is worse, our love
  Is named a sin and published throughout all Italy
  That all may shun us and you are ravished of your goods.

DUCHESS

  Is all our train shrunk to this poor remainder?

ANTONIO

  These poor men which have got little in your service
  Vow to take your fortune; but your wiser birds,
  Now they are fledged, are gone.

DUCHESS

  They have done wisely.

ANTONIO

              Right the fashion of the world.
  From decayed fortunes every flatterer shrinks;
  Men cease to build where the foundation sinks.

DUCHESS

  I had a very strange dream last night.

ANTONIO
  What was it?
DUCHESS
                Methought I wore my coronet of state
  And on a sudden all the diamonds
  Were changed to pearls.
ANTONIO
                          My interpretation
  Is you'll weep shortly for to me the pearls
  Do signify your tears.
DUCHESS
                        The birds that live in the field
  On the wild benefit of nature, live
  Happier than we for they may choose their mates
  And carol their sweet pleasures to the spring.
  Dear Antonio, I've dragged you into this
  And I am sorry.
ANTONIO
                  You are not the cause.
  For since that hour—scarcely now remembered,
  For 'tis obscured by so much later sorrow—
  When, standing in your chamber, I betrayed
  Plain reason urging me to fight for thee
  And went for cunning stratagems, I have lost
  Myself.
  (*Enter Bosola with a letter*)
BOSOLA
              You are happily o'ertaken.
DUCHESS
  From my brother?
BOSOLA
  Yes, from the Lord Ferdinand, your brother
  All love and safety.
DUCHESS
                      Thou dost blanch mischief,
  Wouldst make it white.
BOSOLA His Lordship has had word about the outrageous
  treatment his beloved sister met with at the shrine of Lo-
  retto. His Lordship will take it up with the Cardinal.

DUCHESS (*Reads*) "Dear sister, Why do you not come back
   to Malfi? Bring the right worshipful Antonio Bologna with
   you. I want his head in a business." Strange words.
   (*She shows the letter to Antonio*)

BOSOLA
   Strange? Antonio is an upright treasurer.

DUCHESS
   He is. I perceive my brother's meaning. (*To Antonio*)
   He does not want your counsel, but your head.
   That is, he cannot sleep till you are dead.
   And here's another pitfall that's strew'd o'er
   With roses; mark it, 'tis a cunning one:
   (*Reads*)
   "I have discharged the Neapolitan bonds and am satisfied
   he was falsely accused in this matter. Thus I have made
   sure of his honest service to you, my sister. Let not the
   money trouble him, I had rather have his heart than his
   money."
   And I believe so too.

BOSOLA
             What do you believe?

DUCHESS
   That he so much distrusts my husband's love
   He will by no means believe his heart is with him
   Until he see it: the devil is not cunning enough
   To circumvent us in riddles.

BOSOLA
               Does that mean,
   You will reject that noble and free offer?

DUCHESS
   Yes.

BOSOLA (*to Antonio*)
      And what from you?

ANTONIO
           Thus tell him: I will not come.

BOSOLA
   This proclaims your breeding.
   Every small thing draws a base mind to fear
   As the adamant draws iron. Fare you well, sir;

You shall shortly hear from's.
(*Exit*)
DUCHESS

Dear husband,
If the Lord Cardinal treat us so harshly,
I fear my brother Ferdinand still more.
Therefore by all my love I do conjure you
To take our eldest son and fly towards Milan.
Let us not venture all this poor remainder
In one unlucky vessel.
ANTONIO

You counsel safely.
Best of my life, farewell. Since we must part,
Heaven hath a hand in it, but no otherwise
Than as some curious artist takes in sunder
A clock or watch, when it is out of frame,
To bring it to better order.
DUCHESS (*to eldest son*)

I know not which is best,
To see you dead or part with you. Farewell, boy;
Thou art happy that thou hast not understanding
To know thy misery, for all our wit
And reading brings us to a truer sense
Of sorrow.
(*Pause, she draws the boy back*)
No, give me back my son.
He is weak in the lungs. He'll take some harm.
(*To second son*)
Go, thou, with thy father. Alas, thou art so small.
Haply wilt cry for thy mother i' th' night.
Yet thou art stronger and thou hast far to go.
In the eternal church, sir, I hope we do not part thus.
ANTONIO
Do not weep.
Heaven fashioned us of nothing and we strive
To bring ourselves to nothing. Farewell, Cariola,
And thy sweet armful.
(*To the Duchess*)
If I do never see thee more,

Be a good mother to our little ones
And save them from the tiger. Fare you well.

DUCHESS   Let me look upon you once more, for that speech
came from a dying father.
(*Kisses him*)
Fare you well.
(*He goes out with second son*)
My laurel is all withered.

CARIOLA
Look, madam, what a troop of armed men
Make toward us, with their visors closed.
Why do they hide their faces? They are brigands surely.
(*Enter Bosola, helmeted with a guard*)

DUCHESS
O they are very welcome!
I would have my ruin be sudden
I am your adventure, am I not?

BOSOLA
                              You are.

DUCHESS
Come, to what prison.

BOSOLA
                      To none.

DUCHESS
                                    Whither, then?

BOSOLA   To your palace. Your brother means you safety.

DUCHESS   Safety! With such safety men preserve alive
Pheasants and quails when they are not fat enough to be
eaten.

BOSOLA   These are your children?

DUCHESS
Yes. And their father is a steward.
They were born accursed.

BOSOLA
                        Fie, madam!
Forget this base, lowborn fellow.

DUCHESS
                              Were I a man,
I'd beat that counterfeit face into thy other.

ACT THREE

1

A Room in the Cardinal's Palace.

The Cardinal is reading a book. A monk sits near him telling his beads.

CARDINAL
I am puzzled in a question about hell.
(*Looks at book*)
He says in hell there's one material flame
And yet shall not burn all men alike.
Let him by.
(*Closes book*)
        How tedious is a guilty conscience!
When I look into the fish pond in my garden,
Methinks I see a thing armed with a rake
That seems to strike at me.
(*Enter Ferdinand and his Negro page with two swords*)
        How, now, Ferdinand!
Thou lookst ghastly.
There sits in thy face some great determination.
What is it?
FERDINAND
        I am come to punish thee.
Call your collegium!
CARDINAL
        Collegium? What for?
FERDINAND
'Cause you have published our sister's shame

And publicly dishonored her. And I demand
that now in midst of your collegium
You publicly recant your accusations
in thy dome of Loretto.

CARDINAL

Hast thou gone mad, brother?
Thou thyself didst rage against her most
Intemperately. 'Twas you did call her strumpet.

FERDINAND

I did. But not i' th' market place.
You have so wrought it that the rabble shall soil
Her charms in the tavern and in the baths.
They'll reckon whether her breasts be large or small.
For this you shall pay in full.

CARDINAL

Shall you defend her?

FERDINAND

I shall defend and I shall punish her.

CARDINAL

These are strange words indeed. Why should our sister be
More your concern than mine? As if she were
A rotten tooth in your mouth and not in mine?
Now in her lamentable cause
'Twas not I but my holy office did constrain me:
She has sinned.

FERDINAND

I think your purse constrained you.
You have stolen her lands!

CARDINAL

I see what irks you. Pray hold your temper
And I will faithfully divide revenues with you.

FERDINAND

Thy prayers and proffers are both unseasonable.
Call your collegium.

CARDINAL

In the midst of night?

FERDINAND

Repentance must not wait for sunrise. And
Confessions are worked out best in these quiet

Last hours of the night, and, brother, confess you shall
That thou hast falsely indicted the Duchess of Malfi,
Our sister, out of greed.

CARDINAL

                Now you are mad indeed.

FERDINAND

And you will do more. You will ask the pope to lift
That crooked ban from off her shoulders and you will re-
    store the duchy
And all her rich estates to our sister.
And if you will not do so, I shall kill you.

CARDINAL

That means extortion and I will not stand for't.

FERDINAND

It means extortion and you will stand for't,
Recant or take this sword and draw.
    (*He throws one sword upon him and takes the other*)

CARDINAL

I am a churchman. And I will not fight.
    (*Holds up the book like a sword*)
This holy book is my defense. Pierce it and thou darest.
    (*Ferdinand strikes it aside with his sword*)

FERDINAND

Will you fight or die like a poltroon?
    (*He attacks the Cardinal*)

CARDINAL (*leaping up and snatching sword*)

Help!—Help!—Our guard!

MONK

                Ho, guards! Guards!

FERDINAND

                      You are deceived.

They are out of reach of your howling!
Recant or die!

CARDINAL

        I'll not recant.

FERDINAND

             Die then!
    (*Ferdinand wounds the Cardinal. The Cardinal drops his
    sword*)

CARDINAL

  Thou hast hurt me!

FERDINAND

                     Not enough.

  (*Drives him back and stabs him*)

CARDINAL

                               Oh justice! I am done.

  I suffer now for what hath former been;

  Sorrow is held the eldest child of sin.

  (*He dies*)

2

A Ruin near Milan.

*Enter Antonio and his son. They hold their cloaks close
against them as if walking against the wind.*

ANTONIO

  Yonder lie the ruins of a noble abbey.

  When'er we tread upon these ancient stones

  We set our foot upon some reverend history.

  Here in this open court that now lies naked

  To the injuries of the stormy weather

  Some men lie interred who loved the church so well

  And gave so largely to it,

  They thought it should have canopied their bones

  Till doomsday. But all things have their end.

  Churches and cities, which have diseases like to men,

  Must have like death that we have. Come, boy, we must
    make haste,

  Until we reach Milan.

BOY

  Why can't we stay with mother?

ANTONIO

We are too small to live with greatness.
Our littleness is crushed between the millstones
Of their intemperate actions.

BOY

Shall we not see her more?

ECHO

Not see her more.

BOY

Oh hark to the pretty echo from the ruin!

ECHO

Ruin!

ANTONIO

Two hundred steps, no more, will bring us, son,
To the dreary valley's end, where you will see
The towers of Milan.
Poor boy, well do I know your feet are blistered
Yet we must fly from danger. Do not stay!

ECHO

Do not stay!

BOY

If we run fast, father, think you we will yet die?

ECHO

Yet die.

BOY

What does the echo say?

ANTONIO

It seems to tell us, boy, what is the fate
Of him who is forbid to fight. Alas
Now I remember once, ahawking with my father
Upon the plains of Brittany, our falcon
Spied a hare and coursed it till the poor beast
Was wearied unto death and so, despairing
Turned upon its back and with its stony feet
Hardened by a whole life of timid flight
Beat in the falcon's breast. Yet we must fly.
Although you'll find it to no avail to fly your fate.

ECHO

O fly your fate!

3

A Room in the Duchess' Palace.

Enter Ferdinand and Bosola.

FERDINAND

How doth our sister Duchess bear herself
In her imprisonment?

BOSOLA

Nobly: I'll describe her
She's sad as one long used to it and she seems
Rather to welcome the end of misery
Than shun it; a behavior so noble
As gives a majesty to adversity.
You may discern the shape of loveliness
More perfect in her tears than in her smiles.
She will muse for hours.

FERDINAND

Her melancholy seems to be fortified
With a strange disdain.

BOSOLA

'Tis so and this restraint,
Like English mastiffs that grow fierce with tying,
Makes her too passionately apprehend
Those pleasures she is kept from.

FERDINAND

Curse upon her!
Doth she inquire for her steward-husband and her cubs?

BOSOLA

Call them her children.
For though our national law distinguishes bastards
From true legitimate issue, compassionate nature
Makes them all equal.

FERDINAND

Doth she weep for them?

BOSOLA

Aye, for she is ignorant if they be safe or no.

FERDINAND

She shall learn. Bring her my gift.

She shall be distracted from her sorrow.

Unseen I'll mark how deeply her lecherous sin

Is rooted in her mind.

(*Ferdinand hides upon the balcony. Duchess and attendants and Cariola enter*)

BOSOLA

All comfort to your grace!

DUCHESS

I will have none.

Prithee why dost thou wrap thy poisoned pills

In gold and sugar?

BOSOLA

Your brother,

The Lord Ferdinand, is come to visit you.

In proof that he hath sealed his peace with you, meanwhile;

For your diversion and to cure you

Of your melancholy study of what's past,

The Lord Ferdinand presents you with a rare

And precious gift.

DUCHESS

It is not gifts I'd have

My brother send me. The noblest boon within

His power to grant is friendship to my friends.

BOSOLA

Bring on the gift.

DUCHESS (*to Cariola*)

Methinks I hardly know my brother now

Yet once he loved me well.

(*The servants bring on a huge carved chest. They are preceded by a flute-player playing on his instrument*)

BOSOLA

Here is the key.

CARIOLA

'Tis a costly gift.

DUCHESS

Set it in my bedchamber.

BOSOLA

There's more within.

DUCHESS

Do I open it?

BOSOLA

Aye.

(*She slowly goes to it, unlocks the doors. The bodies of Antonio and her child fall out. Cariola screams. Duchess stands frozen with horror*)

Your brother does present you this sad spectacle

That, now you know directly they are dead,

Hereafter you may wisely cease to grieve

For that which can not be recovered.

(*The Duchess faints. Flautist suddenly perceives what has happened and stops abruptly. Bosola raises Duchess*)

Come, you must live!

(*They try to revive her*)

Remember you are a Christian!

Leave this vain sorrow!

Things being at their worst begin to mend.

The bee when he has shot his sting into your hand

May then play with your eyelid.

CARIOLA

Good comfortable fellow,

Persuade a wretch that's broke upon the wheel

To have all his bones new set!

(*The Duchess faints again*)

My lady! Help! No, don't recall her spirits yet.

This faint is charitable. Help me carry her to her room!

FERDINAND (*from the gallery*)

She is lost! I can not save her.

BOSOLA

Why do you do this?

She hath suffered much.

FERDINAND (*coming down*)

Base varlet, there's too much pity in thy pleading!

BOSOLA

Sir, I have served you well. I have rather sought
To appear true than honest. I swear to you
She hath had eyes for no one but her husband.
Faith, end here. And go no further in your cruelty.
Pray, furnish her with beads and prayer book
And let her save her soul.

FERDINAND

               Damn her, that body of hers,
While that my blood ran pure in it, was worth more
Than that thing which thou wouldst comfort, called a soul.
I see her sin sits deeper than I thought.
To this vile appetite for her own steward
She now adds shameful tears and mourns his death
And in her lecherous grief she naked stands,
The widow of a sweaty stableboy.
To cure such maladies the surgeon's knife
Must cut until it pricks the patient's life.
Your work is almost done.

4

The Courtyard of the Duchess' Castle.

Enter Delio, a physician, and Ferdinand's Negro page.

DELIO

I, Delio Bologna,
Cousin to the late Antonio Bologna
Who was husband to the former Duchess of this realm,
—She, as you know, is kept prisoner within these walls—
I hire you to examine His Lordship, the Duke Ferdinand,
Now lawless ruler of his sister's duchy,
Since of his state of mind the most extraordinary
And damnable rumors shake the ear.

PHYSICIAN
  Is the Duke of a melancholy or choleric humor?
DELIO
  Here the Duke's page will tell you all he knows.
PAGE
  He oft hath had these violent fits of late.
DELIO
  On the morrow of his brother, the Cardinal's, strange
  And sudden death, this boy found him
  All in a cold sweat and altered much in face
  And language.
PAGE
                Since when he hath grown worse and worse
  And yet, at times, he seems himself again.
PHYSICIAN
  What other symptoms
  Doth his disposition show?
DELIO
  One met the Duke 'bout midnight in a lane
  Behind St. Mark's church.
  And he howled fearfully,
  Said he was a wolf, only the difference
  Was a wolf's skin was hairy on the outside,
  His on the inside, bade them take their swords
  Rip up his flesh and try.
  Does it not seem a fearful madness?
PHYSICIAN
  Let me hear more. I must sound the depths
  Of his distraction.
PAGE   Once I did ask him why he loved solitariness. And he
  replied that eagles commonly fly alone. They are doves,
  crows, and starlings that flock together. And on a sudden
  he started most fearfully and cried "What follows me?"
  And then he flung himself upon the ground and said he
  would throttle his shadow.
PHYSICIAN   'Tis most grave.
PAGE   Straightway he sprung up violently and stared about
  him and cried out, "Rogues, knaves, bawds! Oh the world
  is sick. I think only the cold tomb can cure it. Blood's the
  potion for this disease." Then he laughed horribly. Then

he drew his sword, howling, "Hence, hence! There's nothing left of you but tongue and belly, flattery and lechery!" And all must flee before him.

PHYSICIAN   This seems madness indeed.

DELIO (*to the page*)   And what of the book?

PAGE

The Lord Ferdinand did inquire concerning
A certain apothecary who 'tis whispered
Poisoned his mistress with a book.

DELIO

I like it not. I do fear for the Duchess.
So, while you try sound out the Duke, I'll make
Haste to Cortezza there to gather troops and officers
With whom I am popular since the Cyprian war
And who, I know, are loyal to the Duchess.
With them and with your expert statement, I will
Arrest the Duke and boldly free the Duchess.
God's speed! I will be back by daybreak.
(*Exeunt*)

5

A Room in the Duchess' Palace.

Onstage, Duchess and Cariola.

CARIOLA

What think you of, madam?

DUCHESS

Of nothing.
When I muse thus, I sleep.

CARIOLA

Like a madman with your eyes open?

DUCHESS

Dost thou think we shall know one another
In the other world?

CARIOLA

Yes, out of question.

DUCHESS

Oh that it were possible we might but hold
Some two days' conference with the dead!
From them I should learn somewhat, I am sure,
I never shall know here.
What make you of my brother's rage, Cariola?

CARIOLA

He did not like Antonio for your husband.
But you must not think so much.

DUCHESS

Ay, I must.
It's not like him
As I remember him. When we were children
Playing lovers in the park, cutting each other's
Throats with the wooden knives, Ferdinand never was
The highborn rightful groom, but always was
The outlaw highwayman, the brigand dragging
Me from some princely altar. He bore
No pride in his birth. So, why he rages thus,
Against mild-mannered Antonio, my husband,
I can not tell.
(*Enter Bosola*)

BOSOLA

All comfort to your grace!

DUCHESS

I will have none.

BOSOLA

Come, madam, be of cheer, I'll save your life.

DUCHESS

Indeed, I have no leisure to tend so small a business.

BOSOLA

Now, by my life, I pity you.

DUCHESS

Thou art a fool then
To waste thy pity on a thing so wretched
As can not pity itself. Knave, tell my brothers

That I perceive death, now I am well awake,
Best gift that they can give or I can take.

BOSOLA

Does not death fright you?

DUCHESS

                        Who would be afraid on't,
Knowing to meet such excellent company
In th' other world?

BOSOLA

                  Come, you must live.
Who speaks of death? Surely your brother
Would have you live, my lady. He thinks of naught
Save your welfare and desires of you
But one thing, that you should swear
Upon this prayer book never to marry again.
Here is the book and you must kiss it.

DUCHESS

This were easily done. My heart is but
A dead piece of flesh and there is not
'Twixt heaven and earth one wish I'd stay for now.
Only I have two children still. Will not
My brother come and cut their throats?

BOSOLA

Can they prattle?

DUCHESS

         Yes.

BOSOLA   Then he can not call them young wolves. Anyway, he
should consider it a deal without more bargaining. This oath
will satisfy your brother. Kiss the book.

DUCHESS

If it is so
I'll swear it gladly I'll never marry.
Because I hope to meet my husband soon
In heaven, where my brothers can not interfere
With our pleasures. For they'll howl in hell.
To this I swear and kiss the book. Amen.
(*Kisses the book*)

BOSOLA

By this he doth make sure you shall not break your oath.

DUCHESS
    What more?
BOSOLA
                    Your brother, the Lord Duke,
    Now you have brought to rest his mind in this
    Most deplorable case, wants to restore to you
    What never should be taken away, your duchy.
    (*Noise from outside; drums and marching*)
CARIOLA
    My lady, you are free!
FIRST WOMAN (*at the window*)
    The palace guard that held my lady prisoner
    Is marching off.
SECOND WOMAN
                    And her standard flies once more
    From the tower.
BOSOLA
                    Please don your ducal robes, my lady.
    (*Four waiting women enter bringing robes of state and
    coronet*)

                            Please, be robed.
CARIOLA
    My lady, can you stand?
DUCHESS
    What matter? I'll tell thee a miracle:
    I am not mad yet, to my cause of sorrow.
    I am full of daggers, yet I am not mad.
    What noise is that?
    (*Bells. A priest has entered. He reads a Latin proclamation
    lifting the excommunication and restoring her estates*)
DUCHESS
    What means this?
BOSOLA   At the instigation of the Duke, your brother,
    The pope has revoked your excommunication
    And restored your estates.
DUCHESS
    Can this mean, the Holy Church's
    Ban is lifted from me and mine?
BOSOLA
                            'Tis so.

DUCHESS

And my authority restored?

BOSOLA

You are Duchess of Malfi once more.
(*He bows. Exit priest*)

DUCHESS

What says the Cardinal to this?

BOSOLA

Corpses do not speak.

DUCHESS

Ay, but what says the Cardinal?

BOSOLA

His holiness, the Lord Cardinal, prince of Ancona, is dead.

DUCHESS

Dead?

BOSOLA

The Lord Ferdinand
Would not forgive his publishing of your
Misfortunes.

DUCHESS

Bosola, is my brother mad?

BOSOLA

Only in what concerns you.

DUCHESS

My brother, slain by my brother.

BOSOLA

Executed.
Your brother, the Lord Duke, will visit you shortly
And kiss your hand and reconcile himself.
(*Exit. The Duchess stands, frozen*)

CARIOLA

My lady, do not grieve so deeply at your brother's
Violent death.

DUCHESS

I can not grieve.
I have wept my tears. Forgive me if I do not mourn
As would be natural or seemly. Far more
Am I concerned for my brother Ferdinand,
And his coming hither.
If but this drowsiness did not weigh

So heavily upon me. But I must act
And speedily, now I am reinstated,
To defend the living and to bury my dead.
For, now the ban is lifted, I may pick them
From the dunghill and lay them
In consecrated ground and I'll prepare
A princely funeral for my beloved Antonio and my son
And in my widow's weeds I'll walk behind
Their coffins i' th' teeth of all the world.
Teresa, go fetch my children. 'Tis my wish
That they be clad in seemly fashion
To mourn their father. But since I am to meet
A perilous guest to whom the aspect
Of my children may not be pleasing, prithee,
Mariana, seek out the captain of my guard.
Bid him come hither with a score
Of armed men. And since the guest
Comes to forgive me, offering his hand,
—Alas, dripping with blood—and since I myself
Can not forgive him, fetch me from my chamber the poignard,
Once given me by my most capricious brother:
May thus the tiger meet his sister tigress.

CARIOLA
My lady, I rejoice to see you thus determined.

DUCHESS
Yet I can scarcely stand, Cariola. And
One question goes round in my poor head
For which I have no good answer: Why
Did he kill his own brother? Because
He insulted and robbed me?

CARIOLA
                                        That is right.
I marvel greatly he hath taken your part.
'Tis clear he hates you.

DUCHESS
                              Oh Cariola,
I wish I could myself think over it
In such a simple way. Alas, I can not.

My mind is full of shadows. There are wondrous
Questions from early times and half forgot,
And never answered,
Which do concern my brother Ferdinand.

CARIOLA
My lady, you look pale.

DUCHESS
                    Methinks I do begin
To know somewhat I never knew before.
O my poor brother! Cariola, there are sins
With deeper roots than hate.

CARIOLA
                    My lady, you are sick.
Such thoughts are bred of sickness.
When you are sound again, they'll fly out by the window.

DUCHESS
Ay, and I grow sicker, Cariola. Let me be seated.
I think I must die shortly.

CARIOLA
'Tis a denial of God's mercy to speak so.

DUCHESS
My legs grow numb. 'Tis not pain I feel, yet my foot
Seems to be sleeping.

CARIOLA Surely you have eaten somewhat that sits ill upon
your stomach. I will chafe your legs. My lady, you are cold.
(*Suddenly as she kneels to do so*)
The book you kissed! 'Twas the book! Villains! Poisoners!
Murderers!

DUCHESS
                    My oath!

CARIOLA
The oath! He has made sure you will not break it!
(*To the women*)
My lady is stricken. Cry out for help!

DUCHESS
What witchcraft does he practice?

CARIOLA (*as other waiting women rush on*)
Heat water. Fetch some cordial.
The Duke has done this. Fetch water, wine.

My lady is poisoned. Quickly seek a doctor!

DUCHESS

There is none for me. My sickness is mortal.
Methinks I know his secret now. Methinks
I do perceive the cause of this enforcing
Of my chastity and more.

CARIOLA

What speak you, madam?

DUCHESS

This feverish law, put o'er me not to marry,
This spying on me! This tearing off my sheets!
This present in the chest!
And this distracted slaughter of his brother
Who bared my woes in public. All this fury,
His cruelty and his despair! And now the poison
To punish me 'cause I had shared my bed.
'Tis but a fever, unknown to a brother,
'Tis but a fever only lover knows.
Alas, my brother!
He has no friend but death to do his wooing.

CARIOLA

Pray, drink this cordial.

DUCHESS

To what end?
Nay, give it to me for I must live until
My brother comes that I may speak to him
And tell him what I know.
For I do feel such pity with the man
That all is washed away, the ruin he has wrought
My sorrow and his own. Alas
I am so weary I would rest a while.

CARIOLA

No, no, my lady,
From this slumbrous poison no one wakes again.

DUCHESS

Why then I must not sleep. Help me, Cariola.
Let's walk and never let me rest. Thy promise!
I must not die before I meet my brother.

(She is helped up and begins to walk about, supported by

Cariola and the weeping women)
Let someone watch to tell me if the Duke be come.
Make haste. My time is short.
(*Women go to the window to watch*)
                                   Do not weep so loud.
I'm not deaf yet and this noise distracts me.
(*To Cariola*)
I pray thou givest up my little boy
Some syrup for his cold and let the girl
Say her prayers ere she sleep. But I must walk
And when I falter, do thou urge me on. Cry loudly
In my ear: "His soul is lost because he loved you so!"
Oh, I grow giddy.

CARIOLA
                         Lean on me, my lady.

DUCHESS
Now all the coldness
Of this too icy world creeps in about my heart.
My brother is too slow. Tell him, I could not wait.
(*She dies. Women wail. One of the women rushes out.
Shouting from outside, then drums*)
(*Enter Bosola with executioners*)

BOSOLA
Some other strangle the children.
(*Two of the executioners leave*)

CARIOLA
                                   Oh, you are damn'd
Perpetually for this! My turn is next;
Is't not so ordered?

BOSOLA
                         Yes, and I am glad
You are so well prepar'd for't.

CARIOLA
                                   You are deceived, sir,
I am not prepar'd for't, I will not die;
I will first come to my trial, and know
How I have offended.

BOSOLA
                         Come, dispatch her,—

You kept her counsel; now you shall keep ours.

CARIOLA
I will not die, I must not, I am contracted
To a young gentleman.

BOSOLA
                              Here's your wedding ring.

CARIOLA
Let me but speak with the Duke: I'll discover
Treason to his person.

BOSOLA
                              Delays:—throttle her.

FIRST EXECUTIONER
She bites and scratches.

CARIOLA
                              If you kill me now
I am damn'd; I have not been at confession
This two years.

BOSOLA (*to executioner*)
                    When!

CARIOLA
I am quick with child.

BOSOLA
                    Why, then,
Your credit's saved.
(*They strangle Cariola*)
Bear her into the next room.
(*He points to the Duchess*)
Let this lie still.
(*Drumming stops. Enter Ferdinand*)

FERDINAND
Is she dead?

BOSOLA
            She is what
You'd have her. Fix your eye here.

FERDINAND
                              Constantly.

BOSOLA
Do you not weep?
Other sins only speak; murder shrieks out.

The element of water moistens the earth,
But blood flies upwards and bedews the heavens.

FERDINAND

Cover her face; mine eyes dazzle: she died young.

BOSOLA

I think not so. Her infelicity
Seemed to have years too many.

FERDINAND

She and I were twins. She was born some minutes
After me and died some minutes sooner.
Let me see her face again.
(*To Bosola*)
Why didst thou not pity her? What
An excellent honest man mightst thou have been,
If thou hadst borne her to some sanctuary!
Or, bold in a good cause,—oppos'd thyself
Between her innocence and my revenge!
I bade thee, when I was distracted of my wits,
Go kill my dearest friend, and thou hast done't.
For let me but examine well the cause:
Her marriage that drew a stream of gall quite through my
    heart.
Of course, I must confess, I had a hope,
Had she continued widow, to have gain'd
An infinite mass of treasure by her death.
This has an evil sound yet not so evil
As some other reason I'll not speak of.
We'll say the cause was my ungoverned passion,
My cruelty and spite. Only I fear
It is not true.
(*To Bosola*)
                    As to thee, I hate thee for it.
Get thee into some unknown part of the world
That I may never see thee.

BOSOLA

Sir! Let me quicken your memory, for I
Perceive you are falling into ingratitude.
I challenge the reward due to my service.

FERDINAND (*more and more provocatively*)
  I'll tell thee what I'll give thee: a rope.
  And thou shalt hang.

BOSOLA

                    Ha!

FERDINAND
  Ay. Like a bloody fool thou'st forfeited thy life
  And thou shalt die.

BOSOLA
  Is that my pension, scoundrel?
  Draw then or have thy payment too.
  (*Ferdinand does not move. Bosola wounds him*)

FERDINAND
  That was mortal.
  Thou hast done much ill well.
  My sister, oh my sister!
  Here is the cause on it.
  (*He dies*)

BOSOLA (*unbelieving*)
  Didst thou not fight?
  Methinks, I was thy tool in this once more.
  That was the purpose and thy cunning wit
  That I should kill thee, and I did.

6

The Courtyard of the Duchess' Castle.

Enter Captain, Delio, with Duchess' eldest son and soldiers.

DELIO
  Where is the Duchess?
  (*Soldiers come out of the palace, dragging with them Bosola*)

SOLDIER

    The Duchess of Malfi lies within

    Murdered by her brother, the Lord Ferdinand,

    Slain by this knave.

BOSOLA

                    'Twas more a deed of mercy

    Done by a fool unwittingly for nothing.

    I served his tyranny, and rather strove

    To satisfy him than all the world, believe me, sirs.

    For though I loath'd the evil, yet I lov'd

    Him that did counsel it.

DELIO

    'Twas him that slew my cousin too.

    His measure is full—

    Let him be hanged.

BOSOLA

                Dear sir, my estate is sunk

    Below the degree of fear.

    Let worthy minds ne'er stagger in distrust

    To suffer death or shame for what is just:

    Mine is another voyage.

    (*A soldier leads him out*)

CAPTAIN

    Good Delio, we come too late.

DELIO

    Did you find the Duchess' little daughter?

SOLDIER

                      Alas—but dead.

DELIO

    Thus of this mighty family remains

    This child, dragged out of the tumult by a servant.

    These wretched eminent things

    Leave no more fame behind 'em, than should one

    Fall in a frost, and leave his print in snow;

    As soon as the sun shines, it ever melts,

    Both form and matter.—Let's make noble use

    Of this great ruin and join all our force

    To establish this young and hopeful gentleman

    In his mother's right.

CAPTAIN
                    Yet I have heard
  He is not wholly of noble birth?
DELIO
                            An idle rumor,
  As ill founded as all which has befallen those
  Within these ancient and too firmly mortared walls.
  And, were it true, if here should spring
  A new shoot from a hundred-years-old tree
  Whose trunk too long hath twined upon itself
  It were a hopeful portent. Let us now
  Convey to bury these unhappy brethren.
  From hidden causes their misfortunes grow;
  We'll pity when the cause we can not know.

Epilogue

DELIO
  May these deaths enacted here
  Purge by pity and by fear
  Till each chastened conscience be
  From all fatal passions free.
  Hidden hatreds, loves obscure
  Fevers living could not cure
  Pride and jealousy and lust
  Ruined these to squandered dust.
  Here their greatness ended: May
  This portent teach us to survey
  Our progression from our birth.
  We are set, we grow, we turn to earth
  Courts adieu and all delights
  All bewitching appetites!
  Sweetest breath and clearest eye
  Like perfumes go out and die,
  Praise and conversation

Fall silent as we die alone.
Vain the ambition of kings
Who seek by trophies and dead things
To leave a living name behind
And weave but nets to catch the wind.

Notes and Variants

Texts by Brecht

Brecht's version of Webster's *Duchess of Malfi*

1. Backed by his brother the Cardinal, the Duke of Aragon, prior to going to war on her behalf, forbids his widowed sister ever to remarry, and places a spy in her household.

2. Hardly has her brother left than the Duchess tells her steward that she loves him, and they go to bed.

3. The spy discovers this when she becomes pregnant, and he sends a letter to the Duke.

4. The Duke gets the letter just before a battle. Confused by the idea of having to hurry back, he fights badly and is taken prisoner. (Deviation.)

5. After spending some years in captivity the Duke returns and finds that his sister has remarried. He bombards her with threats. The Duchess turns down the steward's offer to fight for her, seeing this as an interference in her dispute with her princely brother; she decides to take refuge with her brother the Cardinal. (Deviation.) Nonetheless she is moved to confide her plan to the spy by his praise for her beloved.

6. The Duke denounces his sister to the Cardinal as a whore. The Cardinal decides to excommunicate her and confiscate her duchy. He recommends a cooler approach to his brother, whose passion astounds him.

7. Having fled to the Cardinal, the Duchess and her family are excommunicated by him and banished.

8. Fleeing once more, and free as a bird, the Duchess comes to realize that her brother the Cardinal acted out of avarice, but fails to understand the Duke and his motives. A letter from him shows her what a deadly hatred he bears her husband, and she sends the latter ahead with one of the children. She is arrested. (The Duchess' uncertainty about the Duke is a deviation.)

9. In his flight the steward complains to his young son about the fate of those who let themselves be persuaded not to fight. (Deviation.)

10. The Duke has the dead bodies of her husband and little son shown to the Duchess. Deeply wounded by her despair, he decides to use the surgical knife to cut deeper. (Deviation.)

11. On seeing her executioners, the Duchess realizes that her brother's pronouncement of the death sentence is a declaration of love, and expresses her sympathy with him. Over her coffin the Duke threatens the executioner for having put his sentence into effect. (The Duchess' realization, a deviation.)

12. Arriving posthaste after hearing of the Duchess' murder, the Cardinal finds the Duke close to madness. During a memorial service organized by the Duke, the Cardinal, to stop him blaming himself, reminds him that the Duchess was no better than a whore, and the Duke kills him for the insult. He in turn is killed by his lieutenant, who has provoked his hostility by a cynical remark. (Deviation.)

[BBA 500/47–49, original in German.]

How *The Duchess of Malfi* ought to be performed

The model to be followed is the Broadway musical which, thanks to certain fiercely competing groups composed of speculators, popular stars, good scene designers, bad composers, witty if second-rate song writers, inspired costumiers, and truly modern dance directors, has become the authentic expression of all that is American. Alienation effects are extensively used by the designers and dance directors, the latter deriving theirs from folklore. The painted backdrops which constitute the main scenery reflect the influence of modern painting, including good surrealist ideas. In the dance numbers, some of them intelligently worked-out mimes, one now and again finds gestic elements of the epic theater. The plot is strongly outlined and provides a sturdy scaffolding for the various insertions.

Unless the groupings in *Malfi* have as much meaning as the dispositions in a musical, and the delivery of the verse arias the . . . .

> [From *Schriften zum Theater* 4, p. 196. The typescript ends thus at the foot of a page so that it is not clear if Brecht left it unfinished or if the rest has been lost.]

Letter to Paul Czinner

Dear Dr. Czinner,

Herewith a few points as to essential alterations.

1. The lighting needs to be much brighter, since long passages spoken in verse are virtually unintelligible.

2. The grouping of the actors should at least be changed so as to prevent them having to deliver scarcely intelligible (and sometimes imperfectly spoken) passages with their backs to the audience.

3. It is essential to return to the adaptation provided by Auden and myself. No cuts should be made without the agreement of both of us. Nor should additional passages from Webster be introduced without our being consulted, since the adaptation consists in a series of carefully considered cuts which were thoroughly and frequently discussed with Elisabeth Bergner, who approved them.

4. Not enough thought has been given to the casting of Ferdinand, as Elisabeth herself says. What is more, the director's conception of the part is a wrong one, as you and Elisabeth both say—so wrong as effectively to obscure and distort the whole sense of the play. You must engage a different Ferdinand.

5. Almost every scene needs to be redirected so as to make the story intelligible to the audience. I suggest that for this you should engage a fresh director. The present director has ignored the adaptation and seems quite incapable of directing in such a way as to allow the audience to follow the plot. (I

understand that the London critics likewise complained of the "obscure plot" in his direction of the original Webster version.)

Would you let me know by Monday, September 30, what you propose to do about these points?

Yours,

Bertolt Brecht

[BBA 1175/01–02. Copy of a letter dated "Boston, September 26, 1946." These appear to represent the changes which Brecht felt were needed before the Boston production could move on to New York.]

Attempted Broadway Production of *The Duchess of Malfi*

The adaptation of John Webster's *Duchess of Malfi* was undertaken at the request of an émigré German actress who had had success on the English stage. The additional verses were translated by Auden, who also saw to it that the original was not unduly maltreated. The actress feared that the New York critics might be provoked by the amputation of a literary monument. However, it turned out that the critics in question were little concerned about careful restoration and largely ignorant of the work (not a single comparison being made with any passage of the original). The production was supervised by an English director and involved old-style declamation in accordance with that so-called Shakespearean tradition whose style derives from the nineteenth century and has of course nothing to do with the Elizabethan theater. The shortcomings of this tradition could be clearly observed. The story narrated by the play was not performed; wherever it came through nonetheless everything possible was done to damp down its startling twists. The characters were flattened out by the pernicious practice of stressing the "eternally human" element, while the shabby attempt to make each event a typical case purged of any operation of chance, so that the audience might blindly follow the workings of "fate," stripped those events of all reality. The actors clung to their purple passages, their arias, for dear life, but without being able to ground them in the action (and for that matter without knowing how to sing). The leading actress refused to let the Duchess' experiences determine her character, nor on the other hand did she stick to one kind of character throughout; thus up to a given scene it was Countess Mitzi and thereafter Mary Queen of Scots. The line taken in the adaptation was that the Duchess' brothers were using her bourgeois love affair as the rope with which to hang her (the Duchess embarks on a bourgeois marriage), but the production saw the "master of the Duchess' household" as a comely princeling, and cut the scene where she tells her bourgeois husband not to interfere in the dispute between her and her noble brothers. The steady aggravation of the tortures to which she is subjected by Ferdinand, himself in love, lost all meaning because his helplessness was not portrayed; while in the final act the actress rejected a scene where the Duchess sees that her death sentence is also her brother's declaration of love. This sprang from a lack of intelligence and stature, and still more from a technical inability to play such episodes. This was something which she shared with the American Antonio and the English Ferdinand. Trained at the Munich Kammerspiele at the end of the First World War and subsequently at Reinhardt's and Barnowsky's theaters in Berlin, she did not command the technique of the German epic theater. As for the rest of the cast, they lacked (and no doubt despised) that of the American musical, which may be entirely phony and provide nothing but empty entertainment in greedy obedience to the fashions of the day, but has nevertheless managed to evolve certain primitive epic methods which could at least serve to present the great Elizabethans in something halfway resembling a contemporary manner.

[From *Schriften zum Theater* 4, pp. 194–6. Not included in GW. The Broadway production opened on October 15, 1946.]

Editorial Note

1. General

The Brecht Archive contains no fewer than five complete or near-complete texts of the play, as well as more entries for subsidiary materials than for any other of Brecht's works apart from *Galileo*. Two of these texts (BBA 144 and 146) predate the 1943 copyrighted version or belong to that immediate period; a third (BBA 1167) has a notation by Elisabeth Hauptmann, "Auden"; a fourth (1177) is a major revision of the 1943 copyrighted text and has manuscript additions and changes most of which have been incorporated in the typed text called "Exemplar Barbara B" (BBA 1419). This last text, then, in the possession of Brecht's daughter, seems to be the one most likely to summarize Brecht's contribution; it shows many signs of his revision, mostly in deleting and adding lines and speeches, tightening scenes and shortening them. The mass of material numbered 1174, however, contains more than two acts of a freshly typed text which includes all of Brecht's changes in 1419 and which apparently was meant to depend upon 1419's unchanged portions to form a complete play. In this text (1174), the manuscript modifications are fewer, though single sheets and groups of sheets following the coherent revised section (1174/01–64) reveal subsequent modifications and/or alternate versions of material in earlier parts of 1174 or in the formerly unchanged parts of the Barbara Brecht script.

Although no certain dates can be put on these last two texts (they are demonstrably later than mid-1943 and were typed by the same New York firm which typed the 1945 and 1946 copyrighted texts), both show careful work by Brecht and represent his continued, perhaps his conclusive, work on the play. Significantly, neither relies very extensively on *The White Devil*: whether this situation indicates that both texts date from a period before (or after) such insertions were contemplated or that Brecht decided not to attempt the amalgamation cannot be judged. Certainly the inclusion of material from *The White Devil*, having been considered by the collaborators part way through their work, was eventually dropped. Possibly the Barbara Brecht script and more probably BBA 1174 date from the latter part of the period during which Brecht is shown by his journal to have worked on the play (i.e., 1945 or early 1946). We have chosen to print as much of BBA 1174 as forms a coherent text and to fill in the gaps with the Barbara Brecht script, modified in places by changes preserved on single sheets in BBA 1174.

The draft plan entitled, "Brecht's version of Webster's *Duchess of Malfi*" (pp. 421–22) gives a general view of Brecht's design for the play and his attitude towards his work on it. Although this story cannot be directly linked with any one of the surviving texts (for example, paragraph 5 describes Ferdinand's captivity whereas all the surviving texts account for the passage of time by delaying Bosola's arrival with news of the Duchess' marriage), most of the major points of Brecht's adaptation appear in the list. Brecht apparently criticizes himself with the word "deviation," specifically the muting of Ferdinand's incestuous jealousy of the Duchess. Each time the action provides an opportunity for explicit recognition or statement of this motive, the characters turn aside. The very basic decision to emphasize this motive (in the original it remains implicit and one among several possibilities) eventually led to the introduction of a prologue (partly from John Ford's *'Tis Pity She's a Whore*) in the Barbara Brecht script and to many other interpolations throughout the play. Brecht later decided to give both the Cardinal and Ferdinand an economic motive (possession of the Duchess' estates) and there are increasingly frequent references to this mercenary incentive from the time of the 1943 copyrighted version (where it is barely mentioned) to our composite text.

A second, more structural, change comes with the very end of the play. Webster's controversial decision to place the Duchess' death in the fourth, rather than the final, act is replaced by a conclusion in which the deaths of brother and sister occur closer together and nearer the play's end. This second modification meant recasting material from the original fourth and fifth acts and also required several adjustments in earlier scenes. Webster's Act IV (all citations in roman numerals refer to J. R. Brown's "Revels" edition of *The Duchess of Malfi*, Methuen, 1964) consists almost entirely of a powerful scene in which Bosola half-tortures, half-comforts the Duchess before executing her. In Act V, interest shifts to Bosola and to an extraordinary series of ironic reversals, unintentional murders, and plans gone astray. While originally he retained a modified version of Webster's Act V (see BBA 1177/84), Brecht finally creates a crescendo of deaths: the Cardinal murdered by Ferdinand (3,1); the Duchess by Bosola, acting for the Duke (3,5); Ferdinand himself by Bosola (3,5). It remains for Delio, in a concluding scene (3,6) to order Bosola's execution and the restoration of the Duchess' surviving son as duke.

Carrying out this second decision had two chief effects: it greatly reduced Bosola's part and led Brecht to create a new scene (3,1) in which Ferdinand kills his brother out of an irrational rage at the excommunication which he himself had proposed and engineered. Through Brecht's drafts, this scene develops from a crudely direct murder (in BBA 1177) to a complicated statement of the Cardinal's remorse and Ferdinand's insane jealousy (in the version here printed). The proper use of Webster's extensive psychological analysis of Bosola puzzled Brecht throughout his work. Eventually, Bosola becomes a much less fully developed character, almost purely the Duke's tool; lingering traces of Webster's treatment occasionally blur his characterization in Brecht's play. An example will clarify Brecht's difficulties and decisions. Immediately after Webster's "excommunication scene" (III.iv), Bosola makes two entrances, the first with an equivocal letter from Ferdinand, asking for Antonio's "head in a business," and the second (after Antonio has escaped) as the leader of a military guard come to arrest the Duchess and her commoner-husband. Brecht appears to have liked the letter episode, and BBA 1177 shows him employing first one of the entrances and then the other, trying to simplify the scene and yet retain Ferdinand's duplicity. Ultimately, in a part of the Barbara Brecht script which shows signs of continued indecision (2,6), Brecht retains Webster's organization, though Bosola's double entrances clearly distressed him. How to dispatch Antonio also posed a problem. In Webster's play, Bosola kills Antonio unintentionally (V.iv), having mistaken him for Ferdinand. This solution Brecht could not use, for it had been decided that the Duchess must receive (as Ferdinand's gruesome "gift") a chest containing the bodies of her husband and child (see 3,3; Webster's analogous scene, IV.i, uses wax-works). Moreover, a remorseful or partially penitent Bosola was not part of Brecht's conception. Many early versions (1177, for example, and the Barbara Brecht script until a manuscript cancellation by Brecht) conclude the "echo scene" (3,2) with Bosola's pursuit of Antonio. In the final version printed here, Antonio's death is neither shown nor implied, merely reported as part of Delio's accusation against Bosola (3,6).

Having diminished Bosola's role, Brecht could write a first act much less complicated than Webster's, although the introduction of set-speech portraits of the major characters still provided problems; the various versions reveal Brecht's experiments in conveying this material. Brecht was more interested than Webster in Duke Ferdinand's foreign wars, and he uses them to explain the curiously long gap (more than two years) between Bosola's discovery of the Duchess' pregnancy and the Duke's return to Malfi. Webster actually mentions two series of battles (in I.i and III.iii), but shows neither; Brecht amalgamates these occasions and suggests a parallel between the Duke's making war for his sister and making war on her. Act 2, scene 2, rather truncated in the version presented here, originally (in BBA 1177, for example) concluded with a more elaborate discussion of war's significance and of Ferdinand's attitudes towards both it and his sister.

Brecht omits completely Webster's subplot, which involves the Cardinal's mistress, Julia. On this point, too, he seems to have wavered: the 1943 copyrighted version omits her; some relevant sections of the next version (1177/56–58) append a conversation between the Cardinal and Julia to the present text's 2,4; the Barbara Brecht text and BBA 1174 make no mention of her. Brecht did, however, salvage one episode from the subplot: Webster's Cardinal murders Julia by demanding that she confirm an oath by kissing a book whose cover has been poisoned (V.ii). Brecht specifies a "prayer book" and employs this device as Ferdinand's weapon against the Duchess (3,5). While Webster's Pescara (a reasonably "good" nobleman who survives the débâcle) and Malatesta (the foolish second husband proposed for the Duchess) both disappear from the adaptation, Delio is given a larger role than in Webster's play. Delio's final restoration of order and especially the epilogue make Brecht's conclusion rather more optimistic than Webster's.

2. Notes on Specific Scenes

The notes on specific scenes in the text which follow offer rejected versions of speeches or portions of scenes, as an illustration of Brecht's methods and evidence of alternatives which he thought promising enough to develop quite fully. In this second regard, BBA 1177 is extremely suggestive. Like 1174, it opens with a coherent and carefully revised partial text, in this case based on the 1943 copyrighted text (thus postdating July 1943) and then becomes a series of loosely related working drafts of scenes and speeches. These working papers reveal more clearly than the analogous material in 1174 just which parts of the play gave Brecht trouble and which interested him most as a field of adaptation and modification. One further textual oddity must be mentioned. File 1178 contains a note by Ruth Berlau: "Material not used—the remainder having been used for complete new script." This note may indicate that an entire text (composed in unknown proportions by Brecht and Auden) has not survived or yet been identified. On the other hand, the note may refer to the 1946 copyrighted version. In any case, the text here printed aims to represent the latest version overseen by Brecht himself. The adaptation seems to have moved along a parabola from Brecht's and Hays's work (revision, rewriting, and addition) to a stretch of Auden's work (including use of *The White Devil* and represented by the 1945 copyrighted text) and a period in which Brecht continued to rework the play. Through various production decisions, with which Brecht disagrees in his letter to Paul Czinner, the final Broadway version returned to almost pure Webster, reduced and clarified with relatively little of the work Brecht had done before Auden's participation and after he joined the project.

Prologue

Most of the material for this prologue comes from John Ford's *'Tis Pity She's a Whore*, which opens with a conversation between a friar and Giovanni (who loves his sister, Annabella). The passages used by Brecht follow (quoted from N. W. Bawcutt's edition, University of Nebraska Press, 1966); all of Brecht's texts for this prologue omit certain inappropriate details from Ford's play, but make no substitutions (see 1.1 49–50, below).

FRIAR

   . . .

No more; I may not hear it.

GIOVANNI

              Gentle father,
To you I have unclasp'd my burdened soul,
Emptied the storehouse of my thoughts and heart,

   . . .

And yet is here the comfort I shall have,
Must I not do what all men else may, love?   (I.i.12–19)

FRIAR

Why, foolish madman—   (I.i.24)

   . . .

GIOVANNI

Shall then, for that I am her brother born,
My joys be ever banish'd from her bed?   (I.i.36–37)

   . . .

. . . tell me, holy man,
What cure shall give me ease in these extremes.

(I.i.40–41)

FRIAR

Art thou, my son, that miracle of wit
Who once, within these three months, wert esteem'd
A wonder of thine age, throughout Bononia [Bologna]?
How did the university applaud
Thy government, behavior, learning, speech,
Sweetness, and all that could make up a man! (I.i.47–52)

. . .

O, Giovanni, hast thou left the schools
Of knowledge to converse with lust and death?
For death waits on thy lust. Look through the world,
And thou shalt see a thousand faces shine
More glorious than this idol thou ador'st:
Leave her, and take thy choice, 'tis much less sin. . . .

(I.i.57–62)

GIOVANNI

It were more ease to stop the ocean
From floats and ebbs than to dissuade my vows.

FRIAR

Then I have done, and in thy wilful flames
Already see thy ruin; Heaven is just.
Yet hear my counsel

. . .

Hie to thy father's house, there lock thee fast
Alone within thy chamber, then fall down
On both thy knees, and grovel on the ground:
Cry to thy heart, wash every word thou utter'st
In tears, and (if't be possible) of blood;
Beg Heaven to cleanse the leprosy of lust
That rots thy soul, acknowledge what thou art,
A wretch, a worm, a nothing: weep, sigh, pray
Three times a day, and three times every night.

(I.i.64–77)

The text which Brecht adapted omits the reference to
Bologna since Antonio and Delio are both of that city, omits
the reference to "the university" since Ferdinand is supposedly
an older man, and omits the word "sweetness" as (presumably)

inappropriate to the Duke. No substitutions have been made, though "Italy" has been tried and rejected as a replacement for "Bologna."

Act One, scene 2

After this scene, several versions (the very early 146 and the late text copyrighted by Auden and Brecht in 1946) insert the dirge from Webster's *White Devil*, here employed as an "interlude." The following text comes from 1174/87:

INTERLUDE

Song by Cariola

Call for the robin red breast and the wren
Since o'er shady groves they hover,
And with leaves and flowers do cover
The friendless bodies of unburied men,
Call unto his funeral dole
The ant, the field-mouse, and the mole.
To rear him hillocks that shall keep him warm,
And (when gay tombs are robbed) sustain no harm:
But keep the wolf far thence, that's foe to men,
For with his nails he'll dig them up again.

Act Two, scene 1

The German text of the soldier's song ("I wrote my love a letter") is in Brecht's GW *Gedichte*, p. 879. Our text gives only the first verse, without its refrain, and the third; the translation is presumably by Auden. The missing portions read approximately:

I never got an answer
And the war went on five years

But that wasn't so surprising.
So I drank instead, supposing:
There she lies, in the embrace
Of the man who took my place.

And we burnt the town around us
When we captured fair Milan
Till its palaces were gutted
And for seven days we looted
And we raped them old and young
For we knew they'd done us wrong.

How could she go on waiting
With the nights becoming lighter and the spring wind
    blowing fresh?
Now it's time I found a lover
He can't make me wait for ever—
Women have such itching flesh.

One of the odd links between the plays in this volume is
the Schweyk song "Onward to Jaromersh hoofing," which not
only appears in Brecht's Schweyk play but evidently inspired
both the present song and Simone Machard's "On my way to
Saint-Nazaire." Nor is Grusha's "Four old commanders/Set
out for Iran" in scene 3 of The Caucasian Chalk Circle all that
remote. The two further poems which follow "Als wir vor
Milano kamen" in GW also relate to the Duchess, though they
were not meant for use in the play. Of these the second,
"Light, as though never touching the floor," will be found in
the selected Poems.

Act Two, scene 2

This scene ends rather abruptly, with the unexplained arrival
of "the Duchess and her brother" in both BBA 1419 and 1174.
Brecht may have intended some further action in this very
short scene, since he never announces Ferdinand's return from
the wars, but merely introduces him in 2,3. In BBA 1177/35–

36, Antonio does not reveal his marriage, and the scene continues:

DELIO
  But who, then, is the father?

ANTONIO
  I can not tell you. Tell me, Delio,
  Hath not this news arrived yet to the ear
  Of the Lord Ferdinand?

DELIO
                        Meseemed his bearing
  Altered the longer he tarried in the field.
  He grew so quiet that he seemed to sleep
  The tempest out as dormice do in winter.
  I could now believe some rumor reached him
  For houses that are haunted are most still.

ANTONIO   Hark, the procession comes.

(*The sound of cheering multitudes is heard outside. The two men go toward the window in order to look down at the street. They are obliged to speak loudly to be heard above the tumult*)

DELIO   The Duke brings home the realm of Cyprus as booty and the people rejoice as if the tailors and pastrycooks were to get some of it.

ANTONIO   What are those wooden beams that stand so high?

DELIO   Prows of Turkish ships our Duke hath set upon carts for the crowd to gape at. Well he knows how the rabble love a brave show.

ANTONIO   'Tis a very forest of captured standards yonder!

DELIO   Ay, they serve well to hide the worn faces of our soldiers. Methinks their joy would have been greater had the war been shorter.

ANTONIO   Enough of this victory. I'd sooner hear the women laugh and jest as they hang upon their husbands' arms and lift their children for a father's kiss.

DELIO   Be still! Here comes the Duke.

(*Enter Ferdinand, Duchess and Bosola*)

The scene then ends with III.i.38–86 of Webster's play.

Act Two, scene 4

In another version, which apparently never developed into an entire text, this scene is followed by a trial, modeled closely on the trial of Vittoria Corombona in Webster's *The White Devil*. Almost an entire scene (also called 2,5) appears on 1174/124–30, at the end of which the Cardinal excommunicates the Duchess and removes her wedding ring. The scene emphasizes the economic motives for the Cardinal's and Ferdinand's deposing the Duchess, but also lightly touches on Ferdinand's incipient madness and his great love for his sister. The following speech (from 1174/131) seems intended to replace Ferdinand's last speech of 2,4 as a preparation for the trial:

CARDINAL   Come, put yourself in tune. It seems she can not be saved. It's a scandal that will shake all Italy. It's up to us, her brothers, to look after her dukedom. We must not hide anything, but proceed openly and fairly. I'll instantly solicit a clerical court and I'll invite all the lieger ambassadors. She is unworthy: her dukedom must be taken away from her and put in the custody of the Holy Church. Brother, let's in to make our preparations.

Act Two, scene 5

BBA 1174/124–30 gives an alternate version of this scene, based upon the trial scene in Webster's *The White Devil*. This alternate version follows; use of this scene would require substituting the speech quoted above in the note to 2,4.

(*Enter French and English ambassadors*)

FRENCH AMBASSADOR
   They have dealt discreetly to obtain the presence
   Of all the grave lieger ambassadors to hear the Duchess' trial
   Trusting our approbation to the proof

Of her black lust shall make her infamous
To all her neighboring kingdoms.

ENGLISH AMBASSADOR
But I would ask what power have the state
Of Ancona to determine a free prince.

FRENCH AMBASSADOR
This is a free state, sir, and her brother, the Cardinal,
Forehearing of her looseness, took occasion
Of their pilgrimage hither to arrest them all,
Duchess and steward and the indeterminate fruit
Of their mismatching, and is in haste
To bring them straight to judgment.

ENGLISH AMBASSADOR
But by what justice?

FRENCH AMBASSADOR
Sure, I think, by none.
These factions among great families are like
Foxes, when their hands are divided
They carry fire in their tails and all the country
About them goes to wrack for them.

ENGLISH AMBASSADOR
Still, she has offended. Who would've thought
So great a lady would [have] matched herself
Unto so mean a person.

FRENCH AMBASSADOR
They that are
Great women of pleasure are oft sudden in their wills
And what they dream they do.
(*Enter officer*)

OFFICER
Pray, silence in the court, their lordships do convene.
(*Enter Ferdinand, Cardinal, guards leading the Duchess,
Antonio, and children into the dock*)

OFFICER (*to Antonio*)   Sirrah, stand off and take your proper
station. This court is not the Duchess' bedchamber. But the
home of justice where you may not stand beside your
betters.

FRENCH AMBASSADOR   Certain people should travel as Dutch
women go to church, bear their stools with them.

OFFICER   The court's in session, signior.

CARDINAL   Stand to the table, gentlewoman, now signior, fall to your plea.

LAWYER   Domine judex, converte oculos in hanc pestem, mulierum corruptissimam.

DUCHESS

What's he?

FERDINAND

          A lawyer that pleads against you.

DUCHESS

Pray, my lord, let him speak his usual tongue.
I'll make no answer else.

FERDINAND

Why, you understand Latin.

DUCHESS

I do, sir, but mongst the auditory
Which come to hear my cause, the half or more
May be ignorant in 't.

CARDINAL

Go on, sir.

DUCHESS

      By your favor
I will not have my accusation clouded
In a strange tongue: all this assembly
Shall hear what you can charge me with.

FERDINAND

Pray, change your language.

CARDINAL

Oh, for God's sake, gentlewoman, your credit
Shall be more famous by it.

LAWYER

Well, then, have at you.
Most literate judges, please your lordships
So to connive your judgments to the view
Of this debauched and diversivolent woman;
Who such a black concatenation
Of mischief has affected, that to extirp
The memory of it, must be the consummation
Of her, and her projections—

DUCHESS
What's all this?

LAWYER
Hold your peace!
Exorbitant sins must have exulceration.

CARDINAL
I shall be plainer with you, and paint out
Your follies in more natural red and white
Than that upon your cheek.

DUCHESS
Oh, you mistake!
You raise a blood as noble in this cheek
As ever was your mother's.

CARDINAL
Observe this creature here, my honor'd lords . . .

DUCHESS
My honorable lord
It doth not suit a reverend cardinal
To play the lawyer thus. If you be my accuser,
Pray, cease to be my judge! Come from your bench!

CARDINAL
You see, my lords, what goodly fruit she seems.
Yet like those apples travelers report
To grow where Sodom and Gomorrah stood
I will but touch her, and you straight shall see
She'll fall to soot and ashes.

DUCHESS
O poor charity!
Thou art seldom found in scarlet.

CARDINAL I pray thee, mistress, are you to deny that you did
use our most unfortunate absence to lead a vicious and
lascivious life?

DUCHESS
You are deceived: 'twas marriage. 'Twas a contract
In a chamber per verba presenti.

CARDINAL
I am resolv'd
Were there a second paradise to lose
This devil would betray it.

DUCHESS

Terrify babes, my lord, with painted devils.
I'm past such needless palsy. For your accusations
Of "vicious" and "lascivious": they proceed from you
As if a man should spit against the wind:
The filth returns in 's face.

CARDINAL Does it? Pray you, mistress, satisfy me one question: While we were absent did nothing leak into the open, blemishing the noble house of Malfi?

(*To Antonio*)

Who made you overseer?

ANTONIO

Why, my honesty; my honesty, I think.

CARDINAL Your lust. And while you were the master of her household, didn't you deal falsely with her in your accounts?

(*Antonio remains silent. Cardinal turns to Duchess*)

Stood not your brother Ferdinand engaged with you
For money
Ta'en up of certain Neapolitan Jews?
And did he not let the bonds be forfeit?

DUCHESS

He did not.

CARDINAL

And whereupon, as you didst testify yourself, our
Brother's bills at Naples were protested?

DUCHESS

They were not.

CARDINAL

But didst say so before your officers.

DUCHESS

To save my husband's life.
Condemn you me for that I do love him?

CARDINAL

And look upon this creature was her husband.

DUCHESS

Had he been in the street
Under my chamber-window, even there
I should have courted him.

CARDINAL Hear you, my lords, how she calls lechery love, a

life in sin she calls a solemn marriage. This whore, foresooth
is holy.

DUCHESS

Ha! Whore! What's that?

(*Murmurs in the court. Ferdinand rises and comes down
slowly to confront the Duchess. Sudden silence*)

ENGLISH AMBASSADOR

There is that in his look
Would wither all that's green, deform all music
Into a witch's whisper.

FERDINAND

What's that? What's that?
Shall I expound whore to you? sure I shall;
I'll give their perfect character. They are first
Sweetmeats that rot the eater, in man's nostrils
Poison'd perfumes. They are cozening alchemy;
Shipwrecks in calmest weather. What are whores?
Cold Russian winters, that appear so barren
As if that nature had forgot the spring.
They are the true material fire of hell.
What are whores?
They are those flattering bells have all one tune
At weddings, and at funerals. They are worse,
Worse than dead bodies which are begg'd at gallows
And wrought upon by surgeons to teach man
Wherein he is imperfect. What's a whore?
She's like the gilt counterfeited coin
Which, whosoever first stamps it, brings in trouble
All that receive it.

DUCHESS

This character 'scapes me.

FERDINAND

But you shall not escape
What you have made yourself. There is no court
Can punish what you are. Had I a sister?
I have a limb corrupted to an ulcer.
And I will cut it off.

(*Exit Ferdinand*)

ENGLISH AMBASSADOR

Some horrid thing
Glared through his human windows as he spoke.
I wish I had not seen it.

FRENCH AMBASSADOR

'Tis said he loved her
Dearer than life. The question of her shame
Wrecks his proud soul. There are your true pangs of death,
The pangs of life that struggle with great spirits.

ENGLISH AMBASSADOR

Hush! The Duchess is about to speak.

DUCHESS

I have no writ to rend
Such incantations save they mean
Like you, grave reasoners, to undo me,
Whose hates are plain. Brother, you had a hope
Had I continued widow to have gained
An infinite mass of treasure by my death.

CARDINAL

See, my lords,
She scandals our proceedings.

DUCHESS

I have houses,
Jewels, and a poor remnant of crusadoes.
Would these make you charitable?

CARDINAL

Hark, with what insolence she offers bribes
To hush the voice of justice. Get this down
In evidence against her plea of innocence.

DUCHESS

Humbly thus,
Thus low, to the most worthy and respected
Lieger ambassadors, my modesty
And womanhood I tender, but withal
So entangled in a curs'd accusation
That my defense must personate masculine virtue.

CARDINAL

This is the tedious prolixity of guilt.
Have done.

DUCHESS

Find me but guilty, sever head from body
We'll part good friends: I scorn to hold my life
At yours or any man's entreaty, sir.

CARDINAL

Speak no more for our opinions are concluded
Hear then, Giovanna, your public fault
Join'd to th' condition of the present time
Takes from you all the fruits of noble pity
Such a corrupted trial have you made
Both of your life and beauty, and been styl'd
No less an ominous fate than blazing stars
To princes. Attend your sentence.

(The Cardinal and the clerical judges rise, so do the rest at a hint of the Cardinal. The Duchess, Antonio and the children are placed before him)

CARDINAL   Herefore, through the authority of the Almighty God, Father of Heaven and His Son, Our Savior, I, Cardinal of Ancona, denounce, proclaim and declare Giovanna Teresa, Duchess of Malfi, and her paramour, Antonio Bologna, together with their children, anathema by the advice and assistance of our Holy Father, the pope, and all the bishops, abbots, priests, and other prelates and ministers of our Holy Church, for her open lechery and sins of the flesh.

FRENCH AMBASSADOR   He hath excommunicated her!

CARDINAL   I curse her head and the hairs of her head, her eyes, her mouth, her nose, her tongue, her teeth, her neck, her shoulders, her breast, her heart, her arms, her legs, her back, her stomach, her womb, and every part of her body from the top of her head to the soles of her feet.

DUCHESS

A rape! A rape! Yes, you have ravished justice
Forc'd her to do your pleasure.

CARDINAL   I dissever and part thee from the church of God and likewise from contracts and oaths of law. I forbid all Christian men to have any company with thee and all her earthly goods I seize in the name of the Holy Church. And as their candles go from our sight so may their souls go from the visage of God and their good fame from the world.

Away with her!
(*Cardinal steps down from the bench*)
(*To an official*)
Take her right hand and raise it!
(*Cardinal takes something off the Duchess' finger*)
(*Exeunt Cardinal and the clerical judges*)

ENGLISH AMBASSADOR
What was it with such violence he took
Off from her finger?

SPANISH AMBASSADOR
'Twas her wedding ring.

Act Three, scene 2

This "echo" scene exists in several versions, all differing from Webster's in the major respect that his scene is between Antonio and Delio. The version included here shows the most signs of Brecht's direct involvement; he certainly accepted it at one stage of the revision. BBA 1177/70 concludes this scene (substantially as it is printed above) with an entrance by Bosola and two murderers. Bosola ends the scene with, ". . . though they fare fast yet death is speedier than they." BBA 1419/83 originally kept this entrance, but then cancels it. Another, different version appears in the text copyrighted by Auden and Brecht in 1946; Brecht did less work on this one, and much is probably Auden's revision of Webster. This alternative scene is printed below.

SON
Father, when shall we rest?
ANTONIO
Courage, dear son,
'Tis but an hour's journey to the inn
Where we may eat and sleep.
SON
My legs refuse
To bear me longer. Let me sit a while,
A little while.

ANTONIO

    Poor child! One moment then,

    Longer we dare not. We must haste. The day

    Already wears its hunted twilight look,

    Come, dry your tears and listen. This fortification

    Grown from the ruins of an ancient abbey

    Gives the best echo you have ever heard

    As plain in the distinction of the words

    As if a spirit answered. You may make it

    A huntsman or a falconer, a musician

    Or a thing of sorrow.

ECHO

    A thing of sorrow.

ANTONIO

    There, did you hear it, son? So soon asleep!

    Sweet innocent who playest in thy dream

    With tops and spangles not those deadly toys

    That princes skirmish with and canst not spell

    The puzzle of these ruins. Here in this court

    Which now lies naked to the injuries

    Of stormy weather, some men be interred

    Loved the church so well and gave so largely to't

    They thought it should have canopied their bones

    Till doomsday; but all things have their end:

    Churches and cities which have diseases like to men,

    That have like death that we have.

ECHO

    Like death that we have.

ANTONIO

    O fearful echo that accuses my life

    Of its long weakness; that has not made its path

    By definite steps but sought its shelter

    In the strong wills of others. Now

    I am caught between their fighting stars, a clerk

    Unpracticed in the sword. O my soul,

    Is't still impossible to fly your fate.

ECHO

    O, fly your fate.

ANTONIO

    Unmoving stones, would you give such counsel

To a bold nature. Echo, I'll not talk with thee
For thou art a dead thing.

ECHO

Thou art a dead thing.

ANTONIO

My Duchess is asleep now
And her little ones, I hope sweetly: O Heaven
Shall I never see her more?

ECHO

Never see her more.

ANTONIO

O dreadful repetition
Methought that on the sudden a clear light
Presented me a face folded in sorrow.
Come, boy, awake. We have delayed too long.

SON

Let me sleep, mother. Kiss me once more.

ANTONIO

Dost thou dream of her
Forgetting where thou art? I'll carry thee
Sleep on, beloved child, believing 'tis her arms
Not thy poor father's.
(*Echo of galloping hooves is heard*)
O hark, the walls
Echo to baying hooves. Where shall the quarry
Turn for salvation now? The hunt is up
And we are gone forever.
(*Exeunt*)

BBA 1174/107 has another version with the note, "Brecht's
rough translation" opposite Antonio's last speech:

ANTONIO

O fearful echo that accuses my life
Of its long weakness; that has not made its path
By definite steps but sought its shelter
In the strong wills of others. Now
I am caught between their fighting stars, a clerk
Unpracticed in the sword.

SON
    Why can't we go with mother?
ANTONIO
    We are too small to live with greatness, son.
SON
    Shall we not see her more?
ECHO
    Not see her more.
SON
    Why does the echo say so, father?
ANTONIO
    It tells us, son, how bitter is the fate
    Of him who is not allowed to fight. The whole day
    (Which now will be ended soon) I have been thinking
    Of another day, when I went ahawking with my father
    Upon the plains of Brittany, and saw our falcon spying a
        hare
    And coursing it till the poor beast
    —Since flying is much easier than running—
    Was wearied unto death and, despairing utterly,
    Turned upon its back and with its stony feet
    Hardened by a whole life of timid flight
    Hammered to pieces our falcon's chest. Lucky hare!
    O 'tis impossible to fly your fate.
ECHO
    O, fly your fate.

Act Three, scene 3

BBA 1174 has variants of the concluding exchange between
Bosola and Ferdinand, showing the way in which Brecht reduced Bosola's express motives and justifications for his actions. Three versions will illustrate Brecht's working methods:

FERDINAND
    Damn her! that body of hers,
    While that my blood ran pure in't, was more worth

Than that which thou wouldst comfort, called a soul.
Curse upon her!
I will no longer study in the book
Of another's heart

BOSOLA
Must I see her again?

FERDINAND
Your work is not yet ended.
To cure such maladies the surgeon's knife
Must cut until it pricks the patient's life.
(*Exeunt*)   (1174/75)

BOSOLA
Right. Give me that scholarship
You promised me and I'll be off to Bologna
And never see her again.

FERDINAND
Your work is not yet ended.
I found her sin sits deeper than I thought.
Vile appetite has turned to lecherous grief.
Such mourning is unbearable.
To cure such maladies the surgeon's knife
Must cut until it pricks the patient's life.
(*Exeunt*)   (1174/80)

BOSOLA
Right. Give me my scholarship and I'll go
To complete my education, never see her again.

FERDINAND
Your work is not yet ended.
I found her sin sits deeper than I thought.
Vile appetite has turned to lecherous grief
With pallidness hardly hidden, impudend [*sic*] tears.
Such mourning is imbearable [*sic*]. Nacked [*sic*] she stands
The widow of a sweaty stableboy.
To cure such maladies the surgeon's knife
Must cut until it pricks the patient's life.

                                                     (1174/79)

Between this scene and the following one, the 1946 text

copyrighted by Auden and Brecht inserts an "interlude" by Bosola. The text comes from Webster's play (IV.ii.178–95) and is spoken by Bosola in an attempt to bring the Duchess "By degrees to mortification." It is cited here from 1174/85:

INTERLUDE

BOSOLA

Hark, now everything is still
The screech-owl and the whistler shrill
Call upon our dame aloud,
And bid her quickly don her shroud!
Much you had of land and rent;
Your length in clay's now competent:
A long war disturbed your mind;
Here your perfect peace is signed:
Of what is't fools make such vain keeping?
Sin their conception, their birth weeping,
Their life a general mist of error,
Their death a hideous storm of terror.
Strew your hair with powders sweet,
Don clean linen, bathe your feet,
And (the foul fiend more to check)
A crucifix let bless your neck.
'Tis now full tide 'tween night and day;
End your groan, and come away.

This text also appears on 1174/109 and 123.

Epilogue

The second half of this epilogue comes from a passage in Webster's *The Devil's Law Case*, slightly modified to suit its new context. The original follows, quoted from Frances A. Shirley's edition (University of Nebraska Press, 1972):

All the flowers of the spring
Meet to perfume our burying:
These have but their growing prime,

And man does flourish but in his time.
Survey our progress from our birth:
We are set, we grow, we turn to earth.
Courts adieu, and all delights,
All bewitching appetites;
Sweetest breath, and clearest eye,
Like perfumes, go out and die;
And consequently this is done,
As shadows wait upon the sun.
Vain the ambition of kings,
Who seek by trophies and dead things
To leave a living name behind,
And weave but nets to catch the wind.   (V.iv.128–43)